International Trade and Economic Growth in the Korean Economy

International Trade and Economic Growth in the Korean Economy

By

Shin-Haing Kim,
Taegi Kim
and Keunyeob Oh

**Cambridge
Scholars**
Publishing

International Trade and Economic Growth in the Korean Economy

By Shin-Haing Kim, Taegi Kim and Keunyeob Oh

This book first published 2023

Cambridge Scholars Publishing

Lady Stephenson Library, Newcastle upon Tyne, NE6 2PA, UK

British Library Cataloguing in Publication Data
A catalogue record for this book is available from the British Library

ISBN (10): 1-5275-2534-1
ISBN (13): 978-1-5275-2534-4

CONTENTS

Part III. Changes in Trade and Industry

Part IV. International Trade and Technology

Part V. Trade, Inequality, and Environment

CHAPTER 1

INTRODUCTION

1. Overview of the Korean Economy

After World War II, Korea was divided into North and South. In 1950, the country experienced the Korean War, and at that time, it was one of the poorest countries in the world. However, since then, the economy of South Korea (henceforth referred to as Korea and South Korea interchangeably) has achieved remarkable economic growth and it has become an advanced country. During the process of rapid growth, exports increased significantly. According to the World Bank, Korea's per capita GDP was only US$82 in 1960, but it grew to US$34,997 by 2021, and Korea's exports increased from US$313 million in 1960 to US$644 billion in 2021. Over the past 60 years, Korea's per capita income has increased by about 426 times, and exports by about 2,050 times. Korea's experience of high growth provides many implications for developing countries that want to achieve economic development.

In the 1960s, the Korean government pursued a policy of fostering industries through export expansion by providing institutional and financial support to the private sector. This included subsidies, tax incentives, and policies to encourage investment in export-oriented industries. Since then, Korea's manufacturing industry has grown rapidly, and the current account turned into a surplus in the late 1980s. However, in 1997, Korea faced a foreign exchange crisis due to factors such as high levels of corporate debt, a weak banking system, and excessive short-term foreign debt. The crisis led to a sharp decline in GDP, a surge in unemployment, and widespread social unrest. However, in the process of overcoming this economic crisis, Korea strengthened corporate governance, strengthened the soundness of financial institutions, and promoted innovation, leading to the fostering of high-tech industries. As a result, today, Korea is a competitive player in global, high-tech industries such as electronics, automobiles, and chemicals.

Korea's rapid growth is largely attributable to the increase in exports. The reasons for Korea's rapid growth have been analyzed in various ways in terms of politics, the economy, and society. However, there is no disagreement in the view that it is thanks to the growth of the manufacturing industry, supported by an export-oriented policy. Korea was able to achieve efficiency in resource allocation through a market opening policy and achieve economies of scale through export expansion. In other words, by exporting products to the international market, it was possible to acquire advanced technology and enjoy the benefits of economies of scale, which led to the growth of the manufacturing industry and the creation of jobs. As companies competed in the international market, new product development and technological innovation took place. However, Korea's openness policy was not completely free trade and was partially used in connection with protection policies to protect domestic industries. Nevertheless, unlike Latin American countries that pursued import-substitution growth policies, Korea continued to pursue a policy of fundamentally opening the market. As a result, it is believed that Korea was able to achieve high growth.

Lucas (1993) describes Korea's rapid growth as a miracle. Factors contributing to this growth include increased exports due to openness policies, rapid improvements in education levels, and high savings rates. It is explained that the accumulation of human capital through increased exports and improved education levels has improved the productivity of workers, becoming a key factor in rapid growth. However, there are also skeptical views about Korea's rapid growth. Krugman (1994) argues that the increase in factor input played a relatively larger role in the growth of East Asian countries, including Korea, than the increase in productivity. The cheap and abundant labor force of the agrarian society was converted into the industrial sector, and the quality of workers was improved through the education system. In addition, rapid capital formation was achieved through a high investment rate based on high domestic savings and foreign investments. As such, it is pointed out that the increase in labor input and investment expansion acted as important factors for economic growth, and the increase in productivity itself was not large. Therefore, in order to achieve Korea's long-term high growth, it is necessary to expand productivity through technological innovation.

Korea has undergone significant changes in its industrial structure during its economic growth. In its early stages, the growth was led by the manufacturing industry. The manufacturing industry accounted for only 12% of the total added value in 1953-60, but it increased to 23% on average in 1971-80. Additionally, there was an increase in the proportion of heavy and chemical industries, while the proportion of light industries decreased. This means that the industrial structure gradually shifted from a simple labor-intensive industry to a capital-intensive industry, and from 1990 onwards, it gradually changed to a technology-intensive industry. In summary, Korea's economy was agriculture-oriented in the 1950s, but later moved to labor-intensive textile, clothing, and shoes industries, and then gradually shifted from capital-intensive shipbuilding, steel, and chemicals to high-tech industries such as automobiles, electronics, and semiconductors. Overall, this change in the industrial structure has shifted Korea from an agricultural-based economy to manufacturing and, more recently, to a high-tech industry. With these changes in the industrial structure, the sophistication of export products also progressed. As the income level increased, the preference for variety also increased, and technological progress led to increased production of product differentiation.

The rapid economic growth and changes in the industrial structure of the Korean economy in its early days were attributed to the accumulation of human capital based on a strong passion for education and the accumulation of capital through high savings rates. In other words, before 1990, the growth of the Korean economy was mainly achieved through an increase in input factors, but after that, economic growth through technological progress became necessary. Early economic growth was achieved by improving the quality of labor and accumulating capital. However, due to diminishing marginal returns, growth through increasing input factors reached its limit, and the growth rate of the Korean economy gradually stagnated. To achieve sustainable economic growth, technological progress is now required rather than an increase in input factors. Since 1990, patent applications and R&D investments have rapidly increased to promote technological progress, which is necessary for the sustainable growth of the Korean economy. The expansion of technological progress is crucial for the continued growth of the Korean economy in the future.

2. Overview of the Volume

This book examines the growth of the Korean economy, both theoretically and empirically, with a focus on international trade. It is divided into 5 parts consisting of 19 topics related to the Korean economy. Part 1 deals with theoretical models of trade and economic growth, while Part 2 explains the growth process of the Korean economy. Part 3 analyzes changes in Korea's trade structure and industrial structure, and Part 4 focuses on technology transfer and diffusion, as well as the effect of exports on increasing productivity. Finally, Part 5 addresses income inequality caused by trade, and environmental issues.

2.1 Theory of Trade and Growth

Part 1 covers the theoretical model of trade and economic growth. Chapter 2 discusses Hicks's neo-Austrian approach to the production process and economic growth theories. Chapter 3 examines the relationship between trade and economic growth, focusing on the positive impact of North-South trade involving capital goods versus consumer goods. Chapter 4 discusses intra-industry trade (IIT), specifically horizontal intra-industry trade (HIIT) and vertical intra-industry trade (VIIT), and analyzes Korea's IIT with other countries. Finally, Chapter 5 explores the impact of intellectual property rights (IPRs) on the welfare and growth of two trading regions in an open economy, utilizing an intermediate final good trade model developed within the framework of the overlapping generation model.

Chapter 2 discusses Hicks's neo-Austrian approach to the production process, which considers time as a scarce factor of production that contributes value to output. The model extends the traditional "point-input point-output" model to a "flow-input flow-output" model, which involves the transition from an old process to a new one through the construction of new equipment. The model also introduces two agents in the economy: an individual worker and a producer. The producer must decide how to allocate their time between the construction and utilization periods, while the individual's allocation problem is related to when they should start engaging in the production of final goods. This chapter also covers topics related to economic growth theories, including Hicks' traverse in a small open economy and the concept of capital gain in a neo-Austrian framework. It concludes by emphasizing the importance of the distance between domestic knowledge levels and the rest of the world in determining which economies will benefit from growth gains from trade.

Chapter 3 discusses the relationship between trade and economic growth, which is not always positively correlated, as suggested by the existing research on this topic. These mixed results are due to differing interpretations of openness and the need to modify its meaning. Specifically, we focus on the positive effect of trade in a North-South trade featuring the trade of capital goods versus consumer goods, and how it can lead to an increase in the economy's growth rate by enabling investment in human capital to match the level of imported capital goods. This chapter concludes that small open economies with a high savings rate and human capital vintage can benefit from knowledge spillovers and reach advanced income levels in a shorter time period, joining the convergence club of the North. Despite many simplifying assumptions and restrictions on the economy's parameters, a neo-Austrian theory is comparable to mainstream neo-classical growth theory. This study introduces a neo-Austrian trade model and highlights its relation to a standard neo-classical trade model and its relevance to the growth experience of the East Asian economies.

Chapter 4 discusses intra-industry trade (IIT) and its causes, specifically horizontal intra-industry trade (HIIT) and vertical intra-industry trade (VIIT). HIIT is caused by product differentiation and economies of scale, while VIIT is caused by differences in product quality. This chapter also examines Korea's IIT with other countries and finds that the increase in IIT is primarily due to the increase in high quality VIIT, indicating that Korea's industrial and trade structure is shifting towards high quality products. A comparison of Korea's trade with China and Japan reveals that the proportion of high quality VIIT is high in trade with China, while the proportion of low quality VIIT is high in trade with Japan. This means that Korea exports superior-quality products to China and imports inferior-quality products from China, while it exports inferior-quality products to Japan and imports superior-quality products from Japan.

Chapter 5 discusses the effects of intellectual property rights (IPRs) on the welfare and growth of two trading regions in an open economy. The literature on IPRs highlights the conflict of interest between the North and South and suggests that global welfare generally declines with the strengthening of IPRs. However, empirical research shows a strong positive correlation between intellectual property protection and economic growth. Using an intermediate final good trade model developed within the framework of the overlapping generation model, this chapter demonstrates that tightening IPRs in the South increases the investment rate, improving the welfare of the two trading regions. This is in contrast to contemporary IPR literature, which shows conflicting results for the two interest groups. The chapter concludes that investment-related intermediate goods trade brings about a favorable outcome for the growth of the South, and the increase in the Southern investment rate by enforcing IPRs reduces the impediment for the case in which the technological efficiency level is properly distanced from that of the North.

2.2 Growth of Korean Economy

Part II discuss various aspects of the economic development of South Korea. Chapter 6 explores the role of exports in financing industrialization and promoting growth. It highlights the export-promotion policy of the 1960s, the heavy chemical industrial policy of the 1970s, and industrial coordination policies of the 1980s as the key factors that contributed to South Korea's sustained growth. Chapter 7 investigates the historical trend of total factor productivity of industries and analyzes economic growth in Korea using industry level data. The chapter confirms the importance of productivity growth in Korea and suggests some policy implications based on the findings. Chapter 8 presents a growth model of firms based on Tobin's q, which shows that "chaebol-incumbents" outperform "non-incumbents" in terms of growth, attributed to their ability to diversify multi-products and realize the "economy of scope." Chapter 9 analyzes investment decisions and adjustment costs of Korean manufacturing firms, finding that group firms have lower adjustment costs and higher investment rates than independent firms.

Chapter 6 discusses the economic development of South Korea from 1960 to 2004, with a focus on the role of exports in financing industrialization and promoting growth. It explains how South Korea, despite lacking natural resources, sustained increased investments through exports and foreign direct investments. The chapter also explores the export-promotion policy of the 1960s, the heavy chemical industrial policy of the 1970s, and the industrial coordination policies of the 1980s. It concludes that South Korea's sustained growth was possible through joint risk-taking by the state and business, investments in human capital, and the adoption of an outward-looking export-promotion strategy.

Chapter 7 investigates the historical trend of total factor productivity of industries and analyzes economic growth in Korea using industry-level data. The chapter focuses on a structural break by checking whether there were regime changes between contributing factors, such as input and productivity, and whether there were any significant changes in the relationship between international trade and those variables. The authors use new econometric methods of time-series, unit-root tests, and cointegration analyses to search for a structural break. The results confirm the importance of productivity growth in Korea, and the authors suggest some policy implications based on these findings.

Chapter 8 presents a growth model of firms based on Tobin's q. The study finds that "chaebol-incumbents" outperform "non-incumbents" in terms of growth, which is attributed to their capacity for diversifying multi-products and realizing the "economy of scope." The paper develops Tobin's q, which incorporates fixed capital goods in the investment decision of a firm, and suggests that the sharing of knowledge embodied in physical capital goods across adjacent industries makes the indivisibility of fixed capital goods divisible. It also discusses the modified version of Uzawa-Hayashi's adjustment cost function and presents an endogenous growth path of a "multi-product firm." Overall, the study highlights the importance of investments in fixed capital goods and diversification for firms to achieve sustained growth.

Chapter 9 investigates investment decisions and adjustment costs of Korean manufacturing firms based on Tobin's q. Regression analyses were performed on panel data of 1,106 Korean manufacturing firms from 1982 to 2015. The results show that group firms have larger investment rates and lower adjustment costs compared to independent firms. Tobin's q is a significant determinant of investment, and the coefficient of Tobin's q is larger in group firms than in independent firms. This implies that group firms can share investment experiences, which can lower the adjustment cost of new investments. Cash holdings and foreign ownership also contribute to increasing investment. The study suggests that Korean chaebols have contributed to the growth of the Korean economy through investment expansion due to low adjustment costs.

2.3 Changes in Trade and Industry

Part III explores changes in trade and industry in Korea, including the growth of Korea's exports, changes in its industrial structure and trade patterns, the relationship between labor mobility and productivity change, and the development of the liquid crystal display (LCD) industry in East Asia. Chapter 10 analyzes the growth of Korea's exports, changes in its industrial structure and trade patterns, and factors affecting trade volume differences by country from 1963 to 2009. Chapter 11 examines the relationship between labor mobility and productivity change in Korea from 1974 to 2014. While the industrial structure has shifted from labor-intensive to capital-intensive industries, labor mobility among Korean industries is gradually decreasing, and the growth rate of labor productivity is slowing down. Chapter 12 discusses the improvement in the quality of Korean exports from 1992 to 2008 and suggests that Korea's industrial structure has shifted from labor-intensive to capital- and technology-intensive industries. Chapter 13 explores the development of the LCD industry in East Asia and various economic development models that can explain it, including the Flying geese model, Bamboo capitalism, and Water lily model.

Chapter 10 discusses the growth of Korea's exports and changes in its industrial structure and trade patterns from 1963 to 2009. The analysis is based on trade statistics and data from the UN Comtrade and World Bank databases. The chapter covers the factors that have contributed to Korea's export growth, how the industrial structure has changed, and what factors affect trade volume differences among countries. The findings show that Korea's global market share has significantly increased due to improved export competitiveness, rather than changes in industrial structure. Intra-industry trade has continued to increase over the period, and the trade volume by country is well explained by the gravity model. The chapter provides a comprehensive analysis of Korea's export industry's dynamic changes and summarizes the main findings of the analysis.

Chapter 11 discusses the relationship between labor mobility and productivity change in Korea from 1974 to 2014. The industrial structure has shifted from labor-intensive to capital-intensive industries, leading to an increase in overall labor productivity. Factors such as workers' human capital levels and movement from low- to high-productivity sectors have also contributed to increased labor productivity. However, labor mobility among Korean industries is gradually decreasing, and the growth rate of labor productivity is slowing down, particularly in the service industry. Despite this, labor is moving from manufacturing to the service industry, including low-productivity sectors within it. The decline in labor productivity across the entire Korean economy is due to the service industry's productivity slowdown and labor movement to the service sector. The study suggests that policy efforts to improve labor productivity in the service industry and vocational training to increase labor mobility are necessary to enhance the entire economy's labor productivity.

Chapter 12 examines the improvement in the quality of Korean exports from 1992 to 2008, using two methods: analyzing the change in the number of export items of superior quality and estimating the quality index. The study found that Korean export quality has improved overall, with high-tech industries showing more significant improvement than low-tech industries. The results suggest that Korea's industrial structure has shifted from labor-intensive to capital- and technology-intensive industries, leading to an improvement in product quality.

Chapter 13 discusses the development of the liquid crystal display (LCD) industry in East Asia and explores various economic development models that can explain it, including the Flying geese model, Bamboo capitalism, and Water lily model. The chapter provides a brief history of the LCD industry in East Asia, analyzes the trade structure and competitiveness of the region using international trade data, and highlights the importance of LCD products in the IT industry. The chapter also mentions the division of labor among the East Asian countries in the LCD industry, with Japan specializing in manufacturing equipment and materials, Korea and Taiwan focusing on intermediary goods like display panels, and China producing final goods with cheaper labor. The LCD industry's current structure is between the Bamboo capitalism and Water lily model, but it is moving from the one to the other.

2.4. International Trade and Technology

Part IV is about topics related to trade and technology on Korea's economic growth. Chapter 14 explores the impact of trade and R&D spillovers on productivity in Korean manufacturing, finding that foreign R&D has a greater impact than domestic R&D and that productivity is higher in export industries. Chapter 15 compares productivity between exporting firms and domestic firms, finding that exporting firms have higher output growth and TFP growth, and that exports contribute significantly to Korea's economic growth. Chapter 16 examines the effects of patent system reforms on knowledge activities and productivity growth in Korean manufacturing firms, finding that policy changes had positive effects on R&D expenditure and patent applications, and increased knowledge and productivity growth.

Chapter 14 discusses the impact of trade and R&D spillovers on Korea's economic growth. The study shows that foreign R&D had a greater impact on productivity in Korean manufacturing than domestic R&D, and that R&D spillovers occurred both domestically and internationally. Japanese R&D had a larger impact on Korean productivity than other foreign R&D stocks. The study also finds that productivity is greater in export and more open industries, and the effects of foreign R&D capital are greater in industries with large import shares or large intra-industry trade shares.

Chapter 15 examines the productivity difference between exporting firms and domestic firms in the Korean manufacturing industry. The analysis covers approximately 150,000 firms from 1984 to 2021. The study finds that exporting firms have a significantly higher output growth rate, and the growth rate of TFP is higher in exporting firms than in domestic firms. Additionally, the productivity increase effect of exports is lower or similar for medium-sized firms but greater for the smallest firms compared to large firms. The study suggests that exports have significantly contributed to Korea's economic growth, serve as an important channel for introducing new production technologies and disseminating knowledge, and policy efforts should focus on enhancing the export capabilities of SMEs to achieve sustainable economic growth in Korea.

Chapter 16 discusses the effects of patent system reforms in Korea on knowledge activities such as R&D expenditure and patent applications, and their impact on productivity growth in Korean manufacturing firms. The analyzed data covers the years 1985-2007 for 216 firms. The results show that R&D expenditure and patents increased faster than output and inputs, particularly in high technology firms. The Korean patent system experienced major policy changes in 1986, 1990, 1995, and 2002, which had positive effects on R&D expenditure and patent applications. Panel data regression with policy dummy variables shows that these policy reforms had a positive effect on increase in knowledge and productivity growth in Korean manufacturing firms, particularly in the high technology sector. Evidence of knowledge spillovers among firms was also detected.

2.5. Trade, Inequality, and Environment

Part V covers discussions on the relationship between international trade and income inequality, as well as topics related to the environment. Chapter 17 investigates the existence of an exporter wage premium in Korean manufacturing firms and finds that while there was a premium before 2010, it has gradually decreased over time and is not significant in recent data. Chapter 18 examines the relationship between international trade and polarization in the Korean economy and finds that there is a positive relationship between the export ratio and polarization, which can widen income gaps. Chapter 19 proposes that imposing a tariff on eco-friendly goods imported from advanced countries can reduce environmental damage and lead to the development of environmentally friendly techniques, helping reduce the growth gap between advanced and developing countries. Chapter 20 analyzes how each country's environmental regulations affect trade patterns, finding that the strengthening of environmental regulations in foreign countries reduces the competitiveness of their products in the overall industry, generating an increase in the exports of Korean products.

Chapter 17 examines the existence of an "exporter wage premium" in Korean manufacturing companies. This wage premium refers to the difference between the wages of exporting companies and domestic companies that cannot be explained by productivity differences. The study uses data from 2007-2016 and examines company characteristics such as size, location, and industry classification in addition to productivity differences. The study found that an exporter wage premium existed before 2010 but gradually decreased over time, and there was no significant premium in recent data. The study also found that the wage premium did not appear in firms with a very large export proportion. Overall, the study contributes to the existing research by analyzing more recent data and considering factors beyond productivity differences that could explain the wage gap.

Chapter 18 examines the relationship between international trade and polarization in the Korean economy. It explores the concentration of export-centric industries and firms within industries, which can result in polarization of the economy. The study uses industry and firm level data and finds a positive relationship between the export ratio and polarization, suggesting that international trade can contribute to polarization and income inequality in the Korean economy. It concludes that international trade can change the production patterns of an economy and result in concentration in export-centric industries and polarization within industries, which can widen income gaps.

Chapter 19 analyzes the environmental problems faced by a developing economy (the South) that trades with an advanced economy (the North). The South has more physical capital, while the North has more human capital, and physical capital-intensive goods harm the environment while human capital-intensive goods are eco-friendly. The study proposes that imposing a tariff on eco-friendly goods imported from the North can reduce environmental damage and lead to the development of environmentally friendly techniques. This can also help reduce the growth gap between the North and the South. The optimal tariff rate is determined by the planner's valuation of natural assets and pollution abatement costs. The study suggests that investing in pollution abatement and preserving natural resources can reduce the urgency of natural disasters and lead to a lower optimum rate of tariff.

Chapter 20 analyzes how each country's environmental regulations affect trade patterns, specifically how Korea's exports are affected by foreign environmental regulations. The study uses regression analysis with various indicators to represent the degree of environmental regulation in countries around the world. The gravity model is used as the basic model, and cross-sectional analysis is performed. The results indicate that the strengthening of environmental regulations in foreign countries reduces the competitiveness of their products in the overall industry, generating an increase in the exports of Korean products. The impact of environmental regulations was greater in environmentally polluting industries and in high-income countries. Overall, the paper supports the hypothesis that environmentally polluting industries will be more affected by environmental regulations.

PART I

THEORY OF TRADE AND GROWTH

CHAPTER 2

HICKS' NEO-AUSTRIAN THEORY

1. Introduction

This chapter provides an overview of Hicks's neo-Austrian technique of the production process, which views the relationship between inputs and outputs of production over time. Unlike traditional production function approaches, this Austrian method considers time as a scarce factor of production that contributes value to output, or views labor inputs as complementary to time. For example, the value of wine improves over time as it matures, and similarly, a tree increases in value as it grows. While there are costs associated with labor during the initial stages of planting a tree or fermenting grapes, the value additions of wine or trees are predominantly a result of the passage of time.

From an economist's perspective, it is important to determine when to harvest the tree or bottle the wine, taking into account the nature of their growth, as well as the prevailing rate of interest and wage rates. Once bottled or cut, a final consumer good is produced. This model is commonly referred to as a "point-input point-output" model. Hicks (1973) extends this simple model into a "flow-input flow-output" neo-Austrian model.

2. A Technique of a Production Process

In neo-Austrian theory, a production process is described as a sequence of inputs $\{a_t\}_0^T$ and outputs $\{b_t\}_0^T$, and has a life period $0 < T < \infty$ after which it comes to an end. Additionally, individuals in the economy have their own corresponding working-life period T, and the economy is inhabited by a population size $A^*(\tau)$ consisting of members of a generation $\tau \in (0, T)$. Each member of a generation engages in the production process, and the size of the population remains unchanged. The production process consists of two periods: the construction period of the physical capital good $(0, v)$ and its utilization period (v, T). The level of activities in the economy, denoted by x_t, represents the aggregate output, capital stock, and aggregate employment at a given point in time.

The aggregate economic output of a generation τ at a time period t denoted by $B^*(t)$ is written as follows:[1]

$$B^*(t) = \sum_0^{T-v}(1 - \delta)^{\tau} b_{\tau}^* K^*(t - \tau); \quad (T - v) > 0; 0 < \delta < 1. \quad (2\text{-}1)$$

The physical capital stock depreciates at the rate of $0 < \delta < 1$. The one produced by a τ-old generation, $K^*(t - \tau)$, contributes to the output by a factor of $(1 - \delta)^{\tau} b_{\tau}^*$.

Likewise, the aggregate capital stock and the aggregate level of employment across the members of a generation are, respectively, as follows:

$$K^*(t) = \sum_0^v a_{\tau}^* x_{t-\tau}; \quad A^*(t) = \sum_0^T a_{\tau}^* x_{t-\tau}. \quad (2\text{-}2)$$

In a steady state, the economy's capital stock remains constant as old capital goods are replaced with new ones at a constant rate of depreciation δ. In the constant technique, the coefficients $\{a_t, b_t\}$, which represent the ratio of total output and total capital stock to employment, remain constant. This

---

[1] To maintain consistency with Hicks' notation, the variables for traditional techniques are denoted by a superscript star (*).

can be verified by substituting $(1+g)^{-\tau}x_t$ for $x_{t-\tau}$ at a steady-state growth rate of g. The ratio of aggregate output $(B/A)^*$ and capital stock $(K/A)^*$ to the level of employment is independent of time t, satisfying Hicks' social accounting principles.

Hicks' social accounting presents a relationship among these variables based on the following accounting identity:

Wages (wA) + Profits (rK) = Consumption (B)+ Net Investment (gK)

at a wage rate w and the rate of profit r for a steady state growth rate of g. This social accounting relationship gives us a distribution of income as explained by per capita capital $(K/A)^*$ and its productivity of $(B/A)^*$ (Hicks 1973, p. 67):

$$(K/A)^* = \frac{(B/A)^*-w}{r-g} = \frac{(B/A)^*-w}{(1-s)r} \qquad (2\text{-}3)$$

The classical savings assumption of the capital fund market, $g = sr$, for a propensity to save in the economy ($0 < s < 1$), holds. Substituting "sr" for "g" on the denominator of the first row of (2-3) generates its second row.

For a given economic endowment, the per capita economic capital stock $(K/A)^*$ and productivity $(B/A)^*$ are inversely related to the wage and profit rates in equation (2-3). This negative relationship between factor prices (w,r) is consistent with the "factor-price-frontier" (or efficiency curve) of the neoclassical aggregate production function approach for a given neo-Austrian production process technique.[2]

However, the negative relationship between wage and profit rates in neo-Austrian theory is based on a different reasoning than the neoclassical approach. In the neoclassical approach, the fall of the interest rate is caused by the decline in the marginal physical productivity of capital of the aggregate production function. On the other hand, the distributional effect in neo-Austrian theory results from the change in the interest rate of the capital fund market. Equation (2-3) reveals the fund market, which is hidden behind the "efficiency curve," as it relates to the determination of the saving rate of the economy. In other words, the capital fund market comes before the aggregate production function in neo-Austrian theory. As we will discuss later, the saving rate is connected to the time preference rate of an individual member of an economy.

3. A Value of a Production Process

There is an underlying occurrence of costs incurred during the construction period and redemptions in the utilization period in Hicks' "flow input–flow output" technology. The capital value of the process at age t is denoted by k_t, and its value at the initial period "0" is denoted by k_0, defined at the gross rate of interest $R = 1 + r$ according to Hicks (1973, p.23):

$$k_0 = q_0 + q_1 R^{-1} + q_2 R^{-2} + \cdots + q_{t-1} R^{-(t-1)} + k_t R^{-t} \qquad (2\text{-}4)$$

where $q_0 < 0$ is the net input for a given wage rate "w" during the construction period "0", and $q_t = b_t - w a_t$ is the net output of the process during the utilization period. This is a discounted stream of earnings of a

---

[2] Hicks prefers to call the "factor–price–frontier" an "efficiency curve."

process at the initial period "0".

The neo-Austrian production process is vertically integrated, meaning there are no markets for intermediates. One of the most challenging problems for neo-Austrian theory is incorporating intermediate markets into practice. One potential solution is to introduce a physical capital good market between the construction and utilization processes. In this case, the gross rate of interest R would also consider the rate of depreciation "δ".

Suppose that the optimal termination period of the process is at T, in the sense that lengthening the process yields a negative value, i.e., $k_0(r, T + \Delta t) < 0.$[3] Then, the value of the process given in equation (2-4) can be decomposed into the construction and utilization periods as follows:

$$k_0(r, T; w) = \sum_0^v q_0 R^{-t} + \sum_v^{T-v} q_t R^{-t} = 0, \qquad (2\text{-}5)$$

for which its first part is the present value of the costs of the construction period, and its second part is the yield of the utilization period at an initial period. The value of the processes at the initial and terminal periods becomes zero: $k_0(r, 0) = k_0(r, T) = 0$ for the yield rate r of the process. Its value is maximized at the end of the construction period (at the beginning of the utilization period) and decreases at the depreciation rate δ. The value of the process changes in time t, varying by the point at which it is evaluated. Figure 2-1 displays it.

Its value at point "v"can be evaluated in two ways: "forward-looking" and "backward-looking." Both are equivalent under the condition $k_0(\cdot) = 0$. Equation (2-6) expresses this equivalency as follows:

---

[3] Its formal proof is provided by Arrow and Levhari (1969) and Burmeister (2009).

Figure 2-1. A value profile for a production process

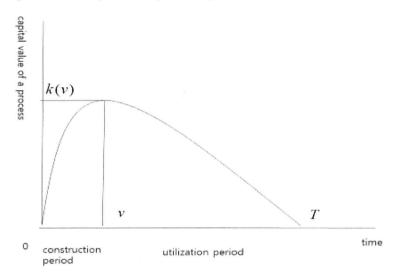

<It reaches its maximum at the end of the construction period "v", as denoted by "$k(v)$". Afterward, its value decreases at the depreciation rate of "δ" up to the terminal period "$k(T)$".>

$$\sum_0^v q_t R^t = \sum_0^{T-v} q_t R^{-t}. \tag{2-6}$$

The left-hand side of Equation (2-6) reflects the accumulated cost of inputs at the gross rate of interest, $R = 1 + r + \delta$, and the right-hand side reflects the sum of the discounted stream of earnings during the utilization period. The former is a "backward-looking" measure, while the latter is "forward-looking" in nature. At the "breaking point" of the process, the price of the capital good produced can be measured either by the forward-looking discounted streams or at accumulated costs. If the interest rate is lower than the yield rate (internal rate) of return in the process, the right-hand side of Equation (2-6) becomes greater than its left-hand side, resulting in capital gains on the process.

4. Production Function

When presenting neo-Austrian theory at seminars, one common question posed by colleagues is the absence of a production function, which is a fundamental element of neo-classical growth theory. In the latter, a factor price frontier is explained based on the marginal productivities of the factors of production. As the capital stock of an economy increases through capital accumulation, the marginal productivity of capital decreases, while the marginal productivity of labor increases. However, from our perspective, the steady state of both factors yields the same outcome.

Neo-Austrian theory diverges from traditional economic theory by emphasizing the importance of the savings-investment relationship, which is typically obscured by the neo-classical production function. In the latter, the capital fund market is separate from the goods market, whereas Hicks' "flow-input flow-output" technique integrates the two. Additionally, a neo-classical production function assumes a homogeneous goods model where there is no distinction between fixed capital goods and variable capital (working capital). While the fixed capital good only appears during the utilization period in the neo-classical approach, it is complementary to labor and prolongs the terminal period of the process in the neo-Austrian approach. As long as the capital goods replace the older depreciated goods and there are no changes in techniques, the savings-investment approach of production is not significantly different from the neo-classical approach.

A departure from the neo-classical approach arises when the fixed capital good is replaced by a new one that differs from the old one. In this case, an incremental increase in the new capital good is preceded by the savings-investment fund market of the neo-Austrian approach, as outlined by Hicks

(1973, p.182):

> According to Savings–Investment theories (and ours in this respect a
> Saving–Investment theory) real wages depend on saving; in Production
> Function theories no such effect appears. The reason is that Production
> Function theories treat New Equipment as an independent variable; in their
> New Equipment (magnitude and composition) the effect of saving is
> concealed.

In neo-Austrian theory, a production process can be distinguished based on
the input costs incurred during the construction period relative to the net
revenues accrued during the utilization period over the profile. A process
that yields higher during the utilization period at a reduced interest rate is
called a "forward-biased" technique, and the one with lower yields is called
a "backward-biased" technique (Hicks, 1973, p.77). This implies that the
equipment emerging from the construction period is more productive at a
lower interest rate.[4] Hicks refers to the input "capital" in a neo-classical
production function as "new equipment," which emerges from a "forward-
biased" technique due to the change in the interest rate of the fund market.
In this respect, the effect of savings is below the production function. In
other words, the history of the physical capital goods used as inputs in the
production function is not revealed as much in neo-Austrian theory.

5. A "Traverse"

Presumably, the construction of new equipment to embody a new technique
requires greater investment. In neo-Austrian theory, the increase in the
capital good should be understood as a substitution of an old production

---

[4] I use the term 'equipment' interchangeably with 'physical capital good'.

process for a new one, which leads to a shift of the economy from a steady state at the old interest rate to a new steady state at the new interest rate.

A new stage of the production process is generated by this substitution, which proceeds through three phases: the preparatory phase, in which the construction of new equipment is prepared; the early phase, in which the old and new equipment coexist; and the late phase, in which the old equipment is completely replaced by the new equipment. Hicks referred to the transition from one steady state to another as the "traverse."

Suppose that the interest rate in the economy is reduced and a "forward-biased" technique is introduced. As the economy undergoes this traverse, the ratios of the input-output coefficients vary over the profile, resulting in a change in the rate of starts in the economy. The economy goes through the three phases, and experiences changes in the rate of starts. During the preparatory phase, a larger amount of labor input is required, resulting in a decrease in the growth rate of the economy. This is because the economy needs to divert resources away from production and towards the construction of new equipment.

In the early phase, the old capital good is substituted for the new one, which is presumably more productive, resulting in a higher growth rate for the economy. Finally, during the late phase, there are no more sources to stimulate an increase in productivity, and the growth rate of the economy decreases from the early phase.

However, neo-Austrian theory is less concerned with changes in the growth rate and stability conditions and more focused on the changes in the economy during non-proportional disequilibrium economic states. There are various repercussions on the traverse of the non-steady state of the economy, such as successive changes in techniques associated with changes in the wage rate, which would cause changes in the value profiles of the different ages. Hicks' Capital and Time caught my attention when seeking to understand the intrinsic nature of "capital gains" and "capital losses." It is a well-established concept in economics that no "capital gains" occur in the steady state in the long run, which is a topic of inquiry in non-steady states. A crossover from one steady state to another, as shown by Hicks' "traverse" in a non-steady state, provides a framework for analyzing the distributional aspects of the economy in transitional environments.

6. Agents of the Economy

In the previous section, it was explained that there are no markets for intermediates in a vertically integrated production process, and no agents participate in the market. Therefore, the interactions among agents in this type of economy are not well understood. This market failure has been cited as one reason why Hicks' Capital and Time has not received much attention in the economic profession.

To better understand the dynamics of this type of economy, two agents will be introduced: an individual worker and a producer. Each agent is given one unit of time and must decide how to allocate it. The producer must decide how to allocate their time between the construction and utilization periods. This decision differs from that of a vertically integrated neo-Austrian process, where the division between the two periods is already given.

The physical capital good that emerges at the end of the construction period is a fixed capital good. The quality of the fixed capital good varies based on the producer's choice of construction period. The longer the period, the higher the quality of the capital good, and its quantity is determined by the rate of starts in the process. A high level of employment resulting from a high growth rate of labor will yield a high rate of starts, and the utilization period begins with a greater amount of the fixed capital good. However, the producer's decision also depends on the market rate of interest, which may differ from the yield rate of the process.

An individual's allocation problem regarding their given unit of time is related to when they should start engaging in the production of final goods in order to earn income. During their early life, individuals acquire knowledge that is available in public or in nature.[5] During this period, their productivity improves and they become human capital of a higher quality. This period of human capital formation is similar to a producer's construction period. In this sense, a producer's utilization period becomes an individual's earning period for the rest of their life.

No final outputs are available during the construction period of the process in which an individual forms human capital and they may need to take out loans to support themselves during this time. This financing problem is not only applicable to the individual, but also to the producer who initiates the production process. This issue will be discussed in more detail later. An individual will engage with the process according to their decision on how to allocate their given unit of time for income-earning activities.

It is tempting to apply a production function during the utilization period, but one drawback is the economy of scale problem that arises from its use.[6]

---

[5] For simplification I abstract from the cost-benefit analysis of education, etc. for human capital formation.

[6] In the aggregate production function of a neo-classical growth model, the economies of scale at an individual firm's plant level are negligible so that it can do away with them.

However, in the context of a production process where there is a match between human capital and physical capital goods, there is an intertemporal complementarity between these two factors that shifts our focus away from the economy of scale problem. Instead, we can use the neo-classical production function, which assumes a homogeneous degree of one at the firm level.

The next question is whether the marginal productivity of the factors of production can be defined at a given utilization moment in the neo-Austrian process. To address this question, I assume that both present and future consumption goods are produced in the economy, represented by capital goods. The neo-Austrian technique for both is identical, with the only difference being the period of construction. A capital good is produced by a technique with a longer construction period that is associated with a higher level of human capital.

Furthermore, I assume that a higher level of human capital can shift to a process with a lower construction period than the one in which an individual is currently engaged. However, an individual must spend more time developing human capital before starting to engage in the production process with a higher level in the construction period. This condition allows for the substitution between the fixed capital good at a given moment in the utilization process and the human capital of the previous process.

With these conditions of intertemporal complementarity, the mobility condition of the human capital production function of a homogeneous degree of one is defined for the inputs of the fixed capital good, and the human capital is integrated into the utilization process.

In Austrian capital theory, capital accumulation begins with natural resources and progresses through a series of intermediate stages until the final stage of consumption is reached. Hicks' book *Capital and Time* (1973) is based on the Austrian approach and allows for the discussion of growth problems in non-steady state developing countries. The vertically integrated economic production process in this approach consists of two parts: a construction period and a utilization period. Intermediates are produced during the construction period, and the final good is produced during the utilization period. Unlike the growth problems of advanced economies, which are usually in a steady-state, the growth problems of developing economies start from scratch. Hicks' neo-Austrian approach provides a framework for examining growth problems within developing economies from the initial period, which is in a non-steady state.

Several articles in this book attempt to link the Austrian approach to the mainstream neo-classical growth model in Hicks' neo-Austrian framework. The inputs of physical capital goods in the neo-classical production function are, in fact, the embodiment of the past history of capital accumulation. Hicks' construction period reveals this history in terms of the Austrian roundabout period of a production process. On the other hand, the utilization period of the production of final goods allows us to deploy the neo-classical production function, which plays a role in bridging both periods. Hicks' "traverse" is the cross-over path from a steady-state of an old technique to a steady-state of a new modern technique due to technical change. The growth of the economy on the "traverse" is expressed by the change in the activity level of the economy, either by a full-employment economy or a fixed-wage economy with a fixed amount of savings. In either case, the growth rate of the economy is higher than that in the steady-state.

During the Austrian roundabout period of production, not only are physical capital goods formed but also human capital. One could consider introducing agents into Hicks' neo-Austrian framework, where a producer initiates the process from the input of natural resources to the output of the final good. An early start-up process is more roundabout, while a late start-up is less so. Each process involves forming physical capital goods during the construction period, and with labor, these capital goods produce final goods during the utilization period. Individuals are faced with deciding which process to engage with, and this choice depends on their individual time preference rate, as described in the relevant model. An individual with a high time preference rate engages with the less roundabout process and earns income earlier in life than someone with a low time preference rate. Conversely, an individual who prefers a low time preference rate delays the start of earnings and earns a higher wage rate later on when engaged with the more roundabout production process. Presumably, the productivity of labor engaging with the more roundabout process is higher than that of the less roundabout process, and therefore more productive labor is matched with a more roundabout process during the utilization period. In this match of physical capital goods with human capital, I refer to the less roundabout process as a physical capital-intensive one and the more roundabout one as a human capital-intensive process. This presentation of production processes in terms of their intensities is more familiar to neoclassical economics. I believe that matching physical capital goods with human capital is a possible linkage of the neo-Austrian approach to a neoclassical growth model.

The capital that is more important for the utilization period depends on the demand for final goods or services. As discussed in Part V of this book, the linkage between the construction and utilization period is related to the market structure of the final goods or services. Another notable aspect of an integrated production process of Hicks' neo-Austrian framework is the liquidity effect on its production process. When the output streams of its utilization process are unable to cover the costs incurred during its construction period, the process becomes unviable. In this regard, the monetary effect on the value of the process occurs during Hicks' "traverse," although not explicitly stated.

7. A "Forward-Biased" and a "Backward-Biased" Technique

A producer's investment includes both the costs of establishing a productive capacity (capacity investment) and the costs of operating that capacity (operational investment), which yield the final outputs. For a given output stream during the utilization period, a technique is characterized by its distribution of cost savings throughout the period: "forward-biased" and "backward-biased." In a forward-biased technique, cost savings come later, while in a backward-biased technique, cost savings come earlier (Hicks, 1973, p.77). A final good is produced later in a forward-biased technique than in a backward-biased one, so the distance from the original factor of production is greater in a forward-biased technique than in a backward-biased technique. Accordingly, the former is referred to as "original-factor-intensive," and the latter as "human-capital-intensive."

Suppose that a human capital technology is described as an increasing function of time, reflecting the Austrian "roundabout period of production." Let h denote the amount of human capital and let "z" denote the ratio of human capital to the natural resources comprised of raw labor and land, such

Figure 2-2. A determination of human capital vintage

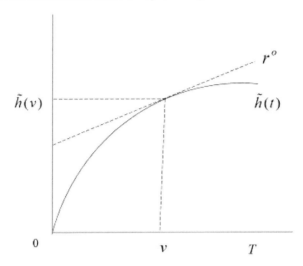

<At a given rate of interest r^o, an individual spends time "v" for their human capital formation and the rest of the period "$T - v$" for earnings.>

that $\tilde{h}(\tau) : \tilde{h}(\tau) \equiv h(\tau)/z$. The productivity of human capital increases at a decreasing rate with respect to time. In particular, it is assumed that $\tilde{h}(t) = t^{\xi} ; 0 < \xi < 1$.

Figure 2-2 illustrates the vintage of the human capital $h(v)$ on the vertical axis with the horizontal time axis of a vintage.

8. Technical Progress

Figure 2-3 illustrates the technical progress for human capital through a shift in the human capital technology function from $\tilde{h}^*(\tau)$ to $\tilde{h}^o(\tau)$. As shown in the figure, an individual increases the time spent on human capital formation by $\tau^o\tau^*$. The individual becomes a higher vintage of human capital of $\tilde{h}^o(\tau^o)$.

Figure 2-3. Harrod's "capital-biased" technical progress

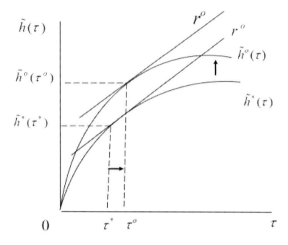

Hicks raises a question about the relationship between a "forward-biased technique" and his "neutral technical progress," and identifies the former with a "Harrod-neutral technical progress." In *Capital and Time* (1973, p. 183), he states that:

> If a change in technique is unbiased, in our sense, if saving is a constant proportion of profits (or of total income), and if there is full employment of a labour supply that is increasing at a constant growth rate, there will be a long-run tendency to a new equilibrium in which the rate of interest is the same as it was before the technical change, and in which distribution, in the sense of (rK/wL) is the same as before. From one steady state to another the Harrod condition is satisfied, for a change in technique which exhibits (our) lack of bias. That is how the Harrod classification fits in.

The surplus of the output expressed by $(B - wA)$ in a Hicks social accounting equation is equal to $(1 - s)rK$. Dividing both sides by the term wA, which represents the earnings redeemed to the original factor of production, a composite of raw labor and land in our case, gives the equality of

$$\frac{B}{wA} = 1 + (1 - s)\frac{rK}{wA},$$

which implies that to maintain Harrod-neutrality, the share of the original factor in the total output must remain constant as the economy's productivity increases. This means that the rate of productivity increase (B/A) is offset by an increase in the wage rate "w", resulting in a constancy of the arc-elasticity of a factor price frontier (Hicks 1973, p.73).

In a previous discussion, I identified a "forward-biased" technique as a "human-capital" intensive one, where the numerator $(B - wA)$ in the social accounting equation of (2-3) increases with the vintage of human capital. The distribution of income, expressed by the ratio of (rK/wL), is positively influenced by the human capital vintage. Therefore, a "forward-biased" technique in neo-Austrian theory aligns with "capital-biased" technical progress from Harrod's perspective.

9. Hicks' Traverse in a Small Open Economy

This section explains Hicks' traverse in a small open economy by incorporating Hicks' flow-input flow-output technology into an overlapping generations model.[7] There is a fixed amount of land in the economy, and individuals live for a unit period. A constant number of new generations are born in a continuum. There are consumer goods and services markets in the economy, and they are perfectly competitive. The consumer good is produced by land and labor in a neoclassical production function. A unit of

---

[7] This section is based on Kim (2009).

capital goods is produced by a fixed bundle of labor, and a given amount of a consumer good is complementary with time. Both the capital goods and human capital truncate concurrently, and the income from the capital goods is shared between the capital goods producer and human capital. The consumer goods and services provided by a capital good enter into a consumer's utility function.

Individuals maximize their streams of income throughout their lives. At the beginning of someone's career, individuals chose a sector in which they would like to work, and sectoral movement may be perceived as difficult or detrimental to their careers. Labor is sector-specific, while capital funds are freely mobile for the small open economy, and the rate of interest is given at the international level. Capital goods producers have static expectations in the sense that they take the price of the capital good of the previous cohort as given.

In order to show the existence of a competitive steady-state, the conditions under which the price of services decreases monotonically with respect to the increase in the knowledge-embodiment period are presented. For this purpose, the knowledge-embodiment period needs to be upper-bounded. We take the upper bound of the knowledge-embodiment period as the one for which half the rate of the increase of the efficiency of the knowledge-embodiment period is equal to the inverse of the life of the capital good. The rate of the increase of the efficiency of the capital good is equalized to the life-period adjusted discount factor at the upper bound with an internationally given rate of interest.

Another condition introduced is that the input of the consumer good for the production of a unit of a capital good is sufficiently small. These conditions ensure that the discrepancy between the rate of increase of the marginal efficiency of the capital good and the life-period adjusted discount factor almost disappears under the first-order condition. Finally, a limited form of the Inada condition is introduced on the efficiency of the capital good. The conditions for local stability of a steady-state competitive equilibrium are as follows: 1) the per capita output function for the consumer good exhibits almost no diminishing marginal productivity with respect to land; 2) the per capita output of the consumer good is finite, even if the per capita land ratio approaches infinity; and 3) the rate of the fall of the marginal efficiency of the capital good with respect to time is finite.

There are barriers for small open economies in adapting to world frontier technology in capital good production. As a result, these economies have a comparative advantage in the production of consumer goods and import capital goods that embody a higher level of knowledge from the rest of the world.

In general, international trade in capital goods results in a lower growth rate for small open economies due to unfavorable effects on the production of research and knowledge (Grossman and Helpman, 1991b; Stokey, 1991; Young, 1991). This is because knowledge spillover effects are limited to the domestic economy. However, as in the endogenous growth model (Romer, 1990; Grossman and Helpman, 1991a), knowledge spillover effects are taken into account and occur through the international trade of capital goods or intermediates, serving as a means of transmitting knowledge between trading economies (Helliwell, 1992; Keller, 2000; Lee, 1994; Xu and Wang, 1999). The knowledge embodied in imported capital goods spills over to domestic human capital, generating favorable growth effects in the small open economy.

It is assumed that economies with a knowledge level above a certain threshold, experience international spillover effects, resulting in growth gains from trade and generating the early phase on Hicks' traverse, in addition to static welfare gains. As a result, the long-run welfare of a small open economy unambiguously improves. In conclusion, this study supports the embodiment hypothesis for growth, which emphasizes investment-specific technological change associated with the accumulation of capital (Greenwood et al., 1997; Rosenberg, 1970).

The distance between domestic knowledge levels and the rest of the world is a critical factor in determining which economies will benefit from growth gains from trade and which will remain in a trap. Economies that are situated closer to the rest of the world with respect to their knowledge level are more likely to converge with the rest of the world through favorable growth effects from international spillovers. This explanation is related to the issue of convergence in growth-related literature.

Continuous introduction of capital goods of a new vintage allows small open economies to sustain Hicks' early phase, exhibiting high growth performances. Economies that heavily engage in the trade of capital goods and intermediates, export manufacturing goods, and possess a knowledge level above critical would experience a high growth path in Hicks' early phase.

This study argues that the high growth performance of East Asian economies over the past several decades can be viewed from this perspective. However, when these economies enter the late phase, their growth rates will fall, resulting in unfavorable expectations on the part of international financial investors. In this regard, the late 1990s financial crisis in East Asia might be interpreted as symptomatic of the end of the early phase and the beginning of the late phase.

10. Capital Gain in a Neo-Austrian Framework[8]

In most cases, developing economies obtain modern techniques through imitation or the transfer of technology from developed economies. On the other hand, developed economies introduce new techniques through innovation. The imitation or transfer of techniques is less costly than inventing new ones, which allows developing economies to benefit from what is often called the "catch-up effect." As structural change associated with introducing a new technique is likely to be more prevalent in a developing economy than a developed one, the problem of capital gains affecting income distribution is more important to the former. The entrepreneur's intertemporal maximization problem can be constructed in such a way that is suited to a fast-growing economy. Another outcome of the model is the provision of an endogenous determination of wage rates, the rate of interest, the actual rate of profits, the entrepreneur's consumption, the propensity to save, and the value of the rate of starts on the traverse.

For a developed economy where a steady state prevails, changes in expectations of future dividends and changes in expected real interest rates are the influential factors regarding capital gains, as exemplified by Donaldson and Mehra's (1984) intertemporal asset pricing model, among others.

---

[8] This section is based on Kim (1994), who develops a general equilibrium asset pricing model with Hicks' neo-Austrian production technology, whereby entrepreneurs maximize their stream of consumption on the Hicksian traverse.

Clark (1923, p. 123) distinguishes the return on capital goods from the interest rates on capital funds. He considers that permanent capital or an abiding fund of productive wealth earns interest. However, particular capital goods or instruments of production that perish through earn rent and not interest. The landowner's earnings correspond to the interest rate on capital funds in Clark's (1923) terms. On the other hand, the rate of return on the traverse equals rents. It is also shown that a discrepancy between the rate of return on the traverse and the entrepreneur's expected rate of return could be interpreted as a causal factor in the rise of capital gains on land. In the steady state, the expected rate of return will be realized, and the problem of capital gains disappears. However, the discrepancy between both arises on the traverse.

The underlying factor of a causal relation between structural change and capital gains is attributed to a difference between an entrepreneur's and landowner's subjective view of the valuation of assets on the traverse. In turn, it comes from the existence of the "bubble." During the early phase in which the "bubble" arises, future consumption is valued less highly than expected at the beginning, and the market value of the asset is undervalued. It causes demand for future income-earning assets to increase.

A credit policy is an important factor in explaining capital gains. By keeping the market rate of interest low through an easy credit policy, capital gains can be achieved over time. While these results are not new, the use of the neo-Austrian approach – a largely neglected one in mainstream economics – sheds new light on the relationship among structural change, economic growth, and the accrual of capital gains. This reminds us of Malinvaud's (1986) passage in his Hicks' lecture: "in theoretical analysis it is indeed often rewarding to look at the same question through different glasses" (p. 371).

In our model, the sequential switching of techniques does not occur in response to changes in wage rates over time. If we were to allow for switching of techniques due to changes in wages, a more complicated analysis would be required. It's possible that the reality is closer to a situation in which continuous adjustments of techniques take place. Complementary to the approach developed in this section, future research on the sequential switching of techniques may enlighten us about the endogenous determination of the traverse.

The effects of differences in construction on income distribution as well as utilization periods are another important area for future research. In this model, a worker is assumed to accept the wage rate passively. However, if workers organize to increase wages and their share of capital gains, then entrepreneurs may be induced to switch to more mechanized techniques, presenting another income distribution problem during the course of the structural change of an economy.

CHAPTER 3

A NEO-AUSTRIAN MODEL
OF TRADE AND GROWTH

1. Introduction

The literature on trade and economic growth is extensive. However, research on these issues often does not offer a consensus among economists. A positive correlation between trade and economic growth is not always ensured, as one might expect. Sachs and Warner (1995) observed a positive effect of an economy's openness on economic growth. Slaughter (2001) found that per capita income convergence is not guaranteed before and after the opening of economies. These differing research outcomes may be partly due to differing interpretations of openness and how data are pooled for this purpose. Traditionally, openness referred to the degree of free trade expressed from tariff and non-tariff levels and other prohibitive trade policy measures. However, the mixed results from trade and growth research on this issue suggest the need to modify the meaning of openness.

Among others, Keller (2000) and Lee (1995) found a positive effect of trade in a North-South trade featuring the trade of capital goods versus consumer goods. In contrast, Eaton and Kortum (2001) found that variations in the relative price of equipment explain productivity differences across countries.[1] In their study, the South, located some distance from the North,

---

[1] Eaton and Kortum (2001) is an extension to an open economy of a De Long and Summers' (1991) empirical result of the positive correlation between the price of

is effectively inhibited from entering into free trade and excluded from its benefits. Their trade model posits the geographical distance of the South from the North in the "capital goods versus consumer goods" trade as an alternative measure of openness.

From a neo-Austrian perspective, a trade of capital goods versus consumer goods implies a dissociation between a capital good's construction phase and its utilization phase in the South. Newly imported goods from the North would then replace the traditional old capital goods of the South. Since knowledge of a higher vintage is embodied in imported capital goods, the South's domestic human capital vintage is considered lower than that of the North. This vintage mismatch adds costs to the operation of the imported capital goods in the South. Thus, a vintage difference between the two is a trade impediment analogous to Eaton-Kortum's geographical distance.

The economy that successfully resolves this impediment through trade benefits from it. During the trade process, the construction period of old capital goods is replaced with the "early phase," where traditional old capital goods coexist with imported modern goods, leading to Hicks' traverse. [2] In the new open economy environment, individuals and firms adapt to new production processes involving imported capital goods, resulting in investment in human capital (Becker, 1962).

Since physical capital goods complement human capital in production, capital accumulation occurs in the South's economy, leading to an increase in the economy's growth rate. Thus, the South's comparative advantage

---

the equipment prices and the economic growth.
[2] The growth effect for the small-open-economy (SOE) on the traverse is discussed in Kim (2009).

changes in favor of capital-intensive goods, as long as the human capital vintage gap between the North and the South persists, and the learning from new imported capital goods is not exhausted. This is similar to how introducing new goods allowed Asian economies to grow beyond the boundedness of the "learning-by-doing" effect of new goods in Lucas' 'Miracle Model' (Lucas, 1993).

An economy that overcomes this impediment can engage in trade and reap its benefits. However, during trade, the construction phase of old capital goods is suppressed, and the economy starts over in the "early phase," where both traditional old capital goods and modern imported goods coexist. This results in Hicks' traverse, where agents in the economy adapt to new situations that differ from those in the traditional economy. To adapt to the production process of new imported capital goods, individuals and firms invest in human capital. Since physical capital goods complement human capital in production, capital accumulation occurs, and the economy's growth rate increases. Therefore, the South's comparative advantage shifts to capital-intensive goods, as long as the human capital vintage gap between the North and the South persists, meaning as long as the South is still learning from the new imported capital goods. This resembles how introducing new goods allows Asian economies to surpass the limits of Lucas' "Miracle Model" based on "learning-by-doing" effects (Lucas, 1993).

In conclusion, the existing research on trade and growth suggests that specific conditions must be met to explain the positive relationship between the two. Although an economy's openness is necessary, it requires sufficient conditions to realize a positive effect, which must be located in the present trade model. High costs of capital goods movement and divergence of human capital vintages among trading nations hinder knowledge spillovers to the South, reducing contributions to productivity increases. Therefore, our analysis focuses on how the economy's agents respond to free trade's opening. The next section presents an overview of the neo-Austrian trade model.

2. Neo-Austrian Trade Model

A standard trade model is typically presented as a model with two goods, two factors (capital and labor), and two countries (one physical capital-abundant, the other human capital-abundant). The model assumes identical preferences over the tradable goods and a production function that is homogeneous of degree one. Both economies engaged in trade share the same technology and preferences, and the flow of goods is directed by the comparative advantage of the economy determined by its endowment factor. According to the Heckscher–Ohlin–Samuelson (standard) trade model, an economy with a relatively higher endowment of capital will export a capital-intensive good and import a labor-intensive one. A welfare-improving doctrine of free trade is well-established in this simplified trade model.

However, clarifying the definition of capital in a standard trade model can be challenging due to the controversial nature of the term. To understand the standard trade theorem using neo-Austrian theory, we need to ask whether an analogous trade theorem can be deduced from the neo-Austrian trade model. Furthermore, we should consider the implications of the neo-Austrian theory for the success stories of East Asian economies. This section aims to provide answers to these questions.

In contrast to the standard trade model, let us consider an economy with two types of goods: present consumption goods (consumer goods) and future consumption goods (capital goods). Goods are identified by the production techniques used. For consumer goods, a backward-biased technique is used, while a forward-biased technique produces capital goods.[3] Three factors are used as inputs for production: land, human capital, and physical capital goods. Physical capital goods are created by accumulating original production factors, such as raw labor and land, during the construction period. In contrast, raw labor is transformed into human capital of higher quality by acquiring publicly available knowledge over time.[4] The supply of land is limited and can only be improved somewhat through irrigation and nurturing. The knowledge of the human capital vintage incorporated onto the physical capital produces the corresponding vintage of the capital good.

Viewed from a production hierarchy perspective, the present consumption good is produced similarly to the original production factors, whereas future consumption-good production is much further removed from the original production factor process, which is where human capital is formed. The former can be referred to as an original factor-intensive good, while the latter is a human capital-intensive good.

An economy is composed of a fully employed population of a specific size. Each member of the economy has free access to the international market for funds at the market interest rate, $r + \delta$, which takes into account the rate of depreciation δ of the physical capital good. Individuals in this economy maximize their utility by allocating their economic life period, T, for

---

[3] Recall that a 'backward-biased' technique is comparable to a 'capital-intensive' technique and a 'forward-biased' one to a 'human-capital-intensive' technique.

[4] A formal cost-benefit analysis of human capital formation, such as investment in education, is not considered for the simplification of the discussion as done in Findlay–Kierzkowski's model.

human capital formation. They weigh their present consumption against their future consumption, based on their time preference rate relative to the market's interest rate. Successful members of a family unit share identical time preference rates. However, an individual with a low-time preference rate values future income more than one with a high-time preference rate. In other words, the former discounts future income less, at a rate of β, which is the inverse of the time preference rate $1/1 + \rho$.

This allocation problem is dependent on the market interest rate, $r + \delta$, relative to an individual's time preference rate, ρ, which we call the relative interest rate. Individuals can consume an amount $c(t + \Delta t)$ by delaying their consumption for a period of Δt at the gross market interest rate, $1 + r + \delta$. At equilibrium, the discounted present value of the amount of consumption, using the discount factor β, should be equal to the present amount of consumption $c(t)$. Therefore, the decision rule for a representative individual under this consideration is expressed as follows:

$$\frac{c(t+\Delta t)}{c(t)} = \frac{1+r+\delta}{1+\rho} = \tilde{r}, \qquad (3\text{-}1)$$

where the right-hand side refers to the *relative interest rate.*

For human capital formation to occur, the amount of consumption an individual obtains in the delay period, Δt, must be greater than what they could have obtained if they had consumed $c(t + \Delta t) > c(t)$ instead. The left-hand side of Equation (3-1) represents the transformation rate of present consumption to future consumption through human capital formation. This rate depends on the level of human capital technology. No individual will allocate their time to human capital formation if the level of human capital technology is so low that $c(t + \Delta t) \leq c(t)$. Conversely, in the neo-

Austrian sense, individuals would allocate more time to human capital formation in an economy with Harrod-capital-biased technological progress.

3. Product Mix and Comparative Advantage

We assume that there are multiple producers in the economy, each with the same planning horizon, T. During the construction phase, they produce physical capital goods by accumulating raw labor over a generation, $\tau \in (0, T)$. In the utilization phase, physical capital goods complement human capital in producing final goods. Therefore, the vintage of physical capital goods is determined by the level of human capital.

An aggregate output over a generation (cohort) $\tau \in (0, T)$ is expressed as the sum of the present and the future consumption goods produced in the economy by all its members:

$$x(\tau) = p_C x_C(\tau) + p_K x_K(\tau), \tag{3-2}$$

where $x_C(\tau)$ and $x_K(\tau)$ refer to the output of consumer goods, C, and capital goods, K, respectively, for a τ generation. In addition, p_C and p_K are the prices given at the domestic economy:[5]

$$x_C(\tau; p) = \sum_{v}^{T} b_{t-\tau} x_{t-\tau}(p);$$

$$x_K(\tau; p) = \sum_{0}^{v} a_{t-\tau} x_{t-\tau}(p); p \equiv p_C/p_K. \tag{3-3}$$

The future consumption amount, $c(t + \Delta t)$, in the numerator of Equation

---

[5] Since the substitution of human capital between the two sectors is allowed, the consumer good output can be presented in typical Cobb–Douglas form, that is, $x_C(\cdot) = \tilde{h}^{\alpha} \sum_{v}^{T} x_{t-\tau}(p)$, where $1 < \alpha < 1$ is a distributive share for human capital.

(3-1), can be achieved by producing consumer goods using physical capital goods that were formed prior to present consumption. Therefore, the total output of the τ-generation's capital goods replaces the future consumption goods in the numerator of Equation (3-1), enabling Equation (3-4) to hold for the capital goods market equilibrium, where

$$\frac{X_K(\tau)}{X_C(\tau)} = \frac{P_C(\tau)}{P_K(\tau)} = \tilde{r}, \tag{3-4}$$

implying that a τ-generation economy accumulates capital at a rate of $\tilde{r}$. When an individual's time preference rate is neutral, such that $\tilde{r} = 1$ is equal to the market interest rate, there is no accumulation of either human or physical capital. In this case, the economy's total output is equally divided between the consumer good (present consumption) and the capital good (future consumption). The savings rate $\tilde{s}$ is thus defined as the share of physical capital goods in total output, given by $\tilde{s} = s/(1-s)$, where s indicates the economy's savings rate.

The first-order condition for human capital formation in Equation (3-1) is connected to the capital goods market in Equation (3-4) through a time lag in the construction period. This link between the two markets determines the savings rate and the price of capital goods associated with an economy's product mix. These variables are influenced by the technology used in human capital formation and the time preference rates of individuals in the economy. In economies with high levels of human technology, specifically those with a Harrod-capital-biased level of technical progress, the savings rate tends to be high, and the price of capital goods is low.

It should be noted that the human capital vintage is high when savings rates are high in low-time-preference-rate economies, in contrast to high-time-preference-rate economies. When an economy's basic needs are significant enough to make time preference rates very high, the relative interest rate becomes smaller than what is needed for capital accumulation.[6] This is often the case for underdeveloped economies, and therefore capital accumulation tends to occur in economies whose developmental stage is at the above-described level, where basic needs are fulfilled, and the relative interest rate is greater than one. As discussed in Section 5, the neo-Austrian trade model is heavily dependent on the economy's time preference rates.[7]

In summary, we have discussed how savings rates, capital goods prices, and the economy's product mix relate to its level of human capital technology and time preference rates. Additionally, Equation (3-3) demonstrates that the endowment of human capital (physical capital) relative to the original factors of production in a steady state can change with the level of human capital technology. Furthermore, the economy's factor endowments tend to be biased towards physical capital goods, as indicated by the increase in the Equation (3-3) numerator when a forward-biased technique is applied.

Suppose two economies have differing levels of human capital technology. For a given relative interest rate, an economy with a high level of human capital technology is endowed with more human capital than one with a lower level. Therefore, a standard trade theorem from a neo-Austrian

---

[6] Unlike the neo-classical growth model, this model allows a change in an agent's discount factor due to adaptation to changing environments.

[7] An economy's time preference rates vary according to the relative amounts of consumer goods available in the present versus the future. In a poor economy that is in dire need of present consumption goods, the time preference rates would be high. Conversely, in an affluent and advanced economy, the need for present consumption goods is much lower. However, when the ratio of consumption goods between present and future consumption is equal to one, the time preference rates of the two economies are comparable.

perspective can be rephrased as follows: [8]

> An economy with a high vintage of human capital (a human-capital-abundant-economy) has a comparative advantage in producing forward-biased-technique goods (human-capital-intensive). In contrast, those with a low vintage of human capital (an original-factor-abundant-economy) have a comparative advantage in producing backward-biased-technique goods (original-factor-intensive).

The factor endowment hypothesis in standard trade theory assumes that the factors of production, whether physical or human capital, are fixed in the economy. In contrast, the neo-Austrian theory takes a more upstream approach, starting with individuals' basic time preferences and the level of human capital technology. What sets the neo-Austrian model apart from the standard trade model is that human capital knowledge is embedded in the production of physical capital goods. As a result, a shift in the aggregate composition towards the physical capital goods sector from the consumer goods sector can drive economic growth.

4. Production Possibility Curves

Assuming we have a small open economy (SOE) in the South, which is a developing economy, that trades with a Northern advanced economy. Let us also assume that this trade is structured as a consumer-capital goods trade, where the advanced economy exports capital goods with a technological edge and imports consumer goods from the South. We propose and will demonstrate that a knowledge spillover process will occur from the North

---

[8] As will be clarified later, human capital is complementary to physical capital, meaning that its value decreases at the same rate as the "δ" of physical capital.

to the South through this trade in consumer-capital goods.

Figure 3-1 depicts a conventional two-dimensional diagram of a production possibility curve, with capital goods on the horizontal axis and consumer goods on the vertical axis. However, in our case, the consumer goods on the vertical axis represent present consumption, while the capital goods on the horizontal axis represent future consumption. The former is based on the goods market, and the latter on the capital funds market. These two markets are related to each other by a time lag, during which the fund market of Equation (3-1) is translated into the capital goods market of Equation (3-4).[9]

In the previous section, we discussed a neo-Austrian theory and its application to a two-sector model economy, which allows for the movement of human capital across sectors. The resulting production possibility curve confirms the conventional outward-convex shape. The production possibility curve for the South is depicted as outwardly convex, with the cutting point at u. Similarly, the North's curve, denoted by $p^o(\tau)p^o(\tau)$, passes through d, bending towards the capital goods axis due to its relatively higher physical-human capital endowment. Conversely, the South's curve bends towards the consumer goods axis due to its higher relative endowment in original factors.

---

[9] The same axis can be represented by different metaphors, depending on whether it refers to the period before or after the construction of capital goods. As previously explained, the use of present and future consumption as representations of the axes is connected to an individual's decision on human capital formation, which is based on the capital funds market. The savings rate of the economy is determined by this decision. The relative price of capital goods in terms of consumer goods can be found by examining the presentation of consumer goods and the capital goods axes.

Figure 3-1. A production possibility curve with a different savings rate

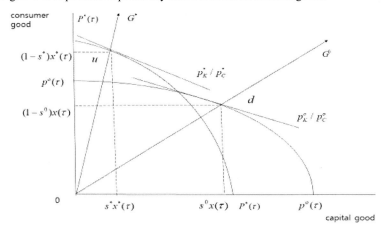

Thus, the Southern production possibility curve starts at point u for its given savings rate s^*, while the Northern curve starts at point d for savings rate s^0. In other words, the respective curves are preceded by the capital fund market equilibrium, and their shapes reflect the allocation of resources with respect to the relative change in the capital goods market price.

Note that the economy's production possibility curve is also defined for a τ cohort. One extreme is where all resources are used to produce consumer goods, and the other is in the opposite direction for capital goods. Human capital moves between sectors in response to changes in capital goods' relative price. With a price increase, an individual engaged in the consumer sector allocates more time to human capital formation to move to the former sector. Thus, human capital moves back to the consumer sector with a drop in the capital goods price, without requiring any additional investment.

Individuals in an economy with high levels of human capital technology, due to technical progress, allocate more time for human capital formation.

This means that the production possibility curve remains the same as "$p^o p^o$", without an increase in the savings rate.

In cases where knowledge is embodied in physical capital goods, the economy's growth rate exhibits Harrod-capital-biased technical progress. The North, which experiences this technical progress, would undergo structural change in their economy associated with the factor endowment in the direction of physical human capital. Therefore, for the given savings rate, the relative capital goods price falls from (p_K^*/p_C^*) at the point u, to (p_K^o/p_C^o) at point d, as indicated in Figure 3-1. Hence, the point d can be reached either by a higher savings rate or technical progress. In either case, the physical capital goods price is lowered, and a higher vintage of human capital is employed in the utilization period of the production process. As a result, the economy's productivity is higher at the product-mix of d than at that of u.

DeLong and Summers (1991) have shown a positive correlation between equipment production and economic growth across economies. [10] Their result suggests that the knowledge embodied in physical capital goods contributes to economic growth. Although this is related to the classic accumulation theory of economic growth, it emphasizes the embodiment of new knowledge on physical capital, which is involved in reducing equipment prices. Thus, the DeLong and Summer model states that growth without the knowledge embodiment of equipment results in capital accumulation that cannot sustain the growth in the long run due to the fall in capital's marginal productivity. Therefore, the balanced growth path

---

[10] This contrasts with the role of the investment rate on the economic growth in one sector of the neo-classical growth model.

along the ray $0G^o$, as shown in Figure 3-1, is unsustainable. In other words, long-run growth is only sustainable if the economy's structural transformation in the physical-human capital-intensive sector becomes feasible.

5. Tradability Conditions

We will now consider the international trade of the two Small open economies in the global economy. These two economies are underdeveloped and share the same objective of achieving a higher income level through industrialization. To achieve this, these economies intend to import capital goods from an advanced economy that are not yet available to them since they are in the nascent stages of development. They also wish to export consumer goods through their use. At their initial development stages, the savings rates of both economies are below those of the world economy (an advanced economy). Thus, these economies share a common neo-Austrian technique, differing only in technology levels.

The small open economy is considered lower income, meaning it falls short of the basic needs of present living consumption. Its discount factor is so low (i.e., the time preference rate is so high) that the relative interest rate is high enough to make the domestic price of consumer goods relative to capital goods above the world economy level. Therefore, it fails to enter our consumer-capital goods trade model. Hence, the feasibility of trade requires a savings rate above the critical level, such that the relative price of consumer goods is lower than the international price.

6. Viability of Trade

Suppose we have a small open economy whose savings rate is equal to the critical rate and is, therefore, in the tradable region. However, meeting the tradability condition does not ensure the viability of trade. The SOE would still need to overcome a technical barrier for trade to be viable. In a neo-Austrian trade model, this problem arises due to a vintage mismatch between domestic human capital and the human capital used for imported capital goods.

Recall that the trade model of consumer-capital goods is related to present consumption for future consumption with a time lag. Trade would not be viable unless the future consumption of imported capital goods is greater than otherwise, as Figure 3-2 illustrates. A small open economy with a savings rate of $s^* > \hat{s}$ engages in trade and exports consumer goods in the amount "ab" for a value of "bc" in capital goods imports at the international price of $(p_K/p_C)^o$. It is expected that a future consumption goods trade in an amount equivalent to "bc" in capital goods will be realized.

This expectation is met as long as there is no difference in the human capital vintage between the North and the South. However, since the human capital vintage of the South is less than that of the North, adjustment costs will occur with the use of the imported capital. Thus, the value of future consumption goods to be produced falls below "bc". Alternatively, a value of "bd" in future consumption goods would be produced with domestic human capital at an expense matching the value of exports, "ab", of present consumer goods. Unless the amount of future consumption goods produced by using imported capital goods is greater than "bd", the trade will be unviable. Therefore, trade viability depends on how high the import capital adjustment cost is for the South.

Figure 3-2. Viable vs. non-viable SOE: Learning effects of international trade

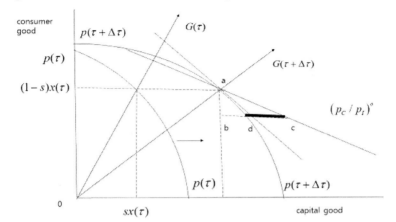

The adjustment costs of human capital *de facto* impede capital-consumer trade. One obstacle to the capital goods trade may arise from the geographical distance between the North and the South, as stated in Eaton and Kortum's model (2001). The difference in the human capital vintage between the North and the South has a similar effect on trade barriers as geographical distance. Trade restrictions caused by geographical distance result in different equipment prices across countries. Moreover, Eaton and Kortum's study finds that about 25% of cross-country productivity differences are due to the relative price of equipment, with half of that ascribed to barriers to the equipment trade. In this study, Equations (3-1) and (3-4) suggest that the capital goods price discrepancy between the South and the North varies with the human capital vintage in the regions.

On the other hand, Parente and Prescott (1994) show that differences in international income levels are explained by a barrier to adopting cutting-edge techniques. This finding confirms the success of East Asian economies due to their low technology barriers concerning economic policies and institutions. Policies and institutions that hinder adapting economies will fail to achieve the high-income levels of advanced economies. A barrier to trade due to the mismatch in human capital vintage can be considered another candidate for Parente and Prescott's (1994) technical barrier.[11]

The adjustment costs of the domestic human capital for the use of imported capital goods can be described as a convex-concave function of the ratio of the two vintages. The distance between the South's human capital and that of the North, expressed by $h(v^*/v^o)$, is shown on the horizontal axis of Figure 3-3. The adjustment cost denoted by the θ term is represented on the vertical axis.

If the distance between the economies is too great, the adjustment costs for a small open economy (SOE) may be excessively high, making it difficult for the economy to meet the trade viability condition. For instance, in Figure 3-3, if the distance is $\hat{h}(\cdot)$, small open economy trade becomes viable. However, trade viability alone is not enough, as the economy still needs to invest in training and education to adapt to imported capital goods to reap the benefits of spillover effects. An economy that successfully adapts can also benefit from Arrow's learning-by-doing effect (1962), leading to increased human capital productivity.

As depicted in Figure 3-3, successful adaptation of the South's human capital shifts the human capital technical function upward, causing forward-biased technical progress, referred to as Harrod capital-biased technical progress. The economy's endowment shifts toward physical human capital,

---

[11] In the early development literature, a barrier is considered a "bottleneck," comprising broader aspects for a developing economy to face to resolve problems such as foreign exchange, infrastructure, entrepreneurship, and skill levels.

Figure 3-3. Adjustment costs of domestic human capital

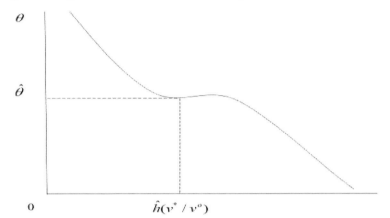

leading to a change in the SOE's comparative advantage for capital goods production. This change is identified as a dynamic comparative advantage against the SOE that fails to meet the viability condition.[12]

7. Relevance of a Neo-Austrian Trade Model: a Focus on the Success of East Asian Economies

The East Asian economies (EAM) comprise Hong Kong, Indonesia, Japan, the Republic of Korea (South Korea), Malaysia, Singapore, Taiwan, and Thailand. The success story of the EAM has caught the attention of many economists interested in determining its causes. Stiglitz (1996) attributes the causes to the following:

- A high savings rate could have partly contributed to their success due to their governments' role in mobilizing resources to ensure a virtuous cycle between growth and savings.

---

[12] The change in the factor endowment of the Korean economy is evident in Hong (1989).

- A high rate of investment associated with the production of heterogeneous and homogeneous capital goods.
- Enormous investment in human capital and skilled labor education to adopt front-edge technologies.

While these economies share common features, they are diverse in their geographical locations, culture, and natural resource endowments. Some of their characteristics are:

- An open economic policy promoting exports for industrialization.
- They have exporting trade structures in manufacturing goods such as textiles, footwear, and sporting goods, and import capital goods and intermediates.
- Most EAMs, except Indonesia and Malaysia, are poorly endowed with land and natural resources. For example, Hong Kong and Singapore are primarily cities.

It is often difficult to explain the growth of economies in a single term and identify the specific policy that brought about a successful result. Harberger (1998) ascribes an economy's growth process with the analogy of a mushroom popping up. Old industries shy away in the back while new ones appear. Many contributing factors interact, and the growth emerges like a mushroom in the morning at a certain stage of its development. How do the common features of the East Asian economies interact with each other and contribute to Stiglitz's attributes? Can the stage of development at which a mushroom pops up be identified?

There is a plethora of research with cross-section regression analyses to find the contributing factors for an economy's growth using pooled data controlled by non-economic factors. One outcome of these studies on EAM growth performance is that the contributing factor is primarily explained by factor inputs such as capital and labor (Kim and Lau 1993; Krugman 1994; Young 1995). These empirical findings imply that EAM growth is factor-driven, and productivity's contribution to growth is negligible.

Lucas' trade and diffusion model (2009) suggests a spillover effect of technology flows from advanced economies into East Asian and Pacific (EAM) economies. [13] This model challenges the growth accounting procedure of productivity measurement. In growth accounting, the residual is the leftover capital accumulation and labor inputs after the economy's growth. It represents the contribution of total factor productivity (TFP) to an economy's growth and is associated with technical progress. As a result, the residual is expected to better explain the growth of advanced economies.

Moreover, the residual is a comprehensive term that includes significant variables such as institutions, policies, cultures, and geographical locations in temperate or tropical regions. The residual can be considered the unknowns in growth accounting. However, once we identify the residual as the rate of technical progress, it becomes necessary to distinguish between embodied and disembodied technical progress. There are doubts about TFP estimates for East Asian economies in this regard.

The need to distinguish between embodied and disembodied technical progress is highlighted by Hulten (1992). He argues that these views of technical progress differ in their capital treatment. In disembodied technical change, new vintages of capital goods are measured by their efficiency units.

---

[13] His calibrated estimate of the effect is about 0.68, which says that a 1% increase in domestic human capital results in 0.68% growth.

For instance, a new vintage of ten units of more efficient capital goods is counted as ten units of the old vintage. This efficiency-adjusted measurement of technical progress results in the loss of productivity effect on the capital accumulation process. In Hulten's growth accounting, the average embodied technical efficiency is considered, which takes into account the efficiency of both the old and new capital goods.

To examine how the technical efficiency of the small open economy is affected in trade with the North, given Hulten's average embodied technical efficiency, let us return to Hicks' social accounting. Remember that the productivity level of the economy is represented by the ratio of the aggregate output level to the aggregate level of employment, and this division equation can be expressed as follows: [14]

$$\left(\frac{B}{A}\right)^* = \frac{\sum_0^{T-v^*} b_\tau^*(1-\delta^*)^\tau x_{t-\tau}}{\sum_0^T a_\tau^* x_{t-\tau}} < \frac{\sum_0^{T-v} b_\tau(1-\delta)^\tau x_{t-\tau}}{\sum_0^T a_\tau x_{t-\tau}} = \left(\frac{B}{A}\right), for(v^* < v).\quad(3\text{-}5)$$

The term, $(B/A)^*$, on the left-hand side of Equation (3-5) represents the productivity of the old capital goods, while the new productivity, (B/A), is on the right-hand side. [15] Since the productivity of the more roundabout process of the forward-biased technique is greater than that of the backward-biased one, the inequality in Equation (3-5) holds. Additionally, Equation (3-5), like Hulten's TFP measure, takes into account the capital depreciation rate. The higher the rate of depreciation of old capital goods, the higher the productivity of the new ones. In other words, the average embodied technical efficiency of the small open economy increases with Northern

---

[14] Note that the comparison of the aggregate productivity level is found for the rate of activities of the economy across the generations for a different calendar time t.
[15] The variables for the old technique are starred. Note that productivity is measured across the members of a generation $\tau \in (0, T)$.

trade.[16] This productivity effect is overlooked when measuring disembodied technical progress.

Recall that the cost share of the production process inputs increases due to the Harrod capital-biased technical progress of the small open economy, which successfully adapts imported capital goods. This magnifies the productivity effect for the small open economy. This favorable productivity effect of international trade is sustained as the new vintage of capital goods enters into trade, as in Lucas' miracle model.

8. Concluding Remarks

The success of the East Asian economies is attributed to their trade structures, which have been highlighted by scholars such as Lee (1995) and Keller (2000) due to their knowledge spillover effects. This study demonstrates that small open economies, which have a savings rate and human capital vintage above a critical level, can benefit from these spillover effects. The economic growth of small open economies is fueled by investment in human capital to match the level of imported capital goods. From a neo-Austrian perspective, the construction period for the small open economy is bypassed in this capital-consumer goods trade, enabling it to reach advanced income levels in a shorter time period. Another aspect of the neo-Austrian perspective on trade is the opening of new environments to the economy's agents, with those who succeed in this challenge joining the convergence club of the North.

Despite many simplifying assumptions and restrictions on the economy's

---

[16] The economy sets off on the 'traverse' in substituting the new vintage for the old one.

parameters, a neo-Austrian theory is comparable to mainstream neo-classical growth theory. This study introduces a neo-Austrian trade model and highlights its relation to a standard neo-classical trade model and its relevance to the growth experience of the East Asian economies.

Producers and consumers must adapt to new environments amid the uncertainty of opening trade, and agents' adaptation ultimately enables the economy to emulate the advanced economy, often referred to as "catching up" in the development literature. In this regard, the neo-Austrian trade model agrees with Nelson and Pack's (1999) assimilation model for the East Asian economies.

As a concluding remark, we will quote Nelson and Pack (1999):

"The message is that other countries could have done as well as the successful NICs if they had made the same investment effort. In contrast, the assimilation account stresses learning about, risking operating, and coming to master technologies and other practices that are new to the country, if not to the world. The marshaling of inputs is part of the story, but the emphasis on innovation and learning, rather than on marshaling."

CHAPTER 4

PRODUCT DIFFERENTIATION, PRODUCT QUALITY, AND INTRA-INDUSTRY TRADE

1. Introduction

Intra-industry trade (IIT) refers to the simultaneous export and import of goods within the same industry. It typically occurs between countries that share similar factor endowments, technological levels, or income levels. In contrast, comparative advantage trade involves countries with different factor endowments or technological levels. Therefore, comparative advantage trade usually occurs between different countries, while intra-industry trade generally takes place between similar countries.

Krugman (1979) explains that product differentiation and economies of scale are the primary drivers of intra-industry trade. When a country specializes in producing a particular product, it can lower production costs through economies of scale. Thus, if two countries specialize in producing different products and trade with each other, both countries can benefit. However, if products of different quality levels are mixed within the same industry, then intra-industry trade is caused not only by simple product differentiation but also by differences in product quality.

In trade within the same industry, the trade caused by simple product differentiation is called horizontal intra-industry trade (HIIT), while that caused by differences in product quality is referred to as vertical intra-industry trade (VIIT). Intra-industry trade, which arises from product differentiation and economies of scale, is related to HIIT. HIIT occurs between countries with similar industrial structures and demand conditions.

On the other hand, Flam and Helpman (1987) and Falvey and Kierzkowski (1987) argue that Intra-industry trade between developed countries (North) and developing countries (South) is an example of VIIT, in which high-quality products from developed countries and low-quality products from developing countries are exchanged within the same industry. The factors driving VIIT are similar to those driving comparative advantage trade, such as differences in technology levels and factor endowments.

This study provides a theoretical examination of the causes of horizontal and vertical intra-industry trade (HIIT and VIIT), and analyzes the two types of intra-industry trade using Korean trade data. Greenaway et al. (1994) classify intra-industry trade as HIIT or VIIT by comparing export and import unit prices. Products whose ratio of export to import unit price falls within a certain range are classified as HIIT, while products whose ratio is outside this range are classified as VIIT. Fontagne and Freudenberg (1997) classify items where the ratio of exports to imports is less than 10% or more than 10 times as comparative advantage trade and the remaining items as intra-industry trade.

Durkin and Krygier (1998, 2000) analyzed data from 20 OECD (Organisation for Economic Co-operation and Development) member countries from 1989 to 1992, showing that VIIT increases with income dispersion. Kandogan (2003) analyzed trade between 10 Central and Eastern European countries and 12 CIS countries during the 1992–1999 period, showing that the factors of HIIT are economies of scale, income similarity, and product diversity, while the factors of VIIT are comparative advantages and income differences. Sharma (2004) found that VIIT accounts for a higher proportion of IIT in Australia due to Australia's advantage in resource-intensive industries. Hurley (2003) showed that VIIT accounts for 70% of all IIT in the trade of the five ASEAN countries.

Oh and Joo (2000) showed that trade between Korea and the OECD is mainly VIIT and that VIIT increases with differences in the size of the economies. Most empirical studies have shown that the proportion of VIIT is higher than that of HIIT in Korea's intra-industry trade (KDI, 2003; Lee, 2003; Kim, 2004; Byun and Lee, 2005; Kim and Zhan, 2006).

This chapter is structured as follows: Section 2 describes HIIT using Lancaster's ideal variety preference function, and Section 3 provides a theoretical explanation of VIIT based on quality differences. Section 4 analyzes changes in intra-industry trade using Korea's trade statistics. Finally, Section 5 concludes this study.

2. Lancaster's Compensation Function in Intra-Industry Trade

Linder's (1961) representative demand theory of international trade views international trade from the demand side, unlike the traditional approach, which views it from the cost side of the economy. This demand-side perspective is linked to the IIT theory developed by Krugman and Helpman. The IIT theory departs from the prediction of trade patterns based on differences in factor endowments or skill levels among trading economies. Instead, IIT is generated among economies with similar incomes, identical factor endowments, and the same level of human capital skills. One advantage of IIT lies in exploring economies of scale through trade between similar economies. The gains from trade benefit trading economies that

experience economies of scale. Thus, the market size of the two trading
economies is the focal point of the analysis, and it is predicted that gains
from trade increase with the size of the market of the trading economies. In
this section, we interpret Linder's representative demand theory of
international trade in relation to Lancaster's compensation function.

Lancaster's (1966, 1979, 1980) variety model of consumer theory
emphasizes the importance of product differentiation in an industrial
economy. In this model, goods are not the objects of a consumer's utility;
rather, a good is identified by the characteristics it possesses. For example,
a consumer derives the characteristics of "sourness," "juiciness," and
"sweetness" from an "apple." These characteristics of an apple are what
enter a consumer's utility function, rather than the apple itself. A "pear" can
be highly substitutable for an "apple," as they share similar characteristics.
In Lancaster's consumer theory, a good is differentiated by the unique
combinations of characteristics it contains.

The sub-utility of a product for a consumer whose ideal variety is x has the
following form.

$$U(D(x), x, \tilde{x}) = D(x)/h(d(x, \tilde{x})), \qquad (4\text{-}1)$$

where $D(x)$ is the consumption level of variety x, $d(x, \tilde{x})$ is the shortest
distance on the circumference of the line between x and $\tilde{x}$, and $h(d)$ is
Lancaster's compensation function. This function describes the compensation
in the consumed quantity that is required to maintain a given utility level
when switching consumption to varieties that are further away from the
ideal product.

Figure 4-1. Ideal variety and effective price

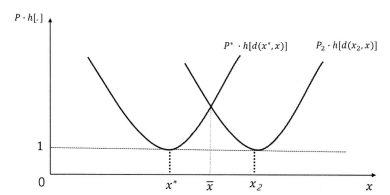

It is assumed that $h(d)$ is a convex function with $h(0)=1$, $h'(0)=0$, and $h'(d)>0$ for $d>0$.[1] An individual prefers the variety that is closest to his/her ideal variety, where closeness is measured by the distance on the line.

Consumers have to pay more to maintain the same utility as the distance of the product supplied in the market becomes farther from their ideal product. Therefore, the effective price increases with the distance. $P(x)h(d(x,\tilde{x}))$ is the effective price at which a consumer who considers $\tilde{x}$ to be the ideal variety purchases x. Each consumer chooses the product with the lowest effective price. Factors influencing consumer choice are the price of the available product and the distance between the consumer's ideal product and the available product.

In Figure 4-1, the horizontal axis represents the ideal variety of consumers, and the vertical axis is the effective price when purchasing products available in the market. The effective price increases as the available

---

[1] See Helpman and Krugman (1985).

product becomes farther from a consumer's ideal product.

Individuals' varied goods preferences are *uniformly* distributed over the economy so that every individual has a *most preferred good* (ideal good) and its density is identical for each of the ideal goods. An available good other than an individual's ideal good needs to be compensated with respect to his or her ideal good from the point of view of the social welfare of the economy. This compensation is explained by Lancaster's compensation function.

Let the ideal good to an individual be denoted by x whose characteristics are specified, and let an available good whose specification does not meet his or her ideal good be denoted by x^*.[2] The prices of these two goods are given and are denoted by $p(x)$ and $p^*(x^*)$, respectively. The distance between the two goods is represented by $u = x - x^*$.[3] Then, there is a dividing good $\bar{x}$ between the two goods in a compensation function $h(\bar{u}) > 0$ such that[4]

$$p^*(x^*)h(\bar{u}) = p(x)h(2\bar{\Delta} - \bar{u}), \qquad (4\text{-}2)$$

where $\bar{u} = \bar{x} - x^*$; $\bar{\Delta} \equiv (1/2)(x - x^*)$; $h'(\cdot) > 0, h''(\cdot) > 0$; $h(0) = 1$.

A compensation function $h(\cdot)$ with the conditions of $h'(\cdot) > 0, h''(\cdot) > 0$ is a convex function with respect to the distance of the available good from the ideal good. The function implies that the available good x^* needs to be

---

[2] An individual is not identified here since the preference distribution of individuals is uniform.

[3] The distance between the goods can be measured by the objective measures of the goods' characteristics, although it is not fully developed here.

[4] This is Lancaster's equation (1979) with modified notations.

provided to him or her whose ideal good is x at the rate of $h(\bar{u})/h(2\bar{\Delta} - \bar{u})$ for a given price ratio of $p(x)/p^*(x^*)$. The distance of the product differentiation range is measured by 2Δ: one half of its range is denoted by $\bar{\Delta}$ in the upward direction, while the other is denoted by the distance $\underline{\Delta}$ in the downward direction.

Then, a consumer whose ideal good is "x" needs to be compensated with a lower price of $p^*(x^*)$ of the available good "x^{*}"; that is, the price ratio of $p(x)/p^*(x^*) > 1$ is required in view of a compensation function of (3.1). If the distance between the two goods is "zero," these two goods are identical (i.e., $h(0) = 1$), and the price ratio becomes "1" and there is no need to compensate the consumer. The range of the production differentiation of trading goods is divided into the two parts by the dividing good $\bar{x}$: the upper range of $[2\bar{\Delta} - \bar{u}]$ and its lower range of $[\bar{u}]$.

3. Vertically Differentiated Goods

So far, we have considered the differentiation of goods based on their different combinations of characteristics. Another way to differentiate goods is by their quality, which is known as vertical product differentiation and is comparable to horizontal product differentiation, where goods are identified by different combinations of characteristics.[5] One of the simplest ways to represent vertical product differentiation is through quality-adjusted prices.

Suppose that the same number of characteristics, say m, is present in the representative goods x and x^* of two trading economies. In the high-

---

[5] In Chapter 4 we consider the 'vertical product differentiation' when the composition of characteristics contained in a good varies.

quality good x produced by the leader, the characteristics are λ times greater than those of the follower.[6] We denote the characteristic vectors of goods x and x^* as "mx1" column vectors z and z*, respectively, where z is for the advanced economy, and z* is a scalar, $\lambda > 1$, multiple of the same column "mx1" for the follower, i.e., $\mathbf{z} = \lambda \mathbf{z}^*$. This implies that the quality-adjusted relative price of the representative good of the follower economy needs to be $1/\lambda$ times lower than that of the advanced economy, i.e., $p(x)/p^*(x^*) > \lambda$, which is the precondition for trade between the advanced economy and the first follower.

In what follows, we refer to the goods of the upper range of $[2\bar{\Delta} - \bar{u}]$ as those with high quality and call them "high vertically differentiated" (HVD) goods and to those of the lower range of $[\bar{u}]$ as "low vertically differentiated" (LVD) goods. We represent the ratio of the two groups of goods by "$d(\bar{u})$" by the compensation functions of each group:

$$d(\bar{u}) \equiv \frac{h(2\bar{\Delta} - \bar{u})}{h(\bar{u})}. \qquad (4\text{-}3)$$

As the dividing good $\tilde{x}$ becomes more distant from its ideal good, the ideal good of a developing economy becomes more distant from that of an advanced economy. Then, it is clear that the quality ratio, $d(\bar{u})$, is a continuously decreasing function of u, and it is concave to the origin by the properties of the compensation function of u: $d'(u) < 0; d''(u) < 0$.

A vertically differentiated good is an indivisible good, which is not only defined by its specifications but also available only in discrete units of a

---

[6] We assume that the characteristics of a good are objectively measurable, although there are some that are not objectively measurable, such as the color of an automobile.

Figure 4-2. Degree of product differentiation of representative demand

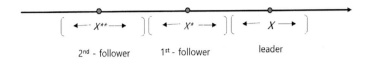

particular size (Lancaster, 1979, p.92). Goods such as automobiles, refrigerators, and electrical equipment, which come in different package forms, are included in this category of indivisible goods. In the case of divisible goods, compensation for the most preferred good can be taken as its fraction. However, the compensation is limited since the characteristics of the good are packaged in a single unit. In our trade model of the vertically differentiated durable good, the compensation for the most preferred good occurs through the provision of the tradable good.[7]

4. Degree of Product Differentiation by Developmental Stage of Economy

So far, it has been assumed that the ideal good of an individual is independent of his or her income, and every individual is given an equal amount of income. However, we can assume that the most preferred good varies with an individual's level of income. It is likely that the degree of product differentiation is greater for individuals with higher incomes. To apply this to the world economy, we divide it into an advanced economy and developing economy on the first tier, with the developing economies divided into other groups of "first followers" and "second followers." We also assume that there are representative individuals whose preferences

---

[7] A trading good of our model can be considered an "outside good" in Lancaster's variety model.

represent the most preferred goods of these economies. This implies that the degree of product differentiation of the most preferred good of a "representative demand" rises as the income level of a developing economy increases. We assume that there are no differences other than incomes among these groups of economies, and that all other factors are identical, such as factor endowments, the level of technology and time-preference rates of the economy. This abstraction of the trade model sheds light on the role of product differentiation of goods in Linder's hypothesis.

Figure 4-2 shows a uni-directional horizontal axis that represents the interval of goods associated with the degree of product differentiation of an economy, with higher degrees of differentiation located to the right of the axis. The different degrees of product differentiation of the "representative demands" are represented by different levels of income on the horizontal line of Figure 4-2. The representative good of an advanced economy with the highest income level is denoted by the good x. The representative good of the first follower with an income level lower than that of the advanced economy is represented by the good x^*, and the representative good of the second follower with an income level adjacent to that of the first follower is denoted by x^{**}. Different kinds of differentiated goods are situated at equally spaced intervals of the representative demands of each of these economies.

How can we explain international trade among these three groups of economies in light of their representative individuals? First, the precondition for trade applies equally to the trade between the second follower and the third follower, as it does to that between the advanced economy and the first follower. In other words, $p^*(x^*)/p^{**}(x^{**}) > \lambda$ needs to be satisfied for trade to take place between them.

Figure 4-3. Quality ratio of representative good of follower

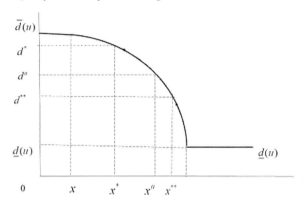

Trade between the advanced economy and the third follower, skipping trade with the first and second followers, is highly unlikely in this model. [8] International trade occurs on the overlapped ranges of product differentiation between the lower range of product differentiation of the "predecessor economy" and the upper range of the "follower economy." Trade increases the degree of product differentiation for the follower, since the imports of highly differentiated goods on the upper range of its product differentiation increase from the predecessor. The upper range of product differentiation widens, while the lower range shrinks in the trade of a follower against its predecessor. As a result, the representative demand good of the follower approaches that of the predecessor, with the degree of product differentiation increasing in the follower economy. This implies that the distance between their representative demands is reduced, and the representative good of the follower comes closer to that of the predecessor

[8] However, trade can be established between the individuals of the low-income group of an advanced economy and those of the high-income group of the third follower in a non-representative individual model.

in terms of its product differentiation.

As a result, the share of high-vertically-differentiated (HVD) goods to those of low-vertically-differentiated (LVD) goods rises for the follower economy. The quality ratio of the follower,$d(u)$, rises as a result of trade. Figure 4-3 depicts the quality ratio, $d(u)$, on the vertical axis with the distance of the representative demand of a developing economy from that of an advanced economy, u, on the horizontal axis.

The quality-ratio schedule is shown by the bold curve $\bar{d}\underline{d}$. The upper bound of the quality ratio for an advanced economy is indicated at $\bar{d}$ on the vertical axis. The representative goods of the group of the advanced economies with the same quality ratio are on the interval of (o, x) to which the conventional version of the IIT model applies. The other extreme of the lower bound of the quality ratio of the representative good is denoted by $\underline{d}$ on the vertical axis. It is located above the distance of $u^{**} = |x - x^{**}|$ for which the degree of product differentiation is so low that the economy is characterized by a negligible variety of goods. Goods of this economy with no product differentiation are defined by the simple unit of characteristicz_0, say, for agricultural foods. [9]

On the range of goods of $[x, x^*]$, there is a dividing good $\bar{x}$ in trade between the advanced economy and the first follower; similarly, on the range of $[x^*, x^{**}]$, there is a dividing good $\bar{x}^*$ in trade between the "follower-1" economy and the "follower-2" economy. The degree of product differentiation of their representative goods increases along the quality-ratio schedule as indicated by the arrows in trade between these two

---

[9] This state of the economy is relevant for a stationary economy.

groups of the economies. [10]

In traditional consumer theory, a decrease in the price of a good increases demand for the good itself, which is called the market depth effect of the price. In addition to this traditional price effect, the degree of product differentiation associated with the widening of the upper range of the interval of the goods increases, resulting in an increase in the number of goods with different product differentiation. In the market-widening effect of trade, a new variety appears to both trading economies, which prevents the marginal utility of a consumer in both economies from falling and consequently increases the volume of trade. Each variety of a good is associated with economies of scale, which do not vanish with the introduction of a new variety, unlike the case of the traditional market depth effect of trade with homogeneous goods. [11]

The following summarizes the properties of trade among advanced and developing economies regarding the international trade of differentiated goods:

① International trade occurs between economies whose representative goods are adjacent to each other.

② The quality ratio for the high vertically differentiated (HVD) good rises for the developing economy, and its representative good

---

[10] The rate at which the follower approaches the advanced economy depends on the elasticity of the rate of change of the quality ratio ($d(u)$) with respect to the distance (u) between the follower's representative good and that of the advanced economy. This elasticity increases as the follower's distance from the advanced economy decreases.

[11] This is comparable to endogenous growth theory in that the decline of the marginal productivity of the intermediate is held off as the new intermediates enter into production.

approaches that of the advanced economy.

③ The economies of scale associated with a variety of a good do not vanish as a result of the increase in the quality ratio of a developing economy.

In the preceding discussion of the representative demand of a good, the production of characteristics to be embodied onto the good is left open. Developing characteristics and a design of the way in which they are combined to give a consumer his or her most preferred one inevitably involves time in production. According to our view, characteristics and their designs are developed during the construction period of a neo-Austrian technique, which links the number of characteristics to the period of their development. [12] The number of characteristics embodied onto the good increases with the construction period relative to the utilization, resulting in the expansion of the product differentiation space of a good.

Varieties of goods are one of the features of an industrially complex economy. However, the product differentiation of goods is inherently involved with economies of scale. The development of new characteristics of intermediates to be embodied onto an indivisible new durable prevents economies of scale from falling off. Neither the marginal utility of a consumer nor the marginal productivity of an intermediate falls in this variety model, so trade expands to both trading economies. Hence, the productivity of an economy is increased by the exploration of the economies of scale, and the increase in the share of high vertically differentiated (HVD)

---

[12] This means that research and development are essential for the development of characteristics. However, we are currently limiting ourselves to the role of time and not taking into account the monopolistic profits associated with research and development.

goods to those of the low vertically differentiated (LVD) goods rises for the follower economy (i.e., for the rise of the quality ratio, , of the follower). This is the way in which the productivity effect of international trade of a developing economy is viewed in Lancaster's variety model.

5. Intra-Industry Trade of Korean Economy

5.1 Measurement of IIT

The IIT index is generally measured using the following Grubel–Lloyd index.

$$IIT_i = 1 - \frac{|X_i - M_i|}{(X_i + M_i)}. \tag{4-4}$$

Here, X is the amount of exports, M is the amount of imports, and i represents the industry. The IIT index has a value between 0 and 1, with 0 meaning no IIT and 1 indicating complete IIT. The IIT index is usually expressed as a percentile (%) by multiplying IIT by 100.

Greenaway et al. (1994) distinguished HIIT from VIIT by using the unit value ratio of export and import goods. If the ratio of the unit value of export goods to that of import goods is more than a certain value, it is called high quality VIIT (VIIT^H), while if the ratio is less than a certain value, it is called low quality VIIT (VIIT^L). This is summarized as follows.

HIIT : $(1 - \alpha) \leq \frac{UV_x}{UV_M} \leq (1 + \alpha)$

VIIT^H : $(1 + \alpha) < \frac{UV_x}{UV_M}$

VIIT^L : $\frac{UV_x}{UV_M} < (1 - \alpha)$,

where UVx is the unit value of export goods and UVm is the unit value of import goods. If the (UV_x/UV_m) of a product is within a certain range (α), it is classified as HIIT, while if it is out of this range, it is classified as VIIT. If (UV_x/UV_m) is higher than $(1 + \alpha)$, export goods are regarded as being of superior quality, while if this value is lower than $(1 - \alpha)$, they are regarded as being of inferior quality. Although there is no criteria for the appropriate value of α, existing studies mainly use 0.15 or 0.25.

In this study, 0.25 was used as the value of α. The IIT index for each group is a weighted average value with trade volume as the weight and is calculated as follows.

$$IIT^G = \sum_{i=1}^{n} w_i \cdot IIT_i^G, \qquad \text{where } w_i = \frac{(X_i + M_i)}{\sum_{i=1}^{n}(X_i + M_i)}. \qquad (4\text{-}5)$$

Here, w is the ratio of the trade volume of the industry to the total trade volume of the country and G represents a product group of HIIT, VIIT^H, and VIIT^L. Here, the sum of VIIT^H and VIIT^L is VIIT. The sum of the weights of the three groups gives 1, so $IIT = HIIT + VIIT^H + VIIT^L$. Therefore, the Grubel–Lloyd IIT index is the sum of the HIIT and VIIT indexes.

5.2 Changes in Korea's IIT

Figure 4-4 shows the annual trends of Korea's IIT index. This is the result of an analysis of trade between Korea and East Asian countries.[13] Figure 4-4 shows that Korea's IIT and VIIT^H continue to increase but that HIIT and VIIT^L do not change much. This indicates that the increase in Korea's

---

[13] The East Asian countries included in this study are Japan, Hong Kong, Singapore, Taiwan, China, the Philippines, Malaysia, Thailand, and Indonesia. Trade with these nine countries accounted for 47.2% of Korea's total trade volume as of 2005, accounting for nearly half of the total trade volume.

IIT

Figure 4-4. Changes in HIIT and VIIT in Korea

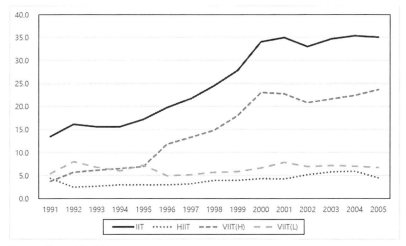

Source: Kim and Ju (2007)

with East Asian countries is mainly due to the increase in VIIT^H. The overall IIT index increased from 13.5 to 35.0, and in particular, VIIT^H, the superior quality index, increased significantly from 3.7 to 23.7. It can be seen that Korea's export structure has been generally shifting toward superior quality.

Table 4-1 shows Korea's IIT index with Japan and China. As of 2005, the total IIT was 23.8 with China and 25.2 with Japan, and the share of HIIT in the total IIT was 38.5% with China and 39.5% with Japan. The value of total IIT and the share of HIIT in the total IIT did not differ significantly between China and Japan.

However, the share of VIIT varied greatly. In trade with China, the proportion of the superior quality index was 49.6, much higher than that of the inferior quality index (11.9%), whereas in trade with Japan, the proportion of the superior quality index was 7.6%, much lower than that of the inferior quality index (52.9%). This shows that Korea is engaged in

Table 4-1. Korea's IIT Index for China and Japan (2005)

	China		Japan	
	Index	Share (%)	Index	Share (%)
HIIT	9.1	38.5	9.9	39.5
VIIT(H)	11.8	49.6	1.9	7.6
VIIT(L)	2.8	11.9	13.3	52.9
IIT	23.8	100	25.2	100

Note: The index is calculated from HS 10-digit trade statistics, and the share is the ratio of specific IIT to total IIT.
Source: Kim (2009)

$VIIT^H$ with China and $VIIT^L$ with Japan. That is, Korea exports superior-quality products to China, which has a low technology level, and exports inferior-quality products to Japan, which has a high technology level. [14]

6. Conclusion

This study explains the causes of intra-industry trade using the concepts of economies of scale and variety preference in the utility function. The production of differentiated products is driven by consumers' preference for variety, and firms' ability to realize economies of scale in production. Specialization and exchange of differentiated products between countries result in lower prices and increased product variety, benefiting both countries. When differentiation takes the form of differences in quality,

---

[14] The quality referred to here is not absolute quality, but rather the relative quality of exports compared to imports. In other words, when Korea exports products of superior quality to China, it means that the quality of Korea's exports is higher than that of products imported from China. Conversely, when Korea exports products of inferior quality to Japan, it means that the quality of Korea's exports is lower than that of products imported from Japan.

vertical intra-industry trade emerges, where high-income countries specialize in producing superior quality products while low-income countries specialize in inferior quality products.

Korea's IIT with East Asian countries continues to increase. However, when the total IIT index is divided into horizontal intra-industry trade (HIIT) and vertical intra-industry trade (VIIT), there is no significant change in HIIT or low quality VIIT, while high quality VIIT steadily increases. This indicates that the increase in Korea's IIT with East Asian countries is primarily due to the increase in high quality VIIT. In other words, it shows that Korea's industrial and trade structure is shifting towards high quality.

A comparison of Korea's trade with China and Japan reveals that the proportion of high quality VIIT is high in trade with China, while the proportion of low quality VIIT is high in trade with Japan. This means that Korea exports superior-quality products to China and imports inferior-quality products from China, while it exports inferior-quality products to Japan and imports superior-quality products from Japan. However, it's important to note that the quality referred to here is the relative quality of exports to imports with the partner country. Exporting high-quality products to China only means that Korea's exports are better than those imported from China, not necessarily better than exports from other developed countries. The interpretation of Korea's IIT with Japan is the same.

CHAPTER 5

INTELLECTUAL PROPERTY RIGHTS, NORTH-SOUTH TRADE, AND ECONOMIC GROWTH

1. Introduction

There are generally two aspects associated with Intellectual Property Rights (IPRs): the incentive aspect, which induces the production of new products or processes, and the transfer of welfare associated with intellectual protection. Deardorff (1992) considers the optimal geographical scope for patent protection and argues that tightening IPRs is welfare-reducing for the South as it restricts the broader geographical coverage of innovation. Using a duopoly model, Chin and Grossman (1988) study the competition between two firms, one from the North and the other from the South. They demonstrate that IPRs improve welfare for the North, while the effect on the South depends on its market share in a third market and the size of the Northern cost-saving innovation.

Diwan and Rodrik (1991) offer a somewhat different perspective by considering the appropriateness of innovation and technology due to differences in the technological needs and preferences of the North and South. Thus, strengthening IPRs may not always harm the South as it can encourage the development of technology suited to the South that would not have been developed without intellectual protection. Moreover, increasing patent protection in the South may not always benefit the North. Therefore, IPRs should be differentiated by industry and the development stage in the South.

Using a dynamic general equilibrium model, Helpman (1993) demonstrates that tightening IPRs is detrimental to both the South and the North, except when the Southern imitation rate is high enough that the favorable terms of the IPR trade effect for the North outweigh the inefficiencies resulting from the restriction on the interregional allocation of production. Overall, the IPR literature addresses the conflict of interest between the North and South and indicates that global welfare generally declines with the strengthening of IPRs.

Empirical research shows a strong positive correlation between intellectual property protection and economic growth (Gould and Gruben, 1996; Torstensson, 1994). Park and Ginarte (1997) find that while IPRs do not directly explain the growth rate, increased intellectual property protection significantly influences the investment rate, particularly the accumulation of factor inputs such as R&D and physical capital. Gould and Gruben (1996) also show that IPRs' growth effect is more robust in an open economy than a closed one, suggesting that IPRs' investment inducement effects in an open economy may be an important link to its growth effect. However, the IPR literature does not explicitly approach the investment aspect related to IPRs using a formal international trade model.

This study examines IPRs' effects on the welfare and growth of two trading regions in an open economy. To achieve this, an intermediate final good trade model is developed within the framework of the overlapping generation model. The production of a final good is intermediate-specific. The North exports intermediate goods in which knowledge is embodied and imports final goods in return from the South. Intermediates are produced in the young age period of a cohort, and the final good is produced in the old age period. Intermediates and labor are complementary. Investment in intermediate goods improves quality, and worker productivity increases in the old age period, while also expanding the knowledge base of the economy, generating spillover effects. For example, knowledge of temperature levels, humidity, and the mixing of substances increases labor productivity in manufacturing final goods related to specific intermediates, such as pharmaceuticals, thus improving overall labor efficiency by increasing the economy's knowledge stock.

An economy's technological efficiency index is established based on the productivity of producing final goods using a given quality of an intermediate good. An economy with a higher technological efficiency level produces more of a final good with a certain amount of the intermediate good of a given quality. Provided that the technological efficiency levels between the North and the South are sufficiently different and the rates of investment in the two regions are high, free trade is likely to be favorable for investment in and growth of the South. A presumption of this argument is that chemical-pharmaceutical trade is more growth-enhancing than apple-banana trade.

In conclusion, tightening IPRs in the South increases the investment rate, improving the welfare of the two trading regions. This contrasts with contemporary IPR literature, which shows conflicting results for the two interest groups.

The structure of this chapter is as follows: Section 2 presents the model, Section 3 considers the trade of intermediate goods, where the North specializes in the production of intermediate goods, and the South specializes in manufacturing consumer goods. Finally, Section 4 presents the concluding remarks.

2. The Model

In the model, there are n final goods that are perfectly substitutable in consumption, but they are differentiated by the intermediates used in their production. There are n firms in the economy, with each firm investing in producing a specific quality of an intermediate good that is used in the manufacturing of the final goods. The amount of labor at any given time in the economy is denoted by L, and it has a constant size due to the birth rate being offset by the death rate. Each worker lives for $2T$ periods, where the first T represents the young age and the second T represents the old age. One unit of labor produces one unit of an intermediate good. Inputs to produce a final good are labor and intermediate goods of specified quality.

The production process is divided into two distinct periods. The first period involves the production of intermediate goods and is carried out by a young worker over a period of T periods. The second period, which lasts for T periods, involves the production of final goods by an old worker. The total life period of a worker is assumed to be $2T$, which is greater than a constant specified later. Leisure does not provide any utility to workers, who derive their utility solely from their work. All firms in the economy are assumed to have the same level of technology for producing both intermediate and final goods.

2.1 Production Technology

We consider a Cobb-Douglas production function of a final good $Y_i(t)$ at time t, which is produced by the inputs of labor $L_i(t)$ and the intermediates of $X_i(t)$:

$$Y_i(t) = A(t)L_i(t)^{\alpha}X_i(t)^{1-\alpha},\ 0 < \alpha < 1 \qquad (5\text{-}1)$$

The amount of labor allocated to the production of the final good i at time t is denoted by $L_i(t)$, and it is equal to the total amount of labor in the economy divided by the number of firms, i.e., $L_i(t) = L/n(t)$. At any given time, denoted by t, there are $2T$ overlapping generations of workers, with T cohorts of young workers producing an intermediate good and T cohorts of older workers manufacturing a final good. Therefore, labor is specific to the firm, meaning that a worker who produces intermediate i in their young age will manufacture final good i in their old age. The total amount of labor at time t is $2TL$. The overall labor efficiency is represented by $A(t)$, and the total amount of effective labor for manufacturing the final goods is $A(t)TL$.

Workers develop knowledge during their young age by utilizing natural resources, which are assumed to be abundant in the economy. [1] This knowledge is embodied in intermediate goods, and their production naturally precedes that of final goods, with a gestation period of T. Firm i invests z_i amount of labor during a worker's young age period T to produce a unit of an intermediate good with efficiency z_i. This increases the worker's efficiency in manufacturing a final good by z_i. The total amount of intermediate goods with efficiency z_i, $x_i(t)$, is obtained by dividing the amount of labor employed in the sector by that engaged in intermediate good production: $x_i(t) = L_i(t)/z_i$. The effective amount of intermediate good i, $X_i(t)$, is a multiple of z_i on x_i: $X_i(t) = L_i(t)$.

---

[1] For example, consider the case of computer chip manufacturing. Embodying knowledge of natural resources such as silicon, which are abundant in the economy, produces chips.

The increase in the amount of investment, z_i, will improve the efficiency of both the intermediate good and the worker. Substituting $L_i(t)$ for $X_i(t)$ in (5-1) yields the output of good i as:

$$Y_i(t) = A(t)z_i^\alpha L_i(t) \qquad (5\text{-}2)$$

We assume that each firm invests the same amount in intermediates, and denote the average rate of investment using z. In a steady state, each generation makes the same amount of investment, which accumulates over time.

Knowledge is embodied in intermediates, which can be disclosed to a competitor through reverse engineering or other forms of imitation. Newly obtained knowledge can be replicated by a competitor and disseminated to the economy at an imitation rate of δ, where $0 < \delta < 1$. A firm's new knowledge is fully disclosed after time $T_c = 1/\delta$, becoming public knowledge. After the knowledge embodied in the intermediate good becomes public, a firm no longer engages in production. The old age period T of a worker should be greater than T_c; otherwise, a worker will not exhaust their knowledge during their lifetime, resulting in a sub-optimal outcome. The amount of knowledge disseminated to the economy is a multiple δ of the average investment rate in the economy, z: δz.

Investing in intermediates increases labor productivity in manufacturing the incumbent final good. At the same time, the overall labor efficiency is increased by the spillover effect. The following differential equation, based on the endogenous growth model of Romer (1990), among others, represents the spillover effects.

$$\dot{A}(t) = (\delta z)A(t)$$

Since each firm's production takes place until the period of T_c, the aggregate production function is represented as follows:

$$Y(t) = A(t) \int_0^{n(t)} \int_0^{T_c} z^\alpha (t - \tau) L_i(t) \, d\tau \, di \, , \, z > 1 \qquad (5\text{-}3)$$

In the steady state, the number of firms in the economy and the effective amount of labor grows at the same rate: $\dot{A}(t)/A(t) = \dot{n}(t)/n(t)$.

Substituting $L/n(t)$ for $L_i(t)$, (5-3) is reduced into the following form:

$$Y(t) = z^\alpha A(t) T_c L, \, z > 1 \qquad (5\text{-}4)$$

In this reduced form of the production function, the α coefficient is interpreted as the rate of investment's effectiveness in producing the final goods.[2] For the given amount of investment z_i greater than 1, the knowledge embodied in intermediates in producing a final good will be more effective, and the coefficient α will be greater. We let α represent the level of technological efficiency of an economy. An economy with a higher coefficient of α is considered more technologically advanced.[3]

2.2 Intermediate Goods Producers

An intermediate goods producer invests in improving efficiency, taking into account the profit accruing during period T_c, which is the inverse of the imitation rate δ. We assume that there is neither uncertainty nor a risk factor in investments for improvement. Equation (5-2) implies that $z_i^{-\alpha}$ units of

---

[2] The coefficient α in (4) is the output elasticity with respect to the rate of investment z.
[3] If $z_i = 1$, the α index becomes neutral, and if $z_i < 1$ the index has a reverse interpretation.

labor are required to produce a unit of a final good.

Hence, the present value of an investment in intermediate good i is represented as:

$$\max_{z_i} -wz_i e^{-rT} + \int_T^{T+T_c}(1 - wz_i^{-\alpha})\, e^{-rt}\, dt\,, \qquad (5\text{-}5)$$

where r and w represent the rate of interest and wages, respectively. Here, w is the efficiency-adjusted wage rate. The wage rate at time period t, $w(t)$, and $A(t)$ grow at the same rate of δz in a steady state. Thus, the efficiency-adjusted wage rate is $w = w(t)/A(t)$.

The first term of (5-5) is the cost of investment, and the second term $(1 - wz_i^{-\alpha})$ represents the profit flow in each period per unit of output from the improved efficiency of the intermediate good. The profits are accrued during period T_c. The following first-order condition indicates that the rate of investment depends on the technological efficiency level, the rate of interest, and the imitation rate:

$$zi = [\alpha\, d(r,T_c)]^{\frac{1}{1+\alpha}} \qquad (5\text{-}6)$$

where $d(r,T_c)$ is the discounting factor for the future income from 0 to T_c periods at the interest rate of r, which will be determined endogenously later:

$$d(r,T_c) = \frac{1-e^{-rT_c}}{r}\quad .$$

The demand for labor increases when investing in the quality improvement of intermediate goods is profitable. This leads to a rise in the wage rate until perfect competition eliminates profits. As a result, the present value of an investment in intermediates becomes zero, resulting in a wage rate with the following formula:

$$w = \frac{z_i^\alpha}{1+\alpha} \; . \tag{5-7}$$

Hence, the demand for labor is perfectly elastic at this wage rate. Substituting equation (5-7) into $(1 - wz^{-\alpha})$ yields the profit rate per unit of output as $\alpha/(1 + \alpha)$. Multiplying this by the total output of (5-4) gives the total amount of profits in the economy: $\alpha z^\alpha A(t) T_c L/(1+\alpha)$. Dividing by the population size $2TL$ results in the per capita profit. Hence the per capita profit accounted by the intermediate good i, π_i, is:

$$\pi_i = \frac{\alpha z_i^\alpha}{2\delta T(1+\alpha)} \frac{L_i}{L} \tag{5-8}$$

2.3 Consumer Preference

Subtracting the aggregate amount of investment $wA(t)L$ from the aggregate output of the economy $z^\alpha A(t) T_c L$ in (5-4) gives the aggregate amount of consumption $C(t)$, expressed as a constant fraction of aggregate income Y (t). That is, $C(t) = [1 - \delta/(1 + \alpha)] Y(t)$. Substituting (5-4) for $C(t)$ and dividing it by the population size $2TL$ gives the amount of per capita consumption $c(t)$:

$$c(t) = \left(1 - \frac{\delta}{1+\alpha}\right) \frac{z^\alpha}{2\delta T} A(t), \tag{5-9}$$

where $0 < (1 - \delta/(1 + \alpha)) < 1$ refers to the propensity to consume.

Goods are differentiated by the intermediates used but are perfectly substitutable in consumption. A representative consumer's problem is to maximize the following utility function for the given price of final good i, denoted by $p_i(t)$

$$u\big(c(t)\big) = \int_0^{n(t)} c_i(t)di$$

subject to the budget constraint of $p_i(t)c_i(t) \leq c(t)$. This solves for $c_i(t) = c(t)/n(t)$ for all i, and $p_i(t) = 1$. For the sake of simplicity, we assume that labor's overall efficiency level is initially equal to the number of goods at period 0, so $A(0) = n(0)$. The variety of goods grows at an equal rate to that of the effective units of labor, implying that any increase in effective labor due to the increase in the economy's overall efficiency is employed in producing new goods. This results in $A(t) = n(t)$.

Hence the amount of the per capita consumption of good i denoted by $\bar{c}_i$ is the same for all i, and remains unchanged for a given rate of investment z in a steady state:

$$\bar{c}_i = \left(1 - \frac{\delta}{1+\alpha}\right)\frac{z^\alpha}{2\delta T}. \tag{5-10}$$

This implies that an increase in investment rate z increases the consumption of good i. An improvement in the overall efficiency of the economy $A(t)$, resulting from the increase in z, simultaneously increases the variety of goods consumed.

It is notable that (5-8) and (5-10) imply that there is a constant relationship between $\bar{c}_i$ and π_i:

$$\frac{\bar{c}_i}{\pi_i} = \left(1 - \frac{\delta}{1+\alpha}\right)\frac{1+\alpha}{\alpha}\frac{L}{L_i}. \tag{5-11}$$

A representative household's intertemporal utility is composed of subsequent generations in the following logarithmic form:

$$\max_{c_t} U(t) = \int_t^\infty \ln u(c(s)) \, e^{-\rho(s-t)} \, ds \quad for \ \ s > t, \qquad (5\text{-}12)$$

where consumption is additively separable over time with a constant time preference rate of ρ, and the elasticity of intertemporal substitution is equal to one. The total amount of investment in the economy divided by the population size yields the per capita capital stock, $k(t)$:[4]

$$k(t) = \frac{z(t)^\alpha}{2(1+\alpha)T} \, A(t), \qquad (5\text{-}13)$$

while the per capita budget constraint is $c(t) + k'(t) = w + rk(t)$.

Hence, the representative household solves the Ramsey rule:

$$r = \rho + g_c, \qquad (5\text{-}14)$$

where g_c represents the growth rate of consumption: $g_c = \dot{c}_t / c_t$.

2.4 Steady State Equilibrium

Every firm in the economy faces the same rate of imitation risk. Wage costs and interest rates are the same for all firms, and each firm sells the final good at the same price. Furthermore, all firms use the same technology to produce intermediate and final goods, and the final goods are perfectly substitutable. Therefore, all firms in the economy have the same profit function and invest the same amount in the production of intermediates. Thus, the investment rate of firm i, z_i, is the same as the average investment rate in the economy, which is used interchangeably with z_i unless there is

---

[4] The capital stock in this economy is in the form of intermediates. It disappears after they are utilized in the manufacturing of final goods. The depreciation rate is 1.

confusion.

In the steady state, each generation on average invests z amount, and the knowledge stock of the economy grows at a constant rate of δz through its spillover effects. Equation (5-13) implies that the growth rate of the per capita capital stock is equal to the sum of the growth rate of the economy's knowledge stock. This is equal to the constant δz, and a multiple α of the growth rate of investment in intermediates:

$$\frac{\dot{k}(t)}{k(t)} = \delta z + \alpha \frac{\dot{z}(t)}{z(t)}.$$

In a competitive steady state of the economy, the investment growth rate is zero in which z_t and c_t satisfy (5-5) and (5-12), respectively, and labor is fully employed at the wage rate of (5-7). Thus, there is a competitive steady state equilibrium of the economy that is unique and stable. In the steady state of the economy, $\lim_{t \to \infty} \dot{z}_t/z_t \to 0$ and the per capita capital stock of the economy approaches δz, that is, $\lim_{t \to \infty} \dot{k}(t)/k(t) \to \delta z$.

The aggregate consumption is a constant multiple $(1 - \delta/(1 + \alpha))$ of the aggregate income $Y(t)$. Consumption and income grow at the same rate of δz. Hence, the economy's interest rate is the sum of the time preference rate ρ and of δz; that is, $r = \rho + \delta z$. Substituting $\rho + \delta z$ for r in (5-6) yields the following investment function for firm i:

$$z_i = F(z_i) = [\alpha d(z_i)]^{1/(1+\alpha)} \qquad (5\text{-}15)$$

where

$$d(z_i; \rho, \delta) = \frac{1 - e^{-(\rho + \delta z_i)T_c}}{\rho + \delta z_i}.$$

A firm's rate of investment z_i is at equilibrium if $F(z_i) - z_i = 0$ in the first-order condition of (5-15). In this competitive steady state of the economy, a constant rate of investment greater than one exists and is unique.

We can see how the investment rate varies across economies with different technological efficiency levels. A comparative static analysis of z with respect to α in (5-15) suggests that the investment rate will be higher for the technologically more advanced economy for $\alpha \ln z < 1$, that is, $z < e^{1/\alpha}$.

3. International Trade

Let's consider two trading regions: North and South. To distinguish them from the South, variables related to the North are starred. The regions are separated by their level of technological efficiencies, with the North being more efficient in manufacturing final goods represented by a higher coefficient α in the North (i.e., $\alpha^* > \alpha$). Other parameters related to production and consumption are assumed to be the same across the two regions, and the same amount of labor stock is given in both economies. This section explains the trade equilibrium and its welfare implications for the two regions, with attention drawn to the welfare effects of strengthening IPRs in the South.

3.1 Trade Equilibrium

Since the North is identified as the economy whose technological efficiency level is higher than that of the South, the rate of investment is higher in the North. The growth rate of the economy is higher in the North in so far as the imitation rate is the same across the two regions. Hence there are a greater number of firms and a greater variety of goods are consumed in the North. The efficiency of intermediates in manufacturing final goods is higher in the

North. Efficiency of the Southern labor in the production of the final good in using the Northern intermediates is raised but it is not as efficient as the Northern labor. There exist adjustment costs, as described by Lucas (1967).

Provided that the Northern intermediates in the South yield more profits due to the low wage rate, compensating for the lower efficiency, international trade of intermediate-final goods can take place, referred to as the tradability condition. The condition depends on the Southern technological efficiency level and investment rates in the two regions, where the Southern investment rate must be greater than 1 but not exceed the Northern investment rate z^*. The range of Southern technological efficiency levels for which the tradability condition is satisfied at the interval of the investment rate between 1 and z^* is called a tradable range.

We assume that there is a matching pair of firms in the two regions engaged in trade, with the Northern firm exporting intermediates to the corresponding Southern firm in exchange for final goods,[5] which keeps a complementarity of intermediates with labor to produce final goods in trade. Since there are more firms in the North, only a subset participate in trade. A good produced by a firm engaged in trade is called a trading good, and a good produced by a firm not engaged in trade is called a non-trading good.

The inefficiencies of Southern labor in adapting to the Northern intermediates arise from the different technological efficiency levels and investment rates between the two regions. The less inefficient the Southern labor is, the smaller the gap with respect to technological efficiency and the rate of investment. This conveys the idea that adaptation to change depends

---

[5] For example, we may consider the case of a matching pair of firms as an exclusive licensor-licensee relationship between the two.

on the educational level of the labor force (see Nelson and Phelps, 1966). The term $\tilde{z}$ in the following production function of firm i captures the ability of Southern labor in using Northern intermediates:

$$Y_i(t) = z\tilde{A}(t)T_c L_i, \qquad (5\text{-}16)$$

where $\tilde{z} = \left(\frac{z^o}{z^*}\right)^{\alpha_* - \alpha} (z^*)^{\alpha_*}$; z^o represents the rate of investment in the South after trade; and $z^o < z^*$, $\alpha < \alpha^*$ (the superscript "o" of the variables refers to those after trade).

A unit of Northern labor produces $z^{*\alpha_*}$ units of a final good with a unit of its own intermediate good. A unit of Southern labor is $(z^*/z^o)^{\alpha_* - \alpha}$ times less efficient compared to a unit of Northern labor. If the rates of investment or the technological efficiency levels are the same in the two regions, the Northern intermediates are used in the South just as efficiently as in the North.

Since $\tilde{z} > (z^o)^\alpha$, using the Northern intermediates in the South must be profitable. Profit from a final good unit using imported Northern intermediates in the South per unit period is $(1 - w^o\tilde{z}^{-1})$, where w^o is the Southern wage rate after trade. For the profit accruing period, T_c, being the same in the two regions, the condition under which trade becomes feasible requires $(1 - w^o\tilde{z}^{-1})$ to be greater than $(1 - w^*z^{*-\alpha_*})$. This is simplified to $w*/wo > z*\alpha*/\tilde{z}$.

Demand for labor is perfectly elastic at the wage rate of $w^* = z^{*\alpha_*}/1+\alpha^*$ in the North and at $w^o = (z^o)^\alpha/1 + \alpha$ in the South. Substituting these for the above yields:

$$\frac{1}{1+\alpha^*} > G(\alpha; z^*), \qquad (5\text{-}17)$$

where

$$G(\alpha; z^*) = \frac{1}{1+\alpha} \frac{(z^0)^\alpha}{\tilde{z}},$$

implying that $G(\alpha;z^*)$, a multiple $1/\tilde{z}$ of the Southern wage rate, does not exceed the constant $1/(1+\alpha^*)$. $G(\alpha)$ is the cost of producing a final good unit in the South, considering the adaptation cost of the imported Northern intermediate good, while $1/(1+\alpha^*)$ is the corresponding cost in the North. Hence, the trade of the intermediate-final goods takes place if $\tilde{G}(\alpha) = 1/1 + \alpha^* - G(\alpha) > 0$.

If the tradability condition is met, Southern workers produce final goods during both their young and old age periods, while Northern workers employed by trading firms only produce intermediates throughout their life. We assume that the intermediates produced by the $\tau+1$ Northern old age cohort are passed on to the next generation, so the τ-old Northern cohort exports the intermediates of the $(\tau+1)$-old cohort instead.

The matching pair of firms engaged in trade operate as a duopoly and share profits in the following manner. A young τ-old South cohort imports the intermediates produced by the $(\tau+1)$-old Northern cohort, and the final goods made using these intermediates are kept for the young τ-old South cohort. During the τ-old period, the South cohort uses the intermediates produced by the contemporaneous Northern cohort, and the profits of this period are paid to the τ-old Northern cohort.

The young τ-old South cohort produces final goods for their own use, while the old age period is dedicated to the North cohort. This profit-sharing arrangement means that the transfer of the $\tau + 1$-old Northern intermediates to the next generation takes the form of final goods through trade with the South.

The portion of trading firms among the total number of firms in the North will eventually become negligible in the long run because the growth rate of firms in the North is higher than that in the South. Therefore, in the long run, the Northern average investment rate remains constant at $z*$, against which a Southern firm maximizes its profits. [6] The Southern investment rate depends on the technological efficiency levels and the Northern investment rate. The greater the Southern investment rate after the trade, the greater the technological gap between the North and the South, and the smaller the Northern investment rate becomes.

This effect of an increase in the Southern investment rate on the tradable range can be explained as follows. It has two opposing effects on the Southern profit rate. On the one hand, the increase in the Southern wage rate due to the increase in the investment rate reduces profits. On the other hand, the increase in productivity is beneficial for profits. Which of these two effects is greater depends on the Southern technological efficiency level's distance from that of the North. In the lower part, the positive productivity effect outweighs the negative wage effect, and a Southern firm's profit increases, shifting the $G(\alpha)$ curve downwards. In the upper part, the wage effect is greater than the productivity effect, and $G(\alpha)$ moves upwards. A downward shift of $G(\alpha)$ in the lower part gives the South a better chance of increasing the investment rate after trade.

3.2 The Welfare Effects of Free Trade

The welfare effects of free trade are explained by the increased profit rate of Southern firms engaged in trade. These firms use Northern intermediates

---

[6] This is in the tradition of the Brander-Spencer (1983) type of game theoretic trade model.

in the South, which positively affects both trading partners. The investment rate remains unchanged for the North, so its wage rate stays the same as before trade. As trading firm profits increase with trade, total income increases, and welfare unambiguously improves after trade. The Northern welfare's improvement comes from the increase in the variety of consumption. Labor released from trading firms is now employed to produce more goods, resulting in an increase in the variety of goods in the North after trade, improving welfare. [7]

For the South, welfare in the short run increases with trade, but the long-run effects are inconclusive. The aggregate output of the economy after trade increases using more efficient Northern intermediates for $\tilde{z} > z\alpha$. The economy's propensity to consume is constant, and consumption increases. However, the Southern economy's growth rate depends on the change in the investment rate after trade. We consider three possible cases: the first is a case in which the Southern investment rate decreases, the second is when there is no change in the investment rate, and the third case is when it increases.

1) $z^0 < z$:

A decrease in the rate of investment lowers the number of goods consumed. In the long run, this negative effect outweighs the short-run positive income effect, and Southern welfare deteriorates.

2) $z^0 = z$:

In this case, we do not need to consider the change in the investment rate. The growth in profits from trade increases per capita consumption for all

---

[7] The increase in variety is the level effect of free trade. It still grows at the rate of δz^* by assumption.

goods, improving Southern welfare.

3) $z^0 > z$:

An increase in the South's investment rate improves welfare by increasing the variety of goods and the consumption of all goods.

The third case is the most desirable outcome for the South. Previous results suggest that this case will most likely occur if the investment rates in both regions are high and the Southern technological efficiency level is sufficiently distant from the North.

3.3 The Welfare Effect of IPRs

We will consider a scenario in which the difference in the imitation rates between the two economies is so small that the tradability condition remains satisfied, and trade takes place between them. Presumably, imitation becomes more difficult in a technologically sophisticated economy. Would an economy's growth rate increase if its rate of imitation is low? The Northern economy has a low imitation rate but a high investment rate, which is favorable for growth. However, the low imitation rate reduces spillover effects, offsetting the growth effect of the increase in investment.

The steady-state growth rate of an economy is a constant multiple δ of the investment rate. Therefore, an economy with a lower imitation rate will have a lower growth rate because the investment elasticity with respect to δ is smaller than 1. In this case, the Southern economy's growth rate will be higher, and the number of firms in the two regions will converge.[8] However, the Northern economy's steady-state consumption level is higher, and consumption convergence will not occur.

A tightening of intellectual property rights (IPRs), such as through strengthened surveillance or monitoring devices, lengthens an investor's profit-accruing period, T_c, resulting in a higher investment rate. Suppose the South strengthens its IPRs, increasing the investment rate and labor productivity, resulting in increased welfare and a growing economy. In particular, this enforcement of IPRs widens the South's tradable range, provided that the Northern investment rate is sufficiently high such that $\tilde{G}(\alpha^*/2) > 0$, where the South's technological efficiency is less than half of the North's.

The impact of Southern IPRs on Northern welfare in our model depends on the profit of a Southern firm in using Northern intermediates. As previously explained, the profit increases if the Southern technological efficiency level is less than half of the Northern one; otherwise, it decreases. When the profit rate for using Northern intermediates increases, more final goods are exported back to the North, making the trade terms favorable for the North. Hence, the variety of goods consumed in the North increases due to the IPRs, for the same reasons previously explained.

In conclusion, strengthening IPRs in the South improves world welfare if the Southern technological efficiency level is less than half of the Northern one. If it's higher, tightening IPRs in the South deteriorates the terms of trade

---

[8] In this argument, it is implicit that the overall productivity of labor at the initial period be greater in the North than in the South so that there are a greater number of goods in the North.

effect for the North. This result differs from the conventional argument that tightening IPRs in the South is unfavorable for its welfare. There may even be a case where it becomes undesirable from the North's point of view.

4. Concluding Remarks

Extending the knowledge developed in the North can increase global welfare, which is the basis of the argument for loosening intellectual property rights (IPRs) apart from its distributional effect between the North and the South. However, this argument assumes that no costs are incurred in the transmission of knowledge. The present model assumes that there are costs involved in adapting Southern labor to the Northern intermediates, as adapting to the imported intermediates in the South requires investment. This links the investment rate with the IPRs and provides the basis for the argument for IPRs' inducive aspect in an open economy. Investment-related intermediate goods trade brings about a favorable outcome for the growth of the South. This is consistent with empirical evidence that shows a positive correlation between the rate of economic growth and IPRs (Park and Ginarte, 1997).

The adaptation cost for using Northern intermediates arises from the complementarity of the intermediates with labor in producing final goods, which is incorporated into our intermediate-final good trade model. It plays the role of impeding the knowledge developed in the North and extended to the South. The increase in the Southern investment rate by enforcing IPRs reduces the impediment for the case in which the technological efficiency level is properly distanced from that of the North. Tightening IPRs makes the South enter the tradable range and explore intermediate good trade opportunities provided the Northern investment rate is sufficiently high. In this respect, IPRs support extending the Northern knowledge embodied in the intermediates to the South. This contrasts with the static argument for loosening IPRs for a wider extension of Northern knowledge.

The profit rate increases with the enforcement of IPRs for the South if the technological efficiency level is in the lower part of the tradable range and the Northern terms of trade improve, positively affecting Northern welfare. Because of the duopoly assumption, the same amount of profit is accrued to the South. The economy also grows by increasing the rate of investment in the South's welfare. In conclusion, tightening IPRs in the South, which has a technological efficiency level that is less than half of the North, increases global welfare.

The model is constructed based on the following assumptions: the increase in the number of goods in the economy correlates with the rate of increase in overall productivity, goods are perfectly substitutable in consumption, profits are shared equally between the North and the South in a special sequence, and the intermediates produced by an older generation are transferred to the next generation. These assumptions make it possible for our economy to cope with a steady state. The restriction on the rate of investment allows us to compare the technological efficiency level of the South with the North regarding the output elasticity with respect to the rate of investment.

This study does not consider the invention-imitation dynamic games that may take place among trading Northern firms and the imitating Southern firms. An R&D race among Northern and Southern firms in an open economy, similar to Segerstrom's (1991) invention-imitation dynamics, can provide more interesting explanations for the effects of IPRs. The analysis of this study can be extended to the case of direct investment by replacing intermediates with capital. In this case, royalties are paid to the Northern parent firms instead of the final goods being exported.

This study argues that investment-related trade can foster the growth of the South, provided that their technological efficiency level falls within the tradable range. This has important implications for the growth of newly industrialized economies (NIEs), which have heavily relied on trade with advanced economies for importing capital and intermediate goods. Fortunately, the technological efficiency levels of NIEs have typically been situated at a favorable distance from the North, allowing trade to bring about positive growth effects. Therefore, strengthening intellectual property rights (IPRs) in these regions may be a more beneficial strategy.

PART II

GROWTH OF KOREAN ECONOMY

CHAPTER 6

FINANCE AND GROWTH OF THE KOREAN ECONOMY FROM 1960 TO 2004

1. Introduction

In 1961, at the start of South Korea's modern economic development, the country had virtually no capital stock. Railroads, plants, dams, and factories left by the Japanese had been destroyed during the Korean War. The majority of fertilizer plants, electric power plants, and mining operations were situated in North Korea, reflecting both natural resource distributions and Japanese investments. Industry in South Korea, in contrast, was focused on agricultural crops and light manufacturing enterprises such as flour mills, breweries, and textile factories. Most of these enterprises, other than public electrical and transportation utilities, were later auctioned to the public. *Per capita* income in 1961 was only 82 US dollars. However, by 1995 it had increased to 10,076 US dollars, and South Korea had joined the ranks of upper-middle income countries.

Previous studies of rapid growth performances in East Asia, including that of South Korea, indicate that capital accumulation was one of the greatest contributing factors to regional growth (Kim and Lau, 1994; Young, 1995). In 1961, per capita capital stock in the South Korean economy was 280 US dollars, a figure that increased to 52,700 US dollars by 1995.[1] These data

---

[1] These figures were computed from Pyo (2002) estimate of capital stock. Capital stocks comprise residential and non-residential buildings, transport and machinery

suggest that the Korean economy was capable of sustaining increased investments throughout the period 1960-2004. In a developing economy, the initial savings rate is usually very low because of low income. How, then, were investments financed over such a prolonged period of time? Foreign aid or loans are primary sources of investment financing for developing economies during their initial development periods. However, financing through foreign aid or foreign loans without the ability to repay the principal or service debts is ultimately limiting. An alternative means of financing is that of exports and of foreign direct investments.

Mountainous South Korea is one of the most densely populated areas in the world. Arable land per capita in 1970 was 0.18 acres, hindering the export of land-intensive products. Some marine products such as agar-agar and seaweed were exported, mainly to Japan, in the 1950s. In an economy with few natural resources, how did exports become the best alternative for financing industrialization? Labor, i.e., human capital, was relatively abundant as opposed to capital and land in the 1960s. Exports of labor-intensive products thus became the natural means of financing industrialization. As this study will describe, South Korea's abundant labor compensated for a lack of natural resources and allowed sustained industrial financing that, in turn, helped increase labor productivity and growth in the economy. In contrast, economies tied to abundant natural resources can ultimately become limited by land-intensive exports. Investment in human capital through education and on-the-job training raises standards of marginal productivity and prevents labor scarcity, as measured by labor efficiency units. A lack of natural resources, which could have been a major

---

equipment, and other construction equipment.

disadvantage to this developing economy, became an advantage here in that it led South Korea to invest in industrialization.

As early as 1977, Ranis suggests an export-substitution policy in his emphasis on the financial aspects of exports. In a similar vein, Findlay (1984) notes that the 'export-led' growth model helps alleviate foreign exchange constraints in a developing economy. An outward-looking export-promotion policy has several advantages over an inward-looking import-substitution policy. First, exports generally remove foreign exchange constraints and facilitate imports of capital goods and intermediates. Second, an export economy spurs entrepreneurialism within the domestic economy through competition in the international market. In this sense, an export-promotion strategy is market conforming in comparison to an import-substitution policy. More importantly, export promotion alleviates foreign exchange bottlenecks for imports.

According to Ranis, a developing economy passes through two stages of development. The first is a primary import-substitution stage, based on import-substitution of light consumer goods by domestic production. The developing economy then reaches the secondary import-substitution stage, at which import substitution of capital goods and other consumer durable goods is attained. At this stage, Ranis further categorized developing economies into two groups of 'deviant' and 'non-deviant'. The deviant category would make an effort to shift from traditional land-based exports to non-traditional labor-based exports. The non-deviant would move toward a capital-intensive growth path, pursuing further secondary import substitution policies and neglecting productivity in a sector with a comparative advantage. Ranis placed Taiwan and Japan in the deviant group, while the Philippines and Latin America were included in the non-deviant group.

The advanced knowledge and technologies embodied in imported capital goods also spillover onto a catch-up economy such as South Korea's, making sustained growth possible. This study examines the growth of the South Korean economy from 1960 to 2004 related to its financial aspects with a focus on investment financing role of exports and its impact.

This chapter is organized as follows. Each section covers a decade, starting from the 1960s. Section II describes the export promotion policy of 1960s that was associated with the five-year economic plans. Section III outlines the heavy chemical industrial (HCI) policy of the third five-year economic plan of 1970s and reviews industrial coordination policies of 1980s. Section IV summarizes the background to the 1997 financial crisis and post-crisis financial turbulence. Section V discusses investment financing role of exports in relation to Ranis' export-substitution policy. Section VI is the conclusion.

2. Export Promotion Policy of the 1960s

After liberation from Japanese occupation in 1945, the Korean government assumed ownership of all Japanese-owned enterprises related to the national infrastructure such as railroads and electric and telecommunications utilities. Following the military coup of 1961, the government developed successive five-year plans focused on self-sustaining economic development and the expansion of basic industries and infrastructure.

The first and second five-year economic plans of 1962-1971 focused on establishing enterprises to supply basic industrial materials. The state-owned Korea Oil Corporation was established in 1962 to help meet the demands of transportation and synthetic fiber manufacturing. The Korea Oil Corporation later merged into the SK Group. Pohang Iron and Steel Company (POSCO), established in 1968, supplied the other basic material for future industrialization, i.e., steel. Agriculture played a key role in the South Korean economy at the start of the 1960s, accounting for 40% of the GDP. To meet agricultural demands, the Korea Fertilizer Corporation was established in 1967.[2]

How were such huge industrial projects financed at the beginning of industrialization? Traditional market-based financial organizations, including the *kye, mujin, and kaekchu*, played important roles. The most popular of these organizations among the public during the 1960s was the *kye*. It pooled resources among members and provided loans to members on either a pre-ordered sequence or by a lottery. The most influential of these market-based financial organizations was the *mujin*, a type of mutual savings and loan institution that was later reorganized into mutual savings and finance companies. Lastly, the *kaekchu* provided short-term financing to fishing households (Cole and Park, 1983, pp. 120-1). While these institutions were too small to finance investments in long-term capital equipment, they could finance short-term capital needs.

Government savings were also insufficient to finance investment projects. However, Brown (1973) has suggested that the effective management of government enterprises with respect to pricing policies contributed to investment financing in that government enterprises did not crowd out the private sector.

---

[2] The company was founded by Samsung and then donated to the government after an Incident Involving illegal saccharine imports.

Because domestic savings were so low, foreign savings provided a major source of investment. From 1962 to 1966, investment funding annually averaged 14.5% of the GNP, and 60% of investments came from foreign funds. The remaining 40% of investment was provided by domestic funds.[3] During the period of 1960s, 26 billion US dollars in foreign capital flowed into South Korea, of which approximately 10 billion US dollars came through official government loans, with the rest through commercial loans.[4]

The military government that had taken control by coup d'état in 1961 promoted an economic developmental regime, in part, to solidify its own legitimacy. One of the first acts of the regime was to nationalize commercial banks. Currency denominations were also altered, and units were changed from Hwan to Won, with a unit of Won equaling ten units of the former Hwan. This change was intended to mobilize domestic savings by forcing citizens to reveal any hidden savings. Further, the government issued loans (called 'policy loans') to supplement industrial targets.

During this decade, the nation's financial infrastructure developed in parallel with the establishment of basic industries. Special purpose banks such as the Korea Development Bank (KDB, established in 1954) provided channels for loans to new corporations. Owing to its specialized purpose, the KDB did not accept deposits as did normal commercial banks. Other special purpose banks such as the National Agricultural Cooperative Federation (NACF), Medium Industry Bank (MIB), Central Federation of Fisheries Cooperatives (CFFC), and Citizens' National Bank were also established to support farmers, fishing industries, small- and medium-sized

---

[3] *AB* computed from Table 6 of Brown (1973, p. 58)
[4] *AB* computed from Table 24 of Brown (1973, p. 215)

firms, and housing developers. The Korea Housing Bank was established in 1967 to finance housing for low-income families. In the same year, the Korea Development Finance Corporation (KDFC) was launched to facilitate the creation of private enterprises by providing medium- and long-term financing. Another special bank, introduced in 1967, was the Korea Exchange Bank (KEB), which dealt with foreign exchange.

The KDB and other special purpose banks provided a major proportion of loans in the 1960s. In 1964, the KDB issued 73% of loans in South Korea; commercial banks issued the remaining 37%. This structure of finance indicates that financial market intermediation played no role in the 1960s. The government retained complete control and extended the role of the KDB, allowing it to borrow loans from abroad and to guarantee foreign loans provided to domestic firms.

In a developing economy poorly endowed in natural resources, exports of manufactured goods are critical sources of funds for investment financing. In the latter part of the 1960s, during the launch of the second five-year plan, the government placed export promotion as its first priority. A package of policy tools including preferential taxes and credits, as well as an escalated tariff structure for imports and intermediates, was applied to encourage exports. The Korea Trade-Investment Promotion Agency (KOTRA), established in 1962, was charged with promoting South Korean exports in foreign markets.

The foreign exchange rate before 1960 was overvalued in the government's attempt to increase the value of imported goods in relation to the domestic currency value of foreign aid counterpart accounts.[5] In just one year, from 1960 to 1961, the exchange rate doubled from 65 won to 130 won per US dollar. The rate then remained stable until 1963.

Thus, the Korean financial market in the 1960s can be characterized as fragmented and unorganized, as is typical of underdeveloped financial markets (McKinnon, 1973). The role of commercial banks as financial intermediaries was absent during this period, which was dominated instead by government industrial policy. Commercial banks did, however, help to carry out government industrial policy. Cole and Park (1983, p. 61) described this financial situation as follows: 'The banks basically issued the guarantees on instruction from the government and took little responsibility for evaluating either the economic or financial feasibility of the project.'

2.1 Interest Rate and Foreign Exchange Rate Realization of 1965

The financial reform of 1965 marked a critical development in South Korea's early economic growth period.[6] The reform confirmed market rates for interest and foreign exchange rates. The interest rate for regular commercial bank loans was raised to 26% per annum in 1965 from 16% of the previous year. This market realization policy successfully restrained inflationary pressures and increased domestic savings. The GNP deflator was reduced to 7% in 1965 from 32% of 1964. The gross domestic saving rate with respect to GNP more than tripled in the four years following the

---

[5] The government's counterpart fund related to special accounts for foreign aid. The over-valued Korean currency before 1960s is one of an interesting example, illustrating an under-effected case of transfer payments.

[6] It was recommended by Gurley, Patrick, and Shaw (1965).

market realization policy, from only 4% in 1964 to as high as 16% in 1968.

The value of the won plummeted when the won/dollar exchange rate increased to 255 won in 1964 from 130 won per US dollar in the previous year. At the same time, a decrease in interest rates on export loans encouraged the export promotion policy. Interest rates decreased from 8% to 6.5%, and had fallen to 6% by 1967. However, the interest rate for general loans increased as a result of the interest rate realization policy (IRP). From 1961 to 1965, the annual interest rate on general loans was 18% and this increased to 23% from 1966 to 1972. Over the same periods, the interest rates on export loans fell from 9% to 6%. The IRP made export loans nearly twice as advantageous as general loans. This circumstance, together with the devaluation of the won, contributed to export promotion. Exports increased and light manufactures such as textiles, plywood, and wigs accounted for 63% of the total.

A negative side effect of the liberalization policy was an increase in costs for domestic firms. Higher interest rates burdened heavily leveraged corporations. Simultaneously, the higher foreign exchange rate added additional costs to imported intermediates and capital goods. Many domestic firms suffered severe financial distress and could not repay loans to commercial banks and private lenders. Nevertheless, the IRP policy was significant in that it introduced market-oriented financial rules to the economy.

2.2 Investments, Financial Distress, and Exports in the 1960s

During the period of 1962-1969 investment increased at an annual average growth rate of 27% with a peak record of 59.5% in 1966 following implementation of the IRP. Concurrently, the trade balance deteriorated at a nearly similar rate of 25% annually due to the import of most capital goods and intermediates. High investment demand together with a trade balance deficit exerted financial strain on the domestic economy, and the demand for loans exceeded the supply. Additional strain was manifested in the curb-market interest rate that exceeded the interest rates of time and savings deposits, and reflected market imperfections. From 1962 to 1969, the discrepancy between the two rate types was 26% on average (See column 4 on Table 6-1). This discrepancy reaches its peak in 1964 over the entire period from 1960 to 2004. Interestingly, the annual investment growth rates, the rate at which the trade balance deteriorated, and the gap between the curb-market and time/savings deposit interest rates increased simultaneously at similar rates.

The real GDP grew annually at 8.8% during this period. At the same time, investments also increased. The IRP of 1965 increased domestic savings and provided a basis for financing investments in exports. In this respect, the primary import substitution stage had been achieved. Nonetheless, high interest rates imposed debt burdens on corporations. In the third five-year plan, government industrial policy was designed to further boost the economy by creating a secondary import substitution stage favoring heavy and chemical industries.

3. Heavy Chemical Industrial Policy of the 1970s

To level the national industrial structure and increase value-added earnings, a third five-year economic plan (1972-1976) was set out that emphasized heavy chemical industrialization. Following the success of the two preceding five-year economic planning policies, South Korea's labor-intensive products had attained a competitive edge in international markets.

Most intermediates and capital goods were imported and were subject to preferential tax treatments, in line with the export-promotion policy. From the third five-year economic plan on, the government also began to put greater emphasis on increasing value-added profits.

However, during this period, the high interest rate IRP policy was still in effect, and a great number of firms were on the verge of financial insolvency. The Heavy Chemical Industrial (HCI) policy faced intense criticism regarding over-investment and the generation of excess capacity in the economy.

This financial danger was lessened by a special emergency measure, decreed on 3 August 1972, that froze private loans borrowed from the curb market for three years and gave corporations five-year grace periods for loan repayments. One of the purposes of the decree was to bring out the private loans of the curb-market to the regulatory financial system. By these measures, many corporations were able to sustain their production, an operation that might not have been possible without the decree. The economy regained its vigor, and exports increased to 80.5 billion US dollars in 1975.

The recycling of oil dollars earned through the export of construction materials to, and wage remittances from, Middle Eastern countries also favorably assisted the overall balance of payments. In 1977, the nation recorded a surplus balance of payments, the first since the launch of the five-year economic plans.

In 1978, domestic savings accounted for 27.2% of the GNP, far exceeding the 3.3% of foreign savings. The strength of domestic savings suggests that the Korean economy could ensure its autonomy independently, without foreign aid. However, the export structure in 1975 still relied heavily on light manufactures such as textiles, even though shares of iron and steel, electrical machinery, and transport equipment were rising. Textile yarn and fabrics accounted for 13% of total exports, followed by electrical machinery and transport equipment at 12%.

The development of financial institutions also proceeded in the 1970s. Non-bank financial institutions (NBFIs) such as life insurance companies, postal savings programs, trusts, and mutual savings and finance corporations (MSFC) were established during this period. These new entities brought unregulated financial markets further under regulation. Merchant banks also formed in 1976 and played a role in diversifying channels of foreign capital.

A variety of financial instruments competed with the curb market to provide short-term financing. Commercial Papers (CPs) were first established in August 1972. They were issued by non-financial corporations, investment and finance companies, and merchant banks. Commercial banks issued their own competition to CPs through certificates of deposit (CDs). The call money market was launched in 1975 to alleviate financial imbalances among commercial banks and financial institutions. Repurchase agreements (RPs) also came into existence in February 1977 and facilitated short-term financing for corporations (Kang 1990).

However, financial deepening, as measured by the ratio of domestic financial assets to the GNP, showed little improvement in the 1970s. Furthermore, the gap between the curb-market and the time/savings deposit rates had narrowed little by the end of the decade. This gap of 27% in 1968 had dropped to only that of 22% a decade later (Table 6-1). These figures indicate that the Korean economy in the 1970s remained repressed under a dualistic financial system.

There were, however, hopeful signals in the economy. Banking activities of 1978 relative to the GDP rose by more than three times that of 1965. Another significant character of the financial sector in the 1970s was a change in the loan structure in favor of the NBFI. The KDB share in the supply of loans and guarantees decreased to 18% in 1978, down from 34% in 1965 (Cole and Park 1983, p. 63). Meanwhile, the deposit share of the NBFIs increased from 16% in 1965 to 28% in 1977.

3.1 Soaring Real Estate Prices and the State-Chaebol Nexus

Several factors can help explain why financial deepening stagnated during the 1970s. A critical factor was soaring inflation, caused by the oil-shocks of 1974 and 1979. The real rate of interest, adjusted for the consumer price index (CPI), fell from 5.3% of the previous year to -19.3% in 1974. This inflationary pressure was reinforced by the balance-of-payments surplus in 1977, the first since the launch of the five-year economic plans. As a result, real estate became a preferred investment. The Seoul land value index in the 1970s increased at an annual rate of 29% and reached its highest rate of 136% in 1978, the highest one from 1960 to 2004 (Table 6-1).

Real estate prices have been blamed for causing growing income discrepancies. Wide-spread public criticism made this issue a topic of repeated socio-political debate. To avoid undesirable real estate speculation, various measures aimed at limiting real estate investments were enforced. These measures were less severe for corporations than for individuals. For this reason, corporations had far greater access to loans than did individuals. Such a situation created favorable situations for corporations to invest in physical capital, including land. Increased investment by corporations led to increased output and resulted in overall economic growth. This growth was a positive effect of rising real estate prices, in contrast to the undesirable effects of slowed financial market growth and greater income discrepancies.

Real estate is well received by banks as collateral because it alleviates problems of moral hazard on the part of borrowers. The increase in land prices put corporations that had provided real estate as collateral in a favorable position when borrowing from banks. Because loans had been allocated by the government since the 1960s, the large firms that had had greater access to policy loans also had more opportunities to obtain real estate. Real estate thus provided large firms with a multiplicative way of expanding their loans. As a result, many large corporations became highly leveraged, a situation that later proved problematic in the 1997 financial crisis.

Real estate also provided another link between the government and big corporations in that the government was a major stockholder of the commercial banks, and the chaebol were large real estate holders. Both the state and the chaebol thus shared a common interest in high real estate prices. To the extent that real estate prices increased not, primarily, as a result of a bubble but, rather, by sustainable fundamentals such as the realization of spillovers from the catch-up economy, the connection formed by real estate collateral between the state and big corporations was solid, sound, and not vulnerable to external shocks. [7] The HCI policy further

---

[7] To the extent to which the price of real estate reflected spillover effects from imported capital goods and intermediates, and the situation suggests that real estate values were based on fundamental value and not on a speculation-driven bubble. This is true in economic circumstances in which interest and wage rates are fixed. In other words, it is considered to be plausible that the spillover effects of a catch-up economy fall on the factor of land from the viewpoint of functional income

strengthened state-chaebol links. A vast amount of the investment required to execute HCI goals was channeled through large corporations. The state-chaebol nexus was further solidified, and replaced financial instruments of savings and those of investment.

The capital market development law was enacted in 1968, followed by an initial public offering law in 1972. Despite preferential treatment in terms of corporate taxes, public stock offerings in corporations were very limited. As of 1979, only five hundred and nine corporations were listed on the stock market, and 80% of those were publicly offered by the designation of the government. The potentially lucrative real estate market had created little demand for an active stock market. However, stocks boomed in 1977, led by stocks in construction corporations. Remittances from Middle East construction ignited a rise in stock prices. In early 1977, the Korean Stock Price Index (KOSPI) was on the level below one hundred by the end of the year, it had risen to one hundred and thirty-seven. However, the following year, the stock market was again depressed when construction stocks crashed (Rhee et al., 2005, pp. 341-4).

Overall, no significant developments in capital markets occurred in the 1970s. Real estate was the favored means of saving and substituted for investments in securities. Cole and Park (1983, p. 109) described the South Korean capital markets in the 1970s as follows:

> The long-term securities markets are, however, very much a product of governmental incentives and direction. While they have led to some broadening of the ownership of the major corporations, they have not generated significant amounts of new capital or reduced the heavy reliance

_____

distribution.

on bank and foreign-loan financing, nor have they had much effect in reducing the direct links between the government and the principal owner-managers of the large corporations.

However, even in this financially repressed decade, the South Korean economy grew. The emergency presidential decree of 3 August 1972 spurred economic growth of 12% in early 1973. Growth held at an average of 9% annually from 1973 to 1977. This growth performance was comparable to the growth rate of 12% in 1966, which had followed the interest realization policy (IRP) of 1965. Similarly, the next five years after 1965 had average annual growth rates of 10%. Growth performances of the latter 1960s and those of the latter 1970s suggest that growth was independent of financial liberalization (Cho, 1989).

Notably, in these two periods, investment rates were also high, independently of the financial environments. The average annual growth rates in investment from 1965-1969 and 1973-1977 were 34% and 20%, respectively. Figure 6-2 shows how increases in investments paralleled those of imports. The simultaneous rises in these variables were supportive of high growth performance.

3.2 Industrial Co-Ordination and Trade Structure Improvement in the 1980s

At the start of the 1980s, excessive investment as a result of the HCI policy, combined with heavy inflation brought on by the 1979 oil-price shock, burdened the Korean economy. In 1980, the GNP deflator increased at a rate of 26%, and the consumer price index soared at an even higher rate of 35%. The political turmoil caused by the assassination of President Park in October 1979 increased economic uncertainty. The growth rate in 1980 plummeted to -5% for the first time since the launch of the five-year plans this was coupled with massive crop failures in the same year. The balance of payments also showed a deficit of 5.3 billion US dollars in 1980, equivalent to 8.7% of the GNP. In the same year, the average debt ratio was on the level of 488 (Song, 1997, pp. 76-7).

Neither domestic savings nor trade surpluses could supply the capital needed for the HCI policy. After the Park assassination, Doo Hwan Chun succeeded to the presidency. The new government's first goal was to resolve the economic insolvency created by heavy indebtedness. Price stabilization was given the highest priority in governmental policy, followed by mitigation of excess capital in the economy through coordination among chaebols.

The production capacities of the semiconductor, automotive, steel, and shipbuilding industries exceeded relative domestic market demand. Such circumstances can create excess competition, and the market structure can become monopolistic. The government intervened to avoid these effects and attempted to reorganize the industrial structure. Hyundai was advised to make automobile manufacturing its core industry, while Samsung was told to concentrate on semiconductors. Likewise, LG was directed to focus on petrochemicals and yield its semiconductor business to Hyundai. The electrical generator business was assigned to Daewoo. Such reorganization of industries among the chaebols was difficult. To implement the plan, the government used cooperation and, sometimes, the threat of cutting off loans.

In an effort to stabilize the economy, the government pursued a tight fiscal policy aimed at reducing the ratio of the government deficit to the GNP.

Credit was also restrained to reduce inflationary pressure. These price stabilization efforts succeeded, and the consumer price inflation rate dropped from an annual rate of 25% during 1980-1981 to 7% in 1982. However, growth rates also fell in 1980 and 1981, reducing the GNP growth rate to -5% and -6% for the above years, respectively.

There was a time lag before the economy realized the benefits of matured investments related to the Heavy and Chemical Industrialization Policy of the third five-year economic plan (1972-1976). Exports gained momentum in the mid-1980s when low interest rates, low oil prices, and low exchange rates of the Japanese yen to the US dollar, in accord with the 1985 Plaza Agreement, gave South Korea a competitive edge in world markets in heavy and chemical manufactures. These favorable factors are often dubbed the 'three-lows' among Korean economists. The rate of return on capital reached a peak level in 1988, the same year the Olympics were held in Seoul.

As the balance of payments turned into a surplus, the burden of foreign debts incurred at the beginning of the 1980s also declined. South Korean exports reached 60 billion US dollars in 1988, and the average debt ratio fell to 296 in the same year (Song, 1997, pp. 76-7). The 1980s thus became an era in which South Korea's export structure began to level and the nation's comparative advantage shifted from labor-intensive manufactures to heavy-chemical industrial products. More than half of the total commodity exports were HCI goods (Hong, 2002, pp. 146-7). These indicators are best exemplified by the rate of increase in the trade balance in 1986. It improved by 733%. This successful performance of the Korean economy indicates that she passes through Ranis' secondary import-substitution stage and the state-chaebol ties were tight and firm as explained by

Amsden (1989, p. 63).[8]

3.3 Financial Reform of the 1980s and Erosion
of the State-Chaebol Nexus

Tight monetary and fiscal policies in 1980 and 1981 kept inflationary pressures under control. The real rate of interest in 1982 was positive for the first time since the 1965 interest rate realization policy. The economic environment of the 1980s provided a favorable situation for undertaking financial reforms. The real rate of interest in 1982 returned to a positive rate of 9% after having suffered negative rates in the latter 1970s. By 1984, the real interest rate had reached 12%. Between 1981 and 1983, the government divested its equity shares in all nationwide city banks, transferring ownership to private banks. Many administrative controls on banking were also eliminated, and entry barriers to financial markets were reduced. Moreover, preferential interest rates applied to policy loans were abolished (Nam, 1994, p. 89).

Significantly, in early 1984, financial intermediaries were permitted to determine their own rates within a given range (Nam, 1994, p. 191).

---

[8] There certainly is an ambiguity between an export-substitution and the import-substitution policy on the second stage as it is read in the following passage of Ranis (1977, pp. 42-3): "We, of course, recognize that these "choices" of growth paths, and of accompanying policy packages, are never quite as clear-cut as all this in real life, but tend to fade into each other at the edges. But while there certainly exist substantial elements of both secondary import substitution and export substitution in the overall production and trade structure of most LDC's, the contrasts painted here are both meaningful and instructive." The above passage suggests that the export substitution policy, not neglecting its financial aspects through exports, needs to be distinguished from the import substitution policy in which the comparative advantage is not well taken into account. The relevance of the heavy chemical industrial policy in this context could be explained in its exerting disciplinary efforts for development of comparative advantages in relation to her possible exports for the future.

Diversified financial services were also provided. Unlawful financial practices through the unorganized market provoked financial reform focused on the development of non-bank financial institutions (NBFI) as a substitute for the informal sector. The NBFIs were largely owned by the chaebol whose shares in commercial banks sharply increased throughout the 1980s.

The ratio of domestic financial assets to the GNP nearly doubled in the 1980s, increasing from two point four in 1980 to four point two in 1990. A salient feature during this period was the increase in the share held by the NBFIs. The ratio of non-bank deposits to the GDP increased to 6% in 1990, from 38% in 1980. Financing through corporate bonds also grew from four point 5% in 1980 to 10.2% in 1987. However, the most notable change in this period was the significant increase in the stock market share of the GDP. It increased to 11% in 1988, from 6% in 1987.

Financial reforms of the 1980s liberalized the financial market to a great extent. The government moved to privatize the banks and even deregulate interest rates within given ranges. The NBFI absorbed non-regulated financial markets, lessening the dualistic financial market structure. The curb-market interest rate exceeded the market rate by only 2.4% in 1987, down from 17% difference in 1977 (Appendix Table 6A-1). Another indicator of the success of the financial reforms was the liquidity supply of the economy increased as measured by the ratio of M3 to GDP. By this indicator it had risen to point eighty-eight in 1988 from point thirty-seven in 1976 (Table 6A-1).

However, the economy had not liberalized to the extent necessary for the financial market to perform intermediary functions in place of the government. The government assigned bonds to the NBFI. Investment trust companies established the Bond Management Fund (BMF) in which individuals could invest by purchasing certificates and participate indirectly in the bond markets. As of 1989, 17 trillion won worth of outstanding Monetary Stabilization Bonds were held by the NBFI (Kang, 1990, pp. 70-1). The amount of commercial bank shares that could be held by an individual was limited to 8% of the bank's total equity stock. In addition, the government continued to appoint top bank management throughout the 1980s. These restrictions discouraged active equity investments by large corporations in these banks. Although the financial markets were not fully liberalized, the influence of the chaebols on the financial markets increased through their ownership of NBFI. Kim (1997, p. 189) and other observers wondered, therefore, whether the state-chaebol nexus could be sustained:

> The chaebol's investment in financial services also highlights a direct competition occurring between the state and the chaebol for the provision of such services. Although direct competition in banking is avoided due to the state's prohibition of chaebol ownership of banks, it still leads us to a basic question of whether a comprehensive developmental state is necessary when the private sector is mature enough to provide certain services such as banking.

The chaebols' influence also increased substantially in the 1980s in the real sector. In 1985, the value-added products of the five largest chaebols accounted for more than 6% of GNP; for the top thirty chaebols, this proportion rose to 12% (Chang, 2003, p. 10). Thus, the 1980s were an era in which the chaebols expanded their influence both in the real and financial sectors of the Korean economy. The chaebols were instrumental in driving economic growth, exploring economies of scale, and also realizing economies of scope.

4. Financial Liberalization and the 1997 Financial Crisis

A democratization of politics accompanied the favorable economic changes of the 1980s. President Tae-woo Roh began his administration with a promise of greater democratization on 29 June 1987, and created an economic environment favorable to economic liberalization. A distinguishing feature of the economy during this period was a drastic increase in the wage rate beginning the mid-1980s. The nominal wage rate of 1985 had increased four-fold by 1994.[9] Profit margins from investment were squeezed out by the higher wage rate, and the rate of return on capital began to fall. The strengthening of labor unions under President Young-sam Kim's democratization regime (1993-1998) further strengthened wages.

Economic deregulation paralleled political democratization and was further intensified by Korea's entry into the Organization for Economic Cooperation and Development (OECD) in 1996. The remarkable performance of the Korean economy in terms of GDP, trade volume, and per capita income had made the nation eligible for OECD membership. The opening of financial markets was a natural outcome of OECD membership and general trends in Korea's political climate.

However, despite growing liberalization, the government-chaebol nexus remained firm, guided by the government's implicit guarantee of chaebol loans, and the government's continuing direct or indirect appointment of bank management personnel. The chaebol-government relationship created negative side effects despite the spectacular growth performances of the Korean economy. Two problems in particular stood out. First, large

---

[9] As computed from Table 5.7 of Song (1997, p. 76).

corporations were highly leveraged, as noted above. In 1997, the top-thirty chaebols had average debt-equity ratios of six hundred (Chang, 2003, pp. 12-3). The second problem related to lack of discipline in the financial sector. Loan decisions were based on government industrial policy, which guided fund allocations, rather than by nonbiased surveillance and evaluation of risks.

The scarcity of loans meant that it was common practice for short-term loans to be rolled over without further restraints. Without full economic reform in lending practices, the financial sector and the implicit state-chaebol nexus were left to market discipline by the financial liberalization policy of 1995, summarized by Woo-Cumings (2001, p. 362) as follows:

> The dilemma in Korea is that the state had to both guarantee and discipline the chaebol. The true "miracle" in Korea in the three decades since the 1960s was that it juggled these conflicting roles. But in the early 1990s the government abandoned its juggling act, without putting in place prudential regulations to rein in the behavior of the nonbank financial intermediaries, which were increasingly providing an internal capital market for the chaebol. This auto-da-fe in favor of the "markets" left Korea defenseless in the face of a massive financial crisis.

The chaebol had grown to the extent that the government could no longer play the role of implicit guarantor or justify the "too big to fail" slogan. Instead, the chaebol had become "too big to bailout" for the state. The state-chaebol nexus, which had helped build the Korean economic success, had become a source of economic fragility and was vulnerable to external shocks. This vulnerability, which had to be dealt with within the fiscal discipline of financial liberalization, contributed to the 1997 financial crisis.

4.1 A Triple Mismatch and Future Prospects

Prior to the 1997 financial crisis, the difference between market and curb rates of interest remained relatively stable. The share of loans provided by the NBFIs also changed little. However, one important shift was the liberalization of the capital account. As noted above, Korea joined the OECD in 1996. Although the capital account was liberalized, large corporations remained highly leveraged, suggesting that the state-chaebol inertia remained intact.

Korea's domestic financial sector was unprepared for the altered economic environment in the wake of the 1995 financial liberalizations. The rollover of short-term loans, creating de facto long-term loans, was still common practice. Financial audits were mere formalities for meeting tax office report requirements. Cross-share holdings of equities and cross-loan guarantees among affiliates and between subsidiaries and the home company of the chaebols were also prevalent. Merchant banks expanded with democratization in politics. These banks were mostly owned by the chaebol and funneled necessary funds to the large corporations. Furthermore, most merchant bank loans were made to firms within the chaebol group. These institutions served as financial intermediaries to fill the gap between the banks and the stock market. Merchant banks even used portions of funds borrowed at low rates from the international financial market to invest in high-yield foreign junk bonds.

In 1997, the top five chaebol owned three merchant banks, six securities companies, three investment trust companies, three life insurance companies, and twelve other financial services (Chang, 2003, p. 58). Profligate management of the merchant banks has been noted as a cause of the financial crisis. Not possessing their own credit and risk assessment capabilities, the domestic financial institutions were exposed to risk from the large corporations of the chaebol.

The debt-GDP ratio of the South Korean economy had continued to decrease since its peak in the early 1980s. The nation had ample capability to repay debts and interest, and the debt service-export ratio was below 10%. The ratio of short-term debt to total external debt, however, reached 50% in 1997, provoking a liquidity crisis on the withdrawal of foreign short-term debts.

As noted above, the chaebol had grown excessively large in relation to the Korean economy in the 1990s. They had begun to outweigh the government in their size and in their role following the HCI policy of the third five-year economic plan. A large inflow of foreign capital further diminished the previous role of the government as a guarantor of foreign loans, a situation exemplified by the government's inability to bail out Hanbo, which was then one of the largest corporations of the top-thirty chaebols in Korea. Thereafter, Sammi, Jinro, and Kia were subject to court surveillance. These failures showed that the government could no longer serve as implicit guarantor of foreign loans. Foreign investors lost confidence in the ability of the Korean economy to protect loans and many loans were withdrawn.

Under such an environment, capital liberalization endangered the capability to repay external loans. Banks were defenseless when requested to repay short-term debt, as opposed to the conventional loan rollover practices. As foreign creditors called in loans and pulled out of the Korean stock market, the domestic exchange rate received a boost from the drastic increase in the exchange rate.

Foreign loans denominated in US dollars were extended to long-term loans in domestic currency (won). The assets and net worth of banks fell greatly because of the depreciated won. This deterioration of bank balance sheets led to further outflow of foreign capital and additional weakening of the won, creating a downward spiral of devaluation.

The state-chaebol nexus, which had taken the place of the savings-investment financial market, could no longer be sustained within financial liberalization. Chang (2003) noted that the ineffective restructuring of economic practices based on the traditional ties between the state and chaebols was a result of this underlying inertia. Thus, a mismatch arose between the state and the chaebols regarding the state's implicit guarantee of chaebol loans. Chang (2003, pp. 35-7) argued the following:

> The Korean financial crisis made it manifest that both chaebols and the government failed to respond to their changing constraints. The transition of chaebols and the government did not entail the scrapping of the old system and starting from scratch. Rather, the routines and practices, organizational forms, and social ties persisted and functioned as sources of inertia … Thus, the crisis of 1997 was due to this mismatch between changing the external environments and internal capabilities of both chaebols and the government. This mismatch was caused by inertia of both institutions.

In summary, a triple mismatch caused the financial crisis of 1997: mismatches of currency, loan maturity, and the state-chaebol ability to cope with the capital account liberalization.

How could future financial markets prevent the occurrence of this interrelated triple mismatch? If the government had avoided implicit guarantees on loans for big corporations in advance of the capital account liberalization, over-borrowing from abroad would not have occurred. Likewise, the crisis could have been avoided if the long-term capital markets had been sufficiently developed to absorb the rollover of short-term loans denominated in US dollars. Eichengreen and Hausman (1999) referred to loan maturity and currency mismatch as the 'original sin', indicative of imperfect capital markets in a developing economy. This 'original sin' model also involves the interrelated foreign exchange and long-term bond markets. Stability of the long-term bond market would deter foreign investors from withdrawing capital out of the host country similarly, long-term confidence in domestic currency would induce foreign investment into the long-term capital market. It is debatable as to which market is more relevant when it comes to ensuring stability in other markets. For instance, McKinnon (2002, p. 235) has argued that East Asian economies need stable exchange rates with respect to the dollar to create economic environments conducive to developing long-term bond markets:

> Only with long-term confidence in the purchasing power of domestic money (against the center country's) would exchange rate expectation be naturally regressive and long-term bond and mortgage markets be possible to organize — both domestically and for commercial (non-sovereign) international borrowing.

If a long-term expectation with respect to reversing the flow of foreign short-term withdrawals had been developed, much of the adjustment costs of the crisis could have been alleviated. After the crisis, South Korea's financial markets experienced substantial changes in the bond market, followed by a general restructuring of the financial sector. [10]

---

[10] IMF program and the changes in the financial market after the crisis are relegated

4.2 Aftermath of the Crisis

Foreign capital returned to Korea after successful recovery from the financial crisis. This return made it easier for the general public to obtain loans from financial institutions. Easy access, which had previously been limited to large corporations or privileged chaebols, was now extended to the general public. One notable outcome was an increase in household debt. Loans to households accounted for 20% of total loans in 1993 and 50% of total loans in 2004. The indiscriminate issue of credit cards to the general public also directly increased household debt. The so-called credit card problem led to a rise in household defaults. However, greater access to credit also generated increased domestic demand, offsetting the recessionary economic downturns related to the financial crisis. A loan repay program in parallel with that offered to corporations was developed for households in danger of credit default.

In the aftermath of the financial crisis, public investments in social overhead capital for schools, public libraries, and highway construction gradually became more market based. One example was the enterprise-city development plan. According to this plan, a large corporation could be given land expropriation rights. Capital gains accruing from the land development would then be used for local public interests. This new plan transferred the traditional state right to use and purchase land to large corporations, mostly chaebols.

This move indicates that the chaebols had gained an even more influential position relative to the state in that they had become involved in regional developmental projects, projects that had been the sole responsibility of the

---

to the Appendix.

government in the 1960s and 1970s.

Investments in social overheads have frequently been carried out by consortiums. The structures and facilities built by the consortium may then be transferred to government, and the costs incurred would be covered either by usage fees or by renting to the government for a certain period. In the former case, the private sector shares in the risk, while in the latter case, the government assumes most risk. This type of investment involves more market-based decision-making with respect to sharing risks the than did investments carried out by the government in the 1970s and 1980s. The success of the enterprise-city proposal depends on the extent to which real estate prices stabilize and balanced development across regions can be achieved.

The rest of this study reviews the investment financing role of exports in the growth experience of the Korean economy within this developmental period in light of the Ranis' export-substitution strategy.

5. Investment Financing Role of Exports

Figure 6-1 exhibits the rate of change in fixed capital stock and that in trade balance from the period of 1960 to that of 2004. The fixed capital stock reached its highest rate of increase by 59.5% in 1966 following the financial liberalization regime of the interest rate realization policy (IRP). Another peak growth rate of the capital stock is marked by the rate of 34.4% in 1978, largely due to the heavy chemical industrial (HCI) policy. The 1990s began with its peak rate of investment by 25.4%. These peak rates of investment are shown in Figure 6-1 together with those of the trade balance improvement rates.

Figure 6-1. Rate of change in fixed capital stock and trade balance, 1960 - 2004 (%)

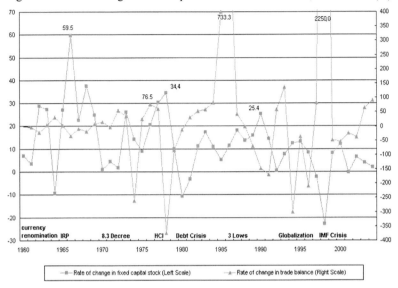

The rate of change of trade balance on Table 6-1 is defined as the change of the trade balance relative to that of income. The counterpart peak rate of the improvement of the trade balance is lagged behind that of the investment rate by about eight to ten years. The rate at which the trade balance improves most rapid during 1970s is recorded by 76.5% of 1976.

This rate increased by about a seven and the half times that of 1986. The most remarkable improvement rate is marked in 1998 by twenty-two and the half times of the previous financial crisis year of 1997. The increase of trade surplus with respect to income lessens the financial strains of the economy.

Figure 6-1 presents events of financial repressions and those of liberalizations in a chronological order during the period from 1960 to 2004 of the Korean economy. It starts from the beginning of 1960s with the financial repression of the currency denomination from Hwan to Won.

These events are shown to occur in the intermediate period between the peak of the investment rate and that of the trade balance improvement rate. The August 3rd Decree of 1972 was promulgated in between the trade balance peak of 1976 and the investment peak of 1966. A trade balance was deteriorated by the rate of 3.9% in the preceding year of the Decree (See Table 6-1). A foreign debt problem of 1980 occurred in between the trade peak of 1986 and the investment peak of 1978. Trade deficit occurred in concurrent with the foreign debt. The financial crisis of 1997 in its time scale is situated in between the trade balance peak of 1998 and the investment peak of 1990. The trade deficit in the crisis year of 1997 increased by the two times that of the previous year.

This recurrent pattern of financial distresses associated with investment and the resolutions by the improvement of trade balances at an approximately decade intervals is consistent with the deviant pattern of developing economies as proposed by Ranis as for the investment financing role of exports.

5.1 A Comparison of Two Peak Rates

In the previous section the two peak rates are compared for explanation of the Ranis' export earning hypothesis for resolution of the financial strains of a developing country. What justification do we have for this explanation? Two scenarios may be suggested with respect to the direction of its causality. One possible hypothesis is that the investment precedes the financial resolutions achieved by the trade surplus. The alternative one is on the view point of the reverse direction. Export earnings provide opportunities for investment expansion which is associated with imports of intermediate and capital goods. The financial distresses related to trade

Figure 6-2. Investments and imports as percent of GDP from 1960 to 2004 (%)

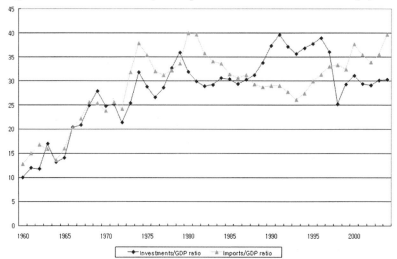

deficits eventually limit the investment. [11]

In the first scenario a 'time to build' model related to trade structure of an economy is implicit in comparing the two peaks. It takes time in construction of buildings and equipments for production of exportables.

This argument is based on the presumption that most of capital equipments and intermediates necessary for production in a developing economy are imported. Figure 6-2 displays the relationship between these two variables. The investment ratio of GDP moves in parallel with that of the import ratio throughout the period of four decades except for the period beginning from 1990s up to the financial crisis period. [12] It suggests that financial returns on

---

[11] This second possibility is suggested by one of the referees.

[12] One of the possible explanations for this divergence could be due to a change in trade structure of the economy. Capital goods and equipment are no longer imported and they are substituted by domestic production. The other alternative explanation

investment are realized by trade surplus. The time intervals of investments-returns are measured by those of the two peaks. This consideration leads us to a presumption that a firm's financial burdens become most severe in the middle of the two peaks before it reaps its export earnings.

One of the most convenient measures for distinguishing between these two scenarios in the present study is the ratio obtained by division of the previous peak growth rate of investment by the lagged one of trade balance improvement. It is interpreted as the amount of the rate of investment for a given rate of improvement of trade balance to be able to finance and is considered to represent the degree of the effectiveness of Ranis' investment financing role of exports. A decrease of this ratio implies that the financing role of exports gradually decreases. As a trade structure of an economy undergoes a change by replacement of imported capital goods with domestic production or as the liquidity supply is sufficient by the financial deepening of the domestic economy this measure of the effectiveness of the investment financing role of export will be decreased.

Over the four decades the peak growth rates of the increase in the fixed-capital stock decreased against the increase of that of the improvement in trade balance. This effectiveness ratio of investment financing of exports decreases to 5% in 1986 and finally 1% in 1998 from 80% in 1976. This investment-related import demand scenario is considered to be more appropriate for the periods up to the end of nineteen eighties.

As the liquidity constraints for firms are alleviated along with the increase

---

is due to the lagged-effects of investments are prolonged. What is significant, however, in the argument of this study is in an exhibition of the co-movement of the investments and the imports by the end of 1980s.

in the supply of liquidity in the economy the financial role of the trade surplus will be diminished. It is noted in the last column of Table 6-1 the liquidity of the economy as measured by the ratio of M3/GDP exceeds one from the beginning period of 1990s. This period of increasing liquidity supply coincides with each other that of the Korean economy passing through Ranis' secondary stage of import substitution.

5.2 A Virtuous Circle of Spillover Effects

In explaining the growth of a catch-up, late-industrializing economy such as that of South Korea, Amsden (1989) attributed successful growth performance to the state, entrepreneurs, a highly qualified workforce, and well-trained bureaucrats and firm managers. These factors contribute to the transfer of technology and applications from contact with foreign marketing personnel, engineers, and scientists, and help the market open. Acquisition of knowledge and know-hows through spillover effects from imported capital goods and intermediates could be another factor which contributes for transfer of technology.

Financing of the investment-related imports by export earnings creates a virtuous circle through which knowledge spillover effects occur to the domestic economy. This process of the investment related imports turns out to be favorable for economic growth of the Korean economy.

The next to the last column of Table 6-1 presents the rate of change in Seoul land value index. This index shows that the Seoul land price had more than doubled by 1977. One of the most influential factors for this hiking price level is the balance of payments surplus due to the recycling of the then oil dollar brought by the construction workers at the Middle East. Besides this surplus from the service account the trade surplus of the previous year is another factor to be taken into account. Subsequent to the trade surplus of 1986 was the rate of the increase of the land value index by 33.5% observed in 1989. In an economy in which financial market is not yet fully developed the land price index can be considered as a measure of capital gains for investments. These accruals of capital gains of investments reinforce the virtuous investment cycle.

A different interpretation for the circle becomes possible, depending on which peak rate one first starts from. Suppose one starts from that of the trade balance. Expansion of overinvestment becomes possible on this trade balance peak because of the expectation of the accruals of future capital gains. This over investment results in a trade deficit and the financial distress occurs. After a lapse of a certain period of time, trade surplus picks it up by exchange rate adjustments. Then the favorable expectation repeats itself generating the investment-related import demand. This scenario is reverse to the first one in a direction of its causality. This export-expansion scenario of the trade peak preceding to the investment peak hinges on price flexibility of the economy. Indeed, the fortunate events of the three lows in the middle of 1980s and the plummeted value of won in 1998 all attributed for the trade surpluses. This would not, however, have become possible without the productive capacity of the economy to meet the foreign demands. In this respect the export-expansion scenario is more relevant for the economy in which productive capacity to meet export demands already exist. Access to liquidity becomes presumably easier in this economy and the role of exports for investment financing is negligible.

However, for the economy in which no sufficient capital equipments are provided and starts from the scratch as it was in the early developmental periods of nineteen sixties and nineteen seventies of the Korean economy the investment-related import demand scenario is considered to be more relevant.

Spillover effects from imported capital goods increase productivity of domestic labor and provide a competitive edge for technologically more sophisticated industries. This continuous injection of spillover effects from the advanced economy makes it possible for an economy to move its trade structure toward more sophisticated ones. Without import of capital goods being able to be financed by exports, economic growth of the early developmental stage could not have been sustained.

The functional distribution of income related to spillover effects is another important issue for the economy on her early developmental stage. In an economy in which the financial market is depressed and the labor market is also suppressed, spillover effects from the abroad would most likely to fall onto the real estate sector as well as on the capital goods. In Korea, land is scarce in its supply relative to labor and its soaring prices as indicated previously are supportive of this conjecture.

Real estates were, therefore, well received as collateral with which to secure loans from financial institutions. Real estate collateral provided by the chaebols to financial institutions helped sustain the state-chaebol nexus until at least the mid-1980s. The exhaustion of spillover effects meant the end of capital gains appropriations. The state-chaebol nexus erodes itself as the capital gains from real estates could no longer be accrued. The eventual bursting of the real estate bubble suggests that a developing economy must pass through Amsden's learning stages (Amsden, 1989), before entering the mature stage.

The recurrent circles of investment, financial distress, and exports followed by soaring real estate prices were conducive to economic growth as long as the positive externalities were involved in the investment. On entering the mature economic stage, once the realization of externalities associated with investments and capital gains were no longer possible, the bubble on which the real estate prices were founded was bound to burst. This occurrence, however, provided a favorable economic environment for financial market deepening, as indicated by the increase in the ratio of domestic financial assets to the GDP. Autonomy of financial intermediation in asset portfolio management as well as in loans could also improve.

The macroeconomic and financial indicators shown in Table 6-1 confirm the conventional wisdom that financial deepening occurs with rises in per capita income (Gurely and Shaw, 1955, 1967; Goldsmith, 1969). The portion of liquid liabilities relative to the GDP, as measured by the M3/GDP ratio, increased from zero point thirty-seven in 1971 to one point sixty-five in 2004. The gap between the curb-market interest rate and the time/savings deposits interest rates was substantially reduced. In 1963 the curb-market rate exceeded the time and savings deposit rates by 31%. This gap almost disappeared in 2004, suggesting that the financial market became integrated and absorbed fragmented informal financial markets after a certain developmental stage. Sustained economic growth throughout four decades of alternating financial regimes also suggests that the type of financial regime had no direct effect on economic growth. However, subdividing the four decades allows examination of any systemic recurrent patterns with respect to investment, financial distress, and trade balances.

Increases in investment throughout the period from 1960 to 2004 have sustained growth of the Korean economy. Starting from the market-oriented financial regime of 1965, financial repression and liberalization alternated, ending with financial liberalization after the financial crisis. Amidst these alternating regimes, financial liberalization and investment increased without any significant interruptions, and economic growth continued, leading the economy to a mature stage of financial diversification. The pattern of investments, imports, financial distress, exports, and soaring real estate prices repeated itself before the spillover effects of the catchup economy were exhausted and before it reaches her maturity.

6. Conclusion

A Rostovian take-off of the Korean economy was possible through risk taking by the authoritarian state led by President Chung-hee Park, in collaboration with the early chaebol founders. Joint risk taking by the state and business connected to the credit supply, which was controlled by the government.

From 1960 to 2004, an alternate sequence of financial repression and financial liberalization occurred at approximately decadal intervals. South Korea's financial market was repressed at the beginning of 1961 with a currency denomination but turned in a more market-oriented direction with the introduction of the interest rate realization policy (IRP) in 1965. High interest rates due to market liberalization, together with the heavy and chemical industrial (HCI) policy of the third five-year economic plan (1972-1976), put financial burdens on corporations and prompted the emergency presidential decree of 3 August 1972. In this period, the financial market returned to repression.

However, the economy grew throughout these two financial regimes, without interruptions. The economy grew at 10% from 1961 until the implantation of the IRP policy. Likewise, the economy grew at 9%, on average, for five subsequent years following the August 1972 emergency decree. The annual rate of investment was high in both of these periods: 34% from 1965 to 1969, and 20% from 1973 to 1977. Commercial banks allocated loans under the state-chaebol nexus, regardless of the financial regime in the 1960s and 1970s. This loan allocation scheme was effective in mobilizing domestic savings and implementing industrial policy. Significant to the IRP, however, was that a market-oriented financial regime was introduced at the initial period of the development stage and helped spur growth momentum for the Korean economy.

Until the 1997 financial crisis, substantial improvements, such as financial deepening and an increase in the variety of financial instruments, occurred throughout the 1980s and 1990s. Unregulated financial markets were absorbed into regulated ones with development of the NBFI. The gap between curb-market and time deposit interest rates was reduced from 20% in 1979 to 12% in 1989. The financial deepening ratio in 1989, measured by the ratio of liquid liabilities to the GDP, was nearly two times that in 1979.

With the success of the HCI policy, the influence of large corporations on the economy increased with respect to output, employment, and loan sizes. Increasing ownership of the NBFIs and commercial banks by the chaebols allowed the chaebols to compete with the government in the financial market. The state-chaebol nexus thus became increasingly eroded, beginning in the mid-1980s.

Labor unions became more active in conjunction with political democratization, and wage rates soared from the mid-1980s. Profits from investment were squeezed out, and the rate of return on capital began to decline. South Korea also became a member of the OECD in 1996, a move that obliged the government to open the capital account. This greater openness was another significant change in the economic environment and influenced the state-chaebol relationship.

The financial crisis of 1997 showed that the government could no longer play the role of guarantor for large corporations. The state-chaebol bond came to its demise, and IMF financial remediation was instituted. The growth and finance pattern of the last four decades suggests that the relationship between the state and business in South Korea has changed as the economy has moved through several developmental stages.

Over these four decades, a systematic pattern of growth in relation to finance has occurred. Financial distress caused by investment has been relieved through increased exports. This investment-cum-export cycle has been repeated at approximately ten-year intervals. After the financial distress of the early 1970s, export performance greatly improved, laying the foundation for the export of light manufactured goods, passing through Ranis' first import-substitution stage. Likewise, after overcoming the financial burdens of the early 1980s created by the recall of foreign loans through the 'three lows', the Korean export structure was leveled up to heavy chemical manufactures such as electrical appliances, ships, steel, semiconductors, and automobiles. By this time, it reached Ranis' second stage of import-substitution. The financial crisis of 1997 was also followed by a recovery marked by an increase in exports of semiconductors, automobiles, information technology equipment, and steel.

Each financial recovery was associated with an increase in exports. Export-led growth of the South Korean economy has relieved harsh financial distress over the past four decades. In this respect, South Korea's economic growth and associated financing from 1960-2004 has exhibited a pattern consistent with Ranis' export-substitution strategy. Financial deepening has occurred, and financial services have diversified, confirming Gurley and Shaw's hypothesis (1955, 1967).

Following the financial crisis, the government has moved from a partnership role to one involved in creating an economic environment favorable for market discipline in the financial and real sectors. Economic restructuring after the financial crisis has been carried out in this context. The Financial Supervisory Commission supervises and coordinates bank mergers and acquisitions. The Fair Trade Commission aims to improve corporate governance and the business transparency of the chaebols. Restructuring problems and the promotion of market discipline have replaced the five-year economic plans launched in the 1970s, and now present new challenges for the Korean economy.

Appendix

Table 6A-1. Major Indicators of Korean Economic Growth

Year	Growth Rate of Real GDP	Rate of Change in Fixed Capital Stock	Curb-Market Real Interest Rate	Real Interest Rate on Time Deposits	A Gap between Curb-Market & Time Deposits Rates	The Ratio of Investments to GDP	The Ratio of Exports to GDP	The Ratio of Imports to GDP	Rate of Change in Trade Balance	Rate of Change in Seoul Land Value Index	Ratio of Liquid Liabilities to GDP
1960	1.2	7.0	n.a.	n.a.	n.a.	10.0	3.4	12.8		n.a.	0.10
1961	5.9	3.5	n.a.	n.a.	n.a.	12.0	5.4	15.0	-2.1	n.a.	0.14
1962	2.1	28.7	n.a.	5.7	n.a.	11.8	5.1	16.8	-21.9	n.a.	0.14
1963	9.1	27.3	26.5	-4.6	31.1	17.0	4.8	15.9	5.1	n.a.	0.11
1964	9.7	-9.3	19.5	-14.9	34.4	13.2	5.9	13.6	30.6	68.0	0.09
1965	5.7	27.1	44.5	8.1	36.4	14.1	8.6	16.0	3.9	33.9	0.12
1966	12.2	59.5	45.6	19.2	26.4	20.4	10.4	20.3	-33.8	n.a.	0.14
1967	5.9	22.6	47.0	22.2	24.8	20.9	11.5	22.2	-8.1	n.a.	0.18
1968	11.3	37.4	43.8	17.7	26.1	24.9	12.8	25.6	-19.6	52.5	0.24
1969	13.8	24.8	42.2	16.6	25.6	27.9	13.5	25.4	7.0	84.1	0.29
1970	8.8	1.0	38.2	12.6	25.6	24.8	13.6	23.8	14.3	4.0	0.28
1971	8.2	4.6	34.5	12.3	22.2	25.2	15.0	25.6	-3.9	28.7	0.37
1972	4.5	1.7	22.1	1.7	20.4	21.4	19.4	24.2	54.7	5.7	0.40
1973	12.0	26.2	30.2	5.3	24.9	25.4	28.7	31.8	35.4	1.6	0.44
1974	7.2	14.1	-3.2	-19.3	16.1	31.8	26.7	37.9	-261.3	30.7	0.39
1975	5.9	8.9	11.6	-9.2	20.8	28.8	26.9	35.4	24.1	31.6	0.38
1976	10.6	20.7	25.3	3.0	22.3	26.6	30.0	32.0	76.5	16.1	0.37
1977	10.0	30.2	26.7	6.6	20.1	28.6	30.4	31.2	60.0	31.7	0.41
1978	9.3	34.4	26.9	4.5	22.4	32.7	28.4	32.2	-375.0	135.7	0.41
1979	6.8	10.0	20.3	0.2	20.1	36.0	26.6	33.6	-84.2	6.4	0.42
1980	-1.5	-10.7	12.7	-7.1	19.8	31.9	32.1	40.0	-12.9	13.4	0.46
1981	6.2	-3.1	11.5	-4.3	15.7	29.9	34.3	39.7	31.6	3.6	0.48
1982	7.3	11.1	21.8	0.7	21.1	28.9	33.2	35.8	51.9	8.7	0.56
1983	10.8	17.4	21.6	4.4	17.2	29.2	33.0	34.1	57.7	57.7	0.58
1984	8.1	10.9	22.2	7.6	14.6	30.6	33.4	33.6	81.8	23.3	0.61
1985	6.8	5.3	21.1	7.4	13.7	30.4	32.0	31.4	400.0	8.1	0.66
1986	10.6	11.5	20.9	7.0	13.9	29.4	35.6	30.6	733.3	3.7	0.73
1987	11.1	18.1	21.3	6.7	14.6	30.3	38.3	31.2	42.0	6.3	0.81
1988	10.6	13.6	14.4	2.7	11.7	31.2	36.4	29.3	0	28.1	0.88

(Table Continued)

Year	Growth Rate of Real GDP	Rate of Change in Fixed Capital Stock	Curb-Market Real Interest Rate	Real Interest Rate on Time Deposits	A Gap between Curb-Market & Time Deposits Rates	The Ratio of Investments to GDP	The Ratio of Exports to GDP	The Ratio of Imports to GDP	Rate of Change in Trade Balance	Rate of Change in Seoul Land Value Index	Ratio of Liquid Liabilities to GDP
1989	6.7	16.0	15.9	4.1	11.7	33.8	30.8	28.7	-70.4	33.5	0.99
1990	9.2	25.4	13.8	1.3	12.4	37.4	28.0	29.0	-147.6	31.2	1.06
1991	9.4	14.4	13.7	0.6	13.1	39.7	26.3	29.0	-170.0	11.2	1.08
1992	5.9	0.6	15.8	3.5	12.3	37.2	26.6	27.7	59.3	-2.8	1.16
1993	6.1	7.7	17.1	3.5	13.5	35.7	26.5	26.1	136.3	-8.7	1.22
1994	8.5	12.5	15.2	2.9	12.2	36.9	26.6	27.4	-300.0	-1.4	1.30
1995	9.2	13.1	17.2	4.2	13.0	37.8	28.8	29.9	-37.5	0.2	1.32
1996	7.0	8.4	6.6	3.8	2.7	39.0	27.9	31.3	-209.1	0.9	1.37
1997	4.7	-2.3	8.6	5.9	2.7	36.1	32.4	33.0	82.4	0.3	1.43
1998	-6.9	-22.9	7.0	5.4	1.6	25.2	46.2	33.3	2250.0	-16.3	1.63
1999	9.5	8.3	8.0	6.2	1.8	29.3	39.1	32.4	-48.1	2.7	1.61
2000	8.5	12.2	6.9	4.7	2.2	31.1	40.8	37.7	-53.7	0.1	1.58
2001	3.8	-0.2	2.8	1.3	1.5	29.4	37.8	35.5	-25.8	1.9	1.64
2002	7.0	6.6	3.8	2.0	1.8	29.1	35.3	33.9	-39.1	15.8	1.69
2003	3.1	4.0	1.8	0.6	1.2	30.1	37.9	35.6	64.3	5.3	1.67
2004	4.6	1.9	1.1	0.1	0.9	30.3	44.1	39.7	91.3	4.1	1.65

* Sources and notes:

1) Growth Rate of Real GDP, Rate of Change in Gross Investments: Bank of Korea, *Economic Statistics System.*

2) Fixed capital stock comprises transport and machinery equipment, residential and nonresidential construction, and intangible assets.

3) Curb-Market Interest Rates:
   1960-1978: Cole and Park (1983, *pp.* 272-3, Table 49).
   1979-1995: Song (1997, p. 164, Table 9.4).
   1996-2004: Annual yield of 3-year corporate bonds on O.T.C, Bank of Korea, *Economic Statistics System*

4) Interest Rates on Time Deposits:
   1960-1978: Cole and Park (1983, pp. 272-3, Table 49).
   1979-1995: Annual interest rates on time deposits at NCB. Bank of Korea, *Economic Statistics Yearbook,* various volumes.
   1996-2004: Annual weighted-mean interest rates on time deposits, Bank of Korea, *Economic Statistics System.*

5) The Ratio of Investments to GDP, the Ratio of Exports to GDP, and the Ratio of Imports to GDP: Bank of Korea, *Economic Statistics System*

6) Trade Balance:
    1960-1969: Bank of Korea, *Economic Statistics Yearbook,* various issues.
    1970-2004: Bank of Korea, *Economic Statistics System.*

7) Capital/Output ratio: Computed from Pyo's capital stock data (2002) for 1960 - 1999.

8) Capital/Output ratio is measured in current Wons where output represents current GDP.

9) Rate of Change in Seoul Land Value Index:
    1964-1974: Cole and Park (1983, pp. 272-3, Table 49). 1975-2004: Ministry of Construction and Transportation, *Construction Statistics.*

10) Ratio of Liquid Liabilities to GDP: Bank of Korea, *Economic Statistics System.* M2/GDP is used for 1960-1970 and M3/GDP for 1971-2004.
    M2 = Ml + Quasi-Money (Time and savings deposits and resident's foreign currency deposits at monetary institutions).
    M3 = M2 + Non-monetary financial institution deposits + Debentures Issued + Commercial bills sold + CD + RP + Cover Bills

Appendix: IMF Program and the Korean Financial Markets after the Crisis

A. IMF Program

At the onset of the 1997 financial crisis, only 6 billion US dollars of foreign reserves were available to meet withdrawal requirements of 200 billion US dollars. An emergency International Monetary Fund (IMF) measure was introduced to relieve the financial distress. The program recommended keeping the domestic interest rate as high as 30% to stabilize the won/dollar exchange rate, which had plummeted to nearly 1,800 won per US dollar in December 1997 from 850 won per US dollar in the pre-crisis period. This prescription was opposite to that suggested at the onset of financial distress periods in the 1970s and 1980s. The IMF measure was aimed at ensuring the stability of the foreign exchange market to restore confidence in the won. The IMF measure caused much debate. Financial programs in the late 1970s and 1980s had shown that low interest rates helped financially troubled firms. It is argued on the part of critics that the IMF policy would cause sound firms, albeit highly leveraged ones, to go bankrupt, thus creating even more economic trouble. Indeed, economic growth plunged to -6.7% in 1998, and the unemployment rate more than doubled to 6.8% in the same year, as compared to a rate of 2.7% in 1997. These data supported the argument for a low interest rate policy.

Nonetheless, the IMF policy helped break the state-chaebol nexus that had existed for nearly four decades during the development of the South Korean economy. The IMF measure shielded economic reformers seeking to create boundaries between the state and chaebol and advance fair competition within the Korean economy.

B. Restructuring and Financial Markets after the Crisis

In the aftermath of the financial crisis, the role of government largely changed to that of a market-based, regulatory role with respect to monetary and fiscal policies. Financial liberalization measures were further reinforced. Domestic corporations were allowed to issue stocks abroad, limitations on foreign ownership of stocks and bonds were abolished, and futures and options markets related to the stock index were permitted to open.

Immediately after the crisis, government policy was aimed at restructuring both the financial and corporate sectors to meet the Bank of International Settlements (BIS) debt-equity ratio imposed by the IMF. A debt-equity swap was the most convenient way to reduce debt leverage for corporations, although this method diluted the ownership share of the chaebol. More transparent accounting practices were required on the corporate level. As such, cross-share holdings of stocks and cross-debt loan guarantees among chaebol affiliates were regulated by the Fair Trade Commission (FTC). [1]

C. Bank Mergers and Acquisitions

Restructuring proceeded in both financial and corporate sectors. Banks, in particular, faced mergers and acquisitions (Rhee et al., 2005, p. 68). What had been nineteen banks prior to 1998 were reformed into five main banks. The Choheung Bank merged with the Shinhan Bank. The Commercial Bank and the Hanil Bank were integrated to form the Hanvit

---

[1] The cross-share holdings and cross-debt guarantees created leverage for the chaebols.

Bank, which later became the Woori Bank. Five banks were also merged to become the Kookmin Bank, and the Seoul Bank was integrated into the Hana Bank. Foreign banks actively participated in acquiring shares of domestic banks.

Lone Star acquired 51% of the shares in the Korea Foreign Exchange Bank. New Bridge Capital bought 49% of Cheil Bank shares. Approximately 70% of Kookmin Bank stocks were held by foreign owners, as were 50% of Shinhan Finance shares. At Hanmi Bank, foreign shareholding reached 86%. The merchant banks, which were blamed for reckless inflows of foreign short-term capital, shrank from thirty in 1997 to three in 2001. Bank mergers and acquisitions increased competitiveness at the international level and facilitated the financial sector restructuring by improving the debt/equity ratio to meet the BIS standard.

The financial supervisory function of the government was also strengthened under the Financial Supervisory Commission (FSC) launched in 1999. The FSC served a financial intermediary role in the market. Two years ahead, the Korea Deposit Insurance Corporation (KDIC) had also been established to protect depositors against possible bank defaults and also to arrange for the merging of banks.

Government emphasis on bank restructuring left investment trust companies unregulated. Loans were channeled into the investment trust companies during the economic crisis. For instance, to avoid the credit crunch immediately after the crisis, Daewoo, one of the biggest conglomerates, issued corporate bonds through investment trust companies (ITCs). After the collapse of Daewoo in July 1999, the flow of funds reversed from the ITCs to the banking sector. In 1998 the total assets held by ITCs reached 214 trillion won, which is more than twice that held in the previous year.

D. Bond Markets

Government-issued bonds of the 1980s were normally assigned to the enforcement of NBFIs. After the crisis, the need to meet the BIS capital ratio induced banks to invest in bonds instead of extending loans to corporations. This situation heightened demand for bonds. Credit risks associated with corporate bonds, however, were seen as high after the Daewoo default. The government intervened to normalize the market. Bonds were categorized as junior and senior tranches, in accordance with their credit risks. Junior bonds with high risks were assumed by the KDB, while senior tranches were more often placed with investors. [2]

Bond investments were an immediate government concern in the post-crisis bank restructuring period. Public funds totaling approximately 147 trillion won were injected into the economy during the period from 1999 to 2002 through bonds issued by the Korea Asset Management Corporation (KAMCO) and the KDIC. KAMCO was in charge of purchasing non-performing loans (NPL) to help normalize financial institutions after the crisis. KAMCO securitized NPLs by issuing asset-backed securities (ABS) and issued approximately 70% of all bonds. Introducing impaired assets to the market through ABS issuances helped develop the capital market after the crisis. However, as Oh and Rhee (2002) have noted, despite government efforts, market autonomy was

---

[2] Interestingly, the KDB allocated loans to target industries in the 1960s and 1970s. Then, some three to four decades later, the role of the KDB changed to the placing of investments in the bond market.

necessary for the creation of future bond markets in which investors would bear the risks, as opposed to the credit subsidization created by government institutions such as the KDB.

In 1998 the government announced measures to develop autonomous bond markets. To set up stable expectations in investors, the government made it a policy to inform the public of the maturity schedules and issuance amounts at the beginning of each year. In 1999, a specialized bond market was established in affiliation with the Korea Exchange market. Another measure served to integrate diverse bonds and establish a leading indicative yield rate for representative bonds. The government promoted the development of the corporate bond market by introducing collateral bond obligations (CBO) and collateral loan obligations (CLO). From 1995 to 1997 the bond market increased by 20 trillion won to 30 trillion won, further jumping to 110 trillion won by 1998 and 660 billion won in 2003, roughly 1.2 times the 2003 GDP (Rhee et al., 2005, pp. 196-7).

E. Stock Markets

Despite the government's push for public stock offerings, the stock market did not operate normally until the latter half of the 1980s. Public enterprises began privatization with the issuance of so-called national stocks. In 1988, Pohang Iron and Steel (POSCO) became the first public enterprise to initiate public offerings. Korea Electric followed with public offerings in 1989. Deregulation allowing foreign ownership in stocks and the introduction of the various forms of financial derivatives after the crisis contributed to a boom in the domestic stock market. The market value of listed companies grew from 151 trillion won in 1994 to

355 trillion won by the end of 2003. This doubling in size amounted to 63% of the GDP.[3] Foreigners owned 40% of the market value of listed stocks at the end of 2003. The Korea Securities Dealers Quotation (KOSDAQ) initiated in 1996 was designed to facilitate equity financing in knowledge-based venture corporations, high-tech corporations, and small- to medium sized enterprises. In addition, by the end of 2003, Korea ranked fifteenth in the world in the size of stock market capitalized values and twelfth in the world in terms of the total value of shares traded at the Korea Stock Exchange (KSE).

Financial derivatives increased in both amount and variety. In 2003 the total value of derivatives trading was 1,788 trillion won, equal to 3.7 times the GDP, and the daily average trading volume in KOSPI 200 futures reached 10,842 billion won.[4] These derivatives are related to currency, interest, and stocks, with currency-related derivatives accounting for 99% of the total.

F. Foreign Exchange Markets

Foreign exchange in the 1960s and 1970s was centralized under government control, which severely limited the amount of foreign exchange. The foreign exchange rate was pegged to the US dollar and, periodically, was raised sharply. After doubling following the IRP of 1965, the exchange rate ranged between 270 won per US dollar and 320 won per US dollar from 1974-1979. The won/dollar exchange rate was fixed at 484 won per US dollar and later raised to 660 won per US dollar in 1980. From 1980 to 1990, the foreign exchange rate was managed by

---

[3] Bank of Korea (2004, p. 252).
[4] Bank of Korea (2004, p. 291).

the basket system. The market average exchange rate system was applied from 1990 until the 1997 financial crisis. Under this system, market exchange rates applied between banks were weighted to yield a market average rate that served as the basis for foreign exchange transactions on the following day. Fluctuations from the base rate were allowed within a certain limit. A limit of 0.4% was imposed on the variability of the exchange rate. This limit was gradually increased to 10%. The exchange rates varied between 700 won per US dollar and 900 won per US dollar in the 1990s prior to the crisis. After the crisis, the exchange rate was allowed to move freely in accordance with market situations. The government entered into the market only to smooth exchange rates. The exchange market, especially as related to derivatives, expanded substantially after the crisis. The amount of currency-related derivatives traded in 2003 reached 1,767 trillion won, equal to about three times the GDP.

CHAPTER 7

SHIFT FROM INPUT-BASED GROWTH TO PRODUCTIVITY-BASED GROWTH IN KOREAN ECONOMY

1. Introduction

In this study, we analyzed the historic trend of total factor productivity in industries and economic growth in Korea using industry-level data. Specifically, we focused on identifying structural breaks by examining regime changes between contributing factors, such as input and productivity, and the relationship between international trade and these variables.

It is widely known that the Korean economy achieved a very high growth rate through an export-oriented strategy, and there have been structural changes among industries toward an increase in the export sector and a decrease in the import sector. Competitive industries with a comparative advantage have risen, while non-competitive industries have declined as a result of international competition. In the earlier stages of economic growth, abundant cheap-wage labor was the main factor for economic growth. However, this was not a sustainable path for further development because wages rose as capital accumulated in the process of economic growth, and more competitive countries emerged in terms of cheap labor.

The Korean economy enjoyed a very high growth rate, exceeding 10% in the 1970s, but the growth rate has been slowing down and is now around 3%, which is not very different from rates in other advanced countries.

According to growth accounting, the determinants of economic growth consist of two main factors: input increases and productivity growth, of which the latter is much more important for long-term economic growth. Krugman (1994) indicated that Asian economies lacked productivity growth, supporting the idea that productivity improvement through technological progress and efficient production were essential for long-term growth in Korea.

In fact, many studies have indicated that the Korean economy has experienced a continuous decline in economic growth rate since the 1980s. However, it is also true that the contribution of inputs, such as labor versus capital, has been decreasing, and total factor productivity (TFP) has contributed relatively more over time. Nonetheless, the contribution share of TFP is still not as large as in advanced countries such as Germany or Japan. For example, the contribution share (the ratio of growth rate contributed by TFP increase to total growth rate) was about 20% in the 1980s, but it had increased to 68% in 2010, which was still lower than in Germany, Japan, and the US (HERI, 2010).

In the 1980s and early 1990s, many economists believed that Asian countries would become leading economies of the world because the average economic growth rates in East Asian and Southeast Asian countries were very high. However, Paul Krugman (1994) noted that the Asian miracle could be just a myth if there were no major changes in the main contribution factor, from input increase to productivity increase. He argued that most of the economic growth in major Asian economies, such as Singapore, Japan, and China, was due to increases in input, not productivity, and that economic growth would not be sustainable without significant changes. This had already been seen in the case of the Soviet Union's economy. He argued that Asian countries needed to focus more on how to improve their productivity for further economic growth. This argument was at the center of attention at that time and gave rise to much debate. In 1997, the so-called Asian currency crisis occurred, and Krugman's argument received further attention.

Here, "productivity" refers to total factor productivity, as reflected in the concepts of Solow's residual. In 1956, Solow calculated the long-run contribution shares among the factors and found that only 1/8 was due to an increase in capital, whereas the other 7/8 was due to productivity improvement in the US economy. This argument suggests that sustainable growth is impossible without productivity improvement.

Since the 1980s, endogenous economic growth theory has proposed a new perspective on economic growth. Unlike neoclassical theory, which assumes that the sources of economic growth come from exogenous technological progress, the new theorists have sought determinants of economic growth within the economic system. Economic growth enables the economy to spend more on research and development (R&D), which in turn leads to technical progress and additional economic growth. This could create a cycle for the economy, in which economic growth appears to be "endogenous." In this cycle, some technology-related factors, such as R&D, technological spillover, and patents, play a critical role in economic growth (Keller, 2002).

Against this backdrop, this study evaluates whether there is a structural break in the trends of economic history in Korea, with a focus on the determinants of economic growth and, in particular, total factor productivity, and if so, when it occurred. We utilize new econometric methods such as time series, unit root tests, and cointegration analyses, to search for a structural break. We also compare differences between periods, with a focus on international trade.

The contributions of the study are as follows. First, it uses time series data from the Korean manufacturing industry and explicitly employs unit root tests with structural break. Second, we propose a structural break test in relation to the cointegration framework. The results confirm those of previous research by highlighting the importance of productivity growth. However, this study is probably the first to apply the structural break model in unit root and cointegration to this area.

Section 2 provides a brief review of the previous literature, theoretical background, and econometric methods, while Section 3 presents data for the Korean economy at the industry level and suggests some trends in the Korean economy. In Section 4, several econometric analyses are presented to evaluate the structural break issue and the relationship between international trade and productivity. Finally, Section 5 provides conclusions and implications.

2. Overview of Korean Economic Growth

Figure 7-1 displays Korea's per capita income (in US dollars) and real GDP growth rate from 1953 to 2021. Per capita income increased significantly from $66.5 in 1953 to $35,373.1 in 2021. From 1953 to 2021 (68 years), the average annual growth rate was 7.0%. As shown in the figure, the growth rate gradually increased until 1970, after which it plummeted during the first and second oil shocks, the 1997 foreign exchange crisis, the 2008 global financial crisis, and the 2020 Covid-19 pandemic, but recovered shortly

Figure 7-1. Per capita gross national income (GNI) and real GDP growth rate

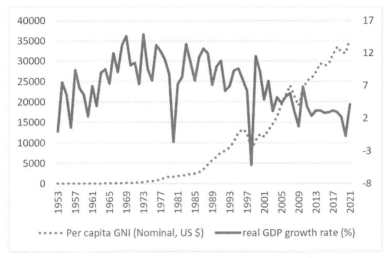

Source: BOK, Economic Statistics System, 2022.

after each event. Nevertheless, the real growth rate had gradually declined since the mid-1970s, when it peaked at approximately 14%.

Table 7-1 displays the average annual real growth rate by industry. The average real GDP growth rate for the period of 1954-2021 is 7%. The mining industry has the highest average real growth rate of 10.37%, followed by the electricity, gas, and water business at 12.15%, and the construction industry at 7.38%, which is higher than the average. On the other hand, the growth rates of other industries are lower than the average. Across all industries, real growth rates have been declining, with the decline in manufacturing and service sector growth rates being a major factor in the decline of GDP growth since 1980.

Table 7-2 shows the demand-side factors that affect real GDP growth. The most significant factor is exports, which account for 15.37% of real GDP growth, followed by fixed capital formation at 10.91%. This indicates that

Table 7-1. Average Annual Real Growth Rate by Industry

	Real GDP	Agriculture, forestry and fishery	Mining and manufacturing	(Manufacturing)	Electricity, gas and water utilities	Construction	Service industry
1954~1960	5.37	3.17	11.81	11.83	14.24	9.00	5.03
1961~1970	9.56	4.76	15.86	16.67	21.99	19.27	9.04
1971~1980	9.35	2.41	15.66	16.37	15.67	10.38	9.00
1981~1990	10.03	4.07	11.84	12.36	17.68	9.81	9.68
1991~2000	7.24	2.09	9.49	9.69	10.23	1.41	7.47
2001~2010	4.69	1.42	6.33	6.38	5.04	1.68	4.63
2011~2021	2.72	0.58	2.79	2.80	1.85	1.19	2.98
1954~2021	**7.00**	**2.59**	**10.37**	**10.71**	**12.15**	**7.38**	**6.86**

Source: BOK, Economic Statistics System, 2022.

increased exports and investments have been the driving force behind Korea's economic growth. While imports have also increased, the rate of growth in exports has outpaced that of imports. This high growth rate in both exports and imports suggests that Korea, as a small open economy, has effectively utilized the economic benefits of international trade.

Table 7-2. Average Annual Real Growth Rate by Demand-Side Factors

	Real GDP	Consumption	Fixed capital formation	Export	Import
1954~1960	5.37	6.21	12.43	12.95	3.74
1961~1970	9.56	7.73	24.27	30.94	19.74
1971~1980	9.35	6.82	15.33	23.30	16.55
1981~1990	10.03	8.19	13.10	11.78	10.91
1991~2000	7.24	6.00	6.28	14.83	11.64
2001~2010	4.69	4.07	3.39	9.82	7.96
2011~2021	2.72	2.52	2.81	4.14	3.91
1954~2021	**7.00**	**5.87**	**10.91**	**15.37**	**10.84**

Source: BOK, Economic Statistics System, 2022.

Figure 7-2. Changes in value-added, capital, and labor in the manufacturing industry.

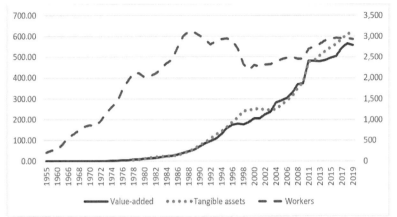

Source: Statistics Korea, KOSIS, Mining and Manufacturing Survey, Industry (Manufacturing), 8th–10th revision, for enterprises with 10 or more employees from 1999.
Notes: The unit of value-added and tangible assets is in trillion Won (nominal value), and the unit of workers is in thousands; Tangible assets are year-end balances, and workers are the monthly average of the number of workers.

Figure 7-2 illustrates the changes in output and inputs in the manufacturing industry, where value-added represents the output, and tangible assets and workers represent the inputs. As we can see, value-added has continued to increase over time. While tangible assets have also been increasing, the number of workers increased rapidly until the mid-1980s but has hardly increased since then. Despite this, value-added and tangible assets have continued to steadily increase, while the number of workers has remained stagnant. Therefore, it appears that the growth of the manufacturing industry in Korea is mainly due to capital input rather than labor input.

3. Literature and Methodology

3.1 Previous Literature

Since the beginning of rapid growth in the Korean economy in the 1960s, there have been many changes to the economy. Although in the early stages, labor and capital inputs were the main factors for economic growth, the economy may have reached a limit for further growth due to the diminishing rate of marginal productivity of these inputs. Thus, it seems natural that there have been structural changes during the process of economic growth.

Most research on structural changes has focused on changes in industry composition with regards to agriculture, manufacturing, and services. In most countries, the share of agriculture decreases, while the service sector tends to gradually increase. For manufacturing, the share initially increases steadily, then declines in later stages. We can see a hump shape for manufacturing industries. This shape can be explained by productivity differences among industries and changes in consumption patterns over time. The former is shown in Ngai and Pissarides (2007), and the latter in Kongsamut et al. (2001).

We can also see the hump shape in the Korean manufacturing industry; the labor share in manufacturing continued to increase at first and then declined. Uy, Yi, and Zhang (2013) used a two-country model to explain the structural changes in the Korean economy. At first, labor moved from agriculture to manufacturing industries because labor productivity in manufacturing became higher than labor productivity in agriculture. However, as the income level increased, the expenditure share of the service sector rose, and the share of manufacturing declined, which caused labor to move from manufacturing to service industries.

We sought to determine whether there was a big break in the economic structure rather than a gradual change using econometric methods. As Krugman (1994) pointed out, the Korean economy may have depended on rapid economic growth based on input increases before the 1990s, and there could have been a big change after the Asian currency crisis, as we noticed that the crisis profoundly shocked Korean society and the Korean economy.

When the economy faces difficulties in growing by putting more input into production, another type of economic growth emerges: productivity initiative growth, made possible by technological advances. These advances may come from increased R&D expenditure within the economy or the adoption of foreign technologies from advanced economies. International trade in goods can facilitate technology spillovers or knowledge spillovers, leading to increased productivity and economic growth. In summary, exports and imports can accelerate economic growth.

Exporting firms introduce advanced technologies through contacts in foreign markets, which can speed up their technological progress, enabling them to grow faster than other domestic firms (Fernandes and Isgut, 2015). In particular, because exporting firms serve larger markets than domestic firms, they can enjoy increasing returns to scale, leading to further productivity gains (Young, 2013). Consistent with this logic, much research has explained why productivity can be higher in exporting firms than in domestic firms. In empirical research on Korean cases, Kim and Kim (2015) found that productivity was higher in exporting firms than in domestic firms.

In addition, previous research has studied changes in the productivity of the Korean economy and its contribution to economic growth (Choi and Lee, 2010; Kim et al., 2009, 2014). In contrast to this research, this study uses time series data and tests for structural breaks in unit root time series. Furthermore, we suggest that the structural break model can be tested by cointegration methods by adding dummy variables. It appears that this study applies the structural break model in unit root and cointegration to the Korean industry for the first time.

3.2 Methodology

In this study, we first calculated the time series of total factor productivity for individual industries and obtained the weighted TFP for the entire industry in question using the output of each industry. We then analyzed the time trend in TFP to assess whether there was a structural break in the trend. To do so, we used several time series analysis methods, such as unit root and cointegration methods.

The augmented Dickey-Fuller (ADF) test is one of the most frequently used testing methods for checking the unit root, but it is known to provide overly favorable results for unit root presence (Oh, 1996; Oh et al., 2006). In particular, misleading results might occur in the case of trending stationary data with a structural break. Indeed, the ADF test tends not to reject the null hypothesis of unit root in too many cases. To reduce the risk of an incorrect decision, many researchers have developed other methods, including unit root tests considering a structural break (Perron, 1997; Zivot and Andrews, 1992). Among these, Zivot and Andrews (1992) and Perron (1997) check the possibility of a break at each time point. Here, we used Gregory and Hansen's (1996) method, which seems to be a revised version of Zivot and Andrews and Perron.

The basic idea of the method can be seen using the following equation (Glynn et al., 2007):

$$x_t = \alpha_0 + \alpha_1 DU_t + \mathrm{d}(DTB)_t + \gamma DT_t + \beta t + \rho x_{t-1} + \sum_{i=1}^{p} \emptyset_i \Delta x_{t-1} + e_t$$

$$(7\text{-}1)$$

Here, D is a dummy variable for the period of time; ones for the data of certain periods and zeros for other periods. The Zivot-Andrews test has the null hypothesis of a 'unit root' against the alternative hypothesis of 'data are stationary with a structural break in the intercept and trend.' The test assumes no particular point of time as the break point. Instead, any point of time could be the breakpoint and the testing method calculates the t-statistic at each point and finds the biggest t-value to compare the t-value with the critical values.

After carrying out the test for the structural break, we used a vector error correction mechanism (VECM) to see the short-run and long-run relationships at the same time, as used in Bai et al. (1998). If we have the variables y_t and x_t, we first estimate the equation $y_t = \theta_1 + \theta_2 x_t + \epsilon_t$ to obtain the estimates for the θ_1, θ_2 and the error ϵ_t.

Next, we estimate the following ECM equation with dummy variable.

$$\Delta y_t = \alpha_0 + \sigma d_t(k_0) + \alpha_1 \epsilon_{t-1} + \sum_{m=1}^{p} \delta_m \Delta x_{t-m} + \sum_{n=1}^{p} \gamma_n \Delta y_{t-n} + \omega_t$$

$$(7\text{-}2)$$

Where Δy_t is the vector of difference term of y and $d_t(k_0)$ is the dummy variable after the breakpoint k_0. This model includes the level variable inside the residual term $(y_{t-1} - \hat{\theta}_1 - \hat{\theta}_2 x_{t-1})$ and difference variable $(\Delta x_{t-m} - \Delta y_{t-n})$ at the same time. Coefficients among the level variables (θ_1, θ_2) can show the long-run relationship, and the coefficient α_1 shows the adjustment speed when the variables diverge from the long-run relationship. $\alpha_1 < 0$ indicates that there is the tendency for reverting to the long-run relationship.

4. Testing Structural Break

4.1 Data

The 44 years of data from 1970 to 2013 were used. Industry data were collected from the Bank of Korea and the OECD database. The current values and constant values of value added, capital stock, and total wages were from the National Account of BOK.[1] Labor numbers by industry are from OECD STAN data.[2] The share of total wages in the value added is used for the ratio of compensation for employees to national income. Export and import data by industry are from UN COMTRADE data. Note that the industry classification for international trade is not the same as the classification of BOK and OECD STAN. Thus, we adjusted the classification by merging and rearrangement and made data sets for nine industries. The concordance is shown in the Appendix 1. In this study, we used value added as output value, and labor and capital stock as inputs.

4.2 Total Factor Productivity

Figure 7-3 shows the trend in total factor productivity (TFP) calculated from the data for manufacturing industries as a whole. We see the TFP had been more-or-less stable but began to rise from the 1990s.[3] In this study, we investigated structural breaks in this trend using econometric methods.

---

[1] Bank of Korea, ECOS database (http://ecos.bok.or.kr/)

[2] http://www.oecd.org/sti/ind/stanstructuralanalysisdatabase.htm. Note that labor data by industry are available only until 2006 in OECD STAN data. Therefore, we used the numbers for labor and capital stock data from the industry input output table.

[3] Because TFP had a rising trend, we carried out a pilot regression on the time trend and obtained the following results. Numbers in parentheses are standard errors.

Figure 7-3. Total factor productivity (TFP)

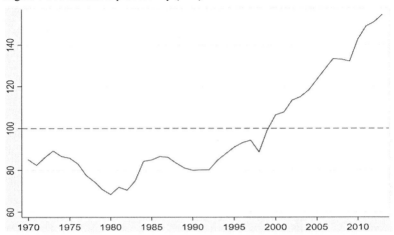

We applied the unit root test with a structural break to identify potential breaks in the data. The t-values for each time point compare the null hypothesis of "no structural break at all" to the alternative hypothesis of "structural break at the point of time." If the t-value is less than the critical value (i.e. the absolute value is larger) at that point, it is possible that there was a structural break. Therefore, we can identify the smallest number to determine where a break exists.

In Figure 7-3, 1999 appears to be the most likely year for a structural break. When we conducted the unit root test with structural break in 1999, we could not reject the null hypothesis (H_0) that "TFP has a unit root with a structural break."[4] This leads to some questions. Could this break have occurred due to an unexpected shock in that year? As a result, we excluded

---

[4] Lag Length for the unit root test was 3 by the Schwarz information criterion (maxlag = 9) and the p-value from ADF test was 0.6978, by which we cannot reject the null hypothesis.

the data for 1999 and instead showed the break occurring in 1998 in subsequent estimations. Based on these results, it seems plausible that the currency crisis in 1997-1998 caused a shock to the Korean economy. However, since labor input had been declining since the early 1990s, and R&D and patenting had increased sharply during the same period, we may conclude that the break resulted from the accumulation of all these factors and was triggered by the external shock of the currency crisis. Next, we calculated the share of contribution to the growth rate by TFP.[5] The contribution share by TFP appeared to be increasing. Generally, the share contributed by TFP was not significant before 1990, and sometimes it even had a negative value. However, it became positive with large values in later periods. We then conducted a test to determine the existence of a structural break and found that the possibility of a structural break was highest in 1991, when the contribution of productivity to economic growth began to rise.[6]

4.3 Ratio of Exports, Imports, and International Trade

To examine the relationship between international trade and productivity, we calculated the ratio of international trade to output. The usual measure of trade dependence is calculated as the ratio of trade to GDP for the entire economy. However, as the service sector is typically not as involved in international trade, we calculated a similar ratio for the manufacturing industry alone, which may result in higher numbers than the usual ones for

---

[5] The numbers and figure are not shown for saving space, but can be provided on request.
[6] We tried other specifications including intercepts, trend, and mixes of the two for checking the robustness. The results were not very different.

the whole economy.

Trade dependence = international trade / output

The trade dependence ratio increased in the Korean economy during the 1970s but showed a turning point and had been declining until the 1990s as the size of the Korean economy grew. However, it started rising again in the mid-1990s. Interestingly, export dependence rose sharply just after the Asian currency crisis of 1997 and the global financial crisis of 2008, whereas import dependence did not. This was not due to an increase in exports, but rather due to a sharp decline in output.

4.4 Structural Break in TFP and other Variables

We investigate the relationship between TFP and other variables, such as international trade and capital intensity, in this section.

Capital intensity and productivity

Firstly, it is not clear whether higher capital intensity increases or decreases total factor productivity, although it may seem natural to assume that labour productivity will increase as capital intensity increases. Only if an economy experiences technological progress or more efficient management as the economy grows with capital accumulation will total factor productivity increase with capital intensity. In that case, we would expect a positive (+) relationship between capital intensity and total factor productivity.

To gain a general understanding of this relationship, we plotted a scatter diagram in Figure 7-4. The horizontal axis shows the capital intensity, and the vertical axis indicates total factor productivity, with both values weighted by the output of an individual industry. On average, we see a

Figure 7-4. Capital intensity and TFP

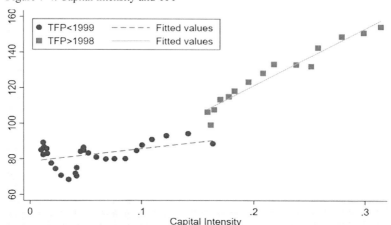

positive relationship between the two variables, which is what we would expect for a developing economy moving in a desirable direction. In fact, total factor productivity and capital intensity increased together, so it is natural to have a positive relationship in the Korean economy. However, we also observe a significant break in the data. We split the data into two groups, as shown in the figure, and added a regression line into the graph after conducting two regressions based on the periods before and after 1999. From this figure, we might conclude that there was a structural break even in the relationship between the two variables. In particular, the slope is very gentle for the earlier period and steeper in the later period.

Export and productivity

Second, we put the data of international trade and TFP in Figure 7-5 using the export dependence defined above.

Overall, the data show a positive relationship between the two variables, but when we split the data into two different periods, we find an interesting pattern. After 1999, we observe a positive relationship, but before then, we see a slightly negative relationship. Of course, we confirmed the relationship using regression in the next section.

Figure 7-5. Export dependence and TFP

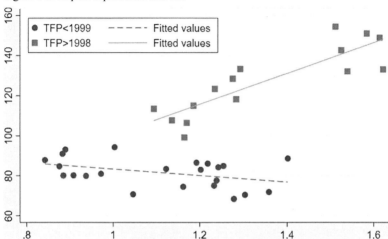

It is widely known that the Korean economy experienced high growth rates, which were possible due to international trade, especially exports. If we plot a scatter diagram between the growth rate of the economy and exports, we can see an explicit positive relationship for the earlier period. However, in our figure, when we plot the relationship between exports and productivity, we do not see a strong positive relationship between the two variables for the same period. We might argue that the economic growth was based on extensive growth or input-based growth. In contrast, the economic growth rate slowed steadily, but we still see a positive relationship between the two variables in the later period. We could argue that this was intensive growth or productivity-based growth in the sense that improved productivity became critical for the economy. From these results, it appears that the Korean economy switched from extensive growth to intensive growth.

An example of error-correction mechanism

We suggest an example of an error-correction mechanism for model 2 with export dependence and a dummy variable (model 2), as follows.

$$\Delta(TFP)_t = 0.037*(TFP_{t-1}-10.610*D_1*Ex_{t-1}-0.202*Ex_{t-1}-3.100)$$
$$+(0.203*\Delta TFP_{t-1}-0.066*\Delta TFP_{t-2})-(0.003*\Delta(D_1*Ex_{t-1})$$
$$+0.003*\Delta(D_1*Ex_{t-2})-(0.083*\Delta Ex_{t-1}+0.162*\Delta Ex_{t-2})$$
$$-0.037+0.128*D_1 \qquad\qquad (7\text{-}3)$$

Here, the long-run relationship between TFP and export dependence was 0.202 for the earlier period and 10.813 (= 10.610 + 0.202). The adjustment speed to the error of the previous period was 0.037.

5. Conclusions

In this study, we investigated whether there was a structural break in Korean economic history, focusing on the manufacturing industry, and whether the factor contributing to economic growth shifted from input to productivity. The Korean economy experienced dynamic and high economic growth since the 1970s, but it seems to have entered a period of relatively sluggish growth. Sources of economic growth are basically input increases and productivity increases, and productivity growth is believed to be much more important than input increases for long-term economic growth, as shown by Robert Solow.

Using various econometric methods, we tested the possibility of the presence of a structural break and found some interesting results from the Korean manufacturing industry. First, there were significant changes in the 1990s, and the productivity trend seems to have experienced a major structural break during that time. Second, input increases were the main factor for economic growth before the break, and productivity increases became much more important as a contributing factor after the break. Third, there was a major change in the relationship between international trade and productivity too. In the later period, the relationship between the two variables became positive and stronger. Finally, we showed concrete relationships between the variables by estimating the cointegrating vectors and ECM.

This study can contribute to the academic community by identifying the structural breaks in the Korean manufacturing industry using explicit econometric tests in the area of unit root and cointegration.

Appendix

Table 7A-1. A Correspondence Table between ISIC (R3) and SITC (R2)

Industry	Name	ISIC (rev. 3)	SITC (rev. 2)
01	Food, Tobacco	15,16	011 012 014 022-025 034 035-037 042 046-048 054 056 058 061 062 071-074 081 091 098 111 112 211 223 263 291 334 411 423 424 431 512 516 592 598 122
02	Textiles, Apparel, Leather	17,18,19	261 263 265-268 411 651-659 847 613 657 842-848 899 611 612 831 851 893 897 899
03	Wood, Paper, Printing	20,21,22	244 246-248 251 633-635 641 251 641 642 657 659 892 642 726 892 898
04	Chemicals, Petroleum, Plastic	23,24,25	323 334 335 341 524 533 671 688 233 245 266 267 271 281 335 431 511-516 522-524 531-533 541 551 553 554 562 572 582-585 591 592 598 651 657 667 882 895 898 233 582-584 621 625 628 744 773 784-786 791 792 848 892-894 899 951
05	Non-metallic products	26	273 335 522 598 651 654 661-666 773 812
06	Iron, Fabricated metal products	27,28	287 671-678 681-687 689 691 699 723 971 679 683 691-697 699 711 718 728 749 812 895 951
07	Machinery, electrical	29,30,31, 32,33	697 712-714 718 721-728 736 737 741-745 749 775 778 786 881 894 951 751 752 759 716 745 771-773 778 812 871 881 884 893 894 899 761-764 772 776 778 881 764 774 821 871-874 881 884 885 897 899
08	Transport equipment	34,35	713 781-784 786 713 714 785 791-793 874 894
09	Other manufactured products	36	269 277 659 667 821 874 894 895 897 898 899 931 961

Note: Arip et al. (2010).

CHAPTER 8

TOBIN'S Q OF A MULTI-PRODUCT FIRM AND AN ENDOGENOUS GROWTH OF A FIRM

1. Introduction

In a textbook version of macroeconomics, the rate of investment is explained by comparing the marginal efficiency of capital (MEC) with the market rate of interest. Investment occurs when MEC is higher than the rate of interest. Keynes' MEC schedule links the monetary sector of the economy to the aggregate activity level of the real sector. Tobin's q bridges the gap between its value in the financial market and the rate of investment in the real sector of the economy at a firm level. It refers to the ratio of a firm's market value in the financial market to its replacement cost (Tobin 1969, p. 21). If this ratio is above 1, then investments take place; otherwise, no investment occurs. Lucas' (1967) adjustment cost theory of a firm paves the way for considering Tobin's with respect to the microeconomic theory of the production function. Uzawa (1969) views the adjustment cost of investments in terms of the effective units of investment. Hayashi (1982) demonstrates the equality between the average and marginal Tobin's q, leading to empirical research on rates of investment related to Tobin's q.

We present a growth model of a firm based on Tobin's q to compare the growth performances of "chaebol-incumbents" and "non-incumbents," particularly given the experiences of the South Korean economy during its developmental stage in the last half-century. We determine that "chaebol-incumbents" outperform "non-incumbents" in terms of growth, disregarding

"Gibrat's law." We attribute this non-proportionate growth pattern between the two to the chaebols' capability to diversify multi-products. [1]

Chaebol investments occur across industries, ranging from automobiles, construction, ship-building, electronics, to semiconductors, including wholesales. These investments contribute to the formation of a centralized group across industries. Amsden (1989, p. 151) views "the economy of scope" as one of the contributing factors for the emergence of chaebols in late industrializing countries such as Korea. Chaebols' capacity to diversify provides them with the "economy of scope." Chandler's (1990) historical perspective on the emergence of "big corporations" inspires us to consider the "economy of scope" that arises from the "economies of scale" generated by investments in fixed capital goods.

Investments in fixed capital goods differ from those in working capital, as reaping the final outputs from investments takes time. To compensate for these costs, certain knowledge embodied in the investment should be shared with the forthcoming production of goods. We believe that knowledge on advanced economies embodied by imported fixed capital goods to small, open economies such as South Korea is transmitted to the latter. This knowledge is shared among adjacent succeeding industries in the production of goods, resulting in the emergence of the "economy of scope" for chaebols through investments in fixed capital goods.

In our model, we develop Tobin's q, which incorporates fixed capital goods

---

[1] The term "chaebol" is often used in reference to the ownership structure of large Korean conglomerates, where a small family holds the majority of stocks and controls the management decisions of the group of firms. However, in this study, the term "chaebol" is used more narrowly to refer only to the production aspect of these conglomerates, and is separated from the issue of ownership.

in the investment decision of a firm. The difficulty arises after the inclusion of fixed capital goods in the typical Cobb-Douglas production function, as it presents the problem of "economy of scale" due to its indivisibility. We suggest that a "multi-production" firm can resolve this issue. The sharing of knowledge is embodied by the physical capital goods across the adjacent products of various industries, making the indivisibility of fixed capital goods divisible by a linear combination of knowledge among them. The firm of our interest, chaebols, can realize the "economy of scope" due to heavy investments in fixed capital goods during the initial period of development. We demonstrate that chaebols' high Tobin's q, which incorporates investments in fixed capital goods, induces their high rates of investment, and their outperformance in growth is due to their realization of "the economy of scope."

This chapter is organized as follows. Section 2 presents a model that incorporates fixed capital goods in the production function, for which a technological frontier of chaebols is introduced. Section 3 discusses the modified version of Uzawa-Hayashi's adjustment cost function. Section 4 derives a modified Tobin's q, including a discussion of the role of fixed capital goods. Section 5 shows an endogenous growth path of a "multi-product firm," and Section 6 provides the conclusion.

2. Model

We propose the concept of a "multi-product" firm that can share variable factor and service inputs provided by fixed capital goods. The marginal physical productivity of the service inputs of fixed capital goods in each product can diminish separately, which relates to the Cobb-Douglas production function in a firm's production theory. However, the law of diminishing returns can be overcome by the "multi-product" firm through the sharing of the services of two adjacent products' fixed capital goods. In fact, Panzar and Willig (1981) have proven the existence of a "multi-product" firm with the "economy of scope" in a competitive market. We view the "economy of scope" of a multi-product firm as a potential solution to the "economy of scale" problem that arises from fixed capital goods in a production function.

We consider that a continuum of industries $\tau \in (0,1)$ exists in the economy. A per capita output $y(\tau)$ is a Cobb–Douglas of the following form:

$$y(\tau) = \begin{cases} 0 \\ [A(\tau)k(\tau)]^\alpha \end{cases} when \begin{cases} k_F(\tau) < k_F^*(\tau) \\ k(\tau) = k_v(\tau) + k_F(\tau), k_F(\tau) \geq k_F^*(\tau) \end{cases} \quad (8\text{-}1)$$

where capital $k(\tau)$ consists of the variable factor input $k_v(\tau)$ and the fixed capital good $k_F(\tau)$, which takes a share $0 < b(\tau) < 1$ of the total. $A(\tau)$ represents the knowledge embodied by capital good τ, and the exponent $0 < \alpha < 1$ is the distributive share for capital.

Suppose that the world production function $\bar{A}k$ is determined by the world frontier technology, and the price of good τ in the international market is denoted by p_τ. Therefore, we consider firm τ in a developing economy whose knowledge level at $A(\tau)$ is below the frontier level of $\bar{A}:A(\tau) < \bar{A}$.

The firm τ of our concern at the initial developmental stage of the economy aims to catch up with the frontier level through investment in the fixed capital goods of $k_F^*(\tau)$. This factor is obtained by satisfying the following equality condition of the marginal productivity of capital with its marginal productivity at the frontier. The output of good τ on the technological frontier is determined by selecting its fixed capital stock $k_F^*(\tau)$, such that the following efficiency condition is satisfied:

$$\frac{1}{(k(\tau_j) - k_F^*(\tau_j))^{1-\alpha}} = \frac{1}{\left[(1 - b^*(\tau_j))k(\tau_j)\right]^{1-\alpha}} = \frac{\bar{A}}{\alpha A(\tau_i)}.$$

Note that the marginal productivity of variable capital does not apply until the total amount of capital is no longer below its fixed amount of capital goods. The efficiency condition implies that the farther the firm of a developing economy is situated from the frontier technology, the higher the amount of fixed capital goods required. We assume that the productivity level of the industry is higher in the order of the continuum of $\tau \in (0,1)$, and increases at a decreasing rate: $A'(\tau) > 0, A''(\tau) < 0$. This assumption suggests that when the productivity level of $A(\tau_i)$ is high, the forthcoming industry τ_j's share of fixed capital $b^*(\tau_j)$ decreases at an increasing rate: $b^{*\prime}(\tau) < 0 ; b^{*\prime\prime}(\tau) > 0$. In addition, we assume that the elasticity of the decrease in the investment share of fixed capital goods with respect to the increase in τ, as denoted by $\eta_{b(\tau)}$, satisfies the following elasticity condition:

$$0 < \eta_{b(\tau)} \equiv -\frac{b^{*\prime\prime}(\tau)\tau}{b^{*\prime}(\tau)} < 2.$$

The elasticity condition is discussed later to explain the endogenous growth path of chaebols.

The technical frontier of a multi-product firm suggests that the highest amount of investment in fixed capital is required at the initial period of development, thus determining a Rostovian "big-push" strategy. This unbalanced growth strategy argues that investments in heavy industries, such as steel, machinery, automobiles, and ships, provide breakthroughs for the growth of a developing economy. The growth of chaebols in the past half-century of the South Korean economy is a success story of this unbalanced growth strategy. It should be noted that chaebols' investment strategy was managed under international environments where prices of goods and inputs are given at international prices. The "big push" was also well incorporated with Park's regime of economic development policy, which was amenable to the market principle (Jwa, 2018).

A "multi-product" firm produces products with the interval of $\tau_{ij} \in (\tau_i, \tau_j)$, using capital stocks of $k(\tau_{ij}) \in (k(\tau_i), k(\tau_j))$. The firm can share the knowledge embodied by the fixed capital goods of two goods, τ_i and τ_j. By sharing such knowledge, the "multi-product" firm can linearize the technological frontier it faces. In small open economies, a firm faces prices of goods τ_i and τ_j given at the level of $p(\tau_i)$ and $p(\tau_j)$, respectively, in the international market. A linear combination of the two prices is denoted by $p(\tau_{ij})$ with the weight of $0 < \xi < 1$, which is determined by the supply conditions of the two goods in small open economies. Moreover, a linear combination of the capitals used to produce the two goods yields $k(\tau_{ij})$.

A production function $y^m(\tau)$ of "multi-product" firm $\tau \in (\tau_i, \tau_j)$, which produces its nearby products τ_i and τ_j, is shown as follows:

$$
\begin{aligned}
y^m(\tau) &= \int_{\tau_i}^{\tau_j} p(s)\big(A(\tau_{ij})k(\tau_{ij})\big)^\alpha ds \\
&; A(\tau_{ij}) \geq \xi A(\tau_i) + (1 - \xi)A(\tau_j) \\
&; k(\tau_{ij}) = \xi k(\tau_i) + (1 - \xi)k(\tau_j) \\
&; \tau_{ij} \in (\tau_i, \tau_j) \\
&\quad 0 < \xi < 1.
\end{aligned} \tag{8-2}
$$

Figure 8-1. Technological frontier of a multi-product firm

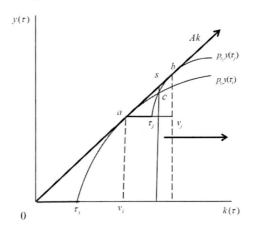

Note: Distance "$0\tau_i$" on the horizontal $k(\tau)$ represents the amount of fixed capital goods in the units of the variable capital of the distance of "$\tau_i v_i$" by the multiple of "$x(\tau_i)$".

While the production functions of products i and j are separately of the Cobb-Douglas form, a multi-product firm exhibits the technology of $A(\tau_{ij})k(\tau_{ij})$. The concavity of the knowledge function when sharing inputs between different products implies that the productivity of $A(\tau_{ij})$ on the second row of Equation (2) is no longer lower than any of the $A(\tau_i)$ and $A(\tau_j)$ of a non-multi-product firm producing products i and j. The input-sharing of different production lines within a multi-product firm allows for the problem of indivisibility of fixed capital goods to be divisible by a linear combination of services provided by adjacent products.[2]

Figure 8-1 displays a technological frontier of a multi-product firm, with the horizontal axis representing the level of capital stock $k(\tau)$ associated with the production of goods $\tau \in (0,1)$. The Ak technology is demonstrated by the

---

[2] These adjacent goods are presumably close substitutes for each other.

line of tangential points of the per capita output of each industry.

The fixed capital goods of firm τ are represented in terms of variable capital units. The horizontal axis represents industries in a sequential order of the required fixed capital goods, which can also be interpreted as the level of development of industries as the knowledge level embodied by the fixed capital goods increases in the rightward direction. Final output of the good τ_i is not produced until after the investment in the fixed capital good $k_F(\tau_i)$, for industry i, is complete. It is represented as the "thick line" of $0\tau_i$ on the horizontal axis. The final output τ_i is produced from investments in variable capital for the interval of "$\tau_i v_i$". Since the fixed capital good is a constant multiple $x(\tau_i)$ of variable capital, the share of fixed capital in total capital, $b(\tau_i) = x(\tau_i)/1 + x(\tau_i)$, increases in a constant multiple of $x(\tau_i)$. This procedure is repeated for the forthcoming industries, in which the share of fixed capital goods in investment decreases.

At point a, the production possibility curve of industry i is tangential to frontier technology A, fulfilling the efficiency condition. Moreover, we superimpose the amount of fixed capital of "$a\tau_j$" for the nearby industry j. We also determine the output at the tangential point of "b" to the frontier technology for the level of variable capital of "$\tau_j v_j$". Accordingly, chaebols can combine the two adjacent techniques of i and j to form the linearized technology at point s on the frontier technology. [3] The linearized AK technology of chaebols deters the fall of the marginal productivity of capital in producing final good i, whereas such technology increases the productivity of creating final good j. A triangular shape, as shown by the

---

[3] Point "s" on line "ab" is determined by the relative price of the two adjacent goods, "i" and "j" on the international market.

area of abc, indicates the efficiency gained by the "multi-product" firm in its operation on the world frontier AK technology.

The sequence of investments is part of a firm's strategy in a developing economy that aims to catch up with the world frontier technology. Thus, this sequence is path-dependent. The linearization of techniques by a "multi-product" firm is not solely attributed to chaebols. Any "multi-product" firm can combine adjacent techniques and linearize them, but this should be at a lower level than the frontier, that is, $A < \bar{A}$. The heavy requirement for investing in fixed capital goods at the initial developmental stage of the economy to access frontier technology is limited to a few, but chaebols succeed in this situation.

An alternative strategy to catch up with the world frontier technology focuses on the supply of parts and components, generally from small and medium-sized firms. This case is relevant to the growth experience of the Taiwanese economy. Grossman and Helpman's quality ladder can also explain the steps that should be followed to reach the frontier.

Our next agenda is to determine whether the "multi-product" firm of our concern is consistent with a competitive equilibrium. Panzar and Willig (1981) suggest that "the economy of scope" is a sufficient condition for the existence of competitive equilibrium prices of multi-products. The "multi-product" firm, which shares the services of fixed capital goods at its disposal, has "the economy of scope" (Appendix 1 provides proof).

In her book *Asia's Next Giant*, Amsden (1989, p. 151) shows that "the economy of scope" and "the capacity to diversify" are crucial for the growth of "chaebols" in late industrializing countries, such as South Korea. We consider Amsden's approach to the growth of South Korean "chaebols," where they can diversify and realize "the economy of scope."[4]

Amsden (1989) suggests that centralizing the knowledge and infrastructure of chaebols at their disposal reduces the cost of entering a new industry. These advantageous situations for the investments of the chaebol incumbents compared to non-incumbents result in asymmetric growth among firms.

We are considering the problem of a developing economy trying to catch up to the world technology frontier. In this scenario, the technology level embodied by physical capital goods is below the world technology level of A. High technology is embodied by the capital goods of advanced economies. Therefore, a trade structure involving the import of capital goods from advanced economies in exchange for the export of consumer goods from developing economies is necessary to reach the world frontier.

The "multi-product" firms in small open economies operate in an economic environment where they export final goods to the international market and import fixed capital goods. These firms rely on imported capital goods from advanced economies to embody the technology required for production, and they strive to reach the frontier technology. In exchange for the consumer goods produced by the firm, capital goods are imported from advanced economies that have the latest technology. Capital goods play a significant role in transmitting technological knowledge across economies.

In the development literature of the 1960s, two competing strategies were used for the development of underdeveloped economies. The first is the

---

[4] Chaebols are often associated with family ownership, in which a small family holds stocks of multiple firms and can control the management decisions of the group. In this study, however, the term "big firm" refers specifically to the production aspect, separate from the issue of ownership.

balanced growth strategy, which provides externalities across domestic industries, as exemplified by Taiwan's growth experiences. The second is the unbalanced growth strategy, which involves a "big push" of heavy industries, such as the steel industry, to overcome the bottlenecks of fixed capital goods. The success story of the South Korean economy over the past half-century, which was led by chaebols, is an example of the "unbalanced growth strategy.

Figure 8-1 illustrates the process of reaching the world frontier *AK* technology. This technology provides the following advantages to economies.

1. The technology is efficient because a linear combination of adjacent technologies yields several outputs.
2. The price level of each good in the world frontier technology is consistent with the international price.
3. Firms using the *AK* technology increase at the growth rate of this technology.

Figure 8-1 illustrates that the world frontier technology, represented by *AK*, is drawn from the origin for a given constant output-capital ratio, *A*. A tangential point of the slope of *A* to the production function of (8-1), $p_i y(\tau_i)$, which presumably has the highest fixed capital requirements, is indicated as *a*.

Investments in future industries unfold over the horizontal time axis in Figure 8-1. Each time a firm enters a new industry, it faces another hurdle in the form of a fixed capital good to cross over. The initial hurdle may be high, but it can gradually decrease as the firm makes further investments along the horizontal axis. This production technology of a "multi-product firm" is based on Rostow's "big-push" doctrine, which suggests that breaking through the bottleneck of development requires an investment rate higher than its critical level.

In the early developmental era, economic environments were favorable to chaebols in this "hurdle race" of fixed-capital good investments in the following aspects:

1. Accesses to international markets for exports of the light-manufacturing consumer goods were favorable for small open economies, such as South Korea.
2. A trade pattern of importing capital goods, in which new technologies are embodied in exchange for exports, was favorable for technology transfer.
3. Government subsidies for the investments in fixed capital goods helped chaebols win the race.

3. Uzawa–Hayashi's Adjustment Cost Function

In an economy, any outputs that are not consumed are typically saved and invested to produce future outputs. A good model can demonstrate that consumption goods effectively become investment goods for production in the next period. In Tobin's q, investment goods are distinguished from consumption goods based on their adjustment costs for production. These costs may arise from administrative overhead expenses or from the efficiency of the investment goods during production. For the former, adjustment costs directly affect the output function of final goods (Lucas 1967), while the latter considers adjustment costs in terms of the effective units of investments (Uzawa 1969, Hayashi 1982). Such costs are reflected in the installation of fixed capital goods, which are relevant to our purpose.

We following Uzawa (1969) and represent the adjustment costs of investments in terms of the efficiency units of capital goods as follows:

$$\tilde{k}(\tau) = \phi(z(\tau))k(\tau) \, ; 0 < \phi(z(\tau)) < 1,$$

where $z(\tau)$ is our multi-product firm's investment rate for industry τ_{ij}.

$$0 < z(\tau) \equiv I(\tau)/k(\tau) < 1.$$

We denote the effective units of investment rate by $\phi(\tau)$ and it is expressed as follows:

$$\phi(z(\tau)) \equiv 1 + b(\tau) \log z(\tau) \, ; 0 < z(\tau) < 1.$$

This expression suggests that no adjustment costs occur when the investment rate is equal to 1. The formula also trivially satisfies one of the conditions for Hayashi's homogeneous degree for the adjustment cost function.

Investments in fixed capital differ from those in working capital, as it takes time to reap final outputs from production. The knowledge to be shared with the forthcoming production of goods compensates for such costs. We consider that the knowledge of advanced economies is embodied in imported fixed capital goods, which is then transmitted to small open developing economies. Knowledge on the production of goods in previous industries is shared with that of the production of goods in the succeeding adjacent industry production. Therefore, investments in fixed capital goods result in the "economy of scope" in chaebols.

Figure 8-2. Effective units of investment[5]

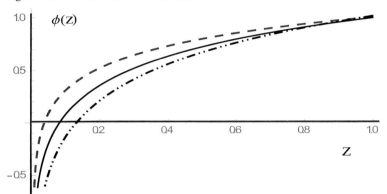

Note: Effective units of investments vary based on the shared fixed capital. The solid curve for $b(\tau) = 0.4$, the dotted curve for $b(\tau) = 0.3$, and the double dotted curve for $b(\tau) = 0.5$. The critical rate $\hat{z}$ for each fixed capital share are $\hat{z}(0.4) = 0.082$, $\hat{z}(0.3) = 0.036$, and $\hat{z}(0.5) = 0.135$.

In Figure 8-2, the effective units of investment $\phi(z)$ are shown on the vertical axis with respect to the investment rate $z(\tau)$ on the horizontal axis. A relevant range of investments is indicated in the investment rates above the critical rate $\hat{z}$. That is, $\hat{z} < z < 1$. Sunk costs emerge for investments below the critical investment rate, i.e., $0 < z < \hat{z}$.. The effective units of capital goods vary based on the shared investments of fixed-capital goods in the total amount of investment denoted by $b(\tau)$. The higher the shared investments of fixed capital goods, the lower the effective units and the higher the critical investment rates are. Figure 8-2 illustrates the critical investment rates for the three cases of the shared investments of fixed capital. This figure indicates that critical rates increase as shares increase from 0.3, 0.4, and 0.5.

No output is possible at an investment rate below the critical investment rate

---

[5] This figure is drawn using the software Mathematica.

$\hat{z}$, in which

$$\varepsilon(\hat{z}(\tau)) \equiv \left(1 + b(\tau)\, \widehat{\log z}\,(\tau) - b(\tau)\right) = 0.$$

We express the viability condition of investment for which $\varepsilon(z(\tau)) > \varepsilon(\hat{z}(\tau))$ as follows:

$$\varepsilon(z(\tau)) = (1 + b(\tau)\, \log z\,(\tau) - b(\tau)) > 0.$$

However, once the firm crosses over the critical investment rate $\hat{z}$, its effectiveness increases at a substantial rate with the increase of investment rate: $\varepsilon'(z(\tau)) > 0$.

4. Role of Fixed Capital Goods in Tobin's q

A multi-product firm, $\tau \in (\tau_i, \tau_j)$, produces nearby products τ_i and τ_j. The firm employs labor in the amount of $L(\tau)$ at the wage rate of w. Intermediates in the amount of $v(\tau)$ are used at the price of $p_v(\tau)$, with fixed capital goods of $k_F(\tau)$, presumably imported at the international price of $p_F(\tau)$. The rental service price of capital goods is r. The composite of the final goods $y(\tau)$ for the two nearby products is sold at prices $p(\tau_i)$ and $p(\tau_j)$. The profit of the firm is shown as Equation (3).

$$\pi(\tau) = y(\tau) - p_v(\tau)v(\tau) - wL(\tau) - rp_{k_F}(\tau)k_F(\tau). \qquad (8\text{-}3)$$

Suppose that our "multi-product" firm has access to the loanable fund market and can invest at the interest rate r.[6] The firm uses loans to invest in fixed capital goods for the production of goods, which involves a trade-

---

[6] We consider that the rental rate of capital goods is at the interest rate in the financial loanable fund market in perfect competition.

off between adjustment costs and efficiency. As the firm increases its investments, adjustment costs also increase. However, the increase in the firm's capital stock enhances production efficiency by reducing adjustment costs. To solve this problem, the firm can use optimization techniques.

$$\max_{k(\tau),I(\tau)} \int_0^\infty \pi(\tau)e^{-\tilde{r}\tau}d\tau$$

$$s.t.$$

$$\dot{k}(\tau) = I(\tau) - \delta k(\tau)$$

$$\tilde{r} = r - \theta - \gamma, \tag{8-4}$$

the constraint of this maximization problem indicates that the capital stock decreases by a rate of $0 < \delta < 1$ due to its use. Therefore, the remaining investments are added to the previous ones. Government subsidies, denoted by θ, have a favorable influence on the investment rate. A reduction in the corporate tax rate, γ, has the same effect as a government subsidy, as it reduces investment costs. The effective rate of interest, $\hat{r}$, is the rate that includes the government subsidy. The rate of reduced corporate taxes is deducted from the market rate of interest.

A modified Tobin's q^m of a "multi-product" firm is of the following expression:

$$q^m(\tau) = \frac{\lambda(\tau)}{p_{K_F}(\tau)} = \frac{\hat{r}b(\tau)}{\varepsilon(\tau)}.$$

The numerator is the capital value, while the denominator is the replacement cost. The second row is determined by the first-order conditions of the firm's maximization problem with respect to the investment rate $I(\tau)$ and the capital stock $I(\tau)$. The numerator is the share of fixed capital goods in investments multiplied by the effective interest rate. Moreover, the denominator is the effective units of the investment rate for the production of good τ. We note that the modified Tobin's q^m is a monotonically decreasing function of $z(\tau)$. Furthermore, an equilibrium investment rate $z^*(\tau)$ exists, in which $q^m(\tau) = 1$ in the interval of $0 < \hat{r}b(\tau) < 1$.[7] Investment occurs if $q^m(\tau) > 1$, and a decumulation of capital stock occurs if $q^m(\tau) < 1$. The modified Tobin's q^m fulfills a sufficient condition for a Tobin's q.[8]

A comparative statistical analysis applied to the modified Tobin's q with respect to the technical coefficient of fixed capital good $b(\tau)$ implies that the higher the share of fixed capital goods, the higher the investment rate. Therefore, the Tobin's q of chaebols, which have succeeded in breaking through high investments of fixed capital goods in the initial period of development, is also high, as well as its investment rate. A high share of fixed capital implies high adjustment costs for potential entrants to the industry.

Investments for the industry are also constrained by the amount of loans, for which the interest rate $r(\tau)$ is paid. The constant d is the rate of depreciation on capital, and the gross interest rate is the sum of the interest and depreciation rates of capital goods, that is, $r(\tau) + \delta$.

5. Endogenous Growth of Chaebols

One often comes across a metaphor in the newspapers describing the growth of South Korean chaebols as "riding a bicycle." If the chaebol stops growing,

---

[7] This condition is fulfilled unless the interest rate is above 100%.
[8] We offer a derivation of the results on request.

it falls. The present model implies that the chaebols' approach to investments is to maintain the accumulation rate from decreasing. Therefore, an endogenous growth path that aligns with chaebols' perception of capital accumulation exists.

Chaebols' aim for capital accumulation modifies its constraint of the previous maximization problem in equation (8-4) as follows:

$$\dot{k}(\tau) = \phi(z^*(\tau); k(\tau))k(\tau) - \delta k(\tau).$$

This constraint is partly related to chaebols retaining ownership control over physical capital goods. The solution for the modified model of equation (8-4) depends on chaebols' ability to acquire a fixed capital stock to achieve this aim. This solution is a plausible proposition for a firm situated at the initial developmental stage of the economy, where the existence of capital goods is almost negligible. The shadow value of capital stock, denoted by λ_k, differs from the shadow value of investment, λ, in the preceding maximization problem, and can be expressed as follows:

$$\dot{\lambda}_k = -\frac{\partial H}{\partial k} = -(A - rp_{k_F}) + \lambda_k[\phi^{'}(k)k + (\phi(k) - \delta)].$$

Note that chaebols' capital accumulation, which is associated with the expansion of industries along the horizontal axis in Figure 8-1, reduces the required rate of fixed capital for the upcoming industry. As a result, the effective units of capital increase, implying that $\partial \phi(\cdot)/\partial k = (\partial b(\tau)/\partial k) \cdot \log z(\cdot) > 0$.[9]

---

[9] Recall the efficiency condition and Figure 8-2. The effective units of capital $\phi(\tau)$ increase for an industry, in which $b^*(\tau)$ is low for a given rate of investment $z^*(\tau)$.

Figure 8-3. Phase diagram of the endogenous growth path of chaebols

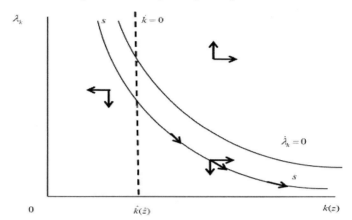

Note: Chaebols accumulate capital for $k(z) > \hat{k}(\hat{z})$. A shadow value of capital good λ_k for chaebols decreases on the time path of ss, for which $\dot{\lambda}_k = 0$. Chaebols with a capital stock below its critical level $\hat{k}$ shrink to the zero level of its capital stock.

Figure 8-3 presents the solution of this problem in terms of a phase diagram of chaebols' growth path. This phase diagram shows that the horizontal axis is capital stock k, while its vertical axis is its shadow price λ_k. Line $\dot{\lambda}_k = 0$ slopes downwards by the following inequality condition:

$$\frac{\partial \lambda}{\partial k}\Big|_{\dot{\lambda}_k=0} = -\lambda_k \frac{[\phi''(k)k + 2\phi'(k)]}{\phi'(k)k + \phi(k) - \delta} = -\lambda_k \frac{\phi'(k)\left[\frac{\phi''(k)k}{\phi'(k)} + 2\right]}{\phi'(k)k + \phi(k) - \delta} < 0. \qquad (8\text{-}5)$$

New industries unfold along chaebols' capital accumulation path on the horizontal axis in Figure 8-1. Therefore, the effective units of capital $\phi(k)$ are replaced as a function of $\phi(\tau)$ such that

$$\begin{cases} \phi'(\tau) = b'(\tau)\,log z^*(\tau) > 0; \\ \phi''(\tau) = b''(\tau)\,log z^*(\tau) < 0. \end{cases}$$

The expression $\dfrac{\phi''(k)k}{\phi'(k)}$ on the second row of Equation (8-4) can be expressed in the elasticity form of required fixed capital goods on the frontier technology with respect to the entrance on new industry τ, $\eta_{b(\tau)}$:

$$-2 < \eta_{b(\tau)} = \frac{\phi''(\tau)\tau}{\phi'(\tau)} = \frac{\phi''(k)k}{\phi'(k)} < 0.$$

In the elasticity condition on $\eta_{b(\tau)}$, the sign of Equation (5) is negative, justifying the downward-sloping endogenous growth path of chaebols denoted as curve "ss" in Figure 8-3.

Line $\dot{k} = 0$ is vertical at the critical capital stock level of $\hat{k}$. Capital accumulates continuously on its right side, while it decreases on its left side. The shadow value of capital goods for chaebols increases above the steady path of $\dot{\lambda}_k = 0$ due to the elasticity condition, while the value decreases below the steady path.

This endogenous growth path is expected from chaebols' linear technology, which holds in an endogenous growth model. A firm with a high share of fixed capital goods in investment has a high growth rate and effective units. Once a firm is on the endogenous growth path, it can continue growing along the path, much like riding a bicycle, as long as it overcomes the hurdles of fixed capital goods.

The result is that chaebols with a capital stock above their critical level of $\hat{k}$ grow along the growth path of ss in Figure 8-3 at a growth rate of $(\tilde{\phi}(z^*) - \delta)\forall 0 < z^* < 1$. As chaebols approach frontier technology, the required amount of fixed capital goods gradually declines, causing their growth rate to fall as the catch-up effect is exhausted.

6. Concluding Remarks

This study examines the growth of South Korean chaebols over the past half-century from the perspective of their investment in a modified Tobin's q. The high proportion of fixed capital goods in their investments gives chaebols a low adjustment cost advantage and allows them to grow at an effective accumulation rate. Among chaebol-incumbents, the effective rate of capital accumulation is particularly high, and they grow at a faster pace than non-incumbents, contradicting Gibrat's law.

The growth of chaebols has allowed them to act as a conduit for the structural change of the Korean economy in this regard. As a late industrializing country that has reached maturity, we expect that fixed physical capital goods will eventually give way to human capital.

Appendix

Let $c(y(\tau_i))$ denote the cost of producing good $y(\tau_i)$. From the Cobb-Douglas function of products τ_i and τ_j, we have the following expression for a unit cost function of product i for a given rental rate r and wage rate w.

$$c(y(\tau_i)) = A(\tau_i)^{-\alpha}\kappa r^\alpha w^{1-\alpha}$$

Similarly, the cost function for good $y(\tau_j)$ is as follows:

$$c(y(\tau_j)) = A(\tau_j)^{-\alpha}\kappa r^\alpha w^{1-\alpha},$$

where $0 < \kappa$ is a given constant in term of α. $A(\tau_{ij})$ is not lower than the technology terms of $A(\tau_i)$ and $A(\tau_j)$. Thus, the following inequality is provided:

$$A(\tau_{ij})^{-\alpha}c\big(\xi y(\tau_i) + (1-\xi)y(\tau_j)\big) = A(\tau_{ij})^{-\alpha}\xi c(y(\tau_i)) + A(\tau_{ij})^{-\alpha}(1-\xi)c(y(\tau_j))$$
$$< \big(A(\tau_i)^{-\alpha}\xi c(y(\tau_i)) + A(\tau_j)^{-\alpha}(1-\xi)c(y(\tau_j))\big).$$

Furthermore, the "economy of scope" exists.

CHAPTER 9

INVESTMENT AND ADJUSTMENT
COSTS OF KOREAN FIRMS

1. Introduction

Corporate investment is a key factor in economic growth. The high growth of the Korean economy is largely due to increased corporate investment. In Korea, the chaebol firms have relatively high investment rates, as compared to general companies.[1] This suggests that chaebol firms have contributed to the high growth of the Korean economy through investment expansion.

Amsden (1989, p. 151) explained that a Korean *chaebol* contributed to centralized knowledge and group resources, which facilitated intragroup transfer of money and personnel. The centralization of knowledge and infrastructure in a business group reduced the cost of entering a new industry. The knowledge and inputs of a business group are shared across business group affiliates. This results in economies of scale (Chandler 1990, 1992; Panzar and Willig, 1981). The adjustment costs of investments in group firms are reduced by sharing the knowledge embodied in the capital goods of extant industries.

Tobin's q theory of investment considers certain adjustment costs

---

[1] A Korean *chaebol* is characterized as a corporate entity comprising a group of firms across industries. It typically covers a wide range of industries, from textiles, chemicals, electronics, motor-vehicles, to ship-building, and, above all, construction. Not only is its scope of industries wide but also it owns a large share of the various industries.

associated with an investment. Adjustment costs refer to costs of installation, costs of reorganizing the plant, and costs of retraining workers to operate the new machines. Tobin's q, which relates the market value of a firm's equity to its replacement costs, explains the investments of a firm (Tobin, 1969). A firm should accumulate more capital when Tobin's q is greater than 1, and should reduce the capital stock when Tobin's q is smaller than 1. That is, a higher Tobin's q is associated with a higher rate of investment by a firm.

Blundell et al. (1992) find that Tobin's q is a significant factor in the explanation of investment, using an unbalanced panel of UK companies over the period 1975-86. Alonso-Borrego and Bentolila (1994) show that Tobin's q is positively related to investment using a panel of Spanish firms over the period 1983-87. Kim et al. (1996), Hong et al. (2007), and Kim et al. (2008) suggest a methodology for calculating Tobin's q for Korean firms, and study the relationship between investment and Tobin's q. Although their data differ, they show that Tobin's q is a determinant in corporate investment.

Tobin's q theory supposes that corporate investment requires adjustment costs. The adjustment cost means a capital loss or an additional cost in the investment process. Due to the adjustment costs, it is not easy for firms to adjust their capital stock to the optimal level immediately. It means that companies with lower adjustment costs can invest more. Cooper and Haltiwanger (2006) argue that understanding the nature of adjustment costs is central to the understanding of investment and is important for the evaluation of policies related to investment. Korea's high growth rate is largely due to its high investment rate, especially the high investment rate of the corporate group. However, we cannot find previous research which analyzed differences in the adjustment cost of investment between group firms and independent firms.

This study examines the investment decisions of Korean firms in view of Tobin's q and investigates the differences in the adjustment costs of investments between group firms and independent firms. We use data for 1,106 firms from 1982 to 2015. All companies are classified into group firms and independent firms, and we examine whether the investment adjustment costs of group firms are lower than those of independent firms.

The results are as follows. First, the rates of investment of group firms are higher than those of non-group independent firms. Second, Tobin's q is a significant determinant of investment, and the adjustment cost of investment is smaller in group firms than in independent firms. Third, the cost advantages of group firms are greater before the Korean financial crisis of 1997. Fourth, a firm's cash holdings and foreign ownership contribute to increasing investment.

Section 2 proposes an investment model, which demonstrates that a firm's rate of investment is an increasing function of Tobin's q, and is related to the adjustment cost of investment. Section 3 presents the empirical results, showing the relationship between the rate of investment and Tobin's q, and the difference in the adjustment costs between group firms and independent firms. Finally, section 4 provides the conclusion.

2. Investment Model with Adjustment Costs

Assume that the technology of the representative firm is given as follows.

$$Y = F(K, L) \qquad (9\text{-}1)$$

where Y, K, and L are output, capital, and labor, respectively. $F(.)$ is a concave neoclassical production function, which has constant returns to scale.

The increase in the firm's capital stock is given by

$$\dot{K} = I - \delta K, \qquad \delta \geq 0, \tag{9-2}$$

where I is the gross capital investment and δ is the rate of physical capital depreciation.

There are adjustment costs in capital investment. Thus, total investment costs are the direct investment costs plus the indirect adjustment costs. Assume the adjustment cost of investment is given by the following function:

$$J_t = G(I_t, K_t) \tag{9-3}$$

J is the adjustment cost of investment and t denotes year. We assume that $G(I_t, K_t)$ has the following properties:[2] $G_I > 0$, $G_{II} > 0$, $G(0, K_t) = 0$, and $G(I_t, 0) = 0$.

The adjustment cost function G is an increasing and convex function of I. This means that the adjustment cost of an investment will be greater, the greater the rate of investment for any given K.

Let cash flow at time t be denoted by Rt. Then,

$$R_t = P_t F(K_t, L_t) - w_t L_t - P_t^I I_t - P_t^I G(I_t, K_t) \tag{9-4}$$

---

[2] The adjustment cost is a strictly convex function of gross investment. Cooper and Haltiwanger (2006) find that a model that mixes both convex and non-convex adjustment costs fits the data best.

where P is the price of final goods, P^I is the price of investment goods, and w is the wage. The adjustment cost $G(.)$ implies that part of production is used up in transforming investment goods into installed capital. [3]

The firm's decision problem is to maximize the firm's market value, i.e., the present value of the future stream of expected cash flows. Thus, the firm's problem can be written as follows.

$$V_0 = \max_{I_t} \int_0^\infty R_t e^{-\int_0^t r_s ds} \, dt; \tag{9-5}$$

$$\text{s.t. } \dot{K}_t = I_t - \delta K_t,$$

where r_s is the nominal discount rate. We can set up a current-value Hamiltonian: [4]

$$H(K, L, I, \lambda, t) = [PF(K, L) - wL - P^I I - P^I G(I, K)] + \lambda(I - \delta K). \tag{9-6}$$

The optimality conditions for investment are:

$$PF_L(K, L) = w; \tag{9-7}$$

$$1 + G_I(I, K) = \lambda/P^I; \tag{9-8}$$

$$PF_K(K, L) - P^I G_K(I, K) - (\delta + r)\lambda = -\dot{\lambda}. \tag{9-9}$$

Then, the transversality condition is:

$$\lim_{t \to \infty} \lambda K e^{-\int_0^t r_s ds} = 0. \tag{9-10}$$

---

[3] There are two approaches to the adjustment cost theory of investments. One is to take the adjustment costs from the output of the good (Lucas 1967), and the other is to consider it in terms of the effective units of investments (Uzawa 1969, Hayashi 1982). We take the former approach.

[4] For simplicity, we omit t.

We define Tobin's q as

$$q = \lambda/P^I. \qquad (9\text{-}11)$$

With the definition of Tobin's q and equation (9-8), we can derive an investment function as

$$G_I(I,K) = q - 1. \qquad (9\text{-}12)$$

Because $G_I > 0$, investment (I) will be positive when q is greater than 1. On the contrary, investment will be negative, when q is smaller than 1.

From equation (9-12), we define the optimal investment, I, as a function of q and K;

$$I = M(q,K). \qquad (9\text{-}13)$$

By implicit differentiation with q in (9-12), we find $\frac{\partial I}{\partial q} = \frac{1}{G_{II}(.)} > 0$, because $G_{II} > 0$. This shows that the optimal investment is an increasing function of Tobin's q. It also shows that firms invest only up to the point where the marginal installation cost (G_I) equals q-1.

Notice that investment is a function of marginal q and of the level of capital. This means that a firm does not need to know anything else about future demand to determine the optimal investment level. All the information about the production function, input prices, and interest rates now and in the future that is relevant to the investment decision is summarized in one number, q. Condition (9-13) shows that if a firm knows Tobin's q and the current capital stock K, it can decide the optimal level of investment.

Hayashi (1982) showed that if, and only if, the adjustment cost function is linear homogeneous in I and K, equation (9-13) reduces to the form:

$$\frac{I}{K} = m(q). \tag{9-14}$$

Let us introduce the case where the adjustment cost function is homogeneous of degree one with respect to I and K. Then it can be written as follows:[5]

$$J = G(I, K) = G\left(\frac{I}{K}, 1\right) = \frac{\emptyset}{2}\left(\frac{I}{K} - \alpha\right)^2 K, \tag{9-15}$$

where $\emptyset$ is an adjustment cost parameter that denotes the size of the firm-specific adjustment cost. A bigger value of $\emptyset$ means that the firm needs more adjustment costs for the same investment than do other firms.

If we use the adjustment function (9-15), equation (9-12) can be rewritten as follows:

$$\frac{I}{K} = \frac{1}{\emptyset}(q - 1) + \alpha. \tag{9-16}$$

This says that the investment rate will be positive if, and only if, $q > 1$. The size of $\emptyset$ is related to the firm-specific adjustment cost and shows how sensitive an investment is to q. Equation (9-16) shows that a firm's investment rate is a function of q and parameters $\emptyset$ and α. That is, q is a sufficient statistic for investment.

The theory above shows that investment depends on q, which is the marginal value of a unit of capital. We call this marginal q. This is not observable. The observable Tobin's q, defined as the ratio of the market value of a firm divided by the replacement cost of its capital, is the average value of a unit of capital. Hayashi (1982) showed that the observable average q will be the

---

[5] See Sommers (1981), Blundell et al. (1992).

same as marginal q when the production function is homogeneous of degree one and the adjustment cost function is also homogeneous of degree one. This study uses Tobin's average q instead of marginal q, like most empirical studies.

3. Empirical Results

3.1. Data

All firm-level data are from the KIS Value database, except for firm investment data and foreign ownership data. Firm investment data are from the FnGuide database, [6] and foreign ownership data are from TS2000 database. [7] Price indexes are from the Bank of Korea database. Characteristics of services or agricultural firms differ from those of manufacturing firms. To analyze investment behavior under similar characteristics, we select only manufacturing companies. Thus, this study covers only manufacturing firms.

The number of firms in our sample comes to 1,106 companies, and the period is from 1982 to 2015. The KISValue database includes data since 1980, but we do not use data for the first 2 years, because many values are missing. Our data are unbalanced panel data, because not all companies existed throughout the period. Some companies were established after 1982, and some closed down before 2015. The total number of samples is 37,604.

---

[6] Both KISValue and FnGuide are databases of financial, statistical and market information on Korean companies. They are very similar to Compustat database of the U.S. Korea's firm level data can be attained from these two databases. (https://www.kisvalue.com; http://www.fnguide.com)

[7] Foreign ownership data were obtained from TS2000 database, since both KIS Value and FnGuide do not report foreign ownership data from 2004. TS2000 database is provided in Korea Company Information (http://www.kocoinfo.com).

Table 9-1. Average Value of Selected Variables.

	Number of samples	I	K	I/K	CF/K	FOWN	Tobin Q
Group firms	2,205	484.5	4294.0	0.096	0.070	12.60	1.033
Independent firms	35,399	14.1	176.8	0.089	0.240	4.61	1.101
Total	37,604	56.4	519.9	0.090	0.226	5.37	1.095

Note: Numbers in the table are simple average values of the whole sample. Investment (I) and capital stock (K) are in billion won (at 2010 constant), and foreign ownership (FOWN) is the percentage share of equity held by foreigners.

We classify all firms into two groups: firms affiliated with business groups (group firms) and firms that are not part of a business group (independent firms). We follow the classification of the KISValue database, which reports whether a firm is included in a business group.[8]

Calculating Tobin's q is not easy because many variables should be considered in measuring it. Even if there are various measurement methods, they are similar each other. The detailed method for calculating Tobin's q in this study is summarized in the Appendix.[9] Nominal values of investments and capital stocks are converted into constant values by the price index.

Table 9-1 provides the average values of selected variables for group firms and Independent firms. The average investment is 484.5 billion won for group firms and 14.1 billion won for independent firms. The average capital stock is 4,294 billion won for group firms and 176.8 billion won for

---

[8] KIS value reports that they classified the company group by the Korean Fair Trade Act.
[9] See Summers (1981), Hoshi and Kashyap (1990), Hayashi and Inoue (1991), Kim et al. (1996), Hong et al. (2007), and Kim et al. (2008) for methods of estimating Tobin's q.

Figure 9-1. Changes in capital stock and investment of group firms and independent firms.

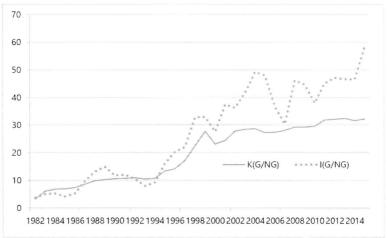

Note: K(G/NG) is the ratio of group firms' capital stock to non-group firms' capital stock, and I(G/NG) is the ratio of group firms' investment to non-group firms' investment.

independent firms. This shows that the group firms are much larger than the independent firms. The investment rate *(I/K)* is higher in group firms (0.096) than in independent firms (0.089), which means that group firms invest more than independent firms. The ratio of cash flow to capital stock *(CF/K)* is higher in independent firms (0.240) than in group firms (0.070), indicating that independent firms hold relatively more cash than group firms. Foreign ownership *(FOWN)* is higher in group firms (12.60) than in independent firms (4.61). The average value of Tobin's *q* is lower for group firms than for independent firms (1.033 *vs* 1.101, respectively).

Figure 9-1 shows how the size of capital stock and investment differ between group firms and independent firms and how they change. The values in the figure are the average values of the group firms divided by the average value of the independent firms. We can see that the ratio of the capital stock between group firms and independent firms increases from 3.2 in 1982 to 32.2 in 2015, and the ratio of investment also increases from 3.8 in 1982 to 58.0 in 2015. This shows that both capital stock and investment grow faster in the group firms than in the general firms. In particular, the investment of group firms increases faster than the capital stock. Overall, the size of the group firms is much larger than that of the independent firms; moreover, the size of the group firms is increasing faster than the size of the independent firms.

3.2. Regression Results

We test the investment function of equation (9-16), which suggests that the rate of investment is related to Tobin's q. The investment function is tested by including an additional variable other than q. The additional variables are cash flow and foreign ownership. Both variables capture liquidity constraints the firm may face. Because of asymmetric information between the managers of the firm and potential creditors, firms sometimes have difficulty in raising external financing. In this case, the availability of internal financing will affect their investment.[10] Foreign ownership also plays a role in reducing financial constraints, and improves accessibility of external financing for investment. Thus, foreign-owned firms have a better capacity to invest more than other firms.[11]

---

[10] Fazzari, Hubbard, and Petersen (1988) argue that when financial markets are imperfect, firms will tend to rely on retained earnings to fund investment before they turn to external funds. Thus, investment increases with higher cash flow or retained earnings. Abel and Eberly (2011) show that investment is positively related to Tobin's q and cash flow, even in the absence of adjustment costs or financing frictions.

[11] Koo and Maeng (2006) and Agustinus (2007) showed that foreign-owned firms invest more than other firms for the case of Korea and Indonesia. Chen, et al. (2017) found that the relationship between foreign ownership and investment efficiency

The investment equation for regression analysis can be summarized as:

$$\left(\frac{I}{K}\right)_{it} = \alpha + \beta_1 \left(\frac{I}{K}\right)_{it-1} + \beta_2 Q_{it} + \beta_3 CFK_{it} + \beta_4 FOWN_{it} + \epsilon_{it}, \quad (9\text{-}17)$$

where $\epsilon_{it} = \alpha_i + \alpha_t + v_{it}$. The error term may contain company-specific effects, α_i, and time-specific effects, α_t, as well as an idiosyncratic shock, v_{it}. From equations (9-16) and (9-17), Q is q-1, where q is Tobin's average q. CFK is cash flow divided by the beginning of the period capital stock, and $FOWN$ is foreign ownership which is the percentage share of equity held by foreigners.

The coefficient β_2 of Q represents $(1/\emptyset)$ of equation (9-16). The larger β_2 is, the smaller is the adjustment cost, $\emptyset$. We use dummy variables to examine the differences between group firms and independent firms. Here, the dummy variable DG is given '1' for group firms and '0' for independent firms. Thus, if the value of the dummy variable is positive (+), it means that the coefficient of β is larger in the group firms, which also means that the adjustment cost of the group firm is smaller.

We use a generalized method of moments (GMM) estimation. The GMM estimator provides consistent estimates of the parameters, even when a lagged dependent variable and other endogenous regressors are introduced into the model, provided that a valid instrument set is used. We use the dynamic panel estimator method in two steps with the no-level option, and the lag values of explanatory variables are used as instrument variables with a maximum time lag of 7 years. [12]

---

becomes stronger in countries with poor institutions.

[12] We use the estimation procedures of the STATA statistical software.

Table 9-2. Regression Results.

	(1)	(2)	(3)	(4)
(I/K)t-1	0.3362***	0.3369***	0.3074***	0.3035***
	(9.39)	(9.47)	(8.94)	(9.31)
Q	0.0274***	0.0266***	0.0252***	0.0247***
	(13.11)	(12.78)	(11.02)	(11.91)
Q*DG		0.0427**	0.0439**	0.0390**
		(2.12)	(2.19)	(2.00)
CFK			0.1381**	0.1395***
			(3.72)	(3.76)
FOWN				0.0564*
				(1.84)
Hansen Test	677.47	624.82	749.66	699.19

Note. 1) The numbers in parentheses are z-values. 2) *, **, and *** denote that the explanatory variable is statistically significant at the 10%, 5%, and 1% levels, respectively. 3) The Hansen test shows the instrument set is valid. 4) AR (1) is statistically significant, but AR (2) is not, indicating that the error term of this model does not show autocorrelation. [13]

Table 9-2 shows the regression results. The sample contains 1,106 firms for 34 years from 1982 to 2015. Column (1) is the results from the basic investment function, and (2) ~ (4) are the results using dummy variables to find the difference between group and independent firms. The coefficient of Q is positive and statistically significant in the range 0.0247-0.274. Even if we add cash flow and foreign ownership as explanatory variables, the coefficient and the significance of Q are almost similar to the results without the variables. The regression results show that Tobin's q is a significant determinant of firm investment.

Regression results (2) ~ (4) show the differences between group companies and independent companies. The dummy variable of *DG* is '1' for firms

---

[13] This interpretation is based on a paper by Arellano and Bond (1991, p.281), because we used STATA statistical software using Arellano and Bond (1991) dynamic panel GMM, which uses the first difference value of the endogenous variable as instrumental variable.

belonging to business groups and '0' for independent firms. Thus, if the coefficient of $Q*DG$ is positive, it means that the coefficient of Q of the group firms is larger than that of the independent firms. Equations (2) ~ (4) show that the coefficients of Q for the independent firms are 0.0247 ~ 0.266, and that those of the group firms are larger than those of the independent firms by 0.0390 ~ 0.0439.[14]

As shown in Eq. (9-16), because the adjustment cost of investment is inversely proportional to the coefficient magnitude of Q, a larger coefficient of Q indicates a lower adjustment cost.[15] In regressions (3) and (4), the mean values of the Q coefficient are 0.0255 for independent firms and 0.0674 for group firms. This difference in the coefficients shows that the adjustment cost of group firms is 1.64 times lower than that of independent firms.

The coefficient of cash flow (CFK) is positive and significant, indicating that the more cash holdings the company has, the more investments they make.[16] Firms with high cash holdings can invest more because they depend less on the external funds. The coefficient of foreign ownership (FOWN) is also positive, indicating that the firms with higher foreign ownership invest more than other firms. Companies with higher foreign

---

[14] The magnitude of the coefficient of variable q varies from study to study. This is because there are differences in the sample of the period, the country, and the companies, and also differences in analysis methodologies. However, most studies are similar to our findings. The coefficient of q in this study is in the range of 0.02-0.07; 0.031 in Summers (1981), 0.013-0.082 in Erickson and Whited (2000), 0.01-0.13 in Abel and Eberly (2002), and 0.049 in Cooper and Haltiwanger (2006). However, there are very large coefficient at 0.5 in Cummmins, Hassett and Hubbard (1994), and very small at 0.0008-0.0046 in Fazzari, Hubbard and Petersen (1988).

[15] Note that (q-1) of Eq. (16) is defined as Q in the regression analysis.

[16] Hoshi et al. (1991) showed that liquidity had a greater impact on investment in independent firms using Japanese firm data.

ownership have relatively higher credit ratings, which makes it easier to access external funds. Therefore, they can invest more.

In Korea, the business environment changed greatly after the foreign exchange crisis in 1997. In order to examine whether there was a difference in investment behavior before and after the foreign exchange crisis, we used a dummy variable. The dummy variable of *DT* is '0' for the period before crisis and '1' for the period after crisis. Thus, if the coefficients of $Q*DT$ and $FOWN*DT$ are positive, it means that the coefficients after the crisis are greater than those before the crisis.

Table 9-3 shows that all the coefficients of Q are statistically significant and positive, as expected. The coefficients of $Q*DG$ are positive, implying that adjustment costs are always smaller in group firms. Moreover, the negative coefficient of $Q*DT$ implies that the adjustment costs of group firms are much smaller in the pre-crisis period than after the crisis.[17] This means that the investment advantages of group firms are greater in the pre-crisis period, when the firms have less investment experience and the development stage is low.

The coefficient of *CFK* is positive and significant. This indicates that cash holdings have a positive impact on investment. The positive coefficient of *FOWN* shows that foreign ownership has an effect on increasing investment, and the positive coefficient of $FOWN*DT$ also shows that the effect is greater after the financial crisis.[18]

---

[17] Since the adjustment cost of investment usually increases as capital stock increases, the increase in firm's capital stock in the post-crisis period might be one reason why the adjustment cost of investment is greater in the post-crisis period.

[18] Koo and Maeng (2006) and Agustinus (2007) showed that foreign-owned firms are less financially constrained than other firms, especially after the financial crisis.

Table 9-3. Regression Results for before and after Crisis

	(1)	(2)	(3)	(3)
(I/K)t-1	0.3357***	0.3054***	0.3025***	0.2946***
	(9.60)	(9.52)	(9.41)	(9.59)
Q	0.0478***	0.0452***	0.0462***	0.0446***
	(3.71)	(3.52)	(3.55)	(3.29)
Q*DG	0.0382**	0.0375*	0.0341*	0.0337*
	(1.96)	(1.92)	(1.82)	(1.72)
Q*DT	-0.0216*	-0.0209*	-0.0220*	-0.0234*
	(1.72)	(1.66)	(1.73)	(1.77)
CFK		0.1404***	0.1385***	0.1416***
		(3.71)	(3.75)	(3.90)
FOWN			0.0563*	0.0501
			(1.86)	(1.49)
FOWN*DT				0.0936**
				(2.58)
Hansen Test	622.68	635.18	696.90	546.97

Note: The same as in Table 9-2.

3.3. Robustness

To test the robustness of the model, we perform panel OLS regression with both individual and time fixed effects. The regression results in Table 9-4 show similar outcomes, even though the magnitudes of the coefficients differ from those of the GMM results. The results show that Tobin's q has positive effects on a firm's investment, and that the coefficient of group firms is larger than that of independent firms, implying that group firm adjustment costs are lower than those of independent firms.

The results of the OLS regressions are similar to those of the GMM regressions, although the estimated coefficients of $Q*DG$ in Table 9-4 are smaller than those of the GMM in Table 9-2. Table 9-4 also shows that the coefficients of $Q*DT$ is negative. It means that the adjustment costs become larger after the crisis, and that the difference in adjustment costs between group firms and independent firms is also larger in before-crisis period,

Table 9-4. Regression Results of Panel OLS

	(1)	(2)	(3)	(4)
(I/K)t-1	0.2352***	0.2350***	0.2341***	0.2272***
	(34.17)	(34.13)	(33.98)	(33.20)
Q	0.0218***	0.0217***	0.0350***	0.0342***
	(22.72)	(22.54)	(6.89)	(6.80)
Q*DG	0.0194***	0.0191***	0.0180***	0.0184***
	(3.34)	(3.31)	(3.10)	(3.20)
CFK	0.0194***			0.0993***
	(3.34)			(16.77)
FOWN		0.0177*	0.0186*	0.0037
		(1.64)	(1.72)	(0.35)
Q*DT			-0.0136***	-0.0141***
			(2.66)	(2.78)
R2	0.370	0.370	0.371	0.382

Note. 1) Numbers in parentheses are t-values. 2) *, **, and *** denote that the explanatory variable is statistically significant at the 10%, 5%, and 1% levels, respectively. 3) The model is estimated including time and firm fixed effects.

which is similar to the GMM results. The coefficients of *CFK* and *FOWN* are positive and statistically significant as expected. Generally, panel OLS analysis also shows that Tobin's *q* has a significant effect on investment, and that the group firms have an adjustment cost advantage in new investments.

As another robustness test, we use another sample that consists of firms that have existed for more than 10 years. This sample contains 770 firms and the total number of observations is 15,180, of which 1,562 for group firms and 13,618 for independent firms.

The regression results for this 770-firm sample are shown in Table 9-5. The statistical significance of the explanatory variables is similar to that in Tables 9-2 and 9-4, except for the coefficient of *FOWN* in panel OLS. We can see that the coefficient of *Q*DG* in Table 9-5 is bigger than those in Tables 9-2 and 9-4; 0.0623-0.0672 in GMM and 0.0296-0.0297 in OLS in

Table 9-5. Regression Results for 770 Firms

	GMM		Panel OLS	
	(1)	(2)	(3)	(4)
(I/K)t-1	0.290***	0.2743***	0.2414***	0.2415***
	(7.56)	(7.91)	(33.88)	(33.89)
Q	0.0249***	0.0210***	0.0200***	0.0200***
	(10.56)	(9.20)	(20.68)	(20.67)
Q*DG	0.0672***	0.0623***	0.0296***	0.0297***
	(3.78)	(3.11)	(4.83)	(4.84)
CFK	0.1680***	0.1735***	0.1151***	0.1154***
	(3.73)	(3.97)	(17.65)	(17.62)
FOWN		0.0849**		-0.0055
		(2.53)		(0.53)
Hansen Test	662.53	521.92		
R2			0.367	0.368

Note: See Table 9-2 and Table 9-4.

Table 9-5, and 0.0337~0.0439 in GMM and 0.0180~0.0194 in panel OLS in Table 9-2 and Table 9-4. This suggests that the adjustment cost of investment in group firms is lower in well established firms than in relatively new firms.

Overall, even if the sample of companies is restricted to companies that have survived for more than 10 years, there is little difference in the results. The results are also not significantly different whether we adopt GMM or panel OLS regression.

4. Conclusions

In this study, we investigate the investment decisions and adjustment costs of Korean manufacturing firms in view of Tobin's q. We also examine whether the adjustment costs of investment are lower in group firms than in independent firms. To answer these questions, we perform regression analyses on panel data of 1,106 Korean manufacturing firms over the period 1982 to 2015.

The results of the analysis are as follows. First, group firms are much larger than independent firms, and the investment rates of group firms are higher than those of independent firms. Second, Tobin's q is a significant determinant of investment, and the coefficient of Tobin's q is larger in group firms than in independent firms, which implies that the adjustment cost of investment is smaller in group firms than in independent firms. Group firms, unlike independent firms, can share the investment experience of other group companies, which can lower the adjustment cost of a new investment.

Third, the group firms have more adjustment cost advantage before the financial crisis of 1997. This implies that the knowledge-sharing effects of group firms on lowering the adjustment cost of investment are larger in the early developmental stage of the Korean economy, when investment experience is not sufficient.

Fourth, cash holdings and foreign ownership contribute to increasing investment. Every firm has financial constraints when it comes to investing. Our results show that firms with high cash holdings or high foreign ownership can invest more since they have less financial constraints.

Our model is based on Tobin's q-theory, which has many strong assumptions regarding technology and adjustment costs, as well as on the efficiency of the stock market. These assumptions are not necessarily consistent with reality. In this respect, the empirical results have some limitations in interpretation. To overcome these limitations, we have used various analytical methods. We divide the sample into two periods of before and after the foreign exchange crisis, limit the sample with firms that survived more than 10 years, and use the regression analyses of both GMM and OLS. The results of these various analyses show that the adjustment costs of group firms are lower than those of independent firms in Korea. Thus, despite some limitations, this study suggests that the Korean *chaebol*s have contributed to the growth of the Korean economy through investment expansion due to low adjustment costs.

Appendix: Estimation of Tobin's q

1. Tobin's q

q = market value of firm capital (V) / Replacement cost of capital (K)

2. Estimation of market value of firm capital (V=E+D)

1) Equity market value (E)

E = (number of ordinary stocks x average annual price of ordinary stock) + (number of preferred stocks x average annual price of preferred stock)

2) Liabilities market value (D=D1+D2+D3+D4+D5)

Market value of debt not paying interest (D1) = (Total current liabilities - Short-term borrowings - Long-term current liabilities) + (Non-current liabilities - Bonds - Long-term borrowings)

Market value of short-term debt (D2) = (short-term interest cost + short-term debt) / (1 + CD interest rate)

Market value of long-term domestic debt (D3) = (long-term domestic interest expense / general bank loan interest rate) $\times$ (1-1/(1+ bank loan interest rate)^3) + Long-term domestic debt book value / (1+ bank loan interest rate)^3

The market value of bonds (D4) = (Interest on Bonds / Interest on 3-year corporate bonds) $\times$ (1-1/(1+Interest rate on 3 year corporate bonds)^3) + Book value /(1 + 3 year corporate bond interest rate)^3

Market value of long-term foreign debt (D5) = (long-term foreign interest expense / (Libor interest rate +1.5%)) $\times$ (1-1/(1+ (Libor interest rate +1.5%))^5) + Long-term Foreign Debt Book Value / (1+ (Libor Rate + 1.5%))^5

3. Estimation of Replacement cost of capital (K= K1 + K2 + K3 + K4 + K5)

Book values (K1) = current assets + intangible fixed assets + investment assets

Inventory Asset (K2):
When inventory increases: $K2_t = INVENT_{t-1} \times (P_t / P_{t-1}) + D\_INVENT_t$
When inventory decreases: $K2_t = INVENT_{t-1} \times (P_t / P_{t-1}) + D\_INVENT_t \times (P_t/P_{t-1})$

Buildings and Constructions (K3) = [$BUILD_{t-1} (P_t / P_{t-1}) + D\_BUILD_t$ + depreciation amount] x (1- δ)

Other Tangible Fixed Assets (K4) = [$MACH_{t-1}$ (P_t / P_{t-1}) + D_MACH$_t$ + depreciation amount] $\times$ (1- δ)

Land market value (K5)
When land assets increase: $K5_t = LAND_{t-1}$ (P_t / P_{t-1}) + D_LAND$_t$
When land assets decrease: $K5_t = LAND_{t-1}$ (P_t / P_{t-1}) + D_LAND$_t$ $\times$ (P_t/P_{t-1})

4. Other variables

Cash Flow (CF) = cash and cash equivalents + short-term financial instruments + short-term investment securities

Investment (I) = Total new fixed assets divided by price index of capital goods

PART III

CHANGES IN TRADE AND INDUSTRY

CHAPTER 10

DYNAMIC CHANGES OF EXPORT SPECIALIZATION INDUSTRIES IN KOREA

1. Introduction

Korea's exports have experienced significant growth, with an average annual rate of 21% over the past 50 years. This growth has exceeded the global export rate, resulting in an increase in Korea's share of total world trade from 0.06% in 1963 to 2.89% in 2020. As Korea's economy has grown, its industrial structure has changed, leading to changes in its major export industries (Balassa, 1979; Maskus, 1983; Kim, 2007). This transformation has been facilitated by technological progress and the accumulation of production factors.

Changes in industry specialization patterns have also impacted Korea's trade patterns. Harrigan (1997) demonstrated that technology and factor endowments are key determinants of trade specialization. If technological progress occurs within an existing specialized industry, the pattern of specialization remains fixed (Lucas, 1988). However, if technological progress occurs through the acquisition of new technologies from other countries, the pattern of specialization changes (Grossman and Helpman, 1991).

Similarly, changes in factor endowments also impact specialization patterns (Findlay, 1970; Deardorff, 1974). The direction of specialization is determined by which production factors increase more. In Korea, capital and technology have been accumulated since the 1960s, leading to a transformation towards a capital- and technology-intensive sector.

This study aims to analyze the dynamic changes in the Korean export industry using long-term trade statistics from 1963 to 2009. We investigate the factors that have contributed to Korea's export growth, how the industrial structure has changed, and what factors affect trade volume differences by country. We employ various methods for the analysis. Trade data are from the UN Comtrade database, and data such as national income and geographical distances between countries are from the World Bank database.

Several previous studies have examined changes in Korea's trade patterns. Oh and Hwang (2003) analyzed the characteristics and changes in intra- and inter-industry trade, as well as changes in specialization structure. Park (2009) empirically analyzed changes in comparative advantage between Korea and China from 1994 to 2003, while Lee and Park (2009) analyzed the change in comparative advantage between Korea, China, and Japan from 1996 to 2005. These studies demonstrate that industries with weak comparative advantages in Korea are becoming stronger. Nam and Lee (2003) analyzed changes in the pattern of comparative advantage according to the accumulation of human capital in Korea and showed that Korea's trade pattern with China is opposite to that of the United States or Japan. Choi and Lee (2010) analyzed changes in trade patterns between major countries and Korea from 1992 to 2009 and derived policy implications.

The chapter is structured as follows. In section 2, we analyze Korea's global market share and growth factors using the fixed market share method. Section 3 examines changes in Korea's trade patterns from the perspectives of comparative advantage and intra-industry trade. In section 4, we analyze

Korea's trade volume by country using the gravity model. Finally, section 5 summarizes the main findings of our analysis.

2. Growth of Korean Trade

2.1 Changes in Global Market Share

Korean exports increased significantly from US$0.175 billion in 1965 to US$644.4 billion in 2021, and Korea's imports also rose significantly from US$0.463 billion to US$615.0 billion during the same period (BOK, ECOS, 2022). Figure 10-1 shows the share of Korean exports relative to total world exports. The world market share of Korea's exports increased from 0.06% in 1963 to 2.89% in 2020, and the world market share of manufactured product exports increased from 0.05% to 3.70% during the same period. This demonstrates that the increase in exports of manufactured products led to an increase in the global market share of Korean exports. Additionally, the increase in Korea's export share indicates that Korea's exports have grown faster than the world's total exports.

2.2 Constant Market Share Analysis

As shown in Figure 10-1, Korea's export market share has been continuously rising in the last decades. The factors that influence the growth of Korean export shares in the global market are analyzed using the constant market share analysis (CMSA). A change in Korea's global market share is written as follows:

$$g - g^* = \sum_i^n \theta_i \, g_i - \sum_i^n \theta_i^* \, g_i^*. \qquad (10\text{-}1)$$

Here, g is Korea's export growth rate, and $g*$ is the world's export growth rate. Therefore, $(g - g^*)$ is a change in the global market share of Korean exports. g_i is the Korea's export growth rate in the i-industry, and g_i^* is

Figure 10-1. Changes in the global market share of Korean exports

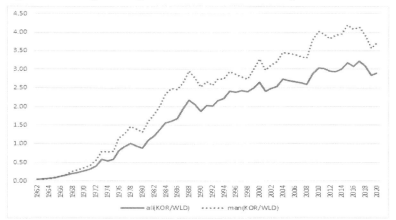

Source: World Development Indicators, 2022
Note: Manufactured goods comprise commodities in SITC 5 (chemicals), 6 (basic manufactures), 7 (machinery and transport equipment), and 8 (miscellaneous manufactured goods), excluding division 68 (non-ferrous metals).

the world's growth in the i-industry. Moreover, θ_i is the i-industry's share in Korea's total exports, and θ_i^* is the i-industry's share in total world exports.

Equation (10-1) is decomposed as follows.[1]

$$g - g^* = \sum_i^n g_i^* \left(\theta_i - \theta_i^*\right) + \sum_i^n \theta_i \left(g_i - g_i^*\right) \qquad (10\text{-}2)$$

On the right-hand side of Equation (10-2), the first term is called the structure effect, and the second term is called the competitiveness effect.[2] The structural effect explains the increase in exports due to the country's export product structure, and the competitiveness effect explains the increase in exports due to increased competitiveness.

---

[1] For details on the constant market share analysis (CMSA), refer to Fontoura and Serôdio (2017), Amador and Cabral (2008), and ECB (2005).
[2] The competitiveness effect is also called the market share effect.

Table 10-1. Constant Market Share Analysis of Korean Exports

Period	Structure effect	Competitive effect	Export growth rate		Difference (Korea-World) (A-B)
			Korea (A)	World (B)	
1964-70	0.6	26.0	37.8	11.1	26.7
1971-80	-1.8	18.3	37.7	21.2	16.5
1981-90	0.1	6.3	12.0	5.6	6.4
1991-00	1.4	2.4	11.0	7.2	3.8
2001-09	-0.6	1.8	9.6	8.5	1.1
1964-09	**-0.1**	**10.2**	**20.8**	**10.7**	**10.1**

The structure effect refers to the difference between Korea's export structure and the global export structure. It becomes positive if Korea's export structure is more focused on high-growth products than the global structure. The competitiveness effect, on the other hand, reflects changes in the relative competitiveness of a country's exports in comparison to the world. It compares the export growth rates of Korea and the world, excluding the impact of differences in the export structure. The structural effect increases exports due to the export structure, while the competitiveness effect increases exports due to improved competitiveness.

Table 10-1 shows the results of the CMSA in Korean exports during the period 1964–2009. The CMSA values calculated annually were averaged over the period. From 1964 to 2009, Korea's exports grew at an average annual rate of 20.8%, while the global export growth rate was 10.7%. Korean growth rate was 10.1% higher than the world export growth rate. This 10.1% difference in export growth rate can be divided into a 0.1% structural effect and a 10.2% competitive effect. This indicates that the increase in the global market share of Korean exports from 1964 to 2009 was due to the expansion of competitiveness rather than the structure of export products.

Korea's average annual export growth rate in the 1960s and 1970s was high at approximately 37%. Korea's export growth rate was higher than the world average; 26.7% in 1964-70 and 16.5% in 1971-80. After 1981, the difference between Korea and the world gradually decreased. However, Korea's export growth rate was still higher than the world average.

Based on the analysis, it appears that the increase in Korea's global market share is primarily due to the competitiveness effect rather than the structural effect. Although the proportion of structural effects was higher in the period from 1991 to 2000 compared to other periods, the competitiveness effect (2.4%) still exceeded the structural effect (1.4%). Therefore, it can be concluded that the overall increase in Korea's global market share can be attributed to an improvement in the competitiveness of its export products rather than structural changes in the Korean export industry.

3. Dynamic Changes in Trade Patterns

3.1 Comparative Advantage Measurement Method

Several indices are used to measure the comparative advantages. This study used Balassa's (1965) revealed comparative advantage index (RCA) below as the comparative advantage index.

$$RCA_i = \frac{X_i / \sum_{i=1}^{n} X_i}{X_i^{w} / \sum_{i=1}^{n} X_i^{w}} \tag{9-3}$$

X stands for export, i for industry, and superscript w for the world. The numerator is the share of the items in Korea's total exports, and the denominator is the share of the items in the world's total exports. The RCA is an index that compares Korea's export structure with the global export structure. If Korea's export share and world export share are the same, RCA equals 1. If Korea's export share is greater than the world export share, RCA will be greater than 1. If Korea's export share is smaller than the world export share, RCA will be less than 1. If RCA is greater than 1, Korea has a comparative advantage in exporting more than the world average, and if it is less than 1, Korea has a comparative disadvantage in that it exports less than the world average.

The value of the RCA index has an asymmetrical characteristic between the range of comparative advantage and the range of comparative disadvantage.[3] Comparative advantage has a wide range from 1 to infinity, whereas comparative disadvantage has a narrow range between 0 and 1. To address this bias, a logarithmic value of RCA is sometimes used, but in this case, the bias problem is mitigated but not completely resolved. To eliminate the bias of the RCA index, a symmetric revealed comparative advantage index (symmetric RCA (SRCA)) is used as shown in following equation.

$$SRCA = \frac{(RCA-1)}{(RCA+1)} \qquad (10\text{-}4)$$

The SRCA index has a value between -1 and 1. If RCA is 0, then SRCA is -1, if RCA is 1, then SRCA is 0, and if RCA is infinite, then SRCA is 1. Therefore, SRCA values between -1 and 0 indicate a comparative disadvantage, and between 0 and 1 indicate a comparative advantage. In SRCA, the ranges of comparative advantage and comparative disadvantage are symmetrical.

---

[3] See Benedictis and Tamberi (2004) for a detailed description of the characteristics of the RCA index.

Figure 10-2. Changes in the distribution of comparative advantage in Korea's export
          industries

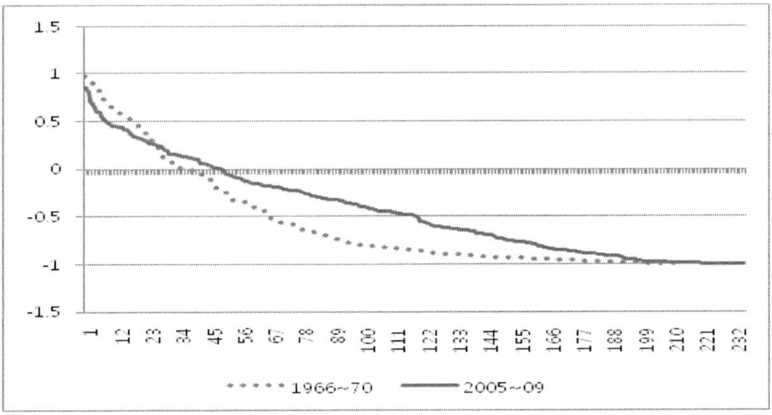

Note: Average SRCA by industry for 1966-70 and 2005-09 plotted in descending order.

3.2 Changes in Comparative Advantage

Figure 10-2 shows the change in the SRCA index distribution of SITC 3-digit industries. The figure shows the average value of SRCA for 1966-70 and 2005-09, calculated at SITC 3-digit and arranged in order of the size of SRCA. In other words, the SRCA for each industry for the period is arranged in order from the largest value to the smallest value. In the figure, values greater than 0 indicate industries with a comparative advantage, and values less than 0 indicate industries with a comparative disadvantage.

The following observations can be made from Figure 10-2. Firstly, the number of industries where Korea had a comparative disadvantage was much larger than the number of industries where it had a comparative advantage. Specifically, the proportion of industries with a comparative advantage was less than 25% of the total industries, with the remaining industries classified as having a comparative disadvantage. This phenomenon is not unique to Korea and has been observed in other countries as well (Proudman and Redding, 2000). In a free trade regime, it is natural for countries to specialize in a few products they are good at and import other products. Secondly, the number of industries where Korea had a comparative advantage increased during the 2005-09 period compared to the 1966-70 period. Thirdly, during the 2005-09 period, the Revealed Comparative Advantage (RCA) index of comparative disadvantage industries increased compared to the past, which was linked to a rise in intra-industry trade.

Changes in comparative advantage by industry were investigated using correlation analysis. The 3-year average data were used to alleviate the specificity of a specific year. For example, the 1965 SRCA by industry is the average value for 1964-1966.

Table 10-2 depicts the inter-year correlation coefficient of SRCA in SITC 3-digit industry, showing that the correlation coefficient decreases as the years increase. For example, the SRCA of SITC 3-digit in 1965 had a correlation coefficient of 0.766 with 1970, 0.541 with 1980, 0.391 with 1990, 0.113 with 2000, and -0.109 with 2009. This shows that the correlation coefficient decreases year by year. Particularly, the negative (-) correlation between 1965 and 2009 shows a reversal phenomenon between the comparative advantage industry and the comparative disadvantage industry in the two years.

Even if a year other than 1965 is used as the base year, the correlation decreases year by year. The correlation coefficient of 1970 with 1980 was 0.700, and decreased to 0.022 with 2009. The results of this correlation analysis show that the comparative advantage structure of an industry is not fixed but changes continuously.

Table 10-2. Correlation between Years of Comparative Advantage Index by Industry

	1965	1970	1980	1990	2000	2009
1965	1.000	0.766	0.541	0.391	0.113	-0.109
1970		1.000	0.700	0.557	0.262	0.022
1980			1.000	0.817	0.521	0.231
1990				1.000	0.774	0.452
2000					1.000	0.790
2009						1.000

Note: The number of industries varies from 193 to 235 depending on the year. A 3-year average of SRCA by industry was used.

The stability of the comparative advantage structure by industry was examined using the Galtonian regression analysis used by Hart and Prais (1956), Cantwell (1989), and Dalum et al. (1998).[4] The regression equation is as follows:

$$SRCA_i^{t_2} = \alpha_0 + \beta_1 SRCA_i^{t_1} + \varepsilon_i, \qquad (10\text{-}5)$$

where t_1 and t_2 are the initial year and the final year, respectively, and i is the industry. This equation is a cross-sectional regression model, using the comparative advantage index for each industry in two years.

If $\beta = 1$, then it denotes that there is no change in comparative advantage during periods t_1 and t_2. If $\beta > 1$, then it indicates that the SRCA in comparative advantage industries increases and the SRCA in comparative disadvantage industries decreases. It means that specialization is strengthened. If $0 < \beta < 1$, then the absolute value of both positive SRCA and negative SRCA decrease, which means that the degree of comparative

---

[4] This analysis shows whether the structure of the industry is stable or is changing into a form of specialization, but does not explain the factors of change.

advantage among industries becomes similar. That is, specialization is mitigated. If $\beta < 0$, then it shows that the comparative advantage is reversed.

Another method to determine whether the specialization pattern is reinforced is to use the SRCA dispersion. The specialization is interpreted as strengthened if the dispersion of SRCA was increased in the latter year compared to the initial year, and the specialization was alleviated if the dispersion of SRCA was decreased. The standard deviation (σ), which measures the dispersion of SRCA, has the following relationship with the regression coefficient (β) and the coefficient of determination (R^2) (Dalum et al., 1998).

$$\sigma_i^{t_2}/\sigma_i^{t_1} = |\beta_1|/|R| \qquad\qquad (10\text{-}6)$$

Equation (10-6) shows that $\sigma_i^{t_2}/\sigma_i^{t_1}$ can be greater than 1 if β is less than 1 but R is very small. Thus, even if the specialization is alleviated when evaluated with the coefficient of β, it can be interpreted that the specialization is strengthened when evaluated by the change in variance $(\sigma_i^{t_2}/\sigma_i^{t_1})$. The judgment by the coefficient and judgment by the variance change are not the same when determining the direction of specialization, The difference is explained by the correlation coefficient R.

The size of the correlation coefficient (R) reveals the mobility of SRCA. A large correlation coefficient indicates that the SRCA ranking of each industry did not change significantly during the two periods, and a small correlation coefficient indicates that the SRCA ranking of each industry changed. This means that the smaller the correlation coefficient R, the greater the mobility of comparative advantage.

Table 10-3. Regression Analysis Results for Specialization

Period	Start	Last	Constant	β	R^2	|β|/|R|	Number of industries
Short-term	1965	1975	-0.009	0.637***	0.327	1.11	198
	1975	1985	-0.127***	0.737***	0.661	0.91	216
	1985	1995	-0.112***	0.649***	0.551	0.87	231
	1995	2005	-0.139***	0.736***	0.609	0.94	231
	2005	2009	-0.026*	0.979***	0.905	1.03	233
Mid-term	1965	1990	-0.157***	0.379***	0.153	0.97	190
	1990	2009	-0.281***	0.405***	0.205	0.90	231
Long-term	1965	2009	-0.451***	-0.094	0.012	0.87	193

Note 1) The SRCA for each year uses a three-year average, including the previous year and the following year. 2) ***, **, * indicating the statistical significance at 1%, 5%, and 10% levels, respectively.

Table 10-3 shows the results of regression analysis using SRCA by industry for 2 years. Regression analyses were performed over 10 years, 20 years, and the entire period. Table 10-3 shows the following facts. First, the coefficient β is less than 1 in any case. In the short-term, the coefficient β is in the range of 0.647-0.979, 0.379-0.405 in the medium-term, and -0.094 in the long term. The size of β becomes smaller in the mid-term and long-term than in the short-term, and, in particular, the coefficient value is negative (-) in the long-term. If β is smaller than 1, the positive SRCA value gradually decreases, and the negative SRCA value gradually increases. This indicates that the SRCA values of all industries will move to zero (0). Additionally, the negative (-) coefficient between 1965 and 2009 indicates that industries with comparative advantages were transformed into industries with comparative disadvantages, and industries with comparative disadvantages were transformed into those with comparative advantages.

Second, the value of R^2 is smaller in both medium and long term than in the short term. The R^2 ranges from 0.327 to 0.905 in the short term, 0.153 to 0.205 in the medium run, and 0.012 in the long run. A small R^2 reveals that the comparative advantage index of each industry is changing, and that the industrial structure is changing. A smaller R^2 in the long term indicates that the structure of the comparative advantage has changed more in the long term.

Third, the value of $|\beta|/|R|$, which represents the change in the dispersion, is less than 1, except in the 1965-75 and 2005-2009 periods. If this value is less than 1, this implies that the initial variance is smaller than the later variance. Therefore, it can be interpreted that Korea's pattern of comparative advantage has changed in the form of mitigating specialization.[5] The relaxation of specialization is related to the increase in intra-industry trade described in the next section.

3.3 Changes in the Import and Export Structure

Before the early 1960s, Korea had an undeveloped export structure, mainly exporting insignificant amounts of fishery products, mineral products, foodstuffs, and raw materials. Since then, exports of manufactured products have gradually increased, and after the 1970s, exports of manufactured products have increased more than those of primary products.

As for Korea's export products, labor-intensive products such as textiles, plywood, and wigs ranked first to third in 1970, but after 2000, capital-intensive and technology-intensive products such as semiconductors, automobiles, and wireless communication devices ranked first to third. This

---

[5] Redding (2002) analyzed the trade patterns of seven OECD countries since 1970, and Worz (2005) used samples of developing and developed countries to show that the degree of specialization of each country was not strengthened.

Figure 10-3. Changes in the composition of Korean exports by industry

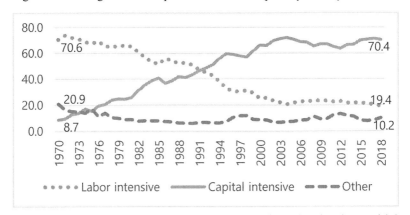

Note: Among SITC 1-digit, "1 beverage and tobacco, 6 manufactured products by material, 8 other manufactured products" are classified as labor-intensive, "5 chemicals and related products, 7 machinery and transportation equipment" are classified as capital-intensive, and the rest are classified as Others.
Source: Statistics Korea, KOSIS, 2019.

indicates that the composition of Korea's export products has gradually shifted from labor-intensive products to capital-intensive products.

Figure 10-3 shows changes in the composition of Korea's export by sector between 1970 and 2018. The export share of labor-intensive products decreased from 70.6% in 1970 to 19.4% in 2018, while the export share of capital-intensive products increased from 8.7% to 70.4% during the same period. Overall, the export share of capital-intensive products gradually increased, while the export share of labor-intensive products gradually decreased. As the country's industrial structure shifted from labor-intensive to capital-intensive, exports also shifted from labor-intensive to capital-intensive.

Next, the entire industry was divided into four sectors: high technology, medium-high technology, medium-low technology, and low technology according to their technological classifications (OECD, 2003, p.155), and the change in export share of each sector was examined.[6]

Table 10-4. Changes in Export Share by Technology Sector

	Low	Medium-low	Medium-high	High	Other	Total
1963-70	69.5	12.7	2.4	3.0	12.3	100.0
1971-80	62.3	17.0	4.9	12.1	3.7	100.0
1981-90	42.9	25.4	12.4	18.2	1.2	100.0
1991-00	25.4	20.1	24.4	29.5	0.6	100.0
2000-09	13.2	18.6	33.2	34.6	0.4	100.0

Note: Industry classification by technology is based on the OECD (2003, 155).

Table 10-4 shows the change in the export share of each sector by period. Comparing 1963-70 and 2000-09, the export share of low tech sector decreased significantly from 69.5% to 13.2%, while the export share of medium-low tech sector increased from 12.7% to 18.6%. In particular, the export share of the medium-high tech sector and high tech sector increased significantly. The share of the medium-high tech sector increased from 2.4% to 33.2%, and the share of the high tech sector increased from 3.0% to 34.6%. The combined export share of the medium-high and high tech sectors was only 5.4% in 1963-1970, but increased to 67.8% in 2000-2009, indicating that Korea's comparative advantage structure has gradually shifted from the low-tech sector to the high-tech sector.

---

[6] Since the OECD's classification by technology is based on the ISIC industry classification, the SITC classification was converted to the ISIC classification using the method of Arip, ct al. (2010) and then linked to the classification by technology.

3.4 Changes in Intra-Industry Trade

Intra-industry trade (IIT) is a phenomenon in which exports and imports occur simultaneously in the same industry.[7] Intra-industry trade is more active in trade of manufactured goods than in trade of primary goods. Moreover, intra-industry trade is more active in developed countries with higher income levels than in developing countries. The reason is that product differentiation and economies of scale are more evident in manufactured products, and diversified consumption is more likely in advanced countries with high income levels. IIT is expected to have increased in Korea because trade in manufactured goods has increased rapidly and income levels have risen.

The Grubel-Lloyd index is used to measure the IIT index.

$$\text{IIT} = (1 - \frac{|X_i - M_i|}{(X_i + M_i)}) \times 100 \qquad (10\text{-}7)$$

The IIT index has a value between 0 and 1. A value of 0 indicates no IIT, and 1 is the highest possible value. Equation (10-7) is expressed as a percentage by multiplying the IIT index by 100.

Figure 10-4 shows the change in Korea's IIT index from 1963 to 2009. The IIT index in Figure 10-4 is the simple average value for each sector after calculating the intra-industry trade index at the SITC 3-digit level. Categories 0–4 of SITC 1-digit are classified as primary products, and 5–8 are classified as manufactured products.

---

[7] For a detailed description of intra-industry trade, see Helpman and Krugman (1985) and Greenaway and Milner (1986). The former contains theoretical research on intra-industry trade, and the latter contains empirical research on intra-industry trade.

Figure 10-4. Changes in Korean intra-industry trade index

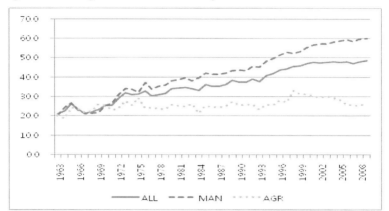

Note: The value is a simple average of the IIT index calculated at the SITC 3-digit level. In the graph, ALL represents all industries, MAN is 5-8 of SITC 1-digit, and AGR is 0-4 of SITC 1-digit.

As shown in the figure, Korea's IIT index has gradually increased. The overall IIT index, which was 21.2 in 1963, rose to 48.5 in 2009. Comparing primary products with manufactured products, the index for manufactured products is higher than that for primary products, and the rate of increase is also greater. In 2009, the IIT index of the manufactured product was 60.1, while that of primary products was only 26.7. The results in Figure 10-4 are consistent with the predictions of the theoretical model that IIT is active in the manufactured product trade and will increase along with the rise in income level.

Table 10-5 shows the IIT index by technology sectors. IIT increased in all sectors, but the IIT index increased more rapidly in the high-tech sector. Examining the changes between 1963-70 and 2000-09, the low-tech sector increased from 27.0 to 43.2, while the high-tech sector increased from 22.1 to 62.0. Overall, the IIT indexes are higher in the high-tech sector than in the low-tech sector. The IIT increase in Korea is thought to be due to an increase in the share of trade in the high-technology sector.

Table 10-5. Average IIT Index by Technology Sector

	Low	Medium-low	Medium-high	High	Other
1963-70	27.0	28.3	10.2	22.1	31.1
1971-80	27.6	38.1	23.9	51.4	26.1
1981-90	28.4	45.5	35.1	55.0	24.9
1991-00	37.2	50.3	44.4	57.0	26.3
2000-09	43.2	53.6	55.4	62.0	21.0

Note: Industry classification by technology is based on the OECD (2003, 155).

IIT is divided into vertical IIT and horizontal IIT according to the quality level of products. Greenaway et al. (1994) calculated the ratio of the unit price of export goods to the unit price of imported goods, and if the ratio is within a certain ratio, it is regarded as horizontal IIT, and if the ratio is above or below a certain ratio, it is regarded as vertical IIT. This is summarized as follows.

horizontal intra-industry trade (HIIT): $1 - \alpha \leq UVx / UVm \leq 1 + \alpha$

high-quality intra-industry trade (VIITH): $1 + \alpha < UVx / UVm$

low-quality intra-industry trade (VIITL): $UVx / UVm < 1 - \alpha$

In this study, 0.15 was used as the value of α to distinguish the range. Therefore, if *UVx/UVm* is higher than 1.15, it is classified as high-quality IIT, and if *UVx/UVm* is lower than 0.85, it is classified as low-quality IIT.

Table 10-6 shows the number of exported products and the ratio of high-quality intra-industry trade for each SITC 1-digit. The number of export products increased in 2008 compared to 1992, indicating an increase in the diversity of Korean export products. Additionally, the share of high-quality products increased in every industry in 2008 compared to 1992. In particular, SITC 7 industries increased from 15.0% in 1992 to 28.8% in 2008, showing

Table 10-6. Changes in the Number of Products and the Proportion of
High Quality

	Total number of export products		Proportion of high quality products (%)	
	1992	2008	1992	2008
SITC 5	964	1436	25.1	37.7
SITC 6	1846	2234	25.3	41.1
SITC 7	1604	1767	15.0	28.8
SITC 8	1402	1459	26.5	43.5
All	5816	6896	22.7	37.7

Note: Proportion of the high-quality products in the total number of export products

a higher relative rate of increase than other industries. This suggests that quality improvement has been rapidly achieved in a capital-intensive industry.

4. Major Importing and Exporting Countries

4.1 Trade Share of Major Countries

Korea's exports and imports are concentrated in a few countries. Table 10-7 shows the share of Korea's exports and imports to the US, Japan, and China. First, the share of exports to the US was 32.7% in 1965 but gradually decreased to 9.6% by 2009. The share of exports to Japan also dropped significantly from 25.1% in 1965 to 5.2% in 2009. The sum of exports to the US and Japan fell sharply from 73.4% in 1970 to 14.8% in 2009. Thus, exports to the US and Japan decreased while exports to China increased, with the share of exports to China increasing from 1.4% in 1991 to 22.6% in 2009, becoming Korea's largest export destination.

Next, examining the share of imports in Table 10-7, the combined share of imports from the US and Japan was 77.4% in 1965 and decreased to 23.8%

Table 10-7. Share of Exports and Imports to the US, Japan, and China

	Share of exports (%)				Share of imports (%)			
	USA	Japan	China	Total	USA	Japan	China	Total
1965	32.7	25.1		57.7	40.4	37.0		77.4
1970	45.4	28.1		73.4	29.5	41.0		70.4
1980	26.4	18.0		44.4	21.9	26.2		48.2
1990	29.9	19.5	1.4	50.8	24.3	26.6	4.3	55.2
2000	21.9	11.9	10.7	44.5	18.2	19.8	8.0	46.1
2009	9.6	5.2	22.6	37.5	8.8	15.0	16.4	40.3

Note: Calculated using UN COMTRADE data. Data for China in 1990 are for 1991.

in 2009. In contrast, the share of imports from China increased rapidly, rising from 4.3% in 1991 to 16.4% in 2009.

Except for 1965, the share of exports in trade with the United States has been greater than the share of imports. This suggests that Korea's trade balance with the United States is a surplus. In contrast, in trade with Japan, the share of imports has been consistently greater than the share of exports. This indicates a trade deficit with Japan. With China, the share of exports is now greater than the share of imports, indicating that the trade balance is a surplus.

4.2 Determinants of Trade Volume

Korea's import and export volumes between the US, Japan, and China are very high. Trade with these three countries accounts for approximately 40% to over 70% of total Korean trade. We will use the gravity model to determine the reason for the high proportion of trade with these trading partners. In addition to GDP and distance, which are the primary explanatory variables of the gravity model, economic integration, trade policies such as tariffs, and cultural similarities such as language are also considered.

The regression model to analyze the determinants of trade volume is as follows.[8]

$$lnEX_j\left(or\ lnIM_j\right) = \alpha_0 + \beta_1 lnGDPj + \beta_2 lnOPEN + \beta_3 lnDist_j$$

$$+ \beta_4 DU + \beta_5 DJ + \beta_6 DC + \varepsilon_j \qquad (10\text{-}8)$$

EX and *IM* are exports and imports, respectively, and *j* represents the partner country. GDP_j is the GDP of the partner country, *OPEN* is *(exports + imports)/GDP* which represents the degree of openness of the partner country, and *Dist* is the distance between Korea and the partner country. *DU*, *DJ*, and *DC* are dummy variables for the United States, Japan, and China, respectively. *DU* has a value of 1 for the United States and 0 for the rest of the world, and the *DJ* and *DC* variables are arranged in the same way. The size of the dummy coefficient indicates that there are other factors not identified as explanatory variables. If this value is positive, it indicates that Korea trades more with this country than is explained by economic factors.

Table 10-8 shows the regression analysis results. The period was divided into two periods before and after 1991, and panel regression analysis was conducted.[9] The total number of sample countries includes 119 countries with high trade volumes with Korea. In the regression analysis, year fixed effects were considered.

Table 10-8 shows that the coefficients of *lnGDP, lnOPEN, and lnDist* are statistically significant, and the estimated signs coincide with the expected

---

[8] Gatto et al. (2011) used the gravity model to analyze changes in US export competitiveness.
[9] The reason the year 1991 was used as a classification criterion is that trade with China began that year.

Table 10-8. Analysis Results using the Gravity Model

	Dependent variable: lnEX		Dependent variable: lnIM	
	1971-1990	1991-2009	1971-1990	1991-2009
Constant	4.26*** (3.63)	0.01 (0.02)	-12.53*** (7.24)	-16.33*** (13.54)
lnGDP	0.91*** (38.40)	0.79*** (56.87)	1.35*** (36.60)	1.36*** (59.19)
lnOPEN	0.64*** (9.68)	0.67*** (13.48)	1.06*** (10.92)	1.35*** (16.29)
lnDist	-1.15*** (13.37)	-0.28*** (5.24)	-0.70*** (5.49)	-0.53*** (6.07)
DU	2.34*** (6.18)	1.41*** (5.23)	0.99* (1.83)	0.31 (0.69)
DJ	-0.13 (0.31)	0.78*** (2.65)	0.60 (1.02)	0.34 (0.70)
DC		1.25*** (4.37)		0.02 (0.04)
R^2	0.707	0.692	0.589	0.676

Note: Fixed effects by year were considered in the panel regression analysis.

signs. Thus, Korea trades more with countries with large GDPs or ones that are open, and less with countries that are farther away. According to the coefficient of *lnGDP*, if the country's GDP increases by 1%, exports increase by 0.79–0.91% and imports increase by 1.35–1.36%. The impact of the partner country's economic size on Korea's trade is greater on imports than on exports. This suggests that while Korea's exports are dispersed in many countries, its imports are more concentrated among a few countries with large economies.

The effect of the openness of a partner country on trade is also greater on imports than on exports. In other words, when a country's openness increases by 1%, exports increase by 0.64-0.67% and imports increase by 1.06-1.35%. The impact of the distance between the two countries on trade varies depending on the period. In both exports and imports, the influence of the distance between countries in the 1991-2009 period is smaller than in the 1971-90 period. In the export equation, the coefficient decreases from -1.15 to -0.28, and in the import equation, it decreases from -0.70 to -0.53. This suggests that due to the development of transportation and communication infrastructure, the distance between countries as an obstacle to trade has been gradually decreasing.

The coefficient of *DU* in the export equation is positive and statistically significant. This signifies that Korea exported more to the US than any other country. Additionally, the coefficient of *DU* decreased from 2.34 before 1990 to 1.41 in the years following, indicating that the proportion of exports to the US has recently decreased compared to in the past. Even in the import equation, the coefficient of *DU* is positive (+), which indicates that the share of imports from the US is larger than that of other countries. The coefficient of *DU* is positive for both exports and imports, but the *DU* coefficient in the export equation is greater than the *DU* coefficient in the import equation. This reveals that Korea exports and imports more with the US than with any other country, but exports more than it imports.

DJ's coefficient is negative for the period 1971-90 and positive for the period 1991-2009 in the export equation. This indicates that exports to Japan were less before 1990 and more after 1990. In the import equation, the coefficient of *DJ* is positive, but not statistically significant.

The coefficient of *DC* is 1.25 and statistically significant in the export equation, but it is 0.02 and not statistically significant in the import equation. This indicates that Korea exports a lot to China, but its imports from China are not particularly high compared with those from other countries.

According to the regression results, the country dummy coefficient is positive (+) overall, indicating that the exports and imports of these three countries are relatively high compared to other countries. However, some country dummy coefficients are not statistically significant at the 10% level. This suggests that the reason why Korea has a lot of trade with these three countries can be mostly explained by the economic size, openness, and distance of these countries.

5. Conclusion

Since the 1960s, Korea's exports have grown rapidly, along with its economy. As a result, both the industry and trade structures have undergone significant changes. This study analyzes the long-term changes in Korea's trade patterns from 1963 to 2009.

The summary of the analysis results is as follows. Firstly, Korea's exports have grown rapidly since the 1960s, and its global market share has risen from 0.05% in 1963 to 3.07% in 2009. The increase in global market share is thought to be due to an expansion in export competitiveness, rather than changes in industrial structure.

Secondly, the comparative advantage of each industry has been continuously changing, with a greater range of change over the long run. In 2009, the export share of industries with high technology intensity had significantly increased compared to 1965. Additionally, none of the 10 major export industries in 1965 overlap with those in 2009.

Thirdly, the overall comparative advantage of the industry has been strengthened, with industries that were previously at a comparative disadvantage experiencing an increase in their comparative advantage.

Fourthly, intra-industry trade has been continuously increasing, which is attributed to the greater diversity of export products and advancements in technology. The number of high-quality IIT products has increased rapidly, with the high-tech sector having a higher and faster growing IIT index than the low-tech sector.

Finally, Korea's trade volume by country is well explained by the gravity model. The data indicates that Korea trades more with larger economies, open countries, and those that are geographically close. Moreover, the influence of distance on trade volume has gradually diminished over time due to the progress of globalization.

CHAPTER 11

INTER-INDUSTRY LABOR MOBILITY
AND LABOR PRODUCTIVITY IN KOREA

1. Introduction

The Korean economy has achieved high growth since the 1960s. During this period of economic growth, the industrial structure has gradually shifted from labor-intensive industries, such as textiles and clothing, to capital-intensive industries. Additionally, as the income level rose, the share of the service industry in the economy continued to increase. These changes in the industrial structure have led to a steady movement of labor among industries.

There are two main causes of labor migration among industries. The first is the wage gap theory, which states that if there is a wage differential among industries, labor will move from lower-wage industries to higher-wage ones. The second is the theory of job opportunities, which suggests that when an industry grows, labor will shift from other industries to it. These changes in the industrial structure lead to labor mobility among industries, which, in turn, causes changes in labor productivity.

Labor productivity in Korea has increased gradually due to several factors. First, the country's industrial structure has shifted from labor-intensive industries to capital-intensive industries, leading to an increase in overall labor productivity. This is because labor productivity is defined as output per capita, and a higher ratio of capital equipment per capita can increase labor productivity. Second, labor productivity has improved as workers' human capital levels have increased. Finally, overall labor productivity has increased as labor has moved from low-productivity to high-productivity sectors.

This study focuses on the relationship between labor movement and productivity change. We analyze labor mobility among industries and changes in labor productivity in Korea from 1974 to 2014, using data extracted from the National Accounts by Industry (Bank of Korea) and the STAN database (OECD). While Lee et al. (2013) have addressed labor mobility in Korea, their analysis period is short, and they have only classified industries into seven categories. Furthermore, they did not analyze the relationship between labor mobility and labor productivity. Although many studies have analyzed labor productivity, none have investigated the relationship with labor mobility (Kim, 2016; Lee, 2013; Hwang, 2008).

The study raises several questions related to labor mobility and productivity. These include changes in labor mobility between industries in Korea, the causes of labor mobility, differences in the growth rate of labor productivity among industries, factors that slow down the growth rate of labor productivity, the narrowing of gaps in labor productivity and wages between industries, and whether this phenomenon differs between the manufacturing and service industries.

This chapter is structured into several sections. Section 2 summarizes previous studies and analyzes the characteristics of each industry. Section 3 analyzes changes in labor mobility and productivity and examines the causes of changes in labor productivity. Section 4 employs regression analysis to examine the factors influencing labor movement, and finally, Section 5 summarizes the discussions.

2. Previous Research and Data

2.1 Previous Research

Structural changes occur during the process of economic growth. As the economy grows, the share of the agricultural sector decreases, while the service sector's share gradually increases, and the manufacturing sector shows a hump-shaped pattern. The hump-shaped pattern refers to the phenomenon where the manufacturing industry's share of labor gradually increases as the economy grows, but at some point, this share decreases. Baumol (1967) and Ngai and Pissarides (2007) explain the reason for the manufacturing sector's hump-shaped growth pattern as a difference in productivity among industries, while Kongsamut et al. (2001) and Laitner (2000) describe it as a change in consumption demand.

In the process of economic growth in Korea, the share of labor in the manufacturing sector increased in the early stage, but later on, it decreased. Uy, Yi, and Zhang (2013) use a two-country model, while Mao and Yao (2012) use a small open economy model to explain structural changes in the Korean economy. They explain that in Korea, the labor force in the agricultural sector moved to the manufacturing sector in the early stages due to the rapid increase in the manufacturing sector's productivity. However, in the later period, as the share of expenditure on services increased due to income growth, the share of the manufacturing sector decreased. Matsuyama (2009) and Sposi (2015) show that the hump-shaped phenomenon emerges during the manufacturing sector's growth process, even in an open economy with multinational models.

Kim (2016) explains that the growth rate of labor productivity in Korea has been slowing since 1990 due to the low labor productivity of the service industry. Labor productivity in the service industry is exceedingly low compared to that in the manufacturing industry, and the gap in labor productivity between these two industries is gradually widening. Furthermore, there is a large gap in labor productivity between large enterprises and SMEs, especially in the manufacturing industry. In Korea, the productivity gap among industries is widening, and productivity is slowing down due to the progress of the population aging (Kim, 2016).

Lee et al. (2013) show that labor mobility has decreased in Korea. This study explains that the decline in labor mobility is due to an increase in the opportunity cost of labor mobility, resulting from population aging and technological progress. Zhou (2008) argues that labor mobility decreases as income increases because labor specialization and differentiation occur as per capita income increases. Chen and Fougere (2009) show that the wage gap has the greatest impact on labor mobility and that mobility in men is more than in women. Lee et al. (2004) show that men have higher mobility than women, and the more experienced people are, the lower their mobility is because the cost of moving is higher.

This study analyzes the current status and causes of structural changes shown in the process of economic growth, focusing on the labor movement and productivity. In particular, we examine the relationship between the change in labor mobility and the slowdown in the growth rate of labor productivity in the Korean economy.

2.2 Data

Data on value added, labor, capital, and wages were obtained from the Bank of Korea's economic statistics database using the 2010 price index to convert values into constant values. The number of workers was estimated using data from the OECD STAN, the National Statistical Office's Economically Active Population Survey, the Mining and Manufacturing Survey, the Ministry of Employment and Labor, and the Enterprise Labor Force Survey.[1]

This study used the industrial classification of the National Account, which includes 17 detailed industries: agriculture, mining, manufacturing (9), and service (6). Due to changes in the industry classification since 1974, the data were organized by connecting the updated classification to the 17 industries.[2]

2.3 Characteristics by Industry

The Korean economy has undergone changes in its industrial structure during its process of rapid growth. Figure 11-1 shows the share of value added by industry. While the share of agriculture and mining decreased, the share of manufacturing increased. The share of manufacturing in total value added has continuously increased from 15.6% in 1974 to 31.9% in 2014. In contrast, the share of agriculture/mining has gradually decreased from 15% in 1974 to 2.5% in 2014. On the other hand, the share of the service industry has remained relatively constant at 65-70% with no significant changes.

Figure 11-2 illustrates the share of labor by industry. The share of employment in the service sector has been steadily increasing among total employment, while that in agriculture and mining continues to decrease.[3]

---

[1] Refer to Kim (2018) for the method of estimating the number of workers by industry.

[2] In 2007, the national account workers in the "15 code (transport/warehouse)" of the service industries were overvalued; therefore, they were redistributed into other industries according to the previous trend.

[3] Shioji (2015) shows that in Japan, labor in the manufacturing sector is decreasing

Figure 11-1. Share of value added by industry

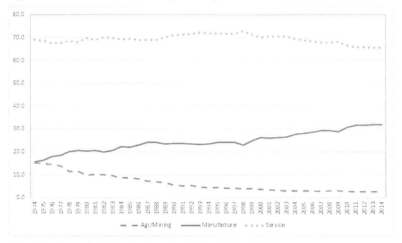

Note: Percentage of added value share (constant price) by industry.

Figure 11-2. Share of labor by industry

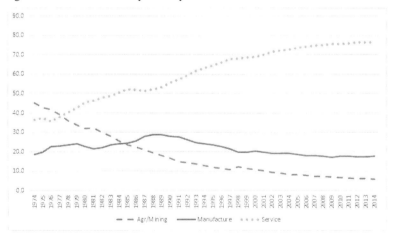

Note: Percentage of labor share by industry.

while labor in the medical, corporate, and information service sectors is increasing. Labor productivity is increasing most rapidly in the electronics industry, but labor is rather outflowing from this industry.

However, the share of manufacturing employment in total employment increased to 28.7% in 1989 and gradually decreased to 17.7% in 2014. The Korean economy exhibits a hump-shaped phenomenon in its economic development process, which is also evident in this trend.

The share of value added and the labor force across industries has undergone changes. The manufacturing industry's share in total value added has been steadily increasing, but its share in total employment rose until 1989 and has been gradually declining since. Meanwhile, the service sector's share in total value added has not significantly changed, but its share in total employment has significantly increased. Labor has shifted from the manufacturing sector to the service sector, but the added value of the manufacturing industry has increased while that of the service sector has remained almost unchanged. Therefore, it is estimated that labor productivity has increased in the manufacturing industry but decreased in the service industry. Such changes in labor productivity among industries have implications for the overall labor productivity of the Korean economy.

Table 11-1 presents changes in value added, labor, capital, and labor productivity by industry from 1974 to 2014. From this table, we can deduce the following:

First, while employment increased in the manufacturing and service industries, it decreased in agriculture/mining. Labor shifted from agriculture/mining to manufacturing and services, with the service sector experiencing the most significant increase in employment.

Second, the overall growth rate of capital (9.4%) is greater than that of labor (2.1%), indicating a gradual shift towards capital-intensive production methods. In particular, there is a large difference between the growth rate of

Table 11-1. Changes in Output, Input, and Labor Productivity by Industry (1974-2014)

	Value added (%)	Labor (%)	Capital (%)	Labor productivity (%)	Labor productivity level (2014)
Agriculture/ mining	1.9	-3.1	3.8	5.1	21.6
Manufacturing	8.5	2.1	11.0	6.4	91.0
Service	6.4	4.0	9.4	2.3	43.3
All	6.5	2.1	9.4	4.3	50.5

Note: 1) Numbers are average annual growth rates. 2) Each industry's average annual growth rate is calculated and then simply averaged for the entire period. 3) The unit of labor productivity level is "million Won."

capital (11.0%) and labor (2.1%) in the manufacturing industry, suggesting that labor was most actively replaced by capital in that sector.

Third, the growth rate of labor productivity in the manufacturing industry (6.4%) is much higher than that of the service industry (2.3%), and the level of labor productivity in the manufacturing industry is 91.0, more than twice as high as that of the service industry at 43.3. However, employment is increasing more in the service than in the manufacturing sector, which leads to a slowdown in labor productivity in the Korean economy.

Lastly, the value-added growth rate of the manufacturing industry is 8.5%, higher than the overall average of 6.5%. Moreover, the labor productivity growth rate (6.4%) and labor productivity level (91.0) are much higher than those of other industries. The labor productivity level of 91.0 million Won in the manufacturing industry is 2.1 times that of the service industry (43.3 million Won) and 4.2 times that of the agriculture/mining industry (21.6 million Won). This indicates that the growth of the manufacturing industry has contributed significantly to the entire economy's growth.

Figure 11-3. Growth rate of labor productivity in Korea

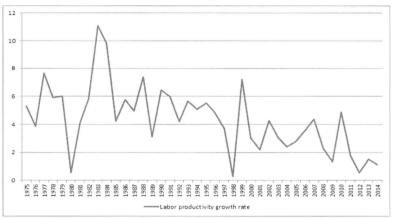

Figure 11-4. Changes in labor productivity levels by industry

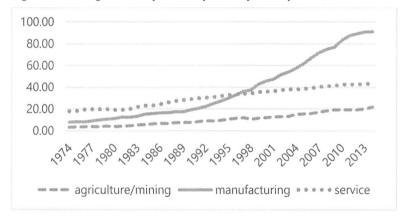

Figure 11-3 illustrates the growth rate of labor productivity in Korea, while Figure 11-4 shows the variation in labor productivity levels across different industries. Figure 11-3 indicates that the growth rate of labor productivity is gradually decreasing. On the other hand, Figure 11-4 reveals that while the labor productivity of the manufacturing industry is rapidly increasing, that of agriculture/mining and service industries is growing at a slower pace.

In 2014, labor productivity in the service industry (43.3) was less than half of that in the manufacturing industry (91.0). The gradual decline in labor productivity in Korea can be attributed to changes in labor mobility and the industrial structure.

3. Labor Mobility and Changes in Labor Productivity

3.1 Decomposition of Labor Productivity Growth

The rise in labor productivity across the entire economy can be attributed to two factors: productivity growth and labor movement. Labor productivity increases when there is an increase in capital input or when technological progress occurs. Moreover, the labor productivity of the entire economy improves when labor shifts from a low-productivity sector to a high-productivity sector.

The factors that increase labor productivity are decomposed as follows (McMillan and Rodrik, 2011):

$$\Delta LP_t = \sum_{i=1}^{n} s_{i,t-1}\, \Delta lp_{i,t} + \sum_{i=1}^{n} lp_{i,t}\, \Delta s_{i,t}, \qquad (11\text{-}1)$$

where LP is the labor productivity level of the entire economy, lp is the labor productivity level of an individual industry, and s is the share of labor in that industry out of total labor. Δ represents the change, i is the industry, and t is the year.

The first item on the right represents the weighted average of productivity changes within an industry, where the weight is the share of labor by industry in the previous year. This item reflects the impact of increasing productivity within the industry. The second item shows the change in productivity caused by labor flow among industries, that is, the effect of the change in productivity caused by structural change. If labor moves to a

Table 11-2. Decomposition of Labor Productivity Growth by Period

	Growth rate (%)			Composition ratio (%)	
	Labor productivity for all industries	Effect within the industry	Effect by structural change	Effect within the industry	Effect by structural change
1974-1980	4.9	2.0	2.9	40.7	59.3
1981-1990	6.3	4.2	2.1	66.7	33.3
1991-2000	4.6	3.5	1.1	76.5	23.5
2001-2010	3.1	2.3	0.8	73.8	26.2
2011-2014	1.2	1.1	0.2	85.4	14.6
Whole period (1974~2014)	4.3	2.9	1.4	66.7	33.3

Note: 1) After calculating the average growth rate and factor decomposition for 17 industries each year, these values were averaged over the period. 2) The composition ratio was calculated from the decomposition of the growth rate.

sector with higher productivity, this item becomes positive (+), indicating that structural changes caused by labor migration contributed to increased labor productivity in the entire economy.

However, an increase in the productivity of one industry may not necessarily increase the productivity of the entire economy. For example, even if labor productivity increases rapidly in the manufacturing sector, but the share of employment decreases and instead increases in the service sector with low labor productivity, productivity growth in the economy as a whole will inevitably slow down. In extreme cases, the movement of labor from high-productivity industries to low-productivity ones may reduce the entire economy's productivity.

Table 11-2 presents the results of decomposing changes in labor productivity in Korea into effects within industries and effects of structural changes. The average annual growth rate of labor productivity from 1974 to

Table 11-3. Decomposition of Labor Productivity Growth by Industry (whole period)

	Growth rate (%)			Composition ratio (%)	
	Labor productivity for all industries	Effect within the industry	Effect by structural change	Effect within the industry	Effect by structural change
Agriculture/ mining	5.1	5.2	-0.1	101.4	-1.4
Manufacturing	6.4	6.0	0.4	94.4	5.6
Service	2.3	1.7	0.6	73.2	26.8
All	4.3	2.9	1.4	66.7	33.3

Note: 1) After calculating the average growth rate and factor decomposition for 17 industries each year, these values were averaged over the whole period. 2) The composition ratio was calculated from the decomposition of the growth rate.

2014 was 4.3%, with 2.9% being an effect within the industry and 1.4% being an effect of structural change. The structural change effect accounts for 33.3% of the total labor productivity increase in terms of composition ratio. However, the share of structural change effects has been declining recently. In the 1970s, the share of the structural change effect was exceedingly high at 59.3%, but it has gradually declined since then, reaching only 14.6% in 2011-2014. While labor movement among industries had previously led to increased productivity of the entire economy, the effect of this structural change is gradually diminishing.

Table 11-3 presents the factor decomposition of labor productivity growth by industry for the entire period. In agriculture/mining and manufacturing, the impact within the industry is considerably more significant than that of structural change. Conversely, the effect of structural change is relatively substantial in the service industry. The contribution of the structural change effect in the manufacturing industry is only 5.6%, while that in the service industry is 26.8%. For agriculture/mining, the effect of structural change is negative (-), indicating a decline in this sector's labor share.

Figure 11-5. Changes in labor mobility in Korea

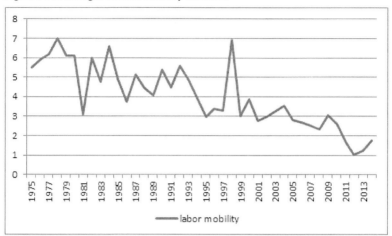

The recent decline in the effect of structural change can be attributed to changes in labor mobility. When labor mobility between industries is low, it becomes challenging to achieve an increase in labor productivity through structural change. One of the methods for calculating labor mobility is as follows (Tehle, 2011):

$$SC_t = \sum_{i=1}^{n} |s_{i,t} - s_{i,t-1}|. \tag{11-2}$$

Here, SC is the labor mobility index representing structural change, and s is the labor share in the industry. This mobility index is the sum of changes in each industry's labor share. If there is no labor movement among industries, the composition ratio of all industries remains unchanged, resulting in an SC value of 0. As labor movement among industries increases, the SC value increases.

Figure 11-5 illustrates changes in labor mobility, indicating an overall decrease. The significant rise in labor mobility in 1998 was due to increased unemployment and re-employment as corporate bankruptcies intensified during the foreign exchange crisis. The overall decline in labor mobility is similar to the reduction in the share of structural change effects in the factor decomposition of labor productivity.

3.2 Convergence of Labor Productivity and Wages

The reasons for labor movement among industries can be explained by two theories: the wage gap theory and the job opportunity theory. The wage gap theory suggests that workers move from low-wage to high-wage sectors, while the job opportunity theory states that labor moves to sectors with expanded job opportunities. The former theory explains the movement of labor on the supply side, while the latter theory explains it on the demand side.

Whether based on the employment opportunity theory or the wage gap theory, labor productivity and wages in each industry are expected to converge if there is labor movement among sectors. This is because labor will move to sectors with higher labor productivity or wages, resulting in a decrease in labor productivity due to inflow into sectors with high productivity and an increase due to the outflow from sectors with low productivity. Therefore, labor productivity in the two sectors will converge. In addition, wages in the high-wage sector will decrease due to labor inflow, while wages in the low-wage sector will rise due to labor outflow, leading to wage convergence between the two sectors. We investigated whether this convergence of labor productivity and wages is evident in the Korean economy. The coefficient of variation was used to measure the convergence phenomenon, which is obtained by dividing the standard deviation by the mean.

Figure 11-6. Coefficient of variation of labor productivity and wages for all industries

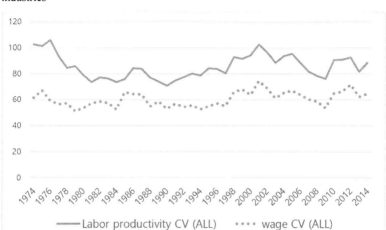

Figure 11-6 shows changes in the coefficient of variation of labor productivity and wages. The coefficient of variation of labor productivity is much greater than that of wages. However, there is no evidence of convergence in wages and labor productivity. The coefficient of variation declined in the 1970s, then moved within a certain range until the mid-1990s, and has been increasing ever since. Overall, there was no convergence in labor productivity or wages in the Korean economy, indicating that the movement of labor cannot be explained solely by the wage gap or employment opportunity theories in the Korean context.

The service sector is the reason why labor productivity and wages do not converge across sectors in the Korean economy. While there was a convergence in the manufacturing sector, there was no convergence in the service industry. In the manufacturing industry, the coefficients of variation in labor productivity fell from 52.7 in 1974 to 37.9 in 2014, and the coefficients of variation in wages fell from 46.8 in 1974 to 29.5 in 2014. This indicates that labor productivity and wages are converging across industries within the manufacturing industry.

On the other hand, the coefficients of variation in labor productivity and wages in the service industry have been increasing recently. That is, both the inter-sectoral gap in labor productivity and that in wages are widening in the service industry. This indicates that labor productivity and wages do not converge between sectors in the service industry.

4. Determinants of Labor Mobility

The factors behind labor movement among industries are examined from the perspectives of wage gap and employment opportunity theories. The regression equation used to verify these factors is as follows:

$$\Delta s_{i,t} = \alpha_0 + \beta_1 \Delta v_{i,t} + \beta_2 \Delta w_{i,t} + \beta_3 \Delta lp_{i,t} + \varepsilon_{i,t}. \qquad (11\text{-}3)$$

Here, s represents the share of labor in the industry, v represents the share of value added, and lp represents the labor productivity of the industry. The wage level of the industry, w, is calculated as "wage in the industry/average of the entire industry." If the coefficient of β_1 is positive (+), then the proportion of labor also increases in an industry where the proportion of value-added increases. This corresponds to the theory of employment opportunities. If β_2 is positive (+), then the proportion of labor in high-wage industries also increases. Additionally, if β_3 is positive, then the proportion of labor in industries with high labor productivity also increases. β_2 and β_3 correspond to the wage gap theory.

Table 11-4. Results of Regression Analysis

	All industry		Manufacturing		Service industry	
Constant	-0.132 (1.21)	-0.061 (0.57)	-0.048 (0.82)	-0.009 (0.17)	0.116 (0.60)	0.074 (0.39)
Δv	0.426*** (8.41)	0.439*** (8.59)	0.345*** (8.56)	0.355*** (8.85)	0.147** (2.01)	0.147** (1.98)
Δw	0.132*** (4.63)		0.067** (2.32)		-0.075* (1.91)	
Δlp		0.061*** (2.99)		0.030 (1.35)		-0.036 (1.34)
R^2	0.144	0.128	0.450	0.443	0.141	0.133
N	680	680	360	360	240	240

Note: 1) This is the result of panel regression analysis considering the year-fixed effect. 2) The values in parentheses are the t-values. 3) *, **, *** indicate statistical significance at the 1%, 5%, and 10% levels, respectively.

Table 11-4 presents the regression results based on panel data for 17 industries from 1974 to 2014.[4] Panel regression analysis was conducted, and year-fixed effects were considered to eliminate economic fluctuation factors.

The coefficients of Δv and Δw are positive and statistically significant when considering the results for all industries. This suggests that employment increases in industries with a high value-added share and those with high wage levels. The results are similar in the manufacturing industry analysis. In contrast, in the service industry analysis, the coefficient of Δv is positive, but the coefficient of Δw is negative. This indicates that employment increased in industries where the share of added value increased but decreased in industries with high wage levels. Consequently, there was no

---

[4] Because labor productivity and wages are highly correlated, multicollinearity problems occur when the two variables are used together as explanatory variables. Therefore, the two variables were used in different regression equations respectively.

convergence of wages among sectors within the service industry.

In the analysis of the entire industry, the coefficient of Δlp, which represents the change in labor productivity, is positive and statistically significant. However, it is not statistically significant in the analysis of the manufacturing or service industries. This indicates that differences in labor productivity do not affect labor mobility in these industries. The fact that structural changes do not have the effect of increasing labor productivity of the entire economy suggests that differences in labor productivity do not significantly affect labor mobility in the manufacturing or service industries.

5. Conclusion

This study analyzes labor mobility among industries and changes in labor productivity in Korea over a period of approximately 40 years from 1974 to 2014, using mainly data from the National Accounts by Industry of the Bank of Korea and the STAN database of the OECD.

The analysis reveals that labor mobility among Korean industries is gradually decreasing and the growth rate of labor productivity is slowing down. Notably, labor productivity in the service industry has been increasing at a much slower pace than in the manufacturing industry, with the service sector's labor productivity being half that of manufacturing in 2014. Despite this, there is a trend of labor moving from the manufacturing to the service industry, with further labor movement to low productivity sectors within the service industry. The decline in labor productivity across the entire Korean economy is due to the service industry's productivity slowdown and labor movement to the sector. The theory of employment opportunities explains that labor is shifting to the service industry with low productivity as employment opportunities increase due to the sector's expansion.

This study presents the following policy implications. Given that the decrease in labor mobility and productivity are related, policy support, such as vocational training, to increase labor mobility is required to enhance labor productivity. In addition, as labor is shifting to the service rather than the manufacturing industry, policy efforts to improve labor productivity in the service industry are necessary to enhance the entire economy's labor productivity.

CHAPTER 12

CHANGES IN THE PRICE AND QUALITY OF KOREAN EXPORT PRODUCTS

1. Introduction

Both the Ricardian model and the Heckscher-Ohlin model explain that differences in labor productivity or factor endowments are the cause of trade. However, they do not consider differences in product quality between countries. Recently, international trade theories have emphasized the importance of quality, but there have not been many empirical studies on product quality due to the lack of detailed trade statistics. As more detailed trade data become available, several empirical studies on quality have been published.

Grossman and Helpman (1991), and Aghion and Howitt (1992), explain theoretically that export quality improves with economic growth. In addition, Flam and Helpman (1987), and Falvey and Kierzkowski (1987), posit that intra-industry trade between developed countries (the North) and developing countries (the South) is due to differences in quality. Hallak and Schott (2008) show a significant positive correlation between income levels and the quality of exports across countries. They demonstrate that the quality level is high in high-income countries and that export quality improves as the economy develops.

Korea has achieved continuous economic growth, resulting in the gradual improvement of export product quality. Kim and Joo (2007) demonstrate this improvement by showing that superior quality trade has gradually increased in Korea's vertical intra-industry trade.[1] In addition, the share of vertical trade in Korean intra-industry trade is high, at about 80%, suggesting that the difference in the quality of exports or imports is an important factor for trade in Korea.[2]

Hallak (2006) uses the unit value of export goods as a proxy variable for product quality. However, since this value is affected by quality as well as exchange rates and production costs, it cannot be considered an appropriate proxy variable for quality. Hummels and Klenow (2005) measure the elasticity of quality using import price and quantity but do not directly estimate the quality index. On the other hand, Hallak and Schott (2008) estimate quality by classifying the quality-adjusted price from the unit price. Furthermore, Aw and Roberts (1986), and Feenstra (1988), measure the quality index by distinguishing the price index from the unit price, which measures the quality index using the composition ratio of exported goods within the industry. In other words, when the proportion of high-quality products increases in the composition of export products within an industry, the quality of the industry is improved, and when the composition of low-quality products increases, the quality is regarded as deteriorating.

This study estimates the change in the quality of Korean exports for 1992-2008, using the most detailed trade data of the HS 10-digit classification.

---

[1] The ratio between export and import unit value is calculated, and if this ratio is above a certain level, it is classified as superior quality intra-industry trade. If it is below a certain level, it is classified as inferior quality intra-industry trade (Greenaway et al., 1994; Fontagne and Freudenberg, 1997).

[2] Empirical studies of Korea's vertical intra-industry trade show that its share is higher than that of horizontal intra-industry trade (Oh and Joo, 2000; Lee, 2004; Kim and Joo, 2007).

The following two methods are used to estimate quality change. First, export quality is analyzed using the unit value of exports and imports. If the unit value of an export good is higher than that of imported goods, the quality of Korean export goods is superior. If the number of these superior goods gradually increases, export quality is improving. Next, the quality index of Korean exports is estimated using Aw and Roberts's (1986) method. An increase in this index indicates that the composition of Korean exports has shifted from low-priced to high-priced products, so it is interpreted that export quality has improved.

The structure of this chapter is as follows. Section 2 analyzes the changes in export quality based on the number of superior quality exports. Section 3 estimates the quality index of exports by industry and examines the changes in export quality by industry group. Finally, Section 4 interprets the meaning of these analysis results and provides a summary.

2. Export Quality Evaluated by the Relative Prices of Exports/Imports

2.1 Data

We used Korean trade statistics classified according to the 10-digit HS classification from 1992 to 2008. To calculate the price of an export product, we divided the export amount by the volume. However, because various products are mixed within a common classification, we needed to use data from detailed classifications to ensure that heterogeneous products were not included in the same classification. Therefore, we used HS 10-digit data, which is the most detailed trade classification available. The total number of HS 10-digit trades in Korea during the 1992-2008 period was 114,340.

Our analysis focused on manufacturing products (classified as SITC 5-8) because product quality is typically more important in manufactured products than in primary goods. This is because the price or quality of primary products is determined by endowed resources, while the quality of manufactured products is determined by the technology level.

2.2 Analysis Methods

If a product is both exported and imported simultaneously, and the export price is higher than the import price, we consider the export product to be of higher quality. This indicates that higher quality goods are exported while lower quality goods are imported. Greenaway et al. (1994) define a product as vertical intra-industry trade if the ratio between the unit value of exported and imported goods is above or below a certain value. Based on this method, we establish the criteria for superior quality products as follows:

Criterion I: $\frac{UV_X}{UV_M} > 1 + \alpha.$

Here, UV_X and UV_M represent the unit value of exports and imports, respectively. While previous studies use 0.15 or 0.25 as the value of α, this study uses 0.15. This means that an export product with an 'export price/import price' ratio of 1.15 or higher is classified as a superior quality export product.

Aiginger (1997) classifies export quality by taking into account not only the unit value ratio but also the difference between export and import volume. Even if the price of export goods is higher than the price of imported goods, if the export amount is not higher than the import amount, the goods cannot be classified as superior quality. According to Aiginger's classification criteria, for export goods to be considered superior quality, they must have

Table 12-1. Percentage of Superior Quality Items by Year

	Total number of export items	Criterion I (%)	Criterion II (%)
1992	5816	22.7	7.8
1993	6050	25.2	8.9
1994	6240	25.0	8.2
1995	6362	25.1	7.8
1996	6554	23.8	6.9
1997	6730	24.8	6.8
1998	6687	23.4	9.5
1999	6757	27.8	10.6
2000	6840	30.2	10.9
2001	6908	31.3	11.1
2002	7030	31.8	10.3
2003	7074	32.4	10.5
2004	7107	33.5	10.9
2005	7145	36.5	11.8
2006	7233	38.7	12.2
2007	6911	40.1	11.9
2008	6896	37.7	11.3

Note: This table displays the percentage (%) of the number of items that meet the conditions of criterion 1 or criterion 2 for the total number of exported items.

a higher price than the imported goods, and their export amount must exceed the import amount. This means that simply having a higher price than imported goods is not enough to classify an export product as superior quality. The export volume must also be higher than the import volume.

Therefore, another criterion for superior quality exports is set as a product in which the export price/import price ratio is higher than $(1+\alpha)$, and the export amount is greater than the import amount. The criteria are as follows:

Criterion II: $\dfrac{UV_X}{UV_M} \rangle 1 + \alpha, \ and \ EX \rangle IM.$

Here, EX is the export amount, IM is the import amount, and α is 0.15.

Table 12-1 displays the changes in the proportion of superior quality products from 1992 to 2008. The proportion of superior exports based on

Table 12-2. Changes in the Share of Superior Quality Products by SITC 1-digit

	Total number of export items		criterion I (%)		criterion II (%)	
	1992	2008	1992	2008	1992	2008
SITC 5	964	1436	25.1	37.7	3.5	6.5
SITC 6	1846	2234	25.3	41.1	8.9	13.1
SITC 7	1604	1767	15.0	28.8	3.1	12.8
SITC 8	1402	1459	26.5	43.5	14.5	11.7

Note: Same as the note in Table 12-1.

criterion I increased from 22.7% in 1992 to 37.7% in 2008. According to criterion II, the proportion of superior exports increased from 7.8% in 1992 to 11.3% in 2006. In both criteria, the share of superior quality products gradually increased, indicating an improvement in the quality of Korean exports.

Table 12-2 shows the total number of exported products and the proportion of superior quality products by SITC 1-digit classification in 1992 and 2008. The number of export products increased in 2008 across all industries compared to 1992, indicating increased diversity of Korean export products. The share of superior quality products based on criterion I increased in all industries from 1992 to 2008. In particular, the SITC 7 industries increased from 15.0% in 1992 to 28.8% in 2008, showing more growth than other industries. The proportion of superior quality products in 2008 for criterion II increased in all industries except those belonging to SITC 8. In particular, in the SITC 7 industries, the rate increased significantly from 3.1% in 1992 to 12.8% in 2008.

Figure 12-1 shows the changes in the proportion of superior quality products in high-tech and low-tech industries. The OECD classification (2007) was

Figure 12-1. Changes in the ratio of superior quality by technology

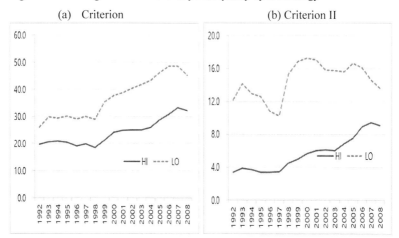

Notes: 1) HI refers to high-technology industries, and LO refers to low-technology industries. 2) In the OECD (2007) classification, ISIC codes 351, 352, 382, 383, 384, and 385 are classified as high-tech industries, and 311, 312, 313, 314, 321, 322, 323, 324, 331, 332, 341, 342, 353, 354, 355, 356, 361, 362, 369, 371, 372, 381, and 390 are classified as low-tech industries.

used to classify technology.[3] The figure shows that the proportion of superior quality products is increasing in both high- and low-tech industries. According to criterion I, from 1992-2008, the proportion of superior quality products increased from 25.8% to 45.2% in low-tech industries and from 19.6% to 32.2% in high-tech industries. For criterion II, it increased from 12.1% to 13.6% in low-tech industries and from 3.4% to 9.0% in high-tech industries. Overall, the proportion of superior quality products was higher

_____

[3] The classification of OECD (2007) classifies high-tech and low-tech industries based on ISIC classification. Therefore, after connecting HS 4-digit with the ISIC classification, the HS 4-digit industry was classified into high-tech groups and low-tech groups.

in low-tech industries than in high-tech industries, but it increased more significantly in high-tech industries.

3. Changes in the Price Index and Quality Index of Export Goods

3.1 Measurement Method of Price Index and Quality Index

As for the price of export goods, the unit value obtained by dividing the export amount by the export volume is often used.[4] However, considering the unit value as the price index of the industry presents a problem. This is due to the mixture of high-priced and low-priced goods within an industry. Even if the prices of various commodities within an industry remain constant, an increase in the exports of expensive commodities results in a rise in the unit value of the industry. Consequently, it can be inferred that the change in the unit value of an industry includes not only the change in price but also the change in quality.

A higher-priced product may be considered of better quality. Thus, if the exported product composition shifts from low-priced to high-priced products, it implies an improvement in the exported product quality within the industry. Aw and Roberts (1986) distinguish between price and quality indices and the industry unit value using the productivity estimation method of Caves et al. (1982). This study also employs this method to measure export price and quality.

The price index is measured as follows:

---

[4] In the trade statistics data, the unit of export volume is recorded as quantity or weight.

$$lnP_{kl} = \frac{1}{2}\sum_{i}^{n}(S_i^{\ k} + S_i^{\ l})(lnP_i^{\ k} - lnP_i^{\ l}). \tag{12-1}$$

P_{kl} is the price index of period k for period l, $P_i^{\ k}$ is the unit value of product i in period k, and $S_i^{\ k}$ is the share of product i in period k. k and l represent time points.

This index is used to measure the price difference between two time points, but there is a problem in that it lacks transitivity. For example, if there is a third point 'm' between 'k' and 'l', then $lnP_{kl} \neq lnP_{km} - lnP_{ml}$, meaning that this index cannot compare multiple time points simultaneously.

Caves et al. (1982) suggest a multilateral translog price index that can simultaneously compare prices at various times. The index is as follows:

$$lnP^{kl^*} = \frac{1}{2}\sum_{i=1}^{n}(S_i^{\ k} + \overline{S_i})(lnP_i^{\ k} - \overline{lnP_i}) - \frac{1}{2}\sum_{i}^{n}(S_i^{\ l} + \overline{S_i})(lnP_i^{\ l} - \overline{lnP_i}),$$

$$\tag{12-2}$$

where $\overline{S_i} = \frac{1}{n}\sum_{i=1}^{n}S_i$, $\overline{lnP_i} = \frac{1}{n}\sum_{i=1}^{n}lnP_i$, and '$n$' is the total number of samples. $\overline{S_i}$ and $\overline{lnP_i}$ are the logarithmic means of all products in the sample, which is a hypothetical observation. If the price index at each time point is calculated based on this hypothetical observation, these indices will have comparable circularity. Therefore, the price index estimated this way has the advantage of simultaneously comparing prices at each time point.

Unit value changes in an industry are divided into export price changes and export quality changes. For example, if the prices of export goods increase, the unit value of an industry rises. This unit value also increases if the composition of export goods changes from low-priced to high-priced products. In the latter case, the unit value rises due to a change in the composition of export commodities without a price change. The unit value of an industry is divided into price and quality as follows:

$$UV^k = P^k A^k. \tag{12-3}$$

Here, UV^k is the unit value, P is the price, and A is the quality. The unit value UV^k is the value obtained by dividing the total export amount by the total export volume of industry k. That is, $UV^k = \sum_i^n P_i^k X_i^k / \sum_i^n X_i^k$.

Taking the logarithm of both sides of the above equation and comparing the two time points, we get the following.

$$[lnUV^k - lnUV^l] = [lnP^k - lnP^l] + [lnA^k - lnA^l] \tag{12-4}$$

Here, $[lnP^k - lnP^l]$, $[lnA^k - lnA^l]$, and $[lnUV^k - lnUV^l]$ are indices comparing price, quality, and unit value between two time points. Let the unit value index be UV^{kl^*}, the price index be lnP^{kl^*}, and the quality index be A^{kl^*}. Re-arranging the above equation, the quality index can be measured with the following equation.

$$lnA^{kl^*} = lnUV^{kl^*} - lnP^{kl^*} \tag{12-5}$$

This equation tells us that the difference in quality between two points in time is calculated by the difference in unit value and pure price. After calculating the price index, the quality index can be computed from the unit value and price indices.[5] Since this index is transitive, it is possible to

---

[5] Aw and Roberts (1988) used this index to measure the price and quality of imported goods, and Faini and Heimler (1991) distinguishes price and quality differences in EU textile and clothing imports. Boorstein and Feenstra (1991) analyzes the quality of U.S. steel imports.

compare several time points simultaneously.

The index of the entire country or industry group is calculated as a weighted average value with the export value of each industry as the weight. The price and quality indices for each industry group are computed as follows:

$$UV_g^{kl} = \sum_{i \in g}^{n} w_i \, UV_i^{kl}, \qquad\qquad (12\text{-}6)$$

$$P_g^{kl} = \sum_{i \in g}^{n} w_i \, P_i^{kl}, \qquad\qquad (12\text{-}7)$$

$$A_g^{kl} = \sum_{i \in g}^{n} w_i \, A_i^{kl}, \qquad\qquad (12\text{-}8)$$

where w_i is the share of industry i in group g.

One thing to note when using this index is that the price index is distorted if there is a missing value for a certain product. This is because the average value of the entire sample is considered when calculating the price index. To avoid such distortions, the sample should be constructed with as few missing values as possible.

3.2 Data Selection

HS 10-digit data was utilized to estimate the price and quality indices of export goods. To ensure reliable data, error data in the subdivided HS 10-digit were trimmed using the methods of Hallak (2006) and Hallak and Schott (2008).[6]

Since the quality or price of a product is more relevant for manufactured products than agricultural products, SITC 5-8 manufactured products were

---

[6] Hallak (2006), and Hallak and Schott (2008), also pointed out that disaggregated trade statistics included erroneous observations and performed the trimming process.

selected. To exclude cases with low trade volume but high price fluctuations, products with an annual export value of less than $10,000 with an HS 10-digit classification were removed. Furthermore, HS 10-digit products with a unit value more than five times or less than a fifth of the product's 17-year geometric average price were excluded. Finally, to measure the price and quality indices, product data must be continuously available throughout the entire period; thus, only products with continuous export data for 17 years were selected.

SITC 3-digit classification and HS 4-digit classification were used as industry standards to measure the price and quality indices. However, if the number of products in an industry is too small, a change in the price of one or two products will have a significant impact on the quality index of the entire industry. Thus, industries containing more than ten export goods were selected to alleviate this issue.

As a result of these adjustments, 100 industries with SITC 3-digit classifications, containing 43,061 samples, and 61 industries with HS 4-digit classifications, containing 14,756 samples, were included in the study.

3.3 Changes in the Price and Quality Indices of Export Goods

Table 12-3 presents the unit value, price index, and quality index for each year. The yearly index is the weighted average of the SITC 3-digit index, where the weight is the export amount of the industry. From 1992 to 2008, the unit value increased by 71.7%, the pure price increased by 54.2%, and the quality increased by 10.6%. After the financial crisis from 1998 to 2003, the unit value of export products was lower than the 1992 level, while the quality of export products was higher than that of 1992. This indicates that although the price of export goods has decreased since the financial crisis, the proportion of relatively high-quality export goods has increased.

The quality index, as defined in this study, depends on whether the proportion of high-priced exports within an industry has increased or decreased. Therefore, different industry classifications can yield different

Table 12-3. Changes in Price and Quality of Korean Export Products

	Unit value index	Price index	Quality index
1992	100.0	100.0	100.0
1993	96.7	97.1	99.6
1994	99.1	98.5	100.6
1995	112.2	109.8	102.4
1996	109.0	105.3	103.4
1997	104.2	100.1	104.1
1998	86.1	84.4	102.1
1999	87.4	83.6	104.5
2000	95.4	89.1	107.3
2001	87.7	83.4	105.3
2002	86.3	81.0	107.0
2003	94.5	88.5	107.4
2004	113.7	105.7	108.3
2005	125.8	116.9	108.2
2006	142.0	132.3	107.7
2007	156.9	143.0	109.6
2008	171.7	154.2	110.6

Note: The index for each year is the weighted average of the SITC 3-digit index, where the weight is the export amount.

values for the quality index. To investigate this, we examined whether the quality index remained consistent with the results presented in Table 12-3 despite variations in industry classification.

Figure 12-2 displays the changes in the quality index resulting from three different industry classification criteria: ten or more export items within the SITC 3-digit classification, twenty or more within the SITC 3-digit classification, and ten or more within the HS 4-digit classification. While there are slight differences among the three indices, they all demonstrate a gradual increase in the quality index over time. This finding provides empirical evidence for the gradual improvement in the quality of Korean export products.

Figure 12-2. Changes in the quality index of different classifications

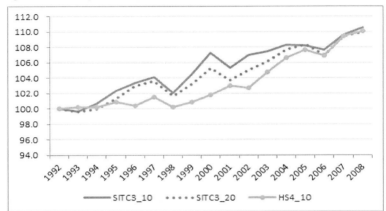

Note: SITC3_10 and SITC3_20 are cases with more than ten or twenty export items within the SITC 3-digit classification, and HS4_10 are cases with more than ten export items within the HS 4-digit classification.

Table 12-4 displays the price and quality indices for each SITC 1-digit industry from 1992-2008. Prices increased across all industries, with the chemical industry (SITC 5) showing the highest increase rate at 106.7%, followed by material-specific manufacturing products (SITC 6) at 66.8%, machinery and transportation (SITC 7) at 21.9%, and other manufactured products (SITC 8) at 35.8%. The quality index increased by 11-13% in SITC 5, 6, and 7 industries but decreased by 17.5% in SITC 8. Therefore, prices increased in all industries, but quality only improved in SITC 5, 6, and 7 and deteriorated in SITC 8.

Table 12-4. Changes in Price and Quality of SITC 1-digit Industries

	SITC 5		SITC 6		SITC 7		SITC 8	
	Price index	Quality index	Price index	Quality index	Price index	Quality index	Price index	Quality index
1992	100.0	100.0	100.0	100.0	100.0	100.0	100.0	100.0
1993	94.2	100.3	96.0	99.3	98.8	102.7	97.6	97.5
1994	108.0	101.2	95.5	101.1	99.3	105.0	97.3	95.6
1995	140.3	100.8	104.8	103.7	104.3	108.8	105.5	93.3
1996	111.5	108.6	104.3	103.4	103.8	108.1	104.9	92.0
1997	103.5	103.0	100.1	102.1	97.8	112.3	101.3	93.5
1998	80.1	102.2	86.2	99.3	82.5	110.4	88.0	93.3
1999	83.3	103.3	82.9	103.4	80.0	113.3	90.9	92.8
2000	99.6	104.0	87.2	105.2	82.2	118.1	94.7	92.7
2001	87.0	104.8	81.8	104.4	79.2	113.2	90.9	90.9
2002	88.3	105.5	79.4	106.8	75.5	114.6	87.3	90.9
2003	103.2	106.0	82.2	108.2	83.3	113.0	91.6	91.5
2004	139.6	106.9	93.9	109.8	94.5	112.9	100.1	91.4
2005	153.7	107.8	109.3	107.9	100.6	112.6	113.7	89.8
2006	174.6	108.4	137.3	108.7	108.3	110.5	121.1	88.1
2007	192.8	110.4	151.6	111.6	113.1	112.4	128.4	86.0
2008	206.7	113.1	166.8	111.5	121.9	113.5	135.8	82.5

Note: SITC 5: chemical industry; SITC 6: material-specific manufacturing products; SITC 7: machinery and transportation; SITC 8: other manufactured products

Figure 12-3 illustrates the changes in the quality index of high- and low-tech industries.[7] The quality index represents the weighted average value of the 4-digit HS quality index, where the weight is the export amount of each 4-digit HS within the group. As depicted in the figure, the export quality of high-tech industries continues to improve, whereas the quality in low-tech industries is gradually deteriorating. This indicates that the quality of Korean export products is improving in high-tech industries rather than low-tech industries.

---

[7] According to OECD (2007) classification, industries are divided into high- and low-tech industries.

Figure 12-3. Changes in quality index by technology

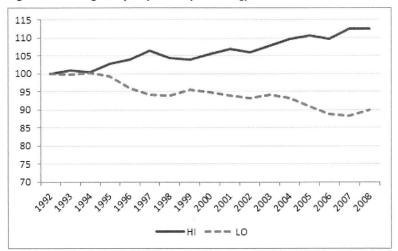

Notes: 1) HI refers to the high-technology industries, and LO refers to the low-technology industries.

We use regression analysis to estimate the growth rate of the quality index for each industry. The regression equation is as follows:

$$log(QID_i) = \alpha_0 + \beta_1 log(EX_i) + \beta_2 D_g * Time. \qquad (12\text{-}9)$$

Here, *QID* represents the quality index, *EX* is the export amount by industry, and *i* represents an individual industry. Since D_g is an industry dummy and Time is a variable representing the year, β_2 is the average annual increase rate of the quality index by industry. We include *log(EX)* to control for the difference in the quality index based on the export amount. A positive (+) coefficient of β_1 indicates that the quality index has increased further in industries with high export volume.

Table 12-5 shows the growth rate of the quality index by SITC 1-digit industry. As shown in the table, the quality of the SITC 5 and SITC 7 industries increased, while that of the SITC 6 and SITC 8 industries decreased. The SITC 5 industry increased by 0.52-0.77%, SITC 7 increased by 0.25-0.43%, and SITC 8 decreased by 0.69-1.07%. The quality of the SITC 6 industry declined, but the coefficient is not statistically significant.[8]

Table 12-5. Quality Index Growth Rate by SITC 1-digit Industry

	(1)	(2)
Constant	25.74*** (9.40)	18.07*** (5.97)
D_{SITC5} * Time	0.0077*** (5.26)	0.0052*** (3.46)
D_{SITC6} * Time	-0.0016 (1.31)	-0.0002 (0.16)
D_{SITC7} * Time	0.0043*** (3.47)	0.0025** (1.99)
D_{SITC8} * Time	-0.0107*** (7.81)	-0.0069*** (4.53)
log(EX)		0.0462*** (5.69)
F-value	35.92***	36.52***
R^2	0.709	0.715

Note: 1) The number of samples is 100 industries * 17 years = 1,700. 2) D_{SITC5} is a dummy variable set to 1 for industries belonging to SITC 5 and 0 for other industries. The rest of the dummy variables are calculated in the same way. 3) Panel regression analysis, including industry fixed effect, was considered. 4) The values in brackets are t-values, indicating that *** and ** are statistically significant at the 1% and 5% levels, respectively.

The coefficient of *log(EX)* is statistically significant and positive (+), indicating that the quality is 0.0462% higher in an industry with 1% more exports.

Table 12-6 displays the growth rate of the quality index for high- and low-tech industries. The quality of high-tech industries increased by 0.63-0.68%

---

[8] While the quality index of SITC 6 appears to have increased in Table 12-3, it appears to have decreased in Table 12-5. This difference is because the index in Table 12-3 is a weighted average value of exports by industry, while the result in Table 12-5 is the average growth rate controlling export volume.

annually, whereas that of low-tech industries decreased by 0.39-0.54% annually. Similar to the findings of Table 12-5, the coefficient of *log(EX)* was statistically significant and positive (+), indicating that quality was 0.015% higher in industries with 1% more exports. The positive (+) coefficient of *log(EX)* suggests that industries with high export volumes experienced a greater increase in the quality index.

Table 12-6. The Growth Rate of Quality Index by high/low Technology

	(3)	(4)
Constant	15.34*** (7.61)	12.36*** (5.18)
D_{HI} * Time	0.0068*** (6.87)	0.0063*** (6.22)
D_{LO} * Time	-0.0054*** (5.35)	-0.0039*** (3.26)
log(EX)		0.0155** (2.32)
F-value	23.33***	23.33***
R2	0.609	0.611

Note: 1) The number of samples is 61 industries * 17 years = 1,037. 2) D_{HI} is a dummy variable set to 1 for high-tech and 0 for other industries. 3) Panel regression analysis, including industry fixed effect, was considered. 4) The values in brackets are t-values, indicating that *** and ** are statistically significant at the 1% and 5% levels, respectively.

The findings from Table 12-5 indicate that quality improvements have occurred in the chemical industry (SITC 5) and machinery and transportation industries (SITC 7), while the results in Table 12-6 demonstrate quality improvements in the high-tech industry. These results suggest that Korea's industrial structure has shifted gradually from labor-intensive industries towards more capital-intensive and technology-intensive industries, leading to an overall improvement in quality across these sectors.

4. Conclusion

This study analyzes the change in the quality of Korean exports using the HS 10-digit trade statistics, analyzed in two ways: first, by analyzing the change in the number of export items of superior quality, and second, by estimating the quality index. Both analyses show that Korean export quality has increased.

Two criteria for superior quality were defined. Criterion I is the case where the ratio of export goods price to import goods price is 1.15 or higher, and criterion II is the case when criterion I is satisfied and exports exceed imports. The superior quality ratio increased from 22.7% in 1992 to 37.7% in 2008 for Criterion I and increased from 7.8% in 1992 to 11.3% in 2006 for Criterion II. The superior quality ratio grew in all industries except the SITC 8 industry and increased more rapidly in the high-tech industry. Overall, the quality of Korean exports improved from 1992 to 2008.

According to the quality index estimation results, the quality of Korean exports increased by 10.6% from 1992 to 2008. The quality index increased in the SITC 5, 6, and 7 industries, and the quality of high-tech industries has continuously improved while that of low-tech industries has gradually deteriorated. Overall, Korean export product quality has improved in high-tech rather than low-tech industries. This suggests that Korea's industrial structure has shifted from labor-intensive to capital- and technology-intensive industries, and quality has improved in these industries.

CHAPTER 13

COMPETITIVENESS OF LCD INDUSTRY OF EAST ASIA: FROM BAMBOO CAPITALISM TO WATER LILY

1. Introduction

East Asian countries obtained higher economic growth than any other areas in the late 20th century and the world is interested in what made this economic success. In particular, the IT industry is considered to have contributed a lot toward this economic development. Thus, it is natural that many theoretical models have tried to explain the process of economic development.

One of the popular models is the 'flying geese model', which focuses on the role of the leading country. This model considers Japan as the leader in the region, and other countries such as Korea or Taiwan as the followers. The leading country transfers their old industries one by one to other followers, and the followers catch up the leader by using the technology and other resources transferred from the leader, as time goes on. This theory seemed to explain quite well the process of the economic dynamics in the past. However, we have seen other cases that the individual countries or firms can develop their own technology which sometimes cannot be transferred easily from the advanced economy. Therefore, we need another model explaining better. This is the background of the need of new models. One problem in this research area is that it is not easy to find any good empirical analysis using the actual data to show which model fits better than other models.

This study investigates the development of the liquid crystal display (LCD) industry in the East Asian region by using international trade data. We try to show what the hard data says about the development model with a case of LCD industry. We first provide brief history of LCD industry in this area, and then, we analyze trade structure and competitiveness by using the actual data. We hope that this analysis will tell us which model best explains the situation of East Asia. As a matter of fact, Linden et al., (1998) already raised the question about the validity of the flying geese model in relation to the LCD industry by looking into the case of Korea and Taiwan.

We have chosen to focus on the LCD industry for the following reasons. First, the LCD industry is a core industry in IT manufacturing. Second, the industry is developed in all East Asian countries, and this region holds an almost 100% market share. Third, the LCD industry started in Japan first and moved to Korea, Taiwan and China, in that order. Last, there exists very active international trade and investment among these countries in the industry.

The East Asian countries, China, Japan, Korea, and Taiwan, have the major market share of the flat panel display (FPD) industry. In particular, these four countries hold more than 90% of the thin-film transistor (TFT-LCD; hereafter, LCD) market, the most important segment of the FPD industry. Considering that the LCD industry is expected to grow further, as new IT products with LCDs are being developed, the market power of these countries would seem set to be strong in the future.

The growth of the LCD market is the result of a combination of many factors. First, the possible applications are very broad. Consider the products with small display panels, such as watches, calculators, cell phones, and digital cameras, and large displays, such as laptop and desktop monitors, personal digital assistants, and LCD TVs. These days, there are LCDs almost everywhere. Furthermore, demand for large displays is accelerating. Additionally, thanks to persistent efforts and technical progress, the LCD industry has overcome various technological difficulties and has won the war against several other FPD technologies, such as plasma display panels (PDPs). Indeed, LCDs now enjoy technological advantages over other FPDs.

The LCD industry in East Asia began in Japan followed by Korean and Taiwan companies. Chinese firms joined this market in the mid 2000s. There has been fierce competition among these countries. Now, it seems that Korea ranks first and Taiwan ranks second. Japan appears to have lost much of its previous market power in the region. However, Japan still has a very strong advantage with regard to LCD manufacturing equipment and materials and China has focused on final products, such as TV sets.

In the context of such strong competition, these four countries have specialized, according to their own comparative advantages and, thus, an international division of labor has occurred. Japan supplies manufacturing equipment and materials, Korea and Taiwan have specialized in intermediary goods, like display panels, and China has focused on producing final goods by putting together other parts, components, and materials with cheaper labor. In some cases, the specialization was possible because of support by the various governments. However, basically, the structure ensues from the principle of comparative advantage.

LCD products are sufficiently important to deserve academic attention and, while East Asian countries have a vital role in the flat panel display market, relatively little research has focused on this industry from a social science point of view. In particular, it is difficult to find any good empirical research using hard data, partly because it is very demanding to manage the data in this area.

This study explores the development of the LCD industry in the region and analyzes the structure of the international division of labor and international cooperation. We also calculate indicators to assess the competitiveness of the countries involved. Then we try to find which model is better to explain the industry in the region.

2. Theories Explaining the Dynamics of Industrial Development among East Asian Countries

In East Asian countries, there was investment- and export-led industrialization from 1960's to 1990's. Most manufacturing industries started in Japan and moved to other countries as the international competitiveness changes. At the early stage, they went to first-tier NIES including Korea, Hong Kong, Taiwan, and Singapore, then to the second-tier countries like China and ASEAN countries. Some scholars called this situation 'Flying geese model'. Japan flies in the front and the other countries flies following the leader. This phenomenon can be shown among the industries in a particular country as in (a), or among the countries in a specific industry as in (b) of the Figure 13-1.

However, since the latter half of the 1990's, the situation changed a lot and we needed a new model to explain the new tendency. After the Plaza Accord of 1985, Japanese firms invested a lot into the South East Asian countries

Figure 13-1.   "Multi-sequential" flying geese paradigm: A graphic presentation

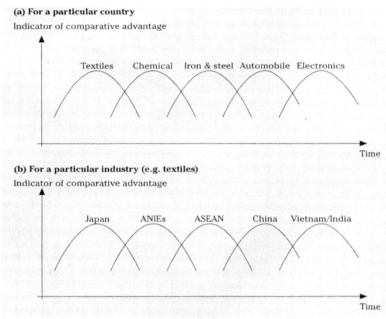

Source: Shigehisa (2004)

according to the international division of labor. Taiwan and Korea developed their own technologies and this made the competition in the region more severe. As a result, the new allocation of production location emerged and international trade of the material and components increased a lot.

A new theory, bamboo capitalism model (Roland-Holst, 2003), has showed up at this time. This model says that individual countries produce a specific part in the industry while they form the international division of labor at the same time. It looks like the bamboo joints. This model seems to explain quite well the situation of industries in the region.

On the other hand, China's role has increased a lot since the late 1990's. As an economy grows and new technologies are developed, it seems natural that the industry can get the benefits from economies of agglomeration and many firms form industrial clusters. But when the economy gets into maturation stage, there could be diseconomies of agglomeration and the firms need a new market to get into. In many cases, the firms look abroad for new market. If firms invested a lot into foreign countries, it is probable that another agglomeration can be emerging in those foreign countries. In East Asia, China was the typical area for new investment and of the agglomeration (Widodo, 2008).

A new model, named the Water Lily model, came out at this stage. This model looks at the water lily leaves coming out one by one from the water, first in the area near to the stalk and then moving outwards, and floating at the same time. In the actual world, the clusters emerged in Japan first, then in Korea and Taiwan, and finally in China. For example, the Pearl River Delta, Yangtze River Delta, and Binhai New Area are in China. The clusters seem to expand to the other areas like the Malay Peninsula, Mekong River Area, and East India Area.[1]

In the Water lily model, the industry cluster experiences the processes of creation, development, and maturation of a product, and then the firms are getting into foreign investment or international trade linked with stalks and leaves coming out when the first stalk gets into maturation stage and falls into the diseconomies of agglomeration. In this stage, the first stalk exports

---

[1] There might be more models for the economic development like 'catch-up model' and 'leapfrogging model' etc. But note that this study is focusing on the movement of an industry (or industries), while those models are explaining the change of technology level or income level.

the materials and components to the second comer. After some time, the second stalk will produce the materials and components and export to the late comers.

We might summarize the three models in Table 13-1.

3. Development of the LCD Industry in East Asian Countries

3.1 Brief History of the LCD Industry in East Asia

Flat panel displays (FPDs) need several key technologies; the driving core is the production of large panels using thin-film transistor liquid crystal displays (TFT-LCDs). These TFT-LCDs can support colorful videos and displays, and the range of applications in which they are used has greatly expanded. As a result, the LCD industry has grown. Japan pioneered the commercialization of the technology into a business. The industry was developed on a commercial scale by Sharp, Toshiba, and IBM (Japan) in the late 1980s. The market for large panels has grown even faster than that of FPDs as a whole, expanding at a rate of 40-50% *per year*, reaching a value of nearly US$ 44 billion in 2004. Japan's position seemed invincible because the technology gap between Japan and other countries made the entry barriers very high. Indeed, the fact that at least US$ 2 billion had to be invested to enter this industry was a serious obstacle for potential new entrants.

However, the industry has an interesting property, that of the "cyclicality" of the market, which does create opportunities for new entrants (Mathews, 2005). Market demand for LCDs has a cycle of upturn and downturn, similar to the semiconductor industry. This cycle depends on the situation of the whole IT industry and the production capacity of the suppliers. The

Table 13-1. Models for the Development in East Asia

	Flying geese model	Bamboo capitalism model	Water lily model
Relevant period	1960-mid 1990	1985 (Plaza Accord)-2001	Late 1990-present
Economic principle	Industrial life cycle -Foreign transfer of declining industry -Theory of comparative advantage	Segmentation of production -Agglomeration and globalization of the firms. -International comparative advantage	Economies of agglomeration -International integration, saving of link cost -Regional comparative advantage
Background	-Enhancement of industry structure in Japan after WWII. -Outward looking policy in NIEs	-Plaza Accord and high Yen -Investments to South East Asian countries by East Asian countries -Entry of China into world economy	-China's accession to WTO and high growth rate -FTA in the region
Economic performance	-Development of Asian countries one by one -Vertical integration with the center of Japan -Export oriented industry	-Stronger linkage with East Asian countries -Complication of vertical integration -Vertical division of labor -Increase in the trade of materials and components inside the region -Increasing materials and components in the region	-Agglomeration in the wider area -Growth in the region and increase in international trade and investment -Very active in the economy of the region

Source: Park (2005)

business cycle in Lcds has been called the "crystal cycle". Figure 13-2 shows this crystal cycle.

The crystal cycle occurs for the following reasons. In times of recession, the price of panels declines, which boosts new demand, in turn, resulting in excess demand and a price surge. Then, suppliers expand their capacity for production. As a result, ultimately, there is excess supply and prices decline again, which, in turn, leads to increased demand and prices rise again. This cyclicality can provide opportunities for new entrants. When the market shrinks, companies producing manufacturing equipment are willing to offer good deals to overcome the situation. This is good news for potential new entrants, who want to buy manufacturing technology and other resources at low cost.

The first downturn in the LCD industry happened in the period 1993-1994. Japanese companies, such as Matsushita and Hitachi, entered the industry. The second downturn in 1995-1996 provided an entrance to Korean companies, such as Samsung Electronics, LG Electronics, and Hyundai Electronics, which had been preparing to get into the market by developing technologies since the end of the 1980s. They had wanted to rely on their own technologies, independent of Japanese companies. For example, Korean producers of laptops were exporting laptop computers to foreign countries at the time but the production and exports were largely dependent on Japanese firms who controlled the supply of LCD monitors to Korea. The Korean firms recognized the importance of LCD technology for their independence from Japan. However, no Japanese company was likely to transfer the technology to Korean firms. Indeed, Korean firms had to develop their own technology. Their efforts were successful and became the base of the Korean LCD industry.

Figure 13-2. Crystal cycle and new entrants in the LCD industry

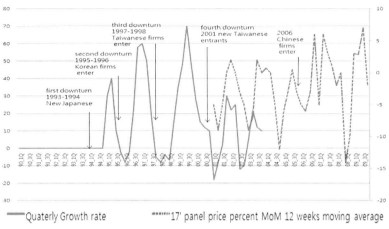

Source: Mathews (2005) and Lee (2010)

Of course, such development was not possible without difficulty. Korean firms have been developed by trial and error and reverse engineering. Some Japanese scholars have insisted that Korean companies obtained core technologies from retired Japanese engineers during the first downturn (Nakata, 2007). It is also possible that Korean companies did obtain some transfer of technologies from Japanese equipment companies. However, it seems likely that Korean firms' experience in the semiconductor industry played a key role in developing LCD technology, because many of the production procedures for LCDs are similar to those of semiconductors.

Though Korean firms did enter the LCD market with independently developed technology, it was not easy to penetrate the market that was already dominated by Japanese incumbents. Indeed, the Korean firms' market share was much smaller than that of Japanese firms' in the beginning, as shown in Figure 13-3, but the gap narrowed very rapidly.

Figure 13-3. Market share by countries in large sized LCD panel (volume base)

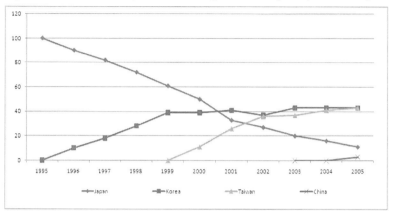

Source: Shintaku (2008)

The upswing that started in 1996 was quickly reversed by the Asian financial crisis in 1997, which was followed by another downturn. A new player, Taiwan, joined the market at that time. As one of the major producers of semiconductors and laptop computers, Taiwan was a big purchaser of display products, and it had tried to enter the market several times in vain because of the high entry barriers mentioned above. The Taiwanese government had designated the display industry as a major strategic industry and made sustained efforts to establish the business of large-panel TFT-LCDs. One of the biggest national research institutes, the Industrial Technology Research Institute (ITRI), was at the center of this policy, but it was unable to access the very latest technology.

At that moment, Japanese companies were willing to transfer their technology by licensing. What caused the Japanese companies to license their technologies to Taiwan?

First, Japan was worried about the challenge from Korea. After the Asian currency crisis, because of the undervaluation of the Korean Won, Korean companies were getting a bigger share in the PC monitor market of Taiwan. Japanese firms wanted to fend off this challenge (Han, 2008).

It is also true that Japanese firms were suffering from high costs (Nakata, 2007). Considering the production costs of TFT-LCDs, Japanese firms had an advantage in materials and components, due to their high levels of technology, but they were not competitive in terms of labor or R&D costs. This situation resulted in a disadvantage of 8% versus Korea and 10% versus Taiwan in terms of total cost. As a result, when the price went down, Japanese firms with higher costs suffered greatly, and it was inevitable that Japanese firms would seek another way to reduce costs and to survive.

Although the newest technologies were not transferred to Taiwan, the transfers that did occur were very important to the development of the Taiwanese LCD industry. Combined with the technological competence in other IT industry segments, the transfers led to very rapid growth of IT in Taiwan (Han 2007; Chang, 2005).

Since 1997, the LCD market has expanded markedly, when LCDs were first used for PC monitors and the boom due to LCD TVs started. At this time, Korean and Taiwanese products were taking market share from Japanese firms and their share overtook Japan's around 2001, as shown in Figure 2.

How did the Korean and Taiwanese rivals catch up with the Japanese panel makers? One reason was differences in investment behavior among those countries. To secure competitiveness in the panel industry, it was very important to invest timely in building manufacturing facilities to produce newer-generation LCD panels. Market demand had been changing to larger and larger panels and producing larger glass substrates became crucial for competitiveness. The producers had to invest a great deal in factories, but the Japanese firms, with the exception of Sharp, were too cautious in deciding whether to invest, especially compared to Korean and Taiwanese companies (Nakata, 2007). In fact, Japanese firms had bad memories with regard to this kind of investment behavior. They had invested large sums before 2000, but lost much of it because of the bursting of the IT bubble in 2001. While Japanese firms were hesitating, competing Korean and Taiwanese firms made aggressive countercyclical investments after 2001, believing that the downturn would be followed by another upswing.

Since the Japanese firms lost market share Japan has not returned to the top position in the LCD panel industry, with the exception of Sharp, which continued to invest in the area. Indeed, since then, Japanese firms have focused on specialized LCDs, such as screens for industrial goods or small LCDs of less than 10 inches.

In the decade 2000-2010, the business cycle in the LCD industry has repeated. A downturn started in 2005, giving another opportunity for China to join the industry. China has a big market for electronics using LCD panels, which could make China a major participant at some point. At first, China focused on the production of earlier generation LCDs and LCD module assembly. Then, the Chinese government decided that the LCD industry was a national strategic industry and substantially supported it. China wanted cooperation with Taiwan for technology transfer, but Taiwan was concerned about technology outflow. The two sides signed an Economic Cooperation Framework Agreement (ECFA) recently (2010) and are expected to cooperate more fully. China has a desire to be a major player in the LCD industry by using its big national market, and it is making efforts to obtain the High-level technologies of sixth- to eighth-generation Lcds.

3.2 International Division of Labor in LCDs of East Asia

As shown above, Korea, Japan, China, and Taiwan are the major players in the world LCD market. In particular, Korea and Taiwan are leaders in panel production. Figure 13-4 shows market share by panel manufacturing companies, where more than 90% of panels are produced by Korean companies, (Samsung, LG Display), Taiwanese companies (CMI*, AUO), and the Japanese company, Sharp (Nam et al., 2010).

Korean firms primarily produce large panels and Taiwanese firms have focused on mid- and small- size panels. China seems to be a little behind these countries in that it is *importing* panels from these countries. Indeed, the major focus in China is the assembly of LCD modules using panels imported from Korea and Taiwan. The weakness and strengths of these countries in the LCD industry are summarized in Table 13-2.

While Korean and Taiwanese firms are leading producers of LCD panels, Japan still has impregnable competitiveness in terms of producing materials, core components, and manufacturing equipment, which are all necessary to make LCD panels. Generally, it is said that the LCD industry consists of three parts: manufacturing equipment, materials and components, and panels. Korean and Taiwanese firms have relied heavily on Japanese firms for equipment and materials and components. As time goes on, the firms have tried to vertically integrate to internalize upstream sectors, but they are still dependent on Japan. For example, even though it is now true that Korean firms export testing and cleaning equipment to China and Taiwan, Korea continues to import core upstream equipment, like lithography

Figure 13-4. Market share of panel manufacturing companies (based on glass output)

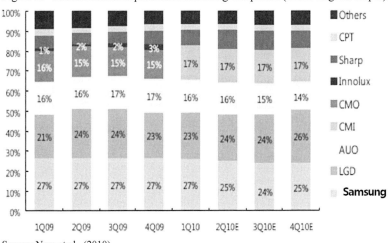

Source: Nam et al., (2010)

Table 13-2. Comparisons of Strengths and Weaknesses of Countries in the LCD industry

	Strength	Weakness
Korea	- Good mass-production capacity - Lowest manufacturing cost - Independence of technology - Vertical integration at firm level - Brand power following Japan - High yields in production	- Lack of backward industry, like PC manufacturing - Dependence of materials and components from Japan and US.
Japan	- Leadership in technology - Wide supply chain in TFT-LCD - High level technology in core parts and equipment production	- High wage costs - No big investment - Lack of government support
Taiwan	- Flexibility in manufacturing - Large demand from backward industry (PCs, etc.) - Low cost of parts through vertical integration - OEMs for laptop and desktop PC monitors	- Dependence on Japanese technology - Imports of core parts and components from Japan - Dependence of manufacturing equipment - Low brand power
China	- Support from the government - Large demand from the home market - Low labor costs	- Relatively low-level technology - Joined the market only after the profit rate became lower

equipment, from Japan. Regarding advanced generation equipment, the technology level of Korean firms has been evaluated as at only 20% of the Japanese level (Joo, 2008).

We can summarize the international division of labor as follows: Korea and Taiwan take most of the large-size panel market, but they rely on Japanese firms for the manufacturing equipment and materials. They are exporting some panels to China, where branches or Chinese firms assemble those parts and components to make final goods. Intermediary goods and capital goods are produced in Korea and Japan. In general, Japan and Korea produce capital-intensive goods and China produces labor-intensive goods (Shintaku, 2008).

4. Trade Structure of the LCD Industry in East Asia

4.1 Concepts and Classification of LCD Industry

LCD displays use two sheets of polarizing material with a liquid crystal solution between them. An electric current passed through the liquid causes the crystals to align so that light cannot pass through them. Each crystal, therefore, is like a shutter, either allowing light to pass or blocking the light. The LCD industry consists essentially of three main parts: the LCD panels, materials and components, and LCD manufacturing equipment. Although it is not easy to decide which items of industry classification should be included, Table 13-3 shows a harmonized system (HS) classification of the industry. Details of the industry are from the National IT Industry Promotion Agency of Korea (http://www.nipa.kr). The classification for LCD equipment is from www.kita.net.

Table 13-3. HS Classification of LCD Industry

LCD panel	853120, 854390, 901380
LCD materials and components	853939, 853940, 853990, 900120, 900190, 901390
LCD equipment	848630, 848690

Table 13-4. Overall Trade Structure

			Export			Import			Trade Surplus		
		Partner	2007	2008	2009	2007	2008	2009	2007	2008	2009
Panels	KOREA	WORLD	168.9	186.2	238.0	28.4	34.7	35.2	140.4	151.5	202.9
		TAIWAN	3.7	0.6	0.6	1.5	1.2	0.8	2.3	-0.6	-0.2
		JAPAN	18.5	10.5	7.2	2.0	2.2	2.9	16.6	8.3	4.3
		CHINA	58.8	70.8	129.6	22.2	28.0	28.8	36.7	42.8	100.8
	JAPAN	WORLD	33.1	38.4	42.1	26.4	19.0	12.4	6.7	19.4	29.7
		TAIWAN	1.6	1.4	1.2	2.0	3.8	1.0	-0.5	-2.5	0.3
		CHINA	15.9	18.4	18.7	6.1	5.2	4.9	9.9	13.2	13.8
	TAIWAN	WORLD	154.3	131.1	114.2	23.0	19.1	14.2	131.3	112.0	99.9
		CHINA	65.1	61.5	70.2	10.8	12.7	9.5	54.2	48.8	60.7
	CHINA	WORLD	210.3	239.5	206.8	425.5	458.0	358.3	-215.2	-218.5	-151.5
Materials and components	KOREA	WORLD	49.9	74.1	30.4	23.7	21.3	19.9	26.2	52.8	10.6
		TAIWAN	2.7	4.0	3.1	1.0	0.8	0.7	1.7	3.2	2.4
		JAPAN	0.8	1.2	1.1	14.6	14.8	14.0	-13.8	-13.6	-12.9
		CHINA	38.4	53.2	20.4	3.6	2.7	2.0	34.9	50.5	18.4
	JAPAN	WORLD	66.2	69.4	52.8	13.5	14.6	10.4	52.6	54.9	42.5
		TAIWAN	14.2	12.3	8.3	0.7	1.2	0.4	13.5	11.1	7.9
		CHINA	19.2	21.8	17.3	3.6	3.8	2.7	15.6	18.0	14.6
	TAIWAN	WORLD	102.8	128.3	71.3	24.7	23.9	18.3	78.1	104.4	53.0
		CHINA	84.6	116.4	59.3	5.4	5.6	5.8	79.2	110.8	53.5
	CHINA	WORLD	24.1	26.2	25.6	90.3	103.3	96.0	-66.2	-77.1	-70.4
Equipment	KOREA	WORLD	5.1	7.4	5.4	15.7	29.8	13.3	-10.6	-22.4	-7.9
		TAIWAN	1.1	2.0	1.1	0.1	0.5	0.2	1.0	1.5	0.8
		JAPAN	0.7	0.9	0.6	9.6	21.8	9.0	-9.0	-20.9	-8.4
		CHINA	1.4	2.8	2.6	0.1	0.2	0.1	1.3	2.6	2.6
	JAPAN	WORLD	33.8	72.8	37.3	6.6	8.0	5.4	27.2	64.8	31.9
		TAIWAN	10.3	28.9	12.4	0.2	0.3	0.5	10.1	28.6	12.0
		CHINA	3.1	8.2	5.2	0.4	0.6	0.3	2.7	7.6	4.9
	TAIWAN	WORLD	1.4	2.0	1.5	11.5	31.1	13.6	-10.2	-29.1	-12.2
		CHINA	1.1	1.2	0.7	0.1	0.2	0.1	0.9	1.0	0.6
	CHINA	WORLD	1.6	2.1	1.6	11.6	17.5	14.5	-10.0	-15.5	-12.9

4.2 Trade Structure in the Data

Some numbers regarding the international trade in display panels are shown in Table 13-4. As for Korea, panel industry is the main exporting industry, of which main partner is China, while Korean exports in MC (materials and components) and ME (manufacturing equipment) are not so much. In particular, Korea shows trade deficit in ME. Japan is not large country in relation to the panel industry, while it is clear that Japan has a trade surplus with all the other countries in ME. For Taiwan, the panel industry and MC is its main exporting industry, while ME is not that significant in Taiwan exports. The three countries export materials and components to China.

In contrast to the general idea that China is not competitive in this industry, China exports more panels than Korea and the other East Asian countries. However, China's imports are almost double of its exports and China has

Figure 13-5. International division of labor in the LCD industry

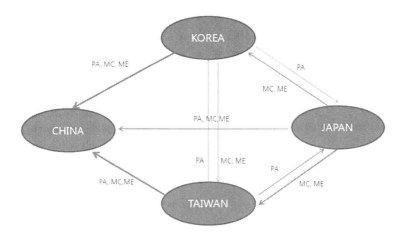

the biggest trade deficit in the panel industry in East Asia. Further, most of China's exports are *not* to the East Asian countries, but to other areas of the world.

From the summary of numbers above, we show the division of labor in Figure 13-5. This is a modification of Shintaku (2008), with more elaboration, and is supported by data. PC-TAS data from UNCTAD were used in terms of the HS six digits. The directions of the arrows indicate the trade surplus and the thickness shows the size of the surplus. This figure shows the structure of the international trade and the division of labor. Korea exports panels to Japan, China, and Taiwan, while Korea imports materials and components, and manufacturing equipment from Japan. China is the big importer of LCDs in the region. We suggest other figures in the appendix in order to focus on the exports part in detail. Those figures show exports to rest of the world, too.

5. International Competitiveness in LCD Industry

5.1 TSI, RCA, RCP

Next, we use a popular indicator, the trade specification index (TSI), to assess the competitiveness and division of labor in the LCD industry of East Asian countries. Trade specification index (TSI) is defined as follows.

$$TSI = \frac{X - M}{X + M}$$

Figure 13-6. TSI's in all LCD industries

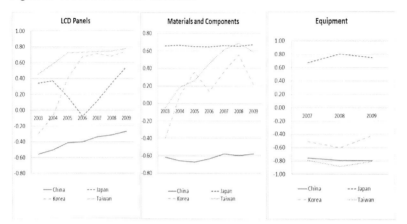

Here X is export of a specific LCD industry and M stands for import. The TSI lies between -1 and 1; if this number is close to 1, the country is very competitive in this industry. If it is close to -1, the country has a negative disadvantage.

The TSI of each country, in relation to trade with the rest of the world and other East Asian countries, is shown in Figure 13-6 (See the Appendix for more details). Japan has very strong comparative advantage in ME and China has no advantage in any industries.

In panel industry (PA), Korea and Taiwan have large scores of TSI, indicating that these two countries are strongly competitive in display panels. Japan has a positive number too. China has negative numbers, although China's exports are very large. In particular, Taiwan's TSI is the largest, showing the strong competitiveness of Taiwanese LCD firms. When looking at the details, all three countries have trade surpluses with China in the panel industry. Note that Korea, while it is known to be a strong player in the panel industry, has a negative number in trading with Taiwan.

In the industry of LCD materials and components (MC), the results were similar. Three countries other than China have positive and large TSI numbers. Interestingly, Japan's TSI is large but stable, between 0.6 and 0.7, while those of Korea and Taiwan have increased sharply. This may suggest that the technology level in these two countries is increasing and that the gap between them and Japan is narrowing.

In LCD manufacturing equipment (ME), Japan has the strongest position and other three countries still seem to be far from a competitive position even though Korea is a little higher than the other two.

Now we calculate another index RCA (revealed comparative advantage). This indicator is calculated by the following formula and might shows relative advantage among the industries. (Here X denotes exports, i is industry, and j is country.)

$$RCA = \frac{X_{ij}/X_i}{X_j/X}$$

From Figure 13-7, we notice that Korea and China have comparative advantage in panel. It is a surprise that China's RCA is shown to be larger than Korea's since we know Korea is number one country in the panel industry. This might be possible because Korea's export in whole LCD industry is very large, thus ratio of panel export can be relatively small. It is interesting that RCA has been decreasing in Taiwan and Japan. Japan and

Figure 13-7. RCA's in all LCD industries

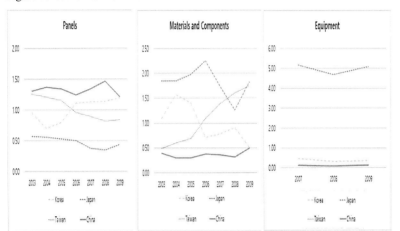

Taiwan are getting more comparative advantage in MC industry, while Japan is focusing on ME. This is similar to what we found by using TSI.

TSI and RCA are two popular indicators for the international comparative advantages. It is worth that we see another index for checking international competitiveness, RCP (Relative Competitive Position) which is a modification of TSI and defined as a ratio of trade surplus to size of international market.

$$RCP = \frac{X - M}{WT}$$

Here, WT is the size of world trade in a specific industry. Figure 13-8 shows that Korea's RCP is highest among three countries. In MC industry, China is the only country showing negative value and in ME industry Japan has positive number alone which shows Japan's competitiveness in the industry. These are very similar to the results above.

Figure 13-8. RCP's in all LCD industries

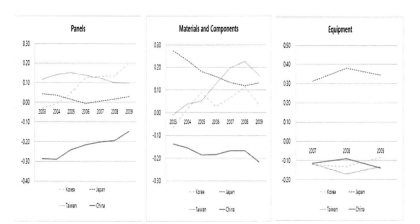

Here, we suggest two other indices which might show the trade structure of LCD industry of East Asian countries. First, we use export ESI (export similarity index) which shows the degree of similarity of the exports items between two countries. Here, i denotes industry, j, k denote country. If this number is big, that means two countries are exporting similar items to other countries.

$$ESI = \sum_{i=1} MIN(X_{ji}/X_j, X_{ki}/X_k)$$

We are going to use another index for showing export concentration. How a countries export is focused on a specific item? There are many indices we can use for this but we use a very popular one; Herfindahl-Hirschman (H-H) Index.

Figure 13-9. Exports similarity and export concentration

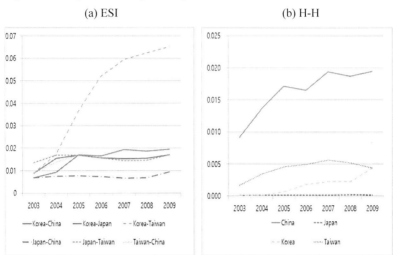

(a) ESI   (b) H-H

5.2 Export Similarity and Export Concentration

Figure 13-9-(a) shows that Korea and Taiwan are exporting very similar items recently. Note that we classify LCD industry only into three sub industries here. If we classify the LCD industry into more small items, we might have different results.

Next, we calculate export concentration index by using H-H index which is defined by

$$H = \sum_{i=1}^{m} S_i^2.$$

Generally speaking, it is desirable to have lower level of this index. We might see the concentration is very high in China, while Japan does not depend its export on a single subindustry.

5.3 Emergence of LCD Clusters in East Asia

So far, the analysis based on the trade data confirmed us the concrete structure of international division of labor in LCD industry of east Asian countries. Note, however, that this structure of international division of labor is not the permanent feature. A new trend has emerged. Some LCD clusters has been formed around the leading panel companies in each countries. To attain local linkage effects and reduce logistic costs and transaction costs, the manufacturing equipment companies and the material and components companies tend to move closer to the panel companies, and they hope to form an LCD cluster.

Each cluster will try to have eventually self-contained features, though some equipment and material will still depend on the foreign upstream sources. Such clusters have already existed in Korea, Japan and Taiwan. Recently, more clusters seem to be added in the near future in China, as the investment for the LCD industry of China expands. The situation seems to approach to the landscape which the water lily model depicts in section II, which might imply that water lily model would get more validity in describing the development of LCD industry in east Asian countries in the future. Figure 13-10 shows the LCD clusters in this area.

6. Conclusions

This study investigates the development of the liquid crystal display (LCD) industry in East Asia and looks for a good model to explain the development of LCD industry in the region. There are a couple of frameworks to describe the economic development in East Asian countries: the Flying geese model, Bamboo capitalism, and the Water lily model. This study provides a brief explanation of those three models and explores the LCD industry and its

Figure 13-10. LCD clusters in East Asian countries

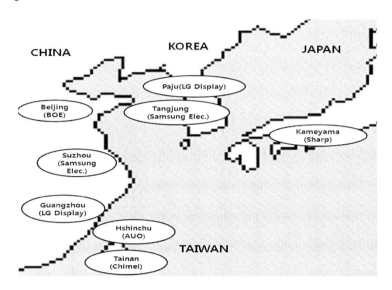

trade structure in East Asian countries (Korea, Japan, China, Taiwan). Trade
data for the LCD industry in East Asian countries were used to show how
the industry operated. In particular, we sought to analyze the international
trade structure and international division of labor using hard data. Basically,
using PC-TAS data from UNCTAD and data from some Korean institutions,
this study indicates the direction and the size of exports, imports, and trade
surpluses among the region.

As is well-known, Korea exports panels to Japan, China, and Taiwan while
Korea imports materials and components and manufacturing equipment
from Japan. However, in contrast to previous research, this study shows that
Korea exports manufacturing equipment to Taiwan and imports panels from
Taiwan. In the panel industry, Korea and Taiwan are the two big players.
However, these two countries rely on Japan for manufacturing equipment

and core materials and components. This indicates that Japan is still very competitive in the industry.

We find that Japan has a comparative advantage in the manufacturing equipment and materials and components while Korea and Taiwan have a comparative advantage in LCD panels and China has LCD modules and final product. This result might indicate that Bamboo capitalism model is better than the Flying geese model in explaining the LCD industry in East Asia.

Note, however, that this structure of international division of labor is not the permanent feature. In the future, the increasing role of China in the LCD industry and the responses of other countries will determine the shape of international division of labor. At present, China is the big importer and the big exporter of LCD in this region. Although China exports many panels and other products, this study shows that China has a long way to go in the sense that China is importing large panels from Korea, materials and components from Japan, and some components from Taiwan and Japan. However, it seems that China will become a major player in the future with the support of a huge domestic market and the Chinese government. China is following the track that Korea and Taiwan took in the past. However, nobody can be sure that Korea and Taiwan can take the position enjoyed by Japan now. This depends on whether these two countries can develop high-end technologies in materials and components, and in manufacturing equipment. Whether and when they shift toward advanced FPD technologies, such as AM-OLED and e-paper, will be critical factors in this regard. Recently, Chinese government gave allowed two leading Korean companies, Samsung Electronics Co. and LG Display, to build the manufacturing factories in China. Samsung and LG are going to build the state of art technology factories in Suzhou and Guangzhou, respectively. Then, LCD clusters with the firms producing components seem to emerge in these two areas. Therefore, there will be many LCD clusters in addition to the following existing clusters; Hanshin area cluster with Sharp factory in Kameyama and in Sakai of Japan, LG factory and Samsung factory in Kyeong-Ki area of Korea, Hsinchu Science Park and Tainan Cluster of Taiwan. Now, it seems reasonable to conclude that the LCD industry in the East Asian area is in between Bamboo capitalism and the Water lily model. The industry structure is moving from one to the other.

Appendix

Figure 13-A-1. Flow of the products in LCD industry

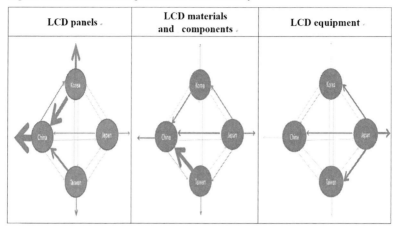

LCD panels	LCD materials and components	LCD equipment

Note: The size of arrows shows the amount of international flows.

Table 13-A-1. TSI in LCD industry

TSI		partner	2003	2004	2005	2006	2007	2008	2009
panels	KOREA	WORLD	-0.30	-0.08	0.40	0.68	0.71	0.69	0.74
		TAIWAN	-0.36	-0.51	-0.07	0.24	0.44	-0.32	-0.17
		JAPAN	-0.58	-0.69	0.47	0.83	0.81	0.66	0.43
		CHINA	-0.43	-0.07	-0.03	0.31	0.45	0.43	0.64
	JAPAN	WORLD	0.34	0.37	0.17	-0.07	0.11	0.34	0.55
		TAIWAN	0.36	0.04	0.33	0.15	-0.13	-0.47	0.11
		CHINA	0.28	0.28	0.28	0.33	0.45	0.56	0.58
	TAIWAN	WORLD	0.45	0.58	0.72	0.73	0.74	0.75	0.78
		CHINA	0.78	0.69	0.76	0.73	0.71	0.66	0.76
	CHINA	WORLD	-0.56	-0.51	-0.41	-0.40	-0.34	-0.31	-0.27
materials and components	KOREA	WORLD	-0.40	0.09	0.36	0.14	0.36	0.55	0.21
		TAIWAN	-0.13	0.09	0.35	0.25	0.47	0.68	0.62
		JAPAN	-0.90	-0.83	-0.86	-0.91	-0.90	-0.85	-0.85
		CHINA	0.80	0.93	0.94	0.84	0.83	0.90	0.82
	JAPAN	WORLD	0.66	0.67	0.65	0.65	0.66	0.65	0.67
		TAIWAN	0.92	0.91	0.83	0.83	0.90	0.82	0.90
		CHINA	0.58	0.56	0.67	0.64	0.69	0.71	0.73
	TAIWAN	WORLD	-0.05	0.18	0.26	0.45	0.61	0.69	0.59
		CHINA	0.92	0.90	0.76	0.77	0.88	0.91	0.82
	CHINA	WORLD	-0.62	-0.66	-0.67	-0.63	-0.58	-0.60	-0.58
equipment	KOREA	WORLD					-0.51	-0.60	-0.42
		TAIWAN					0.87	0.59	0.63
		JAPAN					-0.87	-0.92	-0.88
		CHINA					0.89	0.88	0.94
	JAPAN	WORLD					0.67	0.80	0.75
		TAIWAN					0.96	0.98	0.93
		CHINA					0.76	0.86	0.89
	TAIWAN	WORLD					-0.79	-0.88	-0.81
		CHINA					0.79	0.74	0.73
	CHINA	WORLD					-0.76	-0.79	-0.80

Table 13-A-2. RCA in LCD Industry

	Countries	2003	2004	2005	2006	2007	2008	2009
Panels	KOREA	0.95	0.70	0.80	1.11	1.13	1.14	1.20
	JAPAN	0.57	0.55	0.53	0.50	0.37	0.35	0.44
	TAIWAN	1.26	1.21	1.15	0.96	0.90	0.82	0.84
	CHINA	1.31	1.37	1.34	1.25	1.34	1.47	1.22
Materials and components	KOREA	1.09	1.57	1.41	0.71	0.78	0.91	0.51
	JAPAN	1.84	1.84	1.97	2.25	1.74	1.26	1.83
	TAIWAN	0.49	0.60	0.69	1.10	1.39	1.61	1.75
	CHINA	0.39	0.30	0.30	0.38	0.36	0.32	0.50
Equipment	KOREA					0.46	0.32	0.36
	JAPAN					5.17	4.68	5.09
	TAIWAN					0.11	0.09	0.14
	CHINA					0.14	0.09	0.13

Table 13-A-3. RCP in LCD Industry

	Countries	2003	2004	2005	2006	2007	2008	2009
Panels	KOREA	-0.03	-0.01	0.05	0.12	0.13	0.13	0.20
	JAPAN	0.04	0.04	0.02	-0.01	0.01	0.02	0.03
	TAIWAN	0.12	0.14	0.15	0.14	0.12	0.10	0.10
	CHINA	-0.29	-0.29	-0.24	-0.22	-0.20	-0.19	-0.15
Materials and components	KOREA	-0.07	0.02	0.09	0.03	0.07	0.11	0.03
	JAPAN	0.27	0.23	0.18	0.16	0.13	0.12	0.13
	TAIWAN	-0.01	0.04	0.05	0.13	0.20	0.23	0.16
	CHINA	-0.14	-0.16	-0.19	-0.18	-0.17	-0.17	-0.22
Equipment	KOREA					-0.12	-0.13	-0.08
	JAPAN					0.31	0.38	0.34
	TAIWAN					-0.12	-0.17	-0.13
	CHINA					-0.11	-0.09	-0.14

PART IV

INTERNATIONAL TRADE AND TECHNOLOGY

CHAPTER 14

R&D, TRADE, AND PRODUCTIVITY GROWTH IN KOREAN MANUFACTURING

1. Introduction

Korea's rapid economic growth since the early 1960s can be attributed to the expansion of capital investment and international trade. Increases in physical and human capital investments directly expand output, while trade contributes to growth indirectly. Developing countries like Korea can absorb new technologies developed in advanced countries through trade. Therefore, trade can be considered one of the main drivers of productivity growth, especially for Korea, where trade has grown rapidly.

Numerous studies have examined the relationship between trade and economic growth. Edwards (1998) showed that openness leads to productivity, while Coe and Helpman (1995), Coe et al. (1997), and Keller (2002) demonstrated that international trade plays an important role as a channel for transmitting research and development (R&D) spillovers. Engelbrecht (1997) and Lichtenberg and van Pottelsberghe de la Potterie (1998) are extensions of Coe and Helpman (1995). Braconier et al. (2001) conducted a case study of Swedish firms, focusing on FDI-related R&D spillovers. Keller (2001) provided a review of recent papers on international technology diffusion and the importance of specific channels of technology spillovers. However, few industry-level studies have examined the effects of international R&D spillovers on developing countries.

This study investigates the effects of both R&D spillovers and trade patterns on productivity in Korean manufacturing, using industry-level data. Previous studies on economic growth in Korea have focused on the role of trade policy in productivity growth. Nadiri and Kim (1996) used R&D capital as an input in production, but did not study R&D spillovers. Lee (1996), Feenstra et al. (1999), and Kim (2000) analyzed the relationship between trade policy and total factor productivity.

This study distinguishes itself from previous research in several ways. First, it uses industry-level data from Korean manufacturing to investigate both domestic and international R&D spillovers. Coe et al. (1997) examined North-South R&D spillovers using aggregate data, while Keller (2002) used industry-level data that were limited to eight industrial OECD countries. Second, the study explores the effects of trade patterns on productivity in Korean manufacturing, recognizing that productivity may differ across industries based on their different trade patterns. Third, the study breaks down foreign R&D capital into three subgroups: the United States, Japan, and the other OECD countries. It investigates which country's R&D capital has played the most critical role in Korean productivity, given that Korea has distinct trade structures with these countries, which could affect the impact of their R&D capital on Korean productivity. Finally, the study employs two productivity indexes: the Törnqvist and Malmquist indexes. While most studies use the Törnqvist productivity index, Färe et al. (1994) argued that the Malmquist index is more general than the Törnqvist index, as it allows for inefficient performance and does not presume an underlying functional form for production technology.

The results indicate that there have been both domestic and foreign R&D spillovers in Korean manufacturing. From 1976 to 1996, domestic other-industry R&D and foreign R&D were significant contributors to the productivity growth of Korean manufacturing. The effect of foreign R&D was more substantial than that of domestic R&D, and Japanese R&D had a more significant impact on Korean productivity than other foreign R&D. Generally, exports and openness played a positive role in productivity growth. However, the impact of foreign R&D capital on Korean productivity was more significant in import industries or industries with large intra-industry trade shares.

The remainder of this chapter is structured as follows. Section 2 presents the theoretical background and empirical framework. Section 3 provides a descriptive summary of the primary variables and estimates of the productivity indexes. The empirical results are discussed in Section 4, followed by concluding remarks in Section 5.

2. Theoretical Background and Empirical Specifications

In traditional growth theory, exogenous technology shock is necessary for sustainable economic growth. In new growth theory (Romer, 1986; Grossman and Helpman, 1991a, 1991b and 1991c), however, innovation is determined endogenously, and this enables sustainable long-run growth without exogenous technology shock. There are two types of endogenous growth models: the varieties growth model (Romer, 1990; Grossman and Helpman, 1991a), and the quality-ladder growth model (Grossman and Helpman, 1991c; Aghion and Howitt, 1992). Both models emphasize the role of R&D investment in technology or productivity.

Keller's (2001) survey on technology diffusion shows that domestic and international R&D spillovers are as important for productivity as a country's own R&D activity. Each industry uses intermediates invented not only by its own industry, but also by other industries. Scherer (1982), Griliches and Lichtenberg (1984), and Keller (2002) examined inter-industry domestic R&D spillovers using an inter-industry technology flow matrix. Moreover, in an open economy, domestic industry uses intermediates imported from trade partners, along with those produced by domestic industries. Thus, we can consider foreign R&D spillovers in the context of an open economy.

Based on the theoretical background, we constructed the following empirical model, which considers domestic other-industry R&D and foreign R&D spillovers.

$$lnT_{it} = \beta_0 + \beta_1 \, lnR\&D_{it}^{DS} + \beta_2 \, lnR\&D_{it}^{DO} + \beta_3 \, lnR\&D_{it}^{F} + \varepsilon_{it} \, ,$$
$$\varepsilon_{it} = \mu_i + \eta_t + \nu_{it} \qquad\qquad (14\text{-}1)$$

where the subscripts i and t indicate the industry and year, respectively; lnT_{it} is the log of the total factor productivity index; $lnR\&D^{DS}$ and $lnR\&D^{DO}$ are the logs of the domestic same- and other-industry R&D capital stocks, respectively; $lnR\&D^{F}$ is the log of the foreign R&D capital stock imported indirectly through trade; ε_{it} is an error term, which has three components; μ_i is an unobservable industry-specific factor that reflects the variation across industries; η_t is a time-specific factor varying over time; and ν_{it} denotes the remaining disturbances.[1]

The United States and Japan are Korea's most important trade partners, although Korea has different trade structures with each of these two countries. Korea imports machinery and equipment mainly from Japan, while the United States is Korea's largest market for its exports. Due to these different trade structures, the R&D stocks of the U.S. and Japan may affect

---

[1] Hereafter, ε_{it} has the same three terms.

Korean productivity differently. To examine the different effects of foreign R&D stocks, we divide the foreign R&D stocks ($lnR\&D^F$) in equation (14-1) into three subgroups: foreign R&D stocks from the United States, Japan, and the remaining OECD countries.[2] Thus, the second empirical model becomes:

$$lnT_{it} = \beta_0 + \beta_1 \, lnR\&D_{it}^{DS} + \beta_2 \, lnR\&D_{it}^{DO} + \beta_3 \, lnR\&D_{it}^{F\_USA}$$

$$+ \beta_4 \, lnR\&D_{it}^{F\_JPN} + \beta_5 \, lnR\&D_{it}^{F\_OTH} + \varepsilon_{it} \qquad (14\text{-}2)$$

where $lnR\&D_{it}^{F_{USA}}$, $lnR\&D_{it}^{F\_JPN}$, $lnR\&D_{it}^{F\_OTH}$ are the logs of the foreign R&D stocks from the United States, Japan, and the rest of the OECD countries, respectively.

We also consider trade-related variables in order to explain the determinants of productivity. Kim and Kim (1997), and Lawrence and Weinstein (1999), showed that export industries have higher productivity than net import industries. This may be because export industries are relatively more competitive in the world market than import industries. Exporters acquire knowledge of new production methods and product designs from their international contacts, and this learning may result in higher productivity relative to their more insulated domestic counterparts, especially in developing countries (Aw et al., 1998). Thus, we can expect a net exporter to have greater productivity than a net importer. Secondly, Grossman and Helpman (1991b) have argued that countries that are more open to the world market have a greater opportunity to absorb or imitate the advanced

---

[2] 14 OECD countries are as follows: Australia, Canada, Denmark, Finland, France, Germany, Italy, Japan, the Netherlands, Norway, Spain, Sweden, the United Kingdom, and the United States.

technology generated in advanced countries. According to this argument, opening the domestic market will be positively correlated with domestic productivity growth.[3] Thus, we estimate the following equation:

$$lnT_{it} = \beta_0 + \beta_1 lnR\&D_{it}^{DS} + \beta_2 lnR\&D_{it}^{DO} + \beta_3 lnR\&D_{it}^{F}$$

$$+ \beta_4 lnIMP_{it} + \beta_5 lnOPEN_{it} + \varepsilon_{it} \qquad (14\text{-}3)$$

where $lnIMP_i$ is the log of the share of imports in the production of industry i, and a higher import share implies an import industry;[4] and $OPEN_i$ is the trade share in the production of industry i, and a higher trade share implies a more open industry.[5] The estimates β_4 and β_5 are expected to be negative and positive, respectively.

We expect interactions between the foreign R&D stock and import shares, as well as intra-industry trade. Coe and Helpman (1995) showed that technology spillovers are larger in countries with a higher import share, because imports of foreign technology are proportional to imports of intermediate goods. In other words, since an industry with relatively greater import share imports more foreign R&D indirectly through trade, the interaction term between import share and foreign R&D stock may be positively associated with domestic productivity.

---

[3] For empirical cross-country studies on openness and productivity growth, see Dollar (1992) and Edwards (1998).

[4] Another index for defining net exporter or net importer is the net export index. The correlation between the net export index and the variable *IMP,* used here, is very high.   To examine the effect of interaction between import share and foreign R&D stocks, we used the import share variable as the net importer index.

[5] We can define market openness in several ways, including the presence of a price protection policy or quota protection, as in Kim (2000), although these data are not available for each industry or for the entire period of analysis covered in this study.

Hakura and Jaumotte (1999) argued that technology spillovers in intra-industry trade (IIT) with industrial countries have more of an effect, relative to inter-industry trade, because industries are more likely to absorb foreign technologies when they import products that are similar to items they produce and export themselves.

Therefore, we will investigate the following model to examine the above arguments:

$$\ln T_{it} = \beta_0 + \beta_1 \ln R\&D_{it}^{DS} + \beta_2 \ln R\&D_{it}^{DO} + \beta_4 \ln IMP_{it} + \beta_5 \ln OPEN_{it}$$

$$+ \beta_6 \ln IMP * \ln R\&D_{it}^{F} + \beta_7 IIT * \ln R\&D_{it}^{F} + \varepsilon_{it} \qquad (14\text{-}4)$$

where *IIT* is a dummy variable which has 1 for an industry classified as involved in intra-industry trade and 0 otherwise. Both β_6 and β_7 are expected to be positive.

3. Descriptive Summary of the Data

3.1 R&D and Trade

The data sources and the construction of variables are explained in detail in Appendix 14-B. Here, we summarize some features of the data. Table 14-1 compares the real R&D investment per worker for Korean, U.S., and Japanese manufacturing. Korean R&D investment per worker is smaller than those of the U.S. and Japan. However, Korea's R&D investments have increased more rapidly than those of the U.S. and Japan over the period 1976-1996. For the period 1976-1980, the relative ratios of Korean R&D investment per worker to those of the U.S. and Japan were 0.05 and 0.14, respectively. The relative ratios, however, increased consistently, and had risen to 0.51 and 0.90, respectively, by the period 1991-96.

Table 14-1. Comparison of Real R&D Investment per Worker: US $ of 1990 PPP

Period	Average R&D investment per worker			Relative ratio	
	Korea (K)	USA (U)	Japan (J)	(K)/(U)	(K)/(J)
76-80	133	2,536	943	0.05	0.14
81-85	437	3,499	1,430	0.12	0.31
86-90	1,068	4,106	2,088	0.26	0.51
91-96	2,132	4,193	2,366	0.51	0.90
76-96	**999**	**3,613**	**1,738**	**0.28**	**0.57**

Source: See Appendix 14-B.

Note: The figures show the annual average of the real R&D investment per worker in each period.

The construction of the foreign R&D capital stocks follows both Coe and Helpman (1995, hereafter referred to as CH) and Lichtenberg and van Pottelsberghe de la Potterie (1998, hereafter referred to as LP). In the CH method, the foreign R&D capital stock is defined as the import-share-weighted average of the domestic R&D capital stocks of trade partners. However, Lichtenberg and van Pottelsberghe de la Potterie (1998) propose an alternative measure of foreign R&D stock that is much less sensitive to the level of data aggregation imposed in the CH method. The details of calculating Korea's imported foreign R&D capital stocks are explained in Appendix 14-B.

Table 14-2 shows relative shares and average growth rates of Korean R&D stock and imported foreign R&D stock by industry. In 1986, most Korean domestic R&D is in fabricated metal products (60.5%), and chemical products (18.0%); the total share of these two sectors is 78.5%.[6] These two sectors' share for the imported foreign R&D stock is also very high (90.7% in the CH method, and 94.3% in the LP method). In summary, Korea's domestic R&D and imported foreign R&D are both centered on heavy

---

[6] These compositions are very close to those in 14 OECD countries.

Table 14-2. Comparison of the Domestic and Foreign R&D Stocks

Industry	Korea's R&D stock		Imported foreign R&D stock into Korea				Ratio of imported foreign R&D to Korea's R&D	
			CH method		LP method		CH	LP
	Relative share (A) [a]	Growth rate [a]	Relative share (B)	Growth rate	Relative share (C)	Growth rate	(B/A) [b]	(C/A) [b]
	(1986)	(1976-96)	(1986)	(1976-96)	-1986	(1976-96)	(1986)	(1986)
01	5.5	18.2	2.0	4.8	0.6	10.5	22.7	0.08
02	6.6	9.4	0.5	-0.8	0.6	3.7	4.9	0.07
03	0.7	-2.2	0.4	1.2	0.0	19	30.4	0.03
04	1.1	24.3	1.3	3.4	0.4	8.7	69.5	0.23
05	18.0	19.7	15.9	5.0	25.7	9.5	55.1	0.99
06	2.9	11.6	1.3	5.0	0.8	15.5	29.0	0.2
07	3.5	23.2	3.0	2.5	2.8	9.4	53.3	0.56
08	60.5	23.3	74.8	5.2	68.6	12.1	77.0	0.79
09	1.2	13.6	0.8	4.6	0.4	13.1	41.5	0.22
Lgt	18.1	11.7	6.3	3.8	2.9	9.7	21.8	0.11
Hvy	81.9	22.5	93.7	5.1	97.1	11.5	71.2	0.82
All	**100**	**20**	**100**	**5**	**100**	**11.4**	**62.2**	**0.7**

Source: See Appendix 14-B.

Notes: 1) Lgt is light industry (01-04, 06, 09); Hvy is heavy industry (05, 07, 08); and All is total manufacturing. Industry categories, 01-09, are detailed in Appendix 14-A. [a] Relative shares are percentage and growth rates are annual average growth rates over 1976-96 in percentage. [b] (B/A) and (C/A) are calculated by using the volume of R&D stock , which is used to compute the relative shares of each sector in columns (A), (B), and (C).

industry; the share of heavy industry is 81.9% for domestic R&D stock, and 93.7% (by the CH method) or 97.1% (by the LP method) for the imported foreign R&D stock.

Table 14-2 also shows average growth rates of Korea's domestic R&D stock and imported foreign R&D stock. The growth rate of domestic R&D stock (20.0%) is higher than that of imported foreign R&D stock (5.0% in CH method, or 11.4% in LP method) for all manufacturing. The average growth rate of domestic R&D stock is higher in heavy industry (22.5%) than in light industry (11.7%).[7] The growth rate of imported foreign R&D stock is also higher in heavy industry than in light industry. In Korea, both domestic R&D and imported foreign R&D were mostly concentrated in heavy industry.

The last two columns in Table 14-2 show the ratio of imported foreign R&D stock to Korean domestic R&D stock. Whichever method we use to calculate Korea's imported foreign R&D capital, the ratios are much higher in heavy industry than in light industry. This implies that imported foreign R&D capital is relatively more important in heavy industry than in light industry in Korean manufacturing. We can see that the ratios between the two columns are quite different. In all manufacturing, the ratio in the CH method (62.2 times) is much larger than that in the LP method (0.70 times). This is because the magnitude of imported foreign R&D stock differs markedly between the two calculation methods; the figures by the LP method, however, may be more reasonable.[8]

Table 14-3 presents the trends in trade volume and the intra-industry trade (IIT) index for Korean manufacturing with the 14 OECD countries. In 1986, the export shares of light and heavy industry were similar (47.7% in *Lgt* and 52.3% in *Hvy*), but the import share of heavy industry (84.5%) was much larger than that of light industry (15.5%). Both export and import growth were higher in heavy industry than in light industry, indicating that Korea's trade expansion was greater in heavy industry than in light industry.

---

[7] In 14 OECD countries, the growth rates of R&D stocks in the two sectors are almost the same (3.4% in light industry, and 3.6% in heavy industry).
[8] However, the trends in the two measures are similar. The correlation coefficient between foreign R&D stocks from the CH and LP methods is 0.906, and is significant at the 1% level (obs. = 189).

Table 14-3. Trends of Trade Volume and IIT Index (in percent per year)

Industry	Export		Import		IIT index	
	Relative share (1986)	Growth rate (1976-96)	Relative share (1986)	Growth rate (1976-96)	1976	1996
01	4.0	8.4	4.4	12.5	34.6	29.7
02	35.6	4.7	5.5	7.8	17.8	35.1
03	0.7	-3.7	0.4	26.2	21.8	30.4
04	0.4	10.7	2.7	13.6	25.4	35.4
05	6.4	16.5	19.2	13.8	34.9	45.3
06	1.3	8.7	1.7	19.5	43.0	41.7
07	5.1	12.5	7.9	11.7	23.2	27.0
08	40.8	18.1	57.4	16.1	31.8	58.1
09	5.8	9.2	0.9	15.1	12.7	46.4
Lgt	47.7	5.4	15.5	11.5	26.3	36.0
Hvy	52.3	17.3	84.5	15.2	31.9	47.9
All	100.0	11.9	100.0	14.5	29.3	41.6

Source: See Appendix 14-B.

Note: IIT index is arithmetic mean of Grubel and Lloyd (1975) index defined as $[1 - | X_{it} - M_{it} |/(X_{it} + M_{it})] \times 100$, where X_{it} and M_{it} are exports and imports of industry i at time t, respectively.

The last two columns in Table 14-3 are the average IIT indexes for each manufacturing sector. For all manufacturing, the average IIT index increased from 29.3 in 1976 to 41.6 in 1996. The average IIT index increased in most sectors, and increased more in heavy industry than in light industry. By 1996, the average IIT index of heavy industry had become much larger than that of light industry. This trend may reflect the fact that Korea's trade patterns have become similar to those of the OECD countries, especially in heavy industry.

3.2 Total Factor Productivity

We estimated the Törnqvist and Malmquist productivity indexes for 28 Korean manufacturing sectors over the period 1970-96, using one output and three inputs: labor, physical capital stock, and intermediates. The

Törnqvist productivity index is based on the method of Caves et al. (1982), while the Malmquist productivity index follows the method of Färe et al. (1994).[9] The computer program DEAP 2.1 (Coelli, 1996), which adopts the nonparametric linear programming technique of Färe et al. (1994), was used to estimate the Malmquist productivity index.[10]

The main differences between the Törnqvist and Malmquist productivity indexes are as follows. First, the Törnqvist productivity index presumes that production activity is always efficient, while the Malmquist index does not.[11] Second, calculation of the Malmquist index requires only quantities of inputs and outputs, while the Törnqvist index requires information on cost or income shares, and prices of inputs or outputs. Thus, the Malmquist index requires less data than the Törnqvist index. Third, the Törnqvist productivity index suggested by Caves et al. (1982) is a multilateral index that can compare TFP levels between industries and time periods, but the Malmquist productivity index is not a multilateral index.

Table 14-4 shows the average annual growth rates of output, inputs, and productivity indexes in Korean manufacturing. Over the period 1970-96, the average annual growth rate of real output in total manufacturing was 12.76%, and those of labor, capital, and intermediates were 4.92, 14.08, and 11.78%, respectively. Of the inputs, the growth rate of capital was the largest, and that of labor was the smallest. For all manufacturing for the

---

[9] Ray and Desli (1997) emphasize the importance of variable returns to scale (VRS), but Färe et al. (1997) argued that constant returns to scale captures the long-run while VRS is appropriate for the short-run.   Since our study analyzes the long-run productivity trend over 1970-96, we use the method of Färe et al. (1994).

[10] The Malmquist productivity index can be decomposed into efficiency and technical progress indexes, but in this study we focus only on the Malmquist productivity index.

[11] See pp. 58-61 in Färe et al. (1996) for details.

Table 14-4. Average Growth Rates of Output, Inputs, and TFP in Korean Manufacturing (in percent per year)

Industry	Period	Output	Worker	Capital	Inter-mediate	TFP_TQ	TFP_MQ
01		7.63	1.98	9.37	5.48	1.64	3.19
02		7.81	1.81	11.58	8.65	-0.31	0.10
03		5.10	1.81	9.59	4.90	0.05	0.57
04		11.77	4.50	13.55	11.93	0.77	0.70
05	70-96	12.83	5.06	14.85	12.48	0.53	1.59
06		11.11	3.84	14.03	9.97	1.28	1.99
07		17.48	5.26	15.57	17.11	1.19	1.15
08		20.15	8.65	19.15	19.09	2.42	2.51
09		9.23	1.08	14.76	10.11	-0.17	-0.72
Lgt	70-96	8.37	2.58	10.98	7.48	0.85	1.55
Hvy		16.83	7.22	17.00	16.06	1.49	1.92
All	70-80	16.95	8.53	15.96	15.55	1.95	3.72
	80-90	12.01	3.97	14.44	11.17	1.14	0.58
	90-96	7.01	0.49	10.36	6.50	0.46	0.95
	70-96	**12.76**	**4.92**	**14.08**	**11.78**	**1.29**	**1.87**

Source: See Appendix 14-B.

Note: TFP_TQ and TFP_MQ denote the Törnqvist and the Malmquist productivity indexes, respectively.

entire period, the average growth rate was 1.29% by the Törnqvist productivity index (*TFP_TQ*), and 1.87% by the Malmquist productivity index (*TFP_MQ*).[12]

The growth rates of TFP, as well as output and inputs, in all manufacturing, have gradually declined over time. These results are consistent with the arguments of Young (1995) and Krugman (1994) that the rapid growth in East Asian economies has been derived, in the main, from factor accumulation, while technological progress has had little effect.

---

[12] Although the productivity indexes estimated from the two methods differ, the trends in the two indexes are similar.   The correlation between the two TFP indexes is 0.847 and is significant at the 1% level for 28 industries over the period 1970-96.

Among nine industries, TFP growth was relatively high in industries 01, 06, 07 and 08. Comparing light and heavy industry, TFP growth was higher in heavy industry (1.49 or 1.92%) than in light industry (0.85 or 1.55%). In particular, the growth rate of real output for heavy industry (16.83%) was twice that for light industry (8.37%).

4. Empirical Results

4.1 Domestic and Foreign R&D stock

A two-way fixed-effect method (considering industry-specific and time-specific effects) has been used to treat the panel data in regression models testing the determinants of TFP. [13] Since Korean R&D data are only available for nine manufacturing sectors over the period 1976-96, all the variables for the 28 sectors are aggregated into nine sectors in the regressions.

Table 14-5 shows the regression results using the foreign R&D stocks calculated by the LP method. [14] The estimated coefficients of $lnR\&D^{DS}$ are all positive and statistically significant at the 1% level. This implies that R&D investment in an industry increases the TFP of that industry. The elasticity of the TFP indexes with respect to own-industry R&D ranges from 0.034 to 0.100. [15]

The coefficients of domestic other-industry R&D ($lnR\&D^{DO}$), ranging from 0.076 to 0.137, are positive and statistically significant, and are larger than

---

[13] The Hausman test rejects the hypothesis for two-way random-effect models for the panel data.

[14] The regression results using foreign R&D stocks from the CH method are reported in Appendix 13-C.

[15] The elasticity of TFP with respect to own-industry R&D in Keller (2002) is 0.074 for 13 industries in eight OECD countries over the period 1970-91.

Chapter 14

Table 14-5. Regression Results Using the Foreign R&D Stocks Based on the LP method: Dependent Variable = lnTFP

	Using Törnqvist productivity index					Using Malmquist productivity index				
	(T.1)	(T.2)	(T.2)'	(T.3)	(T.4)	(M.1)	(M.2)	(M.2)'	(M.3)	(M.4)
LnR&D^{DS}	.084***	.100***	.065***	.052***	.034***	.077***	.091***	.065***	.056***	.037***
	(7.69)	(8.30)	(5.77)	(5.17)	(3.37)	(5.80)	(6.22)	(4.37)	(4.16)	(2.92)
LnR&D^{DO}	.111***	.122***	.129***	.127***	.137***	.079**	.093***	.085***	.076**	.109***
	(4.20)	(4.62)	(5.53)	(5.54)	(6.33)	(2.45)	(2.91)	(2.77)	(2.49)	(3.98)
LnR&D^{F}	.124***			.182***	.174***	.125***			.170***	.076**
	(5.68)			(9.28)	(6.31)	(4.74)			(6.56)	(2.19)
LnR&D$^{F\_USA}$		.052***	.074***				.020	.040**		
		(3.47)	(5.75)				(1.10)	(2.33)		
LnR&D$^{F\_JPN}$		.053***	.066***				.094***	.101***		
		(3.72)	(5.37)				(5.48)	(6.25)		
LnR&D$^{F\_OTH}$		.050***	.043***				.049**	.041**		
		(3.17)	(3.20)				(2.57)	(2.35)		
LnIMP			-.177***	-.198***	-.308***			-.163***	-.182***	-.094
			(7.58)	(8.08)	(4.50)			(5.30)	(5.60)	(1.09)
LnOPEN			.125***	.152***	.116***			.191***	.233***	.192***
			(3.06)	(3.64)	(2.97)			(3.56)	(4.21)	(3.90)
LnIMP*lnR&D^{F}					.016**					-.003
					(2.27)					(0.29)
IIT* lnR&D^{F}					.056***					.104***
					(4.68)					(6.84)
R^2	.651	.687	.779	.762	.802	.930	.937	.948	.943	.957
F (28,•) value for no fixed effect	3.83***	4.75***	7.98***	7.38***	9.65***	47.30***	42.19***	20.25***	19.68***	26.76***
F(1,•) value for R&D^{DS} = R&D^{F}	3.44*	7.22***	36.38***	36.01***	21.49***	3.43*	8.74***	20.71***	16.03***	1.05
F(1,•) value for RD$^{F\_USA}$ = RD$^{F\_JPN}$	-	0.00	0.16	-	-	-	6.71**	5.36**	-	-

Notes: 1) The figures in parentheses are absolute t-values. 2) In (T.2), (T.2)', (M.2), and (M.2)', the F test is lnR&D^{DS} = lnR&D$^{F\_USA}$ + lnR&D$^{F\_JPN}$ + lnR&D$^{F\_OTH}$. 3) The estimates of constant term, time and industry dummies are not reported here, for the sake of simplicity. 4) Obs = 178. R&D data are missing for 11 of the 189 observations. 5) ***, **, and * are significant at the 1, 5, and 10% level, respectively.

those of the domestic same-industry R&D stock. These results show that there are domestic R&D spillovers in Korean manufacturing, and that the domestic spillover effects are greater than the effects of own-R&D stock on productivity.

All of the coefficients of $lnR\&D^F$ are positive and statistically significant at the 1% level. Moreover, these coefficients are larger than those of $lnR\&D^{DS}$ and $lnR\&D^{DO}$. Thus, foreign R&D stocks have a greater effect on productivity than domestic R&D stocks in Korean manufacturing. These results are contrary to Coe et al. (1995) and Keller (2002). In both studies, domestic R&D capital stocks had a greater effect on productivity than foreign R&D capital stocks. The differences in the results may come from the different country studies. Coe et al. (1995) and Keller (2002) dealt with R&D spillovers within OECD countries, while this study examines R&D spillovers in Korea. This implies that the domestic R&D stocks of advanced countries are more effective than foreign R&D stocks. By contrast, in developing countries like Korea, R&D investment is relatively small compared with that in OECD countries; thus, foreign R&D stocks can be more effective than domestic R&D stocks.

We tested the hypothesis that the coefficients of the domestic and foreign R&D stocks are equal. The F-value for $lnR\&D^{DS} = lnR\&D^F$ in Table 14-5 shows that we can reject this hypothesis. Thus, the coefficients of $lnR\&D^F$ are significantly larger than those of $lnR\&D^{DS}$, except in (M.4).[16] Here, we

---

[16] Following the suggestion of a referee, we consider the total rather than the marginal effect of foreign R&D stocks, and test the hypothesis of $lnR\&D^{DS} = lnR\&D^F + lnIMP*lnR\&D^F + IIT* lnR\&D^F$ in Equation (M.4). The F value shows that the total elasticity of $lnR\&D^F$ is significantly larger than that of $lnR\&D^{DS}$ at the 1% level.

must note that the empirical models do not consider the effect of foreign other-sector R&D stock because of data limitations. In Keller (2002), the effect of foreign other-sector R&D stock (0.150) is much larger than the effect of foreign same-sector R&D stock (0.047).

Next, we divide foreign R&D capital stocks into three groups - the U.S., Japan, and the remaining OECD countries - and use these segmented foreign R&D stocks instead of $lnR\&D^F$ in columns (T.2), (T.2)', (M.2), and (M.2)' in Table 14-5. In the regression results, the three decomposed variables are all positive and statistically significant, except for the coefficient of $lnR\&D^{F\_USA}$ in (M.2). The coefficient of $lnR\&D^{F\_JPN}$ is the largest of the three coefficients of the foreign R&D stock variables, except in (T.2)'. The last row of Table 14-5 gives the F-statistics for the hypothesis that two coefficients of $lnR\&D^{F\_USA}$ and $lnR\&D^{F\_JPN}$ are equal. According to this test, the coefficients for the U.S. and Japan do not differ significantly when using the Törnqvist productivity index, but they do differ significantly, and the coefficient of $lnR\&D^{F\_JPN}$ is larger than that of $lnR\&D^{F\_USA}$ in the Malmquist productivity index.[17]

Why does R&D investment in Japan have more effect on Korean productivity than such investment in the U.S.? One explanation lies in the difference in the trade structures between Korea and the two countries. Korean imports from Japan exceed those from the United States in heavy industry, which has large R&D investment in both countries. According to our calculation, heavy industry imports from Japan are twice those from the

---

[17] Coe et al. (1997) showed that R&D in Japan has a greater influence on the productivity of Asian countries, because Japan is their most important trading partner, even if R&D spillovers from the U.S. are generally the largest among developing countries.

U.S., suggesting that Japanese R&D stock has a relatively greater effect on Korean productivity than does that of the U.S.

Another explanation may come from the different patterns of patent citations. Korean patents are much more likely to cite Japanese patents than U.S. patents (Hu and Jaffe, 2001); this implies that Korea adopts more Japanese technology than U.S. technology. Hence, we expect Japanese R&D stock to play a relatively larger role in Korean manufacturing than U.S. R&D stock. However, evidence for this is found only in the regressions using the Malmquist productivity index.

4.2 Trade-Related Variables

As we expected, the coefficients of $lnIMP$ are negative and statistically significant in all the equations, except for (M.4). This is consistent with the results of Kim and Kim (1997) and Coe et al. (1997), in which productivity is lower in industries or countries with larger import shares. The coefficients of $lnOPEN$ are significantly positive in all the regression models, implying that productivity is greater in industries with larger trade shares in production.

Columns (T.4) and (M.4) show the interactive effects of trade pattern and foreign R&D capital on productivity. Foreign R&D stock affects domestic productivity via imports. Thus, we expect the effect of foreign R&D on domestic productivity to be larger in an industry with a larger import share. The coefficient of $lnIMP*lnR\&D^F$ is positive and significant at the 5% level in (T.4). This implies that the effect of foreign R&D on productivity is positive in the import industry, even if productivity in the import industry is lower than in the export industry.

The coefficients of $IIT*lnR\&D^F$ are positive and significant at the 1% level, showing that foreign R&D has a greater effect on productivity in an industry with more intra-industry trade. This confirms the argument of Hakura and Jaumotte (1999), who held that an industry with a large intra-industry trade share faces more competition and absorbs foreign technology more easily than do industries with more inter-industry trade.

4.3 Sensitivity Analysis

We tested the robustness of the results in several ways. One was a test using a 5-percent depreciation rate in calculating R&D capital stocks.[18] The results were very similar to those in Table 14-5. The second was to consider the simultaneous bias or endogeneity problem between productivity and R&D stock. Keller (2002) suggested using the instrument variable method to deal with simultaneous bias. However, instrument variables are not available for both long periods and every industry in Korean manufacturing. Therefore, we estimated our regression models for each 5-year observation over 1976-1996, namely, 1976, 1981, 1986, 1991, and 1996. The results for these alternatives were not significantly different from the results in Table 14-5. [3] Only domestic, other industry R&D stock is not statistically significant in some cases, but not in all models. The test of $lnR\&D^{DS} = lnR\&D^F$ cannot be rejected, but the coefficients of $lnR\&D^F$ are still larger than those of $lnR\&D^{DS}$.

Lastly, we estimated regression models using foreign R&D capital stocks calculated by the CH method. The results are in Table 14-C1 in Appendix 14-C. We briefly summarize the similarities and dissimilarities between the

---

[18] These results can be obtained from the authors by request.

two results in Tables 14-5 and 14-C1. In general, the estimates in Table 14-C1 are similar to those in Table 14-5. The main difference is that the elasticity of TFP with respect to the domestic R&D capital stock is smaller in Table 14-C1 than in Table 14-5, while the elasticity with respect to the foreign R&D capital stock in Table 14-C1 is increased (although it is somewhat reduced in the model using the Malmquist productivity index). This might occur because, as shown in Table 14-2, the foreign R&D capital stock calculated by the CH method is larger than that calculated using the LP method. In the Törnqvist productivity index models, most of the estimates are statistically significant, while the degree of significance is lower in the Malmquist productivity index models. The significance of the trade-related variables is essentially the same as in Table 14-5.

Comparing the results of the CH and the LP methods in our regression analyses, we can say that the LP method is better for constructing foreign R&D stock because, as shown in Tables 14-5 and 14-C1, the LP method improves R^2, which means that the LP method fits the model well. Moreover, even if all the coefficients of $lnR\&D^{DO}$ are statistically insignificant in the Malmquist productivity index in Table 14-C1, they are all statistically significant in Table 14-5, which uses the foreign R&D capital stock by the LP method.

5. Concluding Remarks

Trade has played an important role in Korea's rapid economic growth since the early 1960s. Trading with developed countries provides an opportunity to absorb advanced technology developed by these partners, thereby increasing productivity. In new growth theory, technology transmission through trade is linked to productivity. Although Coe and Helpman (1995),

Coe et al. (1997), and Keller (2002) empirically analyzed international R&D spillovers through trade within developed countries as well as between North and South, these studies did not examine industries in developing countries.

We investigated the effects of R&D spillovers on productivity using data from the Korean industry. Our findings suggest that domestic and foreign R&D have played an essential role in the productivity of Korean manufacturing from 1976 to 1996. Specifically, foreign R&D stock had a greater impact on productivity than domestic R&D. Furthermore, foreign R&D stock from Japan was more important than that from the US or other OECD countries. This could be due to the different trade structures between Korea and its trade partners. We also observed that domestic other-industry R&D contributed more to productivity than domestic own-industry R&D in Korean manufacturing, suggesting that there have been both domestic and foreign R&D spillovers.

When examining the relationship between trade patterns and productivity, our results showed that productivity was greater in export and open industries. The effects of foreign R&D capital were also more substantial in industries with significant import shares or intra-industry trade shares. Even if productivity was lower in an import industry, the effects of foreign R&D capital on productivity were greater in the import industry, as imports are a vehicle for foreign R&D spillovers. The effects of foreign R&D capital on productivity were also more significant in industries with large intra-industry trade shares, as foreign technology can be more easily absorbed in industries that import similar products to those they produce and export.

While this study focused on the effects of domestic and international R&D capital and trade on the productivity of Korean manufacturing, we believe that other variables, such as domestic market structure or direct foreign investment, are additional determinants of domestic productivity. This opens up another avenue for further research.

Appendix 14-A. Industry Classification of Manufacturing Sectors

9 Ind	28 Ind	ISIC Rev. 2	STAN industry category	SITC classification
	(31)		Food, Beverages & Tobacco	
01	01	311/2	Food	01-09 (0482), 211, 2232, 2239, 2632, 2681, 291, 4(4314), 5921.
	02	313	Beverages	0482, 11.
	03	314	Tobacco	12.
	(32)		Textiles, Apparel & Leather	
02	04	321	Textiles	2223, 261, 263(2632), 2667, 2672, 2682, 2686, 2687, 65(6576), 8451, 846(8465).
	05	322	Wearing Apparel	6576, 842, 843, 844, 845(8451), 8465, 847, 848.
	06	323	Leather & Products	61(6123), 831.
	07	324	Footwear	6123, 851.
	(33)		Wood Products & Furniture	
03	08	331	Wood Products	2460, 248, 63, 6597.
	09	332	Furnitures & Fixtures	82.
	(34)		Paper, Paper Products & Printing	
04	10	341	Paper & Products	251(2511), 641, 642(6423).
	11	342	Printing & Publishing	2511, 6423, 892.
	(35)		Chemical Products	
05	12	351	Industrial Chemicals	2331, 266, 2671, 2814, 51, 52, 53, 56, 58, 591, 5981, 6514, 6517.
	13	352	Other Chemicals	4314, 533, 541(5419), 55, 57, 592, 598, 882.
	14	353	Petroleum Refineries	334, 3351, 3354.
	15	354	Petroleum & Coal Products	323, 3352, 3353.
	16	355	Rubber Products	62.
	17	356	Plastic Products, nec	893.
	(36)		Non-Metallic Mineral Products	
06	18	361	Pottery, China etc	6639, 666, 8122.
	19	362	Glass & Products	664, 665.
	20	369	Non-Metallic Products, nec	661, 662, 663(6639).
	(37)		Basic Metal Industries	
07	21	371	Iron & Steel	67(677).
	22	372	Non-Ferrous Metals	2881, 68, 6999.
	(38)		Fabricated Metal Products	
08	23	381	Metal Products	677, 69(6954, 6973, 6999), 711, 7187, 7492, 8121, 8951.
	24	382	Non-Electrical Machinery	6954, 6973, 712, 713, 718(7187), 72, 73, 74(7492, 7493), 75, 7784, 8946, 951.
	25	383	Electrical Machinery	716, 76, 77, 8748, 8983.
	26	384	Transport Equipment	713, 714, 7493, 78, 79, 8941.
	27	385	Professional Goods	5419, 87(8748), 88(882), 8974, 8996.
	(39)		Other Manufacturing	
09	28	390	Other Manufacturing	667, 6993, 89(8941, 8946, 8951, 8974, 8983, 8996), 961.

Note: Figures in parentheses are excluded from the sub-classification of each industry.

Appendix 14-B. Data Sources and Construction of Variables

This study used a number of different data sources: (1) data on output, inputs and their prices for estimating productivity indexes of Korean manufacturing; (2) R&D data for Korea and OECD countries by industry; and (3) bilateral trade data by industry and trade partner for 14 OECD countries.

B.1 Inputs and Output Data

The data on output, number of workers, value-added, and wage compensation for Korean manufacturing for the period 1970-96 come from the OECD STAN database (2000). The STAN database is classified into 28 manufacturing industries based on the 3-digit ISIC Rev. 2. Since the OECD STAN data are reported in current values, we estimated a price index for each variable to calculate a constant value. The output deflator for each industry was obtained from the Bank of Korea (BOK), and deflators for intermediate goods were created by averaging the price deflators of 55 inputs using their weights. The weight of each input is defined as the relative share of purchases by each industry to the input, based on the Input-Output Tables of the BOK (1998). Using these price indexes, each current value is converted into a 1990 constant value. The data on physical capital stock in terms of 1990 constant values are from Pyo (1998).

B.2 R&D and Trade Data

The Korean R&D data are from various issues of Science and Technology Statistics published by the Ministry of Science and Technology, Korea, while the R&D data for 14 OECD countries are from the OECD ANBERD database (2000). The nominal values of R&D expenditures in the national currency were converted into a constant 1990 value using the GDP deflator from the OECD Economic Outlook (2002). Then, these constant R&D expenditures were converted into U.S. dollars using the 1990 purchasing power parity exchange rates. Data for Korean R&D investment were only available for nine industries after 1976. Therefore, we reclassified the variables for all 28 sectors (three-digit ISIC) into the nine sectors (two-digit ISIC) that corresponded to the Korean R&D data for 1976-96 (see Appendix 14-A for details).

R&D capital stocks were calculated from the R&D expenditures using the perpetual inventory method. We assumed a depreciation rate of 5% or 10% for every industry. In constructing Korea's imported foreign R&D capital stock, the CH and the LP methods were used. In the CH method, foreign R&D stock of industry i at time t, S_{it}^{f-CH}, is defined as follows:

$$S_{it}^{f-CH} = \sum_{j \neq i} S_{ijt}^{f-CH} = \sum_{j \neq i} \frac{m_{ijt}}{m_{it}} S_{ijt}^{d} \quad \text{for each industry } i \qquad \text{(B1)}$$

where S_{ijt}^{d} is industry i's domestic R&D stock of trade partner j, m_{ijt} is the import flow of industry i from one of its trade partners j, and m_{it} is the total imports of industry i at time t from all of its trade partners, namely, $m_{it} = \sum_{j \neq i} m_{ijt}$.

On the other hand, in the LP method, foreign R&D stock of industry i at time t, S_{it}^{f-LP}, is calculated as follows:

$$S_{it}^{f-LP} = \sum_{j \neq i} S_{ijt}^{f-LP} = \sum_{j \neq i} \frac{m_{ijt}}{y_{ijt}} S_{ijt}^{d} \quad \text{for each industry } i \qquad \text{(B2)}$$

where y_{ijt} is industy i's output level of trade partner j at time t. LP (1998) argues that this formulation reflects the intensity as well as the direction of international R&D spillovers.

The trade data used to calculate the bilateral trade shares of the industries are from the World Trade Flows Database CD-ROM (Feenstra et al., 1997; Feenstra, 2000). The industry code of trade data is the SITC Rev. 2, but the R&D data are based on ISIC Rev. 2. Therefore, we matched the four-digit SITC to the three-digit ISIC using the OECD classification (refer to Appendix 14-A). Then we constructed Korea's imported foreign R&D stocks for the nine industries.

Appendix 14-C. Alternative Empirical Result

Table 14-C1. Regression results using the foreign R&D stocks based on the CH method: Dependent Variable = lnTFP

	Using Törnqvist productivity index					Using Malmquist productivity index				
	(T.1)	(T.2)	(T.2)'	(T.3)	(T.4)	(M.1)	(M.2)	(M.2)'	(M.3)	(M.4)
LnR&D^{DS}	.056***	.073***	.044***	.034***	.031***	.053***	.057***	.038***	.043***	.039***
	(5.08)	(6.34)	(3.22)	(2.86)	(2.92)	(3.88)	(3.98)	(2.23)	(2.82)	(2.99)
LnR&D^{DO}	.061**	.067**	.065**	.059**	.063**	.042	.047	.031	.023	.060*
	(2.21)	(2.44)	(2.43)	(2.18)	(2.41)	(1.21)	(1.37)	(0.91)	(0.67)	(1.88)
LnR&D^{F}	.185***			.193***	.227***	.110**			.117***	.036
	(4.76)			(5.32)	(4.18)	(2.27)			(2.51)	(0.53)
LnR&D$^{F\_USA}$		.080***	.085***				.022	.025		
		(4.29)	(4.79)				(0.95)	(1.12)		
LnR&D$^{F\_JPN}$		.060***	.045***				.065***	.048**		
		(3.53)	(2.74)				(3.06)	(2.29)		
LnR&D$^{F\_OTH}$		.021	-.007				-.005	-.029		
		(1.27)	(0.42)				(0.26)	(1.30)		
LnIMP			-.121***	-.127***	-.772***			-.118***	-.113***	-.423
			(4.16)	(4.76)	(3.50)			(3.21)	(3.31)	(1.56)
LnOPEN			.108**	.133***	.063			.194***	.213***	.137**
			(2.19)	(2.76)	(1.43)			(3.09)	(3.46)	(2.52)
LnIMP*lnR&D^{F}					.046***					.024
					(3.07)					(1.32)
IIT* lnR&D^{F}					.182***					.282***
					(6.14)					(7.74)
R²	.631	.644	.685	.682	.756	.922	.925	.931	.929	.950
F (28,•) value for no fixed effect	3.44***	3.31***	3.64***	4.07***	6.71***	42.22***	30.98***	14.23***	13.82***	21.14***
F(1,•) value for R&D^{DS} = R&D^{F}	9.14***	7.45***	6.52***	15.43***	12.01***	1.12	0.37	0.02	2.02	0.00
F(1,•) value for RD$^{F\_USA}$ = RD$^{F\_JPN}$	-	0.70	2.88**	-	-	-	2.00	0.59	-	-

Notes: 1) See notes in Table 14-5. 2) ξ is rejected at the 20.0% significance level.

CHAPTER 15

EXPORTS AND PRODUCTIVITY GROWTH IN KOREAN MANUFACTURING FIRMS

1. Introduction

Since the 1960s, Korea has achieved high economic growth that is notable worldwide. It can be said that trade played a key role in this rapid economic growth. Korea's exports increased significantly from $175 million in 1965 to $644.4 billion in 2021. The growth rate of Korea's exports has far exceeded that of world exports, with Korea's exports accounting for 2.9% of the world's total in 2021.

Exports promote economic growth in many ways. According to endogenous growth theory, exports promote technological progress by allowing countries to acquire new technologies from other nations. Grossman and Helpman (1992) explain theoretically that trade facilitates the diffusion of knowledge, promotes productivity, and drives economic growth. In general, trade has a positive effect on economic growth through economies of scale, inflow of technology, and increased competition.

Exporting firms increase their productivity by acquiring technology through exchanges with other countries, while domestic firms do not. Therefore, their productivity is relatively low compared to that of exporting firms. As openness expands, the productivity gap between exporting firms and domestic firms widens.

The reasons why exporting firms are more productive and grow faster than domestic firms are as follows. First, exporting firms can improve their productivity by acquiring various advanced technologies through contact with overseas markets. Since exporting firms compete with excellent foreign firms, there is a strong incentive for technology acquisition and development. Exporting firms maintain high productivity compared to domestic firms by concentrating their resources on technology development necessary to compete with foreign firms. Therefore, exporting firms can maintain high productivity compared to domestic firms with a relatively low level of technology (Aw et al., 2000; De Locker, 2007).

Secondly, only firms with a certain level of productivity can enter the export market. Exporting firms typically have higher productivity than domestic firms before entering the export market, as noted by several studies (Aw and Hwang, 1995; Clerides, Lach and Tybout, 1998; Bernard and Jensen, 1999a, b). This is because firms with low productivity are less likely to survive in the competitive global market. Additionally, to sell products abroad, exporting firms must incur fixed costs that are not required in the domestic market. To maintain profitability after paying such additional costs, productivity must be higher than that of domestic firms. According to Roberts and Tybout (1997), the difference in productivity between exporting and domestic firms is mostly due to sunk costs required to enter the export market.

Thirdly, exporting firms benefit from increasing returns to scale, as they operate in the global market. Expanding production for export leads to economies of scale, which in turn increase productivity. This phenomenon has been observed in developing countries that have implemented export-oriented growth policies (Krueger and Tuncer, 1982; Chenery, 1983;

Young, 1995). Studies show that as exports expand, the productivity of exporting firms tends to increase due to these economies of scale. Therefore, exporting firms are able to achieve higher levels of productivity compared to domestic firms that do not operate in the global market.

As previously explained, exporting firms typically exhibit higher productivity levels compared to their domestic counterparts. For instance, De Locker (2007) demonstrates that export firms in Slovenia have 8-13% higher productivity than domestic firms. However, Bernard and Jensen (1999) found that exporting firms in the US have higher growth rates or profit rates than domestic firms, but productivity and wage growth rates are higher in domestic firms. Furthermore, Hung et al. (2004) discovered that in the case of the US manufacturing industry from 1996 to 2001, productivity growth was not due to exports, but rather due to increased competition resulting from imports.

Lee and Choi (2009) conducted an analysis of Korean manufacturing firms from 1992 to 2003 using a matching technique. Their study showed that there is a learning effect resulting from export activities, and this effect leads to an increase in total factor productivity. Furthermore, they found that this learning effect persists for a long time. Jeon et al. (2013) analyzed Korean manufacturing firms from 2006 to 2008 and demonstrated that firms with both export and foreign direct investment exhibit the highest productivity, followed by export firms, and domestic firms have the lowest productivity.

This study aims to analyze the productivity and productivity growth rate differences between exporting and domestic firms using data from the Korean manufacturing industry from 1984 to 2021. Additionally, it seeks to investigate whether the effect of exports on productivity varies depending on the firm size.

The structure of this chapter is as follows. Section 2 explains data and characteristics of exporting firms, Section 3 analyzes the difference in total factor productivity between exporting and domestic firms, and Section 4 analyzes the effect of exports on total factor productivity using regression analysis. Finally, Section 5 briefly summarizes the above discussion.

2.   Data and Characteristics of Export Firms

2.1 Data

This study uses firm level data of the Korean manufacturing industry for the period 1984-2021. The firm data was obtained from KIS Value and FN Guide. To ensure the reliability of the research results, firms with uncertain data and firms with a short duration were excluded from the study. Only firms with data for at least 5 years during the 37-year period of 1984-2021 were included in the analysis.

This study estimated total factor productivity using value-added as the output variable. In cases where value-added data were missing, value-added was estimated using sales. To estimate value-added, the study first calculated the average value-added rate (i.e., value-added/sales) for each company. Then, the value-added was estimated by multiplying this rate by the sales. To adjust for inflation, current value-added was converted into real value-added using the producer price index by industry.

In estimating total factor productivity, this study used labor and capital as input factors. Total assets data was used for capital stock, and the number of employees was used for labor. Capital stocks at current prices were converted into capital stocks at constant prices using the price index of final capital goods. Nominal wages were converted into real wages using the consumer price index. If the total wage was missing, it was estimated from the value-added using the average labor share of the firm. Export data were obtained from the export items of KIS Value and FN Guide.

Price index data such as producer price index, capital goods price index, and consumer price index and exchange rate data were extracted from the economic statistics system of the Bank of Korea.

2.2 Classification of Export Firms

There is no clear criterion for distinguishing between export firms and domestic firms. All companies that export cannot be classified as export companies. It is questionable whether a company that exports a very small proportion of total sales or exports only for one or two years can be regarded as an export company. Therefore, we classified exporting firms as follows.

During the period of 1984-2021, companies that had export experience for more than 10 years, or more than half of the duration, were considered as exporting firms. Additionally, the exporting firms were divided into two categories based on the percentage of exports in their total sales. Firms that export more than 0% were classified as exporting firms under "Criterion I," whereas firms that export more than 50% of their sales were classified as exporting firms under "Criterion II." Criterion I is a more lenient standard, while Criterion II is more rigorous.

3. Characteristics of Export Firms

Table 15-1 presents the average values of major variables for domestic and exporting firms. The table shows that there are more domestic firms than export firms. Under Criterion I (0%), there are 6,796 domestic firms and

Table 15-1. Summary of Major Variables for Domestic and Export Firms (2021)

	All	Criterion I (0%)		Criterion II (50%)	
		Domestic firm	Export firm	Domestic firm	Export firm
Number of firms	8,542	6,796	1,746	8,057	485
Sales*	1,523	562	5,265	804	13,458
Value-Added*	350	123	1,233	180	3,175
Assets*	1,826	585	6,655	911	17,028
No. of employees**	181	102	488	129	1,049
Assets/No. of employees	10.1	5.7	13.6	7.1	16.2

Note: 1) The values of each firm were simply averaged by group. * The unit is 100 million KRW. ** The unit is person.

1,746 export firms. Under Criterion II (50%), there are 8,057 domestic firms and 485 export firms. The number of firms classified as exporting firms decreases as the criteria become more stringent.

Table 15-1 presents that export firms are generally larger in size compared to domestic firms. For instance, under 'Criterion I (0%)', the average sales of domestic firms were 56.2 billion won while export firms had an average sales of 526.5 billion won, which is approximately nine times more than domestic firms. Similarly, under 'Criterion II (50%)', domestic firms had average sales of 80.4 billion won, while export firms had an average sales of 1345.8 billion won, which is roughly 16 times more than domestic firms. In addition, exporting firms had higher average values of other variables such as value added, assets, and number of employees compared to domestic firms. Specifically, value added of exporting firms was 10-17 times more than that of domestic firms, the size of assets was 11-18 times more, and the number of employees was 5-8 times more. This trend is not limited to Korea but can be observed in other countries as well.

Export firms are typically larger than domestic firms due to the fixed costs required to establish a foundation for exporting abroad. In other words, in order to cover these fixed costs, firms must reach a certain size threshold. Additionally, the size of exporting firms tends to be larger in Criterion II than in Criterion I. This suggests that firms that export extensively are also generally larger in size.

Exporting firms tend to have a higher asset/employee ratio, which indicates greater capital intensity. In Criterion I, the asset/employee ratios for domestic and exporting firms are 5.7 and 13.6, respectively. In Criterion II, these ratios increase to 7.1 and 16.2, respectively. Furthermore, the asset/employee ratio of export firms is more than twice that of domestic firms, suggesting that exporting firms in Korea are significantly more capital-intensive than their domestic counterparts.

3. Comparison of TFP between Domestic and Export Companies

3.1 TFP Estimation Method

Total factor productivity (TFP) is conceptually the difference between output and input. In this study, the multilateral translog index of Caves et al. (1982) was used as a TFP measurement method.[1] This is an index made to enable cross-sectional comparison of Tornqvist-Theil's index, and is appropriate for the analysis of this study using time series and industry data.

Total factor productivity (TFP) represents the difference between output and input, and is a measure of how efficiently firms are able to use their

---

[1] Refer to Kim and Jang (2002) for the calculation method of the output index and input index.

Table 15-2. Decomposition of Output Growth Rate by Period

	1984~ 1990	1990~ 2000	2000~ 2010	2010~ 2021	Whole period (1984~ 2021)
Output	8.35	-0.03	6.51	1.83	3.65
(Labor)	0.11	-4.53	1.23	-0.03	-0.88
(Capital)	4.14	2.08	2.66	2.45	2.68
Total factor productivity	4.11	2.41	2.62	-0.59	1.85

* The growth rate here is the exponential growth rate.

resources. In this study, we used the multilateral translog index developed by Caves et al. (1982) as a method for measuring TFP. This index is specifically designed for cross-sectional comparison of Tornqvist-Theil's index, and is particularly appropriate for the analysis of this study, which utilizes time series and industry data to assess the relative productivity of domestic and export firms.

When calculating total factor productivity (TFP), the choice of output and input factors is critical. Sales and added value are both commonly used as measures of output. However, when using sales as output, it is necessary to have data on intermediate goods. Unfortunately, many firms do not disclose data on intermediate goods, which can make it difficult to use sales as a measure of output. Therefore, in this study, added value was used as output, and capital and labor were used as input factors.

3.2 Changes in TFP of Korean Manufacturing Firms

Table 15-2 provides a summary of the growth rate of total factor productivity (TFP) for Korean manufacturing firms over the period 1984-2021. The data shows that the average annual growth rate of output (value added) during this period was 3.65%, with labor contributing a negative -

0.88% and capital contributing 2.68%. The remaining increase in production was due to an increase in TFP, which contributed 1.85% to the overall growth rate. These results suggest that the increase in production was achieved by the increase in capital input and total factor productivity, and labor did not contribute to the increase in production at all. The negative growth rate of labor input indicates either a decrease in the absolute amount of labor input or a decrease in the labor input ratio in the production function. Overall, these findings provide important insights into the drivers of productivity growth in the Korean manufacturing sector over the past few decades.

The rate of increase in output varies from period to period, with the highest rate of 8.35% observed during 1984-1990. However, during the period of 1990-2000, there was a negative growth of (-0.03%) due to the foreign exchange crisis. The growth rate of capital is higher than the growth rate of labor, indicating a shift towards capital-intensive production methods. Additionally, during the periods of 1990-2000 and 2010-2021, the growth rate of labor input is negative, suggesting that labor did not contribute to the increase in output during these periods.

The growth rate of TFP is gradually declining, with rates of 4.11% in the period 1984-90, 2.41% in the period 1990-2000, 2.62% in the period 2000-2010, and -0.59% in the period 2010-2020. The growth rate of TFP for the entire period 1984-2021 is 1.85%.

3.3 TFP Growth Rates between Exporting and Domestic Firms

Table 15-3 presents the growth rates of output, input, and total factor productivity for both export and domestic firms. Firstly, it is evident that the output growth rate of export firms is higher than that of domestic firms. In

Table 15-3. Growth Rate of Output, Input and TFP of Export and Domestic Firms

	All	Criterion I (0%)		Criterion II (50%)	
		Domestic firm	Export firm	Domestic firm	Export firm
Output	3.65	3.25	5.71	1.77	6.77
(Labor)	-0.88	-0.96	-0.17	-1.37	-0.16
(Capital)	2.68	2.41	4.02	1.72	4.26
TFP	1.85	1.80	1.86	1.42	2.66

Note: output is value added, inputs are labor and capital.

Criterion I, domestic firms show a growth rate of 3.25% while export firms show a growth rate of 5.71%. Similarly, in Criterion II, domestic firms show a growth rate of 1.77% while export firms show a growth rate of 6.77%. The higher output growth rate of exporting firms in Criterion II compared to Criterion I suggests that firms with a high export share experienced a faster increase in output.

The growth rate of labor input for domestic firms is -0.96% in Criterion I and -1.37% in Criterion II, while for export firms it is -0.17% in Criterion I and -0.16% in Criterion II. It can be observed that the labor input growth rate is decreasing for both domestic and export firms, but the decrease is more significant for domestic firms.

The growth rate of capital input is increasing in both domestic and exporting firms, but the growth rate is greater in exporting firms. Under Criterion I, the growth rate of capital input for domestic and exporting firms is 2.41% and 4.02%, respectively, and under Criterion II, it is 1.72% and 4.26%, respectively. It is clear that the growth rate of capital input is positively correlated with the share of exports.

The growth rate of labor input is negative (-) and the growth rate of capital input is positive (+) in both domestic and export firms, indicating a reduction in labor employment and an increase in capital input in the production of goods. In other words, production methods have gradually become more capital-intensive.

The growth rates of TFP of domestic and export companies are 1.80% and 1.86%, respectively, under Criterion I, and 1.42% and 2.66%, respectively, under Criterion II. The productivity growth rate of exporting firms is higher than that of domestic firms, and is higher in Criterion II than in Criterion I. This suggests that exports have the effect of increasing productivity, and that the effect is greater in firms that export more.

According to the research findings, exporting firms tend to experience faster growth than domestic firms, and the growth rate of total factor productivity (TFP) is also higher among exporting firms. When breaking down the factors contributing to increased output, capital has a positive effect, while labor has a negative effect, indicating a shift toward more capital-intensive production methods. It's worth noting that the growth rate of output is higher under Criterion II than under Criterion I. In addition, the growth rates of labor, capital, and TFP are also higher under Criterion II. These results suggest that the positive impact of exports on output and productivity is even greater among firms with a higher proportion of exports.

Figure 15-1 displays the productivity level changes of exporting and domestic firms over time. The figure reveals that in the initial stage, the total factor productivity of exporting firms was either similar to or lower than that of domestic firms. However, in the later period, the total factor productivity of exporting firms surpassed that of domestic firms. These findings suggest that the total factor productivity of exporting firms increased more rapidly than that of domestic firms.

Figure 15-1. Changes in total factor productivity

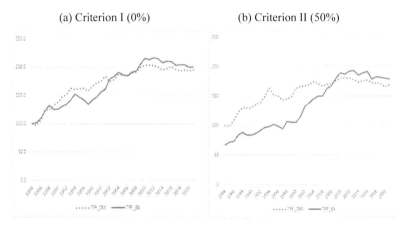

(a) Criterion I (0%)   (b) Criterion II (50%)

Note: TFP_DM is TFP of domestic firms, and TFP_EX is TFP of exporting firms.

4. Regression Analysis

4.1 Regression Model

To compare the performance of exporting firms to that of domestic firms, we conducted a regression analysis using the following model.

$$dTFP =_= \beta_0 + \beta_1 \log(LAB) + \beta_2 \log(CAPS) + \beta_3 DE_i + \beta_4 DS_j + \varepsilon$$

In the equation above, *dTFP* represents the growth rate of total factor productivity, while *log(LAB)* and *log(CAPS)* denote the log values of labor and capital stock, respectively. To account for the impact of input factors on total factor productivity, we included labor and capital stocks as explanatory variables in the regression model.

DE_i is a dummy variable with a value of 1 for export firms and 0 for domestic firms. The variable i indicates the type of criterion, with 1 representing Criterion I and 2 representing Criterion II. Additionally, DS_j is a dummy variable that reflects the size of the firm. The variable j takes on the values 1, 2, 3, and 4, with 1 indicating the largest firms and 4 indicating the smallest. We classified firms based on their average number of employees in the last three years, with Group 1 consisting of firms with 300 or more employees, Group 2 consisting of firms with 100 to 300 employees, Group 3 consisting of firms with 30 to 100 employees, and Group 4 consisting of firms with 30 or fewer employees.[2]

4.2 Effect of Exports on Total Factor Productivity

Table 15-4 presents the regression results of the impact of exports on total factor productivity.[3] The table shows that the coefficients of the dummy variable DE for exporting firms are all positive and statistically significant, indicating that the growth rate of TFP is higher in exporting firms than in domestic firms. Specifically, in Criterion I, the coefficient of DE ranges from 2.68 to 3.28, while in Criterion II, the coefficient of DE ranges from 5.85 to 6.11. The coefficient value of DE is higher in Criterion II, suggesting that the growth rate of TFP is higher in firms that export a greater proportion of their output. These findings demonstrate that exports have a positive effect on firms' productivity, and this effect is greater for firms that export more.

---

[2] Firm size can be classified based on assets, sales, or number of employees, but there is no universally accepted criterion. In this study, we classified firm size into four categories based on the number of employees.
[3] The reason why the R2 value is very small at 0.015-0.018 in the regression results is because the number of explanatory variables is relatively small compared to the sample size of approximately 155,000. Generally, when there are few explanatory variables in relation to the number of samples, the R2 tends to be small.

DS_2, DS_3, and *DS_4* are dummy variables that represent the size of the firm.[4] The coefficients of *DS_2, DS_3*, and *DS_4* are all negative (-) and statistically significant, indicating that the growth rate of TFP is lower in smaller firms compared to larger ones. Moreover, the coefficient values decrease from *DS_2* to *DS_4*, suggesting that the TFP growth rate decreases as firm size decreases.

Using the interactive variable of *DSj*DE*, we examined whether there is a difference in the effect of exports on productivity growth depending on the size of the firm. In equation (3), the coefficient of *DS_2*DE* is -0.798, which means that the effect of exports on productivity growth is lower in Group 2 than in Group 1 by −0.798. In other words, since the *DE* coefficient of 2.815 represents the effect of exports on productivity growth in Group 1, the effect becomes '2.815-0.798' in Group 2. This indicates that the effect of exports on productivity growth is lower in smaller firms, and the effect becomes weaker as the firm size decreases.

The coefficient values are mostly negative (-) in Group 2 and 3, while positive (+) and statistically significant in Group 4. This suggests that in the smallest firms, the positive effect of exports on TFP is greater than that of large firms. In other words, the effect of exports on the increase in productivity is greatest in the smallest firm groups.

The coefficient of the *DSj*DE* variable for Group 4 is 3.528 in Criterion I and 11.030 in Criterion II. The coefficient in Criterion II is larger than that in Criterion I. This indicates that for Group 4, the effect of exports on increasing TFP is greater when there is a higher proportion of exports.

The regression results indicate that exporting firms experience a positive

---

[4] DS1 is not included in the regression equation, since Group 1 is the reference.

impact on productivity growth, with a stronger effect observed for those that export more. Furthermore, the impact of exports on productivity varies by firm size, with the smallest firms experiencing the greatest productivity gains.

Table 15-4. Effect of Exports on Total Factor Productivity

Dependent variable	Criterion I (0%)			Criterion II (50%)		
dTFP	(1)	(2)	(3)	(4)	(5)	(6)
lnLAB	-3.045***	-4.884***	-4.966***	-2.924***	-5.001***	-5.074***
	(0.206)	(0.235)	(0.237)	(0.207)	(0.239)	(0.240)
lnCAPS	-0.848***	-0.979***	-0.953***	-0.796***	-0.996***	-0.975***
	(0.176)	(0.180)	(0.180)	(0.175)	(0.179)	(0.179)
DE_i	3.282***	2.680***	2.815***	5.852***	5.581***	6.112***
	(0.319)	(0.320)	(0.783)	(0.492)	(0.493)	(0.841)
DS_2		-5.456***	-5.184***		-5.741***	-5.482***
		(0.474)	(0.720)		(0.483)	(0.524)
DS_3		-9.268***	-9.303***		-9.938***	-9.942***
		(0.537)	(0.737)		(0.549)	(0.581)
DS_4		-11.014***	-11.506***		-12.067***	-12.368***
		(0.699)	(0.874)		(0.724)	(0.751)
DS_2*DE_i			-0.798			-2.654**
			(0.906)			(1.166)
DS_3*DE_i			-0.036			0.130
			(0.913)			(1.232)
DSl_4*DE_i			3.528**			11.030***
			(1.442)			(2.721)
Constant	40.336***	56.992***	57.162***	40.398***	58.954***	59.112***
	(2.332)	(2.513)	(2.555)	(2.346)	(2.546)	(2.551)
Observations	155,803	155,803	155,803	154,265	154,265	154,265
R-squared	0.015	0.017	0.017	0.015	0.018	0.018
F	61.34	64.97	60.88	61.70	66.21	62.42

Note: 1) This is the regression result considering the year-fixed effect. 2) Values in ( ) are standard errors. 3) *, **, *** indicate statistical significance at the 10%, 5%, and 1% levels, respectively.

5. Conclusion

This study analyzes the difference in productivity between exporting firms and domestic firms using data from the Korean manufacturing industry. The analysis was conducted using data from approximately 150,000 firms covering the period from 1984 to 2021.

To examine the effects of exports on productivity, we classified all firms into two categories: exporting firms and domestic firms. There are no agreed-upon criteria for classifying exporting firms. In this study, we defined exporting firms as firms that exported for more than 10 years or for more than half of the analysis period. Additionally, firms exporting 0% or more were classified as Criterion I, and firms exporting 50% or more were classified as Criterion II.

The analysis results reveal that the output growth rate of exporting firms is significantly higher than that of domestic firms, indicating that exporting firms have grown at a faster pace than domestic firms. In terms of the growth rate of production factors, the labor growth rate is negative (-) and the capital growth rate is positive (+) for both domestic and exporting firms. This suggests that the production method in the Korean manufacturing industry has shifted towards a more capital-intensive method.

The growth rate of TFP is higher in exporting firms than in domestic firms. In addition, the growth rate of TFP is higher in firms with a higher export intensity. These results indicate that exports have the effect of contributing to productivity growth, and that the effect is greater in firms with a higher export intensity.

The regression analysis results can be summarized as follows: the growth rate of TFP tends to be lower for small firms than for large firms. Exporting firms have a higher TFP growth rate compared to domestic firms. Moreover, among exporting firms, the TFP growth rate increases with a higher proportion of exports. Interaction analysis shows that the productivity increase effect of exports is lower or similar for medium-sized firms as compared to large firms. However, the effect is greater for the smallest firms as compared to large firms.

This study suggests several important economic implications. Firstly, the higher productivity growth rate in exporting firms indicates that exports have significantly contributed to Korea's economic growth. Secondly, the finding that the productivity growth rate is higher for firms with a greater proportion of exports suggests that exports serve as an important channel for introducing new production technologies and disseminating knowledge. Finally, the greater productivity increase effect of exports in small enterprises highlights the need for policy efforts aimed at enhancing the export capabilities of SMEs to achieve sustainable economic growth in Korea.

Appendix

Table 15A-1. Variables and Codes

Name/Code	Data source
KIS	
Stock	
Name	
Company registration number/0A1170	
KSIC/0A1133	
Date of Establishment/0A1030	
Total Sales/121100	
Value added (total)/204090	
Number of employees/105000	KIS VALUE
Total assets/115000	
Labor cost/2040201	
Operating profit (loss)/125000	
Value added rate/2041402	
Labor income share/2041803	
[Export]/121195	
Export Total/ 0A2031	
*Exports (*) (thousand Won)	FN GUIDE
Producer Price Index	
Consumer Price Index	Bank of Korea, Economic Statistics System
Exchange Rate	
Capital Goods Price Index	

* 1) Labor cost is the sum of [the labor cost and welfare cost reported in the 'statement of the costs of goods manufactured'] and [the labor cost reported in the 'Income Statement']. 2) The value-added ratio is 'value added (total)/sales'. 3) Labor income share is 'labor cost/value added (total)'.

CHAPTER 16

THE IMPACT OF PATENT SYSTEM REFORM ON INNOVATION AND PRODUCTIVITY OF KOREAN FIRMS

1. Introduction

The endogenous growth theory developed by Romer (1986), Lucas (1988), and Grossman and Helpman (1991) identified technical changes and knowledge spillovers as the principal sources of continuous economic growth. As opposed to previous theories of economic growth under conditions of constant returns, these models demonstrated how the economy can consistently expand as a consequence of R&D investment and human capital growth, both of which would tend to raise the knowledge capital stock.

The Korean economy experienced rapid growth and significant structural changes beginning in the 1960s. Much of this economic growth appears to have been attributable to the enlargement of the stock of production inputs (labor and capital) rather than to productivity growth. In order to achieve sustainable economic growth, Korea must enhance the productivity growth associated with technological progress. Many researchers have previously pointed out that this task would require increases in knowledge. Both R&D investments and patents can be considered measures of knowledge (Griliches, 1990).

Korea's patent system experienced a major policy change in 1986. The underlying objective of the patent system was to restrict patentees' rights in order to obtain foreign technology until 1986, but after 1986 the policy shifted toward protecting inventions and strengthening patent rights. We surmise that R&D expenditures and patent applications have expanded as a consequence of strengthening Korea's patent system. We also expect that this increase in R&D expenditures exerts positive effects on firm productivity.

A large body of research regarding the effects of R&D on productivity has been accumulated.[1] Literature focusing on the firm level indicates that R&D generally has a positive effect on productivity (Griliches and Mairesse, 1984; Wang and Tsai, 2003; Wakelin, 2001). Some studies have shown that there are knowledge spillovers among industries and among countries using R&D data at the industry level (Keller, 2002; Kim and Park, 2003; and Singh, 2004; Kim, Maskus and Oh, 2009), and using patent data (Bottazzi and Peri, 2001; Jaffe, 1986; Kwon, 2004).

The principal objective of this study is to determine whether the strengthening of Korea's patent system induced increases in R&D expenditures or patent applications, and then to determine whether or not this increase in knowledge caused productivity growth in the Korean manufacturing sector. We employed Korea's 1985-2007 firm-level data, which encompasses data from 216 firms. The numbers of Korean patent applications and patent grants have been increasing rapidly since the early 1990s. This may be attributable to the sizeable amount of R&D expenditures undertaken by private firms and public institutions, although the strengthening

---

[1] For an early literature survey, see Griliches (1995).

of patent protection policy by the Korean government may also play a role (Luthria and Maskus, 2004; Jung et al., 2004).

This study differs from the currently existing literature in the following ways. First, this study analyzes the effects of strengthening patent systems on innovation in Korean manufacturing firms. Second, we evaluate the effects of innovation on productivity growth using firm-level data. We extract each firm's patent data from the raw Korean patent dataset. Finally, we evaluate the effects of knowledge spillovers on productivity at the firm level. It is quite difficult to find studies addressing knowledge spillovers at the firm level, because the measuring index for knowledge spillover at the firm level is not a simple proposition. We utilized Jaffe's (1986) technology proximity index to determine the effects of knowledge spillover among firms.

Our results reveal that, during the time period studied, productivity growth rates were higher in high technology firms than in firms in other sectors. Next, according to our regressions, the strengthening of the Korean patent system exerts positive effects on innovation, and induces increases in R&D expenditures and patents. This increase exerted significantly positive effects on productivity growth in Korean manufacturing firms. Additionally, we detected evidence of knowledge spillovers among firms, in that innovation in other firms increased TFP in any other particular firm.

This chapter is structured as follows. Section 2 presents a theoretical model supporting the empirical analysis, whereas Section 3 describes changes in the Korean Patent System and the data sources. Section 4 presents the results using panel regressions with fixed effects. Finally, Section 5 provides our concluding remarks.

2. Model

The patent system attempts to provide incentives to inventive efforts in order to encourage technological development, which stimulates economic growth. This study assesses this notion using Korean firm-level data. The empirical analyses conducted herein consist of two steps. First, we determine whether the strengthening of the patent system results in increases in R&D investment and patent applications. Second, this study attempts to address another question: do increases in R&D investments and patent applications have a positive effect on total factor productivity? If the above two analyses reveal positive and significant results, we can safely assert that a strengthening of the patent system does indeed positively affect economic growth in Korea.

The Korean patent system has been strengthened over time since its establishment in 1946. A particularly dramatic shift in the Korean Patent System occurred in 1986. Prior to 1986, the primary purpose of the patent system was to restrict patentee's rights in order to obtain and diffuse foreign technology easily; however, after 1986, the policy shifted toward protecting inventions, thus becoming more similar to the patent systems of advanced countries.

In order to determine whether the strengthening of the patent system encourages R&D investments and patent applications, we utilize the following equation:

$$ln\ KN_i = \alpha_0 + \beta_1\ ln\ SIZE_i + \beta_2 D + \varepsilon_i\ . \qquad (16\text{-}1)$$

Here, KN denotes knowledge stock whose proxy variables are R&D investments or patent applications, SIZE is the output (or employment) of a firm, and D is a dummy variable indicative of policy change. D is 1 for years after changes in the patent system, and 0 for years before.

In order to visualize the effects of knowledge on productivity, we consider the following production function, which is suggested in the endogenous growth model (Romer, 1986; Grossman and Helpman, 1991)

$$Y_i = A \, L_i^\alpha K_i^\beta \, n^\gamma \,. \tag{16-2}$$

Here, Y, L, and K are output, labor, and capital, respectively. The variable n indicates the number of intermediate goods, although it could also be regarded as an indicator for the quality level. If this production function displays constant returns to scale in labor and capital, the sum of α and β should be unity. The overall production function is subject to increasing returns because of the existence of the intermediate inputs n.

Here, n is an increasing function of knowledge stock, because intermediate goods are developed and improved by access to the existing knowledge stock. That is, as the knowledge stock increases, new intermediate goods are developed or the quality of intermediate goods is improved. Thus, we obtain:

$$Y_i = A \, L_i^\alpha K_i^\beta \, KN_i^\gamma. \tag{16-3}$$

Here, KN denotes knowledge.

This equation may be readily represented in log form as

$$\ln Y_i = A + \alpha \ln L_i + \beta \ln K_i + \gamma \ln KN_i. \tag{16-4}$$

We utilize R&D investments or patent applications as proxy variables for knowledge, because R&D expenditure is input to produce knowledge and patents are an output of knowledge (Pakes and Griliches, 1984). The coefficients α, β, and γ are the elasticities of output with regard to labor, capital, and knowledge, respectively.

Our measure of productivity, TFP (total factor productivity), is defined as the residual between output and inputs of labor and capital in the production function, as follows:

$$lnTFP_i = lnY_i - \alpha \ln L_i - \beta lnK_i. \qquad (16\text{-}5)$$

Here, *TFP* denotes total factor productivity. From equations (16-4) and (16-5), we can see that TFP has the following relationship to the quantity of knowledge.

$$lnTFP_i = lnA + \gamma \, lnKN_i. \qquad (16\text{-}6)$$

Coefficient γ is also the elasticity of TFP with regard to knowledge. This coefficient illustrates to what degree R&D investments or patents, the proxy variable of knowledge, contribute to the productivity of a firm.

In this study, we consider knowledge spillovers among firms. Knowledge spillovers allow us to escape diminishing returns and cause economic growth to proceed at an undiminished rate into the future (Romer, 1986; Grossman and Helpman, 1991). The equation regarding knowledge spillovers can be expressed as follows.

$$lnTFP_i = \alpha_0 + \beta_1 lnKN_i + \beta_2 lnKNO_i + \varepsilon_i \qquad (16\text{-}7)$$

Here, *KNO* denotes the knowledge spillover from other firms. The expected coefficients of β_1 and β_2 are positive, as we anticipate that knowledge accumulation will exert positive effects on productivity.

3. The Data

3.1 Data Sources

Our study utilizes the data of 216 manufacturing firms, each of which have more than 10 patents, over the years 1985-2007, and all of which have been registered in the Korean Stock Exchange Market over the specified time period.[2] The data for output, labor input, capital stock, and intermediate goods at the firm level are derived from the KISVALUE (Korea Investors Service-Financial Analysis System) database (2008).[3] Since the values in the KISVALUE database are in current terms, we converted current values into constant values using price indices from the Bank of Korea (BOK, 2008). As a price index for R&D investment, we used the average values of the producer price index and wage index, as in the studies of Coe and Helpman (1995), and Hall (1990). Data regarding unit labor cost from the OECD (2007) were used as the wage indices.

Patent application data for each firm were obtained from the KIPO (Korea Intellectual Property Office) database. We employed the raw dataset of patent application, which included more than one million patents. Every patent application included the name of its applicant firm. We matched each individual firm's patent application with the input and output data from KISVALUE by using the firms' names.

---

[2] One of the problems here may be the absence of a large amount of pre-patent reform data. The authors attempted to extend the data back in time. However, we found that the data for the previous time were not perfect, in that a great deal of data were missing from the KIS value dataset. Additionally, there were not enough patents to analyze the effects for the time period.

[3] The KISVALUE codes for each variable are listed in Appendix.

3.2 Calculation of Spillovered Knowledge

To assess knowledge spillover, we calculated other-firm knowledge using Jaffe's (1986)' method. Jaffe (1986) measured the magnitude of spillovers using a function of the technological distance between firms. He utilized the distribution of firms' patents over patent classes and defined the spillover pool as the weighted sum of all other firms' R&D, with the weights set proportional to the technological proximity.

Jaffe (1986) evaluated the similarity between firms using patents of firms classified by international patent classification (IPC) codes. If two firms applied for patents for similar IPCs, they are considered to have a substantial mutual effect on one another. Thus, the patent similarity between two firms can be calculated via the following correlation coefficient.[4]

$$Prox_{ij} = \frac{F_i F_j'}{\sqrt{(F_i F_i')(F_j F_j')}}$$

Here, F_i and F_j are the IPC patent vectors of firms i and j, respectively. $Prox_{ij}$ is the proximity or correlation between firms i and j. If every patent applied for by the two firms belongs to the same IPC category, $Prox_{ij}$ is 1. Additionally, if two firms applied for completely different IPC categories, $Prox_{ij}$ is 0. Thus, $Prox_{ij}$ is between 0 and 1. It becomes closer to unity as the technologies of two firms become more similar to each other.

---

[4] See Jaffe (1986) for the details.

The spillover knowledge from other firms can be calculated using the proximity index as the weight. Other-firm R&D (*RNDO*), and other-firms patents (*PATO*), can be calculated as follows.

$$RNDO_i = \sum_{j \neq i} Prox_{ij} RND_j$$

$$PATO_i = \sum_{j \neq i} Prox_{ij} PAT_j$$

The weight increases with greater proximity between the firms, and this means that knowledge of closer firms increases the mutual influence of the forms on each other. For example, a new patent or new semiconductor knowledge will have a greater effect on the technology development in semiconductor-related firms than on firms in the food industry.

3.3 Data Description

Table 16-1 shows the shares of output, R&D expenditure, and patents by technology sector in 1985 and 2007. We classified all firms into technology sectors in accordance with OECD guidelines (2007). In our sample, the numbers of firms were as follows: 29 in the high-technology sector (HI), 110 in the medium-high technology sector (MH), 43 in the medium-low technology sector (ML), and 34 in the low-technology sector (LO). Share of output, R&D expenditure, and patent applications have increased rapidly in high-technology firms over the years 1985-2007. Average R&D intensity was quite high in high-technology firms in 2007, even though those of all firms increased during that period. R&D intensity is the ratio of R&D expenditure to output.

Table 16-1. Share of Output, R&D Expenditures, Patent Applications by Technology Group

	N of Firms	Output		R&D Expenditures		Number of Patent Applications		R&D Intensity	
		1985	2007	1985	2007	1985	2007	1985	2007
High Technology	29	12.3	30.6	7.1	71.4	55.2	66.5	0.09	4.57
Medium-High Technology	110	43.0	42.9	62.4	24.4	28.9	28.3	0.24	1.11
Medium-Low Technology	43	32.8	21.4	20.0	3.5	12.1	4.7	0.10	0.32
Low Technology	34	11.9	5.1	10.5	0.8	3.8	0.6	0.14	0.30
Total	216	100.0	100.0	100.0	100.0	100.0	100.0	0.16	1.96

Source: KISVALUE Database (2008), and KIPO Database (2008)

Note: 1) Classification of each technology group is based on OECD (2007): High Technology (30, 32, 33), Medium-High Technology (24, 29, 31, 34, 35), Medium-Low Technology (23, 25, 26, 27, 28), Low Technology (15, 16, 17, 18, 19, 20, 21, 22, 36, 37). The numbers in parentheses are ISIC code (rev 3).   2) R&D intensity=R&D/output*100

The share of R&D expenditures was highest in MH firms in 1985, but in 2007, that of HI firms became highest as the share increased from 7.1% in 1985 to 71.4% in 2007. The shares of patent applications were largest in HI firms in both 1985 and 2007. In 2007, over 90% of total R&D expenditures and total patent applications were undertaken in two groups: high-technology firms and medium-high technology firms. Firms in these two sectors were responsible for 73.5% of total manufacturing output. Table 16-1 shows that the firms in the high-technology sector grew faster than those in the low-technology sector.

Table 16-2 shows the growth rate of variables by the four technology sectors during the 1985-2007 period. For total firms, output increased 11.6% annually on average, and capital input increased faster than labor input. The average annual growth rate of labor was 1.6%, and that of capital stock was 11.5%. This implies that the capital-labor ratio in production increased in Korean firms during the specified period. The average annual growth rates

Table 16-2. Annual Average Growth Rates of Output, Inputs, R&D, and Patent (1985-2007)

	N of Firms	Output	Labor	Capital Stock	R&D Expenditures	Number of Patents	TFP
High Technology	29	27.1	5.6	19.6	37.9	21.1	11.23
Medium-High Technology	110	11.4	1.2	11.2	19.0	19.9	1.56
Medium-Low Technology	43	7.0	-0.7	8.0	14.7	15.0	0.40
Low Technology	34	6.1	-0.8	8.8	10.4	9.9	0.80
Total	**216**	**11.6**	**1.6**	**11.5**	**24.2**	**20.0**	**2.51**

Note: Output, capital stock, and R&D expenditures are in constant terms, and labor is the number of employed labors. TFP is the simple average of those of the firms in each group.

of R&D expenditures and patents were 24.2% and 20.0%, respectively. R&D expenditures and patents increased more rapidly than outputs and inputs.

The output growth rate in HI sector was 27.1%, more than twice that of the total firm rate. Additionally, R&D expenditures and patents increased more rapidly in the HI sector. As for the average annual growth rate of TFP, the highest growth rates were attained in HI firms (11.23%).[5] TFP in other sectors was substantially lower, and the average TFP growth rate for total firms was 2.51%. Table 16-2 shows that during the period studied, knowledge is accumulated more rapidly in HI firms, and the TFP growth rate is also higher in high-technology firms than in the low-technology sector.

---

[5] We estimated the total factor productivity indices based on the method of Caves et al. (1982), which is a multilateral index that allows for comparisons of TFP levels among industries and time periods.

4. Empirical Results

4.1 Changes in the Korean Patent System

The Korean Patent System has been revised 16 times since it was first established in 1946. The most profound policy change in the system occurred in 1986. Until 1986, the underlying objective of the patent system was to restrict patentee's rights in order to obtain foreign technology more easily, but after 1986 the policy shifted toward protecting inventions and strengthening patent rights.[6] Two things can be mentioned regarding this 1986 policy shift. First, in the 1986 Uruguay Round, the strengthening of intellectual property rights was one of the major issues addressed. The Korean government was compelled to strengthen the patenting system, following the examples of patent systems in advanced countries. Secondly, the demand for patent protection rose with Korea's economic development and technological evolution. Korea's industrial structure needed to move toward a capital-intensive or technology-intensive model in order to achieve sustainable economic growth, and the government thus attempted to encourage R&D investment with a robust patent system for this purpose. The Korean patent system thus has undergone continual strengthening, beginning in 1986.

Jung et al. (2004) measured the index of the strength of the patent system using the method developed by Ginarte and Park (1997). The results of that study demonstrated that the Korean patent system had been substantially

---

[6] Maskus and McDaniel (1999) and Cohen et al. (2001) showed that the weak patent system in Japan from the 1960s to the mid-1990s positively affected Japanese productivity growth, as it played a pivotal role in diffusing technical information among Japanese manufacturing firms.

strengthened as the indices changed from 3.99 in 1986, to 4.28 in 1990, 4.67 in 1995, and 5.00 in 2002.

Major changes in the patent system for each year are as follows: In 1986, the patent system allowed substance patents, and the patent period extended from 12 years to 15 years. In 1990, the patent system added food to the list of patentable subjects and introduced a domestic priority rights system. In 1995, the list of patentable objects was again expanded and the patent period was extended form 15 years to 20 years. Korea also became a member of the WTO TRIPs in 1995. In 2002, Korea joined the UPOV (International Union for the Protection of New Varieties of Plants).

This study considers the effects of patent system reforms imposed in the years 1987, 1990, 1995, and 2002. It appears likely that the stronger patent protection regime in Korea, implemented beginning in 1986, has encouraged R&D expenditures and patent applications (Luthria and Maskus, 2004; Maskus, 2000).

4.2 Trends in the Patent System, R&D, and Patents

Here, before addressing the effects of patent system, some relevant trends in R&D investment and patent applications by Korean manufacturing firms are sketched using line graphs. As the data used herein were firm-level panel data, we regressed the R&D or patents on the year dummy variables under consideration. That is to say, we used a year dummy to match each year and then estimated the regression coefficients for each year dummy.

4.2.1 R&D Investment

Figure 16-1 shows the results. *RNDT*, *RNDL*, and *RNDP* are the simple trend of R&D, the trend of RND with the control variable 'labor', and the trend of RND with the control variable 'production' in the regression model, respectively. As the three lines evidence quite similar trends, only one figure need be interpreted as a representative case. If the trend evidences rapid increase in the years 1987, 1990, 1995, and 2002, we can assert that the IP policy change resulted in immediate effects on the R&D or patents. Here, *DRND* is the increase in R&D for the year, and *DPAT* carries a similar meaning.

Figure 16-1 shows that firms' R&D investment (*RNDT*) increased rapidly during the early 1990's, and then stalled at a near plateau during the mid-nineties. R&D trended upward for several years, from 1999 to the beginning of the 2000s. After 2003, R&D decreased dramatically until recent years. This movement trend appears comparable for the other variables, RNDL and RNDP. At the bottom of the figure, the differences are plotted for the sake of clarity.

If the strength of the patent system encouraged R&D, we should be able to detect significant positively-sized R&D changes (*DRNDT*) occurring around incidences of relevant policy changes. In particular, as the policy change is generally announced prior to actual change, the firms or people generally prepare for these changes in advance. Therefore, as a reasonable response, it is not unusual to find R&D investment changes prior to policy change. We must keep in mind that if the policy changes are in the form of changes in the clauses of IP laws, these effects could prove permanent.

According to the bottom of Figure 16-1, we can find the positive values of difference in R&D (*DRNDT*) for the years 1986, 1987, 1989, 1990, 1991,

Figure 16-1. Changes in R&D expenditures

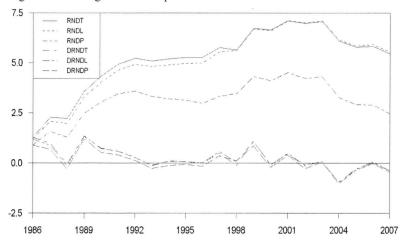

1997, 1999, and 2001.[7] We might consider the positive values around 1987 as the Korean patent system becomes stronger (introduction of substance patent). The change to the patent system in 1990 also appears to have influenced R&D, judging from the positive values observed around that year. However, accession to WTO and IPR policy changes in Korea do not appear to have increased the R&D activity of Korean firms in the figure. The Korean government enforced the IPR laws quite seriously to fulfill the WTO criteria, and a great many people were punished for IPR infringements in the first half of the 1990s.

However, R&D does not seem to have immediately responded substantially to this policy change. In contrast, after a couple of years of this change, positive values were observed in 1997, which may indicate the effects of the 1995 change. In 1998, we experienced negative R&D growth (that is,

---

[7] Here, the sizes in the Figure 15-1 and Figure 15-2 are the estimates for the year dummy variables with or without the control variables.

Figure 16-2. Changes in Patent applications

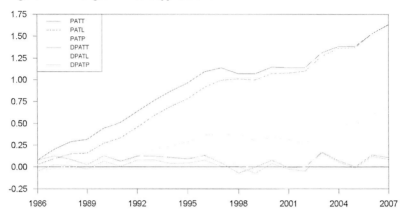

DRNDT is negative value) owing to the Asian currency crisis. Here, if we control the regression with firm size (LABOR) or production (PROD), the change appears not to be negative. This may indicate that the reduction in R&D was not the result of R&D behavior, but rather was caused by a downturn in the business cycle.

From 1999 to 2001, there was a large worldwide venture business boom, and we can see an upshift in R&D, followed by a major reduction in R&D after the craze. The strengthening of the IPR was not sufficiently powerful to offset this reduction in R&D.

4.2.2 Patents

What were the effects on patents? In Figure 16-2, the number of patent applications is provided. Patent trends appear similar to each other both with and without the control variables. In general, the years 1987, 1988, 1990, 1992, 1993, 1994, 1995, 1996, 2000, 2003, 2004, 2006, 2007 show increases in patents. This does not correlate precisely with year-to-year changes in R&D activity. However, we can interpret the figures as follows. The reforms of 1986 seemed effective in encouraging patent applications. In Korea, from the beginning of the 1990's, the government exerted major efforts to prepare for Korea's accession to the WTO on the IPR policy side, and the positive values in the years 1992-1996 may represent the results of these efforts. Even though the currency crisis resulted in negative effects in 1998, the venture business boom increased R&D significantly, and this gave rise to an upshift in patents in the 2000s. Of course, this rise could have been perpetuated by the patent reform of 2002.

4.3 Regression Analysis Using Policy Dummy Variables.

We implemented regression analysis to evaluate the effectiveness of policy changes in Korea. R&D investment and the number of patent applications were utilized as the dependent variables. The policy changes could be indicated by the year dummy variables for the timing of the reform. For example, if we wish to assess the effects of 1987 policy reform, we used ones for the years after 1987 and zeroes for the years before 1987. If the regression coefficients are positive and significant at the given criterion, we may conclude that the policy change was effective. We considered the years 1987, 1990, 1995, 2002 as the years of IPR policy reforms.

The fixed effects model was used in the panel data regressions. The individual fixed effects are included in this section, which leaves no constant terms in the regression.[8]

---

[8] We tried to do GMM developed by Arellano-Bond (1991), but we could not obtain more interesting results, thus report the results using fixed effects model.

Table 16-3. Effects on R&D Expenditure

	Dependent variable = RND			
	(1)	(2)	(3)	(4)
LABOR	1.061 (6.142)		1.053 (6.090)	
PROD		1.482 (11.297)		1.477 (11.246)
1987	1.871 (5.862)	1.317 (4.096)	1.873 (5.866)	1.319 (4.103)
1990	2.207 (8.674)	1.500 (5.759)	2.207 (8.675)	1.503 (5.767)
1995	1.265 (6.166)	0.344 (1.612)	1.318 (6.220)	0.384 (1.741)
1998*			-0.375 (-0.996)	-0.266 (-0.713)
2002	0.315 (1.611)	-0.360 (-1.830)	0.260 (1.281)	-0.396 (-1.950)
R^2	0.481	0.490	0.481	0.490
Obs.	4,968	4,968	4,968	4,968

Note: *1998 dummy has one only in 1998 and has zeroes in the other years. Numbers in ( ) are all t-values.

4.3.1 Whole Firms

First of all, the regressions for the whole firms were implemented with the explanatory variables of policy dummies and control variables. The size of labor employment and the values of production of each firm were used as control variables. We hoped that production in each year might partially reflect the business cycle effects, as well as the size effects, of the firms. All values are expressed in constant values.

Let us consider models (1) and (2) in Table 16-3. Note that both the control variables *LABOR* (employment) and *PROD* (production) have positive coefficients, which could indicate that these values exert a positive influence on R&D activity. This is consistent with our expectation in the model. Turning to the coefficients for dummy variables, the sizes of the coefficients are 1.3~1.8% and 1.5~2.2% for the 1987 and 1990 dummies, respectively. The 1990 reform is shown to have exerted a slightly greater influence than the 1987 reform. The coefficients of the 1995 dummy variable are dependent on the model. When labor is utilized as a proxy variable for the firm size, the coefficient is 1.265, but in the other case it looks insignificant. Finally, the 2002 dummy is not significant at the 5% significance level. This could be the result of the disappearance of the venture business boom around the beginning of the 21st century.

Incidentally, Korea sustained a sizeable shock to its economy at the end of 1997, due to the Asian currency crisis. This crisis gave rise to substantial curtailments of production and R&D activity in 1998. This shock was recovered in a short time. Thus, we used an additional dummy for the year 1998, and reported the results in columns (3) and (4). The currency crisis dummy in the table does not appear very significant.

We then analyzed the patent application data. In a fashion similar to that of the R&D activity, we regressed the patent data on the policy change dummies controlled with some variables.

Table 16-4 shows that patent applications were closely related to employment, R&D, and production. For example, according to model (2), patents increased by 0.466% when the firm's production increased by 1%. By way of contrast with the R&D side, the 1987 reform does not appear to have significantly affected patent applications. As the principal reform in 1987 was the introduction of substance patents, it would be expected that this area might take some time to yield results in the form of new patents. Reforms in 1990, 1995, and 2002 were all influential with regard to patent

Table 16-4. Effects on Patent Application

	Dependent variable = PAT			
	(1)	(2)	(3)	(4)
LABOR	0.521 (19.707)		0.522 (19.713)	
RND	0.008 (3.620)		0.008 (3.628)	
PROD		0.466 (23.365)		0.466 (23.376)
1987	0.122 (2.509)	-0.002 (-0.055)	0.122 (2.505)	-0.003 (-0.063)
1990	0.334 (8.562)	0.139 (3.515)	0.334 (8.560)	0.138 (3.504)
1995	0.506 (16.110)	0.199 (6.155)	0.501 (15.453)	0.192 (5.738)
1998*			0.034 (0.598)	0.046 (0.814)
2002	0.395 (13.26)	0.152 (5.086)	0.400 (12.903)	0.158 (5.127)
R²	0.783	0.788	0.783	0.788
Obs	4,968	4,968	4,968	4,968

Note: Numbers in ( ) are all t-values.

applications. Note that, even though we obtained negative coefficients in the R&D parts above, the coefficients here are positive numbers. We might interpret these positive numbers as the effects of increased R&D during the venture boom period prior to 2002, because increased R&D expenditure naturally increases patents.

Columns (3) and (4) show cases with the currency crisis included as a year dummy, but no significant coefficient was detected when some controlling variables were used. This result enables us to present the following interpretation: even though there was a reduction in patents in 1998, the reduction in the number of patents in that year might not be attributable to the shrinkage of patenting behavior, but rather to a downturn in the business cycle.

Table 16-5. Effects on R&D by Sectors

| | Dependent variable = RND2 | | | |
| | (1) | | (2) | |
	High Tech	Low Tech	High Tech	Low Tech
LABOR	1.112 (5.747)	0.659 (1.782)		
PROD			1.430 (9.955)	1.247 (3.482)
1987	1.670 (4.286)	2.276 (4.127)	1.108 (2.830)	1.844 (3.247)
1990	2.456 (7.908)	1.759 (4.007)	1.716 (5.405)	1.260 (2.728)
1995	1.394 (5.572)	0.988 (2.776)	0.376 (1.439)	0.429 (1.144)
2002	0.744 (3.130)	-0.539 (-1.561)	-0.047 (-0.197)	-0.852 (-2.532)
R^2	0.448	0.516	0.460	0.519
Obs	3,197	1,771	3,197	1,771

Note: Numbers in ( ) are all t-values.

4.3.2 Analysis by Technology Sectors

The effects of policy change differ depending on the characteristics of industries. For example, it is quite simple to copy a new technology in the computer game software industry or in the pharmaceutical industry if no patent protection exists. By way of contrast, in some other industries significant physical capital is required for the production of generic products, and nobody worries overly about patent infringement (Gould and Gruben, 1996).

Sometimes, a very high level of technology is needed just to copy the relevant products. Considering this, we split the industry into two sections according to technology level—high-technology industry and low-

Table 16-6. Effects on R&D by Sectors

	Dependent variable = Patents			
	(1)		(2)	
	High Tech	Low Tech	High Tech	Low Tech
LABOR	0.556 (17.632)	0.363 (7.319)		
RND	0.006 (2.292)	0.007 (2.268)		
PROD			0.468 (20.119)	0.375 (7.809)
1987	0.157 (2.491)	0.075 (1.017)	0.022 (0.360)	-0.013 (-0.171)
1990	0.383 (7.530)	0.254 (4.297)	0.168 (3.283)	0.120 (1.939)
1995	0.545 (13.374)	0.425 (8.881)	0.194 (4.598)	0.239 (4.747)
2002	0.453 (11.734)	0.264 (5.696)	0.171 (4.373)	0.126 (2.787)
R^2	0.807	0.678	0.811	0.678
Obs	3,197	1,771	3,197	1,771

Note: Numbers in ( ) are all t-values.

technology industry.[9] Generally, the IPR protection is considered more important in the high-technology industry. With regard to R&D investment, as is shown in Table 16-5, all the reforms but the 1987 reforms affected the high-technology industry more than the low-technology industry.

With regard to patents, we can observe similar effects (Table 16-6). The only exception is the 1995 reform case with the value of the firm's

---

[9] We used the OECD industry classification criteria. Here, High Technology and Medium-High in OECD criterion are merged into High Technology, whereas Medium-Low Technology and Low Technology are merged into Low Technology. However, it remains unclear as to how something as broad as electronics could be fit into one category. For instance, some subsectors within electronics are extremely high-tech, others are medium-tech, and some are low-tech. We have, however, been unable thus far to find a better categorization scheme than the OECD classifications.

production as a control variable. Overall, the IPR reforms appear to have had a bigger impact in the high-tech industry, as anticipated.

4.4 Effects of R&D and Patents on TFP

In the previous section, we determined that the strengthening of patent protection affected R&D activity and patent production. Now let us examine the effects of R&D and patents on productivity in Korean firms. We included the R&D and patents of other firms in order to assess the cross-firm effects of technology spillover. We applied a fixed effects model with both the individual fixed effects and the time-fixed effect.

Note that many aspects of firms' external environments were changing in the late 1980s and early 1990s other than domestic patent reform, and that these other changes could have driven both the increase in R&D and the increase in patenting. For example, after 1985, the Japanese yen appreciated sharply with respect to the dollar. The Korean won, partly pegged to the U.S. dollar, did not. The timing of the exchange rate shift roughly coincided with the first step in Korean patent reform. Interestingly, the Korean won appreciated in the 1990s, and this would seem to have occurred at roughly the same time that growth in R&D spending leveled off. We might consider these effects by controlling directly for the exchange rate or by identifying a subset of R&D-investing and patenting firms for whom foreign markets were unimportant.

Furthermore, the Korean economy faced a lot with several economic shocks over the last two decades, which included incentives for R&D and patenting; thus, we would rather control for them so as to more convincingly estimate the true marginal impact of domestic patent reform. However, we found that the export data of individual firms were not stable and we were unable to attain

Table 16-7. Effects of R&D and Patents on TFP: Whole Firms

	Dependent variable = TFPID			
	(1)	(2)	(3)	(4)
RND	0.003 (3.657)	0.001 (2.368)		
RNDO		0.468 (39.969)		
PAT			0.030 (5.601)	0.027 (5.022)
PATO				0.168 (7.899)
R^2	0.665	0.749	0.666	0.670
Obs	4,968	4,968	4,968	4,968

Note: Numbers in ( ) are all t-values.

any meaningful results from in this work. Additionally, it proved quite difficult for the authors to identify certain shocks and other incentives that would be helpful in explaining the increases in R&D and patents.[10] Thus, we employed both the individual fixed effects and the time-fixed effect in order to control for all these changes in the external environment.

The regression coefficients for the explanatory variables of R&D and patents are all positive and significant in Table 16-7. R&D investment and patents appear to exert positive effects on the increase in total factor productivity in the Korean firm-level data. Interestingly, the R&D of other firms (*RNDO*) was more influential than the within-the-firm R&D (*RND*) to the productivity, and this situation is similar in the case of patenting. This result is consistent with the industrial-level data analysis (For example, Kim et al., 2009, and Lach, 1995).

---

[10] We appreciate the reviewer's reminding us to think about these points.

Table 16-8. Effects of R&D and Patents on TFP by Sector

| | Dependent variable = TFP | | | |
| | (1) | | (2) | |
	High Tech	Low Tech	High Tech	Low Tech
RND	0.0008 (0.788)	0.0001 (0.230)		
RNDO	0.485 (33.673)	0.095 (4.755)		
PAT			0.018 (2.556)	0.003 (0.687)
PATO			0.230 (7.908)	0.064 (3.185)
R^2	0.771	0.571	0.693	0.568
Obs	3,197	1,771	3,197	1,771

According to Table 16-8, the R&D (and patents) of other firms appears to increase productivity more profoundly than R&D (and patents) within the firm, and this holds true for both the high-tech and low-tech sectors. Furthermore, these effects are larger in the high-tech industry than in the low-tech industry. For instance, a 1% increase in the R&D of another high-tech industry affects productivity by 0.485%, whereas the value of this case is 0.095 in a low-tech industry.

5. Conclusion

This study evaluates the effects of patent system reforms in Korea on knowledge activities such as R&D expenditure and patent applications, and then attempts to determine whether increases in knowledge exerted productivity growth in Korean manufacturing firms. We used Korea's firm level data, which encompassed 216 firms over the years 1985-2007.

The results of our descriptive analysis revealed that R&D expenditures and patents increased more rapidly than output and inputs. For all firms, the average annual growth rates of R&D expenditures and patents were 24.2% and 20.0%, respectively, whereas output increased by an annual average of 11.6%. Thus, the average R&D intensity, which is defined as the ratio of R&D expenditure to output, has increased from 0.16 in 1985 to 1.96 in 2007, and the R&D intensity of the high technology sector has increased particularly rapidly, from 0.09 to 4.57, from 1985 to 2007. In 2007, 71.4% of total R&D expenditures and 66.5% of total patent applications were undertaken by high-technology firms. As for the average annual growth rate of TFP, the highest growth rates were achieved in high technology firms (11.23%). TFP in other sectors was much lower, and the average rate of TFP growth in the total firms was 2.51%. This demonstrates that, during the period studied, knowledge was accumulated more quickly in high technology firms, and the TFP growth rate was also higher in high technology firms than in the low technology sector.

The Korean Patent System experienced a major policy change in 1986, when the policy shifted from weak system to a strong system based on the protection of inventions and patent rights. Since 1986, the Korean patent system was continually strengthened. Major reforms in the patent system have been undergone in the years 1986, 1990, 1995, and 2002. The government attempted to encourage R&D investment with a strong patent system in an effort to achieve sustainable economic growth. The 1986 reforms appeared to have been effective in terms of encouraging patent application. From the beginning of the 1990's, the government assiduously prepared for Korea's accession to WTO on the IPR policy side, and as a result, the numbers of Korean patent applications and patent grants have increased rapidly since the early 1990s. Even though the currency crisis resulted in negative effects in 1998, the venture business boom increased

R&D greatly, thus giving rise to an upshift in patents in the 2000's. Of course, this rise might have been accelerated by the patent reforms of 2002.

The results of panel data regression with policy dummy variables demonstrated that the policy reforms exerted a positive effect, increasing R&D expenditure and patent applications, and also that these increases in knowledge lead productivity growth in Korean manufacturing firms. When we split the industry into two sections according to technology level, the IPR protection is generally considered more important in the high technology industry. The regression results demonstrate that the IPR reforms had a more profound impact in the high technology sector firms than in the low technology sector firms, as had been expected. We also detected evidence of knowledge spillovers among firms, in that innovation in a certain firm was shown to increase the TFP of other firms.

Appendix

Table 16A-1. KISVALUE Item Code for Each Variable

Variable	KISvalue Source	KISvalue item code
Output	Profit-and-loss account	Sales (121000)
Intermediate Input	Manufacturing cost account	Raw Material Cost (151000) + Expenses (153000) – [Depreciation Cost (153130) + Tax and public charges (153150) + Rent (153160) + Welfare (153240)]
	Profit-and-loss account	Sales cost and Management cost (124000) – [Labor Cost (124100) + Tax and public charges (124214) + Rent (124215) + Depreciation Cost (124216)]
Capital Stock	Balance sheet	Tangible Assets (113200) + Intangible Assets (113400) + Postponed Assets (114900)
Labor	Balance sheet	Number of Employees (105000)
Wage	Manufacturing cost account	Labor expenses (152000)
	Profit-and-loss account	Labor costs (124100)
R&D Expenditures	Profit-and-loss account	Research cost (124406) + Current R&D cost (124410) + Current Development Cost (124420)
	Manufacturing cost account	Research and R&D Cost (153141)

Table 16A-2. Price Index for each Variable

	Item
Output Price Index	Producer's Price Index (KSIC 2-digit Industry)
Price Index for Intermediate Input	- Price index for Raw Material Cost is the weighted average index of raw material index and intermediate input index, where weight is reported in BOK price index dataset. - Rest of values in intermediate inputs are deflated by producer's price index for all industries.
Price index for Capital Stock	Price index for final capital good
Price index for R&D	0.5×manufacturing producer's price index + 0.5×wage index

Sources: Price index are from Bank of Korea Database (2008), and wage index are from OECD (2008)'s Korean unit labor cost.

PART V

TRADE, INEQUALITY, AND ENVIRONMENT

CHAPTER 17

WAGE PREMIUM OF EXPORTING FIRMS

1. Introduction

Exporting firms in many countries tend to pay higher wages than domestic firms. This may be attributed to exporting firms' greater productivity, among other factors. Theories regarding differences in productivity between exporting and domestic firms can be broadly classified into three categories: self-selection, learning effects, and economies of scale theories. Self-selection theory posits that firms with high productivity will enter into export markets, while learning effects theory posits that productivity may improve as a result of the export process; meanwhile, economies of scale theory encompasses both aspects. Regardless of which theory is applied, when exporting firms achieve greater productivity than their domestic counterparts, their wages will naturally be higher, as demonstrated by several existing studies based on actual data. However, even considering differences in productivity, the gap between exporting companies' wage levels and those of domestic companies is often greater than the productivity difference. This gap is termed the 'exporter wage premium'.

This study aims to investigate the wage premium in Korean manufacturing companies, as well as the reasons for its existence, by using actual data. The study focuses on the following aspects: first, a comparative analysis of Korean export and domestic manufacturing companies is performed, taking into account company characteristics such as size, location, and industry. While studies to date have attributed the wage gap to differences in productivity, we expand the discussion to encompass other factors—that is, the productivity effect is controlled by the inclusion of per capita labor productivity as an explanatory variable. The wage gap that emerges even after controlling for the productivity effect is called the exporter wage premium. Second, using 10-year panel data from the companies in question, we not only confirm the existence of the exporter wage premium but also calculate changes over time and explicitly demonstrate the premium's size.

Our analysis comprised the following steps. First, we extracted data from KISVALUE—a financial database of Korean companies—and organized the data according to per capita wage, per capita value added, export share in sales, company size, company location, and industry classification. The wage and value-added data were converted from nominal variables into real variables using the Consumer Price Index (CPI) and Producer Price Index (PPI). Second, the Breusch-Pagan test confirmed the existence of heteroscedasticity, so we performed the analysis using robust standard error.

The present study is different from previous studies in various respects. First, this research examines the wage gap between exporters and domestic firms for Korean manufacturing firms in the period 2007-2016. While most existing studies are based on data from the 1990s and earlier, the present study reflects more recent conditions. Second, earlier approaches focused on differences in productivity between exporters and domestic firms and attributed the wage gap to this difference. However, this study considers the productivity gap as a variable that represents corporate heterogeneity and examines the wage gap between exporters and domestic firms that exists even after controlling for its effects. Company characteristics including size, location, and affiliated industry were considered as part of this process. Our analysis determined that exporter wage premium existed prior to 2010 but declined gradually over time, and it was difficult to identify a significant premium in recent data.

In the following, the theoretical background and previous empirical studies are presented in the section 2, the data are explained in 3, the wage gap is analyzed through regression analysis in 4, and finally the conclusion is presented in the section 5.

2. Theoretical Background and Previous Literature

2.1 Wage Gap due to Productivity Differences

Melitz (2003) developed a trade model that considers heterogeneous firms and argued that various barriers and conditions impede firms' entry into the international market. This theory has become a basic model for many studies investigating the difference between export and domestic firms.

Many empirical studies were conducted before Melitz (2003). Bernard and Jensen (1995) analyzed data from US firms and found that exporting firms were larger than domestic firms and had higher capital intensity and per capita investment. Moreover, the wages of exporting companies were 14.5% higher and the welfare level was 32.7% higher. Bernard and Wagner (1997) reported that German exporting firms had high labor productivity for similar reasons. Bernard and Jensen (1997) analyzed the resource utilization rate of US exporting firms and reported that exporters' productivity was twice that of domestic firms, resource use was 12-19% lower, and wages were significantly higher. Clerides and Lach (1998) studied exporting companies in developing countries, including Colombia, Mexico, and Morocco, and observed that exporters tended to show high productivity.

Based on these empirical analysis results, Melitz (2003) developed a hypothesis regarding differences in firm productivity based on the monopolistic competition model and constructed a heterogeneous firm trade theory, according to which firms with high productivity achieve higher profits because of their lower production costs, whereas firms with lower productivity have lower profits due to higher production costs. Given that any firm's profits ultimately depend on productivity, there exists a certain level of productivity that distinguishes positive and negative profits. Firms whose productivity exceeds this level achieve positive profits, while firms whose productivity falls below that threshold report negative profits. Consequently, companies with negative profits will ultimately fail to sustain production and suffer expulsion from the market. Conversely, firms recording positive profits due to high productivity will remain in the market, and new firms will enter the market when they anticipate that positive profits will ensue. In such a market environment, only firms whose productivity surpasses a certain level can thrive in the domestic market in a closed economy before trade opening.

When markets open up and trade becomes possible, companies must invest extra money to engage in export. First, it is necessary to verify the existence of an international demand for their products and determine the regulations and quality standards that apply in the overseas market. It is also necessary to find buyers willing to sell the product overseas, and to install a sales logistics system and bear the transportation costs associated with international delivery. Firms that cannot bear these costs will be unable enter the export market even if it is open; only firms whose productivity is sufficiently high to allow them to meet those costs will be able to export. As such, just as survival in and exit from the domestic market are determined by a specific productivity level, entry and non-entry into the export market are similarly dependent on productivity. This scenario constitutes the so-called self-selection theory. In a highly competitive international market, only companies with a certain level of competitiveness can begin exporting, and exporting companies are thus already highly productive before they enter the export market. Therefore, exporting companies' productivity is typically higher than that of domestic companies.

A range of other factors may also account for exporting firms' high productivity relative to their domestic counterparts. Here, we cite the example presented by Kim (2007), whereby through the acquisition of various advanced technologies through contact with overseas markets, exporting companies can accelerate their technological progress and improve their productivity compared to domestic companies. Exporting companies have considerable incentives to engage in technology acquisition and development, which allow them to contact foreign companies with superior competitiveness and various clients in the global market. Exporting companies occupy an advantageous position compared to domestic firms in that they fully recognize the necessity of technological tools and direct their resources toward the necessary technological development. They are thus able to maintain high productivity rates compared to domestic companies whose market size is small, and whose competitors operate at a relatively low technological level. This logic may be termed the learning effect theory.

Economies of scale theory can also account for the difference described above. Given that exporters operate in both domestic and overseas markets, their market size is typically larger than that of domestic enterprises. Therefore, increasing returns to scale may occur in production, and productivity may increase. When an exporting company increases its production factor input and expands its production to generate exports, it may achieve an economy of scale and thereby enhance its productivity. This phenomenon is primarily witnessed in developing countries that pursue export-oriented economic growth policies. As governmental support is largely directed toward exporting companies, such companies' productivity typically increases in response to their increased production factor input.

Companies choosing to remain in the domestic market typically show poorer productivity and inferior business environments. As markets opens up, which intensifies competition with foreign companies, domestic companies' profits may decline. For example, the demand for labor may increase as other firms enter the export market and generate high profits, thus raising wages. For domestic enterprises, such wage increases may contribute directly to their diminished profits.

2.2 Wage Gaps due to Factors other than Productivity

Where productivity differences emerge between exporting and domestic firms for any of the reasons described above, a wage gap between these firms will naturally ensue. In this study, we control the effects of productivity differences to analyze the wage gap. Note that a wage gap may be present between exporting and domestic firms even when they have the same productivity level; this phenomenon is known as the exporter wage premium. This study intends to empirically analyze these aspects.

McDonald and Solow (1981) were perhaps the first to suggest a profit-sharing negotiation framework within which companies might determine wages in the course of trade. According to that study, international trade affects wages via two key pathways. In addition to wage fluctuations due to changes in corporate profits, the income distribution ratio may change due to changes in workers' bargaining power even at the same level of profit. First, international trade affects wages through changes in a firm's earnings and profit levels. As markets open, exporting companies' profits increase; accordingly, wages also increase. For domestic companies, meanwhile, imports from overseas reduce the demand for their products and intensify market competition, leading to declining profits and a reduction in workers' income. Second, international trade affects wages via changes in the profit-sharing ratio. Exporting companies' labor demands increase as they begin to engage in export, and companies have little choice but to offer high wages in a bid to attract workers. Therefore, as workers' ability to negotiate for profit-sharing increases, the labor income share of exporting firms may exceed that of domestic enterprises.

In developing countries, the wage gap between exporting and domestic firms may also be attributed to external pressures. This is succinctly illustrated by the so-called Blue Round, which became an issue in the international trade field before and after the launch of the World Trade Organization (WTO) in the 1990s. North American and European interest in working conditions in developing and underdeveloped countries subsequently grew, and an anti-sweatshop campaign was launched targeting factories with poor working conditions. In developing countries, where workers work in poor conditions and have frequent accidents, wages are generally extremely low. For concerned consumers, international labor standards offer a remedy to substandard working conditions and low wages in developing countries. In many cases, this may exert pressure on developing countries to improve working conditions and increase unskilled laborers' wages. For example, these movements substantially improved conditions for Indonesian workers (Harris and Scorse, 2006). At that time, pressure from foreign governments and the international community was exerted against Nike, Reebok, and Adidas through the Indonesian government. In particular, the US government announced its intention to withdraw the Generalized System of Preferences (GSP) if the Indonesian government failed to improve working conditions. Ultimately, the Minimum Wage Act was passed, such that the actual wage paid to unskilled laborers in exporting companies could rise.

Through the above-described process, exporting companies are more easily subjected to international pressures, including from anti-exploitation movements and International Labor Organization (ILO) recommendations, than their domestic counterparts, and the wage gap between exporting and domestic companies can thus be widened.[1]

2.3 Existing Empirical Studies

Numerous empirical studies have analyzed company data to demonstrate that exporting firms pay higher wages than domestic firms, and that there is a wage gap between exporting and domestic firms. Bernard and Jensen (1995) analyzed the productivity and wage characteristics of US exporters and domestic firms from 1976 to 1987, and Meller (1995) analyzed five major factors affecting food, wine, and wood production in Chile during the period 1986-1989. Based on data from each industry, Meller found that the exporting companies' wages were higher than those of domestic companies. Arnold and Hussinger (2005, Germany) and Loecker (2007, Slovenia) obtained similar results for their respective countries. Liu et al. (1999) used

---

[1] Following the collapse of Rana Plaza in Bangladesh in 2013, similar pressures from international organizations and the international community arose in Bangladesh, with similar results.

balanced panel data from Taiwanese electronics companies for the 5-year period 1989-1993 and reported that exporters' wages were 15.5% higher. Greenaway and Yu (2004) also found that the wage gap for exporters in the UK chemical industry was 7.6%, while that for exporters in other industries was 1.5%.

While the above studies did not consider workers' characteristics, Schank et al. (2007) used German employer/employee data and controlled for worker and firm characteristics to demonstrate that wages increased according to the export share. For example, blue-collar (white-collar) employees working in a plant with an export-sales ratio of 60% earn approximately 1.8% (0.9%) more than similar employees in otherwise identical non-exporting plants. Alvarez and Lopez (2005) analyzed 7,132 manufacturing companies in Chile, and Van (2005) analyzed manufacturing companies in nine African countries. These studies report wage gaps. Bernard and Jensen (2004), Aw and Batra (1995), and Bernard and Jensen (1999) also detected wage gaps in exporting firms.

Several studies have reported results that differ from most of those detailed above. Tsou, Liu, and Huang (2006) found that the export wage premium for skilled labor was positive, while the export wage premium for unskilled labor was negative, for Taiwanese manufacturing firms. Using data from Denmark, Munch and Skaksen (2008) demonstrated that exporter wage premiums exist only in exporting firms that employ skilled labor. In addition, Were and Kayizzi-Mugerwa (2009) and Breau et al. (2006) found that the export wage premium disappeared after controlling for workers' age, gender, education, race, and nationality.[2]

Several empirical analyses have been conducted in Korea since Kim and Kim (1997) observed that the productivity growth rate was higher in the export goods industry. For example, studies by Lee et al. (2009) and Chun et al. (2013) revealed that exporting firms had higher productivity than domestic firms; foreign direct investment firms also had higher productivity. Meanwhile, Kim and Kim (2015) found that the increase in total factor productivity was higher for export than domestic firms, although the absolute level did not differ significantly between the two types of firm.

 Kim et al. (2005) analyzed the problem of wage inequality and argued that although wages were higher in industries with low tariff rates, it could not be stated with certainty that trade liberalization affected wage inequality. Ok et al. (2007) compared intra-industry trade data among Korea, China, and Japan and verified that trade structure can affect the wage gap.

3. Data

3.1 Data Description

Using unbalanced panel data obtained by firms in the Korean manufacturing sector during the period 2007-2016, this study investigates whether the wages that exporting companies pay are higher than those paid by domestic companies, and whether this difference can be attributed to factors other than productivity. The data were extracted from KISVALUE, provided by the Korea Investors Service. For the period 2007-2016, we collected 20,202

---

[2] Chinese studies regarding the wage differential between exporting and domestic companies are also ongoing. For example, Fu and Wu (2013) suggested that exporting companies in Hong Kong, Macao, and Taiwan pay relatively low wages compared to other companies. Regional differences have also been found.

pieces of data for 5,044 listed and unlisted (externally audited) companies, excluding companies with missing data. To compare and analyze the wages of exporters and domestic companies based on Bernard and Jensen's (1995) method, we extracted and organized data pertaining to per capita wage, value added per capita, export share, and company size, location, and industry. Firms were divided into large companies and small and medium-sized enterprises (SMEs). Companies located in Seoul, Gyeonggi-do, and Incheon were further classified as Seoul metropolitan; the rest were classified as non-Seoul metropolitan. Wages and value added per capita were calculated using the CPI and PPI for conversion into real variables. In the absence of any explicit criterion for distinguishing export and domestic companies, this study defined export companies based on the proportion of sales accounted for by exports, as in Kim and Kim (2015), as follows: $\geq 0\%$, $\geq 20\%$, or $\geq 50\%$.

3.2 Current Wage Gap Status

First, we analyzed the current status and trend of the wage gap between export and domestic companies. Figures 17-1 (a) and (b) present the real average wage calculated by CPI and the real weighted average wage based on the number of employees for export and domestic companies classified using the $\geq 0\%$ criterion.

Between 2007 and 2009, the average wages of both export and domestic companies fell; more specifically, in 2009, export companies' wages fell by 6% and the wages of domestic companies fell by 4.5%. During this period, the global economic recession precipitated by the 2008 financial crisis affected Korea's export and domestic markets. Since 2009, wages for export and domestic companies have risen, but as domestic companies have increased more rapidly than export companies, the wage gap between export companies and domestic companies in 2011 was minor.

Figure 17-1. Average wages

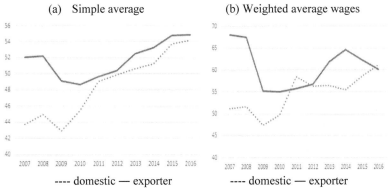

(a) Simple average (b) Weighted average wages

---- domestic — exporter   ---- domestic — exporter

Note: The unit is 'Mil. KRW'.

Source: KISvalue

Between 2012 and 2016, the wages of exporters and domestic companies increased by 12% and 13%, respectively, so there was almost no wage gap between exporters and domestic companies in 2016. As Figure 17-1 (b) illustrates, when the number of employees was weighted, wages for both exporters and domestic companies decreased in 2009, and wages for domestic companies increased from 2010. However, for exporters, wages began to decline again in 2014, and in 2016 the weighted average wage of exporters was lower than that of domestic companies.

Figure 17-2 (a) shows the labor productivity of export and domestic companies. In 2007, the labor productivity of exporting companies was much higher than that of domestic companies, but the labor productivity gap gradually narrowed due to the global economic downturn that followed the 2008 financial crisis, and the labor productivity gap subsequently disappeared in 2011.

From 2011 to 2016, labor productivity changed slightly, but the gap in labor productivity between export and domestic companies was only moderate. The situation differs slightly for the weighted average labor productivity, as

Figure 17-2. Average labor productivity

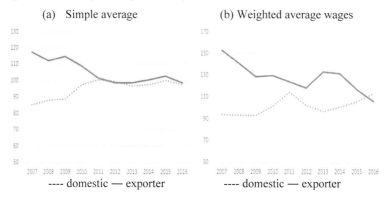

      (a)   Simple average   (b) Weighted average wages

      ---- domestic — exporter   ---- domestic — exporter

Note: labor productivity=per capita value-added.
Source: KISvalue

shown in Figure 17-2 (b). Compared to 2007, the weighted average
productivity of domestic companies has increased slightly over the last 10
years, but export companies' productivity has fluctuated and appears to be
lower than that of domestic companies in 2016. This can be explained not
only by the economic environment, but also by changes in the proportion of
large companies in operation.

To demonstrate the impact of company size and location, Figure 17-3
compares the real average wages of large companies and SMEs, while
Figure 17-4 shows the difference in average wage according to location.
Owing to the financial crisis, wages for large companies in 2008 showed
little change compared to 2007, while wages for SMEs increased by 3.1%
in that year. In 2009, wages for large and small companies fell by 3.7% and
4.6%, respectively. Wages of large companies and SMEs have been
increasing since 2010, with large companies' wages being 24-34% higher
than those of SMEs.

Figure 17-3. Average wages of large firms and SMEs

    (a)   Simple average   (b) Weighted average wages

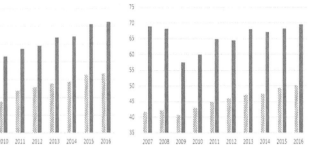

Source: KISvalue

Figure 17-4. Average wages for Seoul Metropolitan and other areas

    (a)   Simple average   (b) Weighted average wages

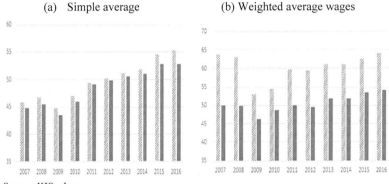

Source: KISvalue

Figures 17-4 (a) and (b) compare the real wages of manufacturing companies in the Seoul metropolitan area and elsewhere. Contrary to expectations, wages in the Seoul metropolitan area are lower than elsewhere in the Seoul area; this may be attributable to the size and industries of manufacturing companies in the Seoul metropolitan area. Large companies account for < 20% of all companies in the Seoul metropolitan area, while other areas include much larger companies. Further details are provided in the Appendix 17-1 and Appendix 17-2. In terms of the distribution of industries to which the companies belong, most of the high-waged

industries are located in the non-Seoul metropolitan area, while those with
lower wages are concentrated in the Seoul metropolitan area.

4. Results and Discussion of Empirical Analysis

4.1 Panel Regression Analysis of Exporter Wage Premium

We performed a regression analysis to test for the existence of export wage
premiums in Korean manufacturing companies. Given that the heteroscedasticity
problem frequently occurs in panel data, a heteroscedasticity test was
conducted first, Using the BP test (Breusch and Pagan, 1979), we detected
heteroscedasticity. Several approaches may be adopted to solve the
heteroscedasticity problem, including Robust ordinary least squares,
weighted least squares (WLS), and feasible generalized least squares (FGLS);
among these approaches, the Robust OLS method is the simplest and most
commonly used, and was thus used in this study.

Bernard and Jensen (1995) compared wages between export and domestic
companies after controlling for industry, size, and location. This study also
considers differences in companies' characteristics and analyzes whether
exporters have wage premiums compared to domestic companies under the
same conditions, with labor productivity variables included as control
variables.

$$Ln\ Wage = \beta_0 + \beta_1\ Expdum + \beta_2\ Ln\ Productivity + \beta_3\ Size + \beta_4\ Region$$
$$+ \beta_5\ Industry + \beta_6\ Year + \varepsilon_{it} \qquad (17\text{-}1)$$

$Ln\ Wage$: real wage

$Ln\ Productivity$: per capita value added

$Expdum$: dummy for exporter (1 for exporter, 0 for domestic)

$Size$: dummy for firm size (1 for large firm and 0 for SMEs)

Region: dummy for location (1 for Seoul metropolitan area and 0 for other areas)

Industry: dummy for industry

Year: dummy for year

In this model, β_1 represents the wage gap between export and domestic firms. If β_1 is statistically significant and positive, exporting firms have higher wages than domestic firms, even when labor productivity, firm size, firm location, industry, and year are identical.

To distinguish export and domestic companies, referring to the method of Kim et al. (2015), the ratio of exports to sales was defined as $\geq 0\%$, $\geq 20\%$, or $\geq 50\%$. Given that the data used in this study are panel data, we applied the Hausman test to select an appropriate model after considering both fixed-effects (FE) and random-effects (RE) models. Table 17-1 presents the results of regression analysis of CPI-adjusted data for the FE and RE models. A two-way model including industry and year as FE was used.

Although not reported in Table 17-1, the Hausman test yielded a p-value of 0.00. Therefore, as the hypothesis that there is no difference between FE and RE was rejected at the 1% significance level, interpretation of the results based on the FE model was preferable. When export and domestic companies are classified based on the $\geq 0\%$ criterion described above, the coefficient for the *Expdum* variable was significant at the 10% or 1% level, depending on the model. However, when exporting companies were defined as $\geq 20\%$ or $\geq 50\%$, the results were not significant. The final column of Table 17-1 presents the results of regression analysis including the export ratio (exports/sales) of a company as an explanatory variable; these results were also non-significant.

Table 17-1. Results from Panel Regression

	lnWage(0%)		lnWage(20%)		lnWage(50%)		lnWage	
	(1) FE	(2) RE	(3) FE	(4) RE	(5)FE	(6) RE	(7) FE	(8) RE
Expdum	0.010* (0.006)	0.016** (0.005)						
Expdum20			0.007 (0.007)	0.008 (0.006)				
Expdum50					0.002 (0.008)	0.002 (0.007)		
Exratio							0.000 (0.000)	0.001 (0.000)
lnPro	0.189** (0.003)	0.228** (0.003)	0.189** (0.003)	0.228** (0.003)	0.189** (0.003)	0.228** (0.003)	0.188** (0.003)	0.228** (0.003)
Size		0.194** (0.009)		0.197** (0.009)		0.199** (0.009)		0.197** (0.009)
Region		0.020** (0.007)		0.020** (0.007)		0.020** (0.007)		0.020** (0.007)
Cconst	14.31** (0.062)	13.49** (0.072)	14.31** (0.062)	13.49** (0.072)	14.31** (0.062)	13.49** (0.072)	14.31** (0.062)	13.49** (0.072)
Obs.	20,202	20,202	20,202	20,202	20,202	20,202	20,202	20,202
R^2	0.267	0.264	0.266	0.264	0.266	0.264	0.266	0.264

Source: standard errors in parenthesis. We selected FE model by Hausman test in all the cases.
Note:* $p < 0.10$, ** $p < 0.05$, *** $p < 0.01$.

For all other variables, the same results were obtained regardless of the criteria used for classifying export and domestic companies. According to Table 17-1, if productivity is 1% higher, wages will increase by 0.189% when other variables remain constant. According to the results of the RE model, the wages of large corporations are 19% higher than those of SMEs, while the wages of companies located in the Seoul metropolitan area are 2% higher than those of companies located in non-metropolitan areas. However, as the Hausman test results indicate, it may be difficult to interpret the results of the RE model. These results differ from the descriptive statistics presented above, which indicate that, on average, wages in Seoul's non-metropolitan areas are higher than those in the Seoul metropolitan area. In other words, when only the region where the company is located was taken into consideration, the average wage was higher in the non-Seoul metropolitan area because the effect of the other variables was controlled. This is likely because the proportion of large corporations is higher, while the proportion of export companies is higher in the non-metropolitan than Seoul metropolitan region. As the table in Appendix 1 illustrates, in the Seoul metropolitan area, large companies account for 11-17% of all enterprises, while in non-Seoul metropolitan areas the proportion is 21-27%.

4.2 Pooled OLS

We classified companies as exporting or domestic based on the annual export share. Accordingly, the same company may be classified as an exporting company in some years and as a domestic company in other years. Wage premium analysis, including that reported herein, analyzes structural relationships; additional analysis was performed to solve the problem of variability in company status among years. The analysis was performed again for companies classified as exporting or domestic companies throughout the analysis period, i.e., excluding companies that experienced a change in status at least once. The results are presented in Table 17-2.

The number of observations decreased from 20,202 to 14,479. The results in Table 17-2 again indicate that productivity is a significant determinant of wages, and the results for company size and location were in the expected direction. The export wage premium also had a significant positive value. However, when the definition of an exporting company was an export ratio $\geq 50\%$, although the wage premium of the exporting company maintained a positive value, it was not statistically significant.

Table 17-2. Regression for Consistently Exporting Firms

	(1)	(2)	(3)	(4)
Expdum	0.028***			
	(0.006)			
Expdum20		0.021***		
		(0.007)		
Expdum50			0.008	
			(0.009)	
Export ratio				0.0003***
				(0.0001)
lnPro	0.314***	0.314***	0.314***	0.314***
	(0.004)	(0.004)	(0.004)	(0.004)
Size	0.150***	0.154***	0.159***	0.155***
	(0.006)	(0.006)	(0.006)	(0.006)
Region	0.025***	0.025***	0.025***	0.025***
	(0.005)	(0.005)	(0.005)	(0.005)
Constant	11.868***	11.872***	11.873***	11.874***
	(0.084)	(0.084)	(0.084)	(0.084)
Obs.	14,479	14,479	14,479	14,479
R^2	0.439	0.438	0.438	0.438

$^*p < 0.10$, $^{**}p < 0.05$, $^{***}p < 0.01$.   standard errors in parentheses.

4.3 Regression Analysis by Year

Regression analysis was performed by year to examine changes in the wage gap between exporting and domestic companies over time (Table 17-3). After controlling for industry, region, and company size, the coefficient of labor productivity fluctuated from 2007 to 2016 (range: 0.26-0.35). The wages of large enterprises were 0.13-0.16 higher than those of SMEs.

While Figure 17-4 shows that the real average wage in the Seoul metropolitan area was lower than that in the non-metropolitan area, the regression analysis indicates that wages in the Seoul metropolitan area were higher than those in the non-metropolitan area when industry, company size, exporting firm dummy, and labor productivity were controlled for.

Table 17-3. Exporter Wage Premium by Year

	*ln*Wage				
	2007	2008	2009	2010	2011
Expdum	0.03**	0.06***	0.04***	0.02*	0.01
	(0.01)	(0.02)	(0.02)	(0.01)	(0.01)
*ln*Pro	0.34***	0.27***	0.29***	0.29***	0.31***
	(0.02)	(0.02)	(0.02)	(0.02)	(0.03)
Size	0.15***	0.16***	0.16***	0.13***	0.13***
	(0.01)	(0.02)	(0.02)	(0.02)	(0.02)
Region	0.03**	0.03**	0.02	0.01	0.02*
	(0.01)	(0.01)	(0.01)	(0.01)	(0.01)
Constant	11.32***	12.47***	12.29***	12.13***	11.95***
	(0.30)	(0.30)	(0.33)	(0.41)	(0.52)
Obs	2,460	2,160	1,981	1,968	1,940
R^2	0.476	0.388	0.417	0.393	0.399
	2012	2013	2014	2015	2016
Expdum	0.01	0.01	-0.01	-0.02	-0.00
	(0.01)	(0.02)	(0.02)	(0.02)	(0.02)
*ln*Pro	0.35***	0.31***	0.35***	0.30***	0.27***
	(0.02)	(0.03)	(0.02)	(0.03)	(0.03)
Size	0.13***	0.16***	0.15***	0.16***	0.16***
	(0.02)	(0.02)	(0.02)	(0.02)	(0.02)
Region	0.02	0.02	0.02**	0.02	0.00
	(0.01)	(0.01)	(0.01)	(0.01)	(0.01)
Constant	11.45***	12.10***	11.21***	12.01***	12.87***
	(0.37)	(0.53)	(0.45)	(0.55)	(0.56)
Obs.	2,145	2,411	2,084	1,714	1,339
R^2	0.428	0.399	0.438	0.413	0.379

Note:* $p < 0.10$, ** $p < 0.05$, *** $p < 0.01$. Standard errors in parentheses

As noted previously, Table 17-1 presented the results of two-way FE models including individual industry and year as FE. Figure 17-5 presents estimated coefficients for exporter wage premium by year based on dummy variables.

Figure 17-5 illustrates an interesting phenomenon. Prior to the global financial crisis, the wage premium of exporters rose from 3% in 2007 to 6% in 2008. As such, the wages of exporting companies were approximately 6% higher than those of domestic companies after controlling for labor productivity, company size, company location, and industry. As the wage

Figure 17-5. Changes in export wage premium

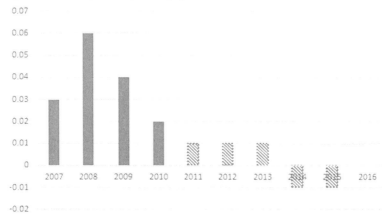

Note: statistically significant ▨ statistically insignificant

premium of exporting companies began to decrease from 2009, however, the difference became insignificant (from 2011 onward); from 2011 to 2013, the wage premium of exporting companies was only 1% higher. From 2014 to 2016, the coefficient of the export dummy variable was negative, indicating that the wage premium of exporting companies maintained a positive value during the first half of the analysis period. However, more recently, it has shown a negative value.

Figure 17-5 shows that, overall, the wages of exporting companies were not higher than those of domestic companies in the Korean manufacturing sector. How might we explain this phenomenon? In the case of developing countries, such as Bangladesh and China, exporting companies not only make higher profits than domestic companies, but also have better working conditions and—accordingly—higher wages in many cases. In the case of Korea, exporting companies were able to pay higher wages in the past for the various reasons presented above. However, Korea passed that point a long time ago; export companies no longer appear to have a wage premium.

The results of our empirical analysis can be explained as follows. First, the economic situation of Korean exporting companies has deteriorated since the international financial crisis. [3] Second, Korea's export-oriented economic policy is diminishing rapidly. This phenomenon has occurred not only in Korea, but also in countries that previously operated mainly based on exports, such as China, in line with the deterioration of the international economic situation. Therefore, there is currently no reason for a wage gap between exporting companies and domestic companies to appear. Third, the fourth industrial revolution should be considered: as the wage level continues to rise in tandem with economic development, it is more efficient for companies to adopt various machines or computer systems rather than workers as a means of reducing costs, particularly in response to the increasing wage burden. In particular, export companies are more motivated to cut costs. Moreover, because they enjoy access to international markets and are able to more rapidly and efficiently acquire cutting-edge technology, export companies adopt artificial intelligence technology at an earlier stage as a means of replacing manpower. Therefore, it is less necessary for exporters to pay high wages, and hire high-skilled workers to ensure the quality of exporters' products.

The results of this study can be summarized as follows. Exporting companies in Korea's manufacturing industry exhibited a wage premium in the past, but this has gradually declined and is now almost non-existent. For

---

[3] According to the Korea Development Institute (KDI), Korea's annual exports have stagnated in terms of volume, and the growth rate is far below that expected by the International Monetary Fund (i.e., Korea's export situation is deteriorating; KDI, 2015).

this reason, the analysis of the entire panel data set identified no significant wage premium for Korea's export companies.

5. Conclusion

Numerous theoretical and empirical studies have verified that exporting firms pay higher wages than domestic market-oriented firms.[4] In this study, the wage gap between exporters and domestic firms was reanalyzed using relatively recent data from Korea. Perhaps the most important cause of the wage gap is the difference in productivity. Most existing studies reported that exporting firms had higher productivity than domestic market-oriented firms, which may be due to learning or self-selection effects. When productivity is high, workers in exporting companies will naturally be paid more than those employed by domestic market-oriented companies. The data also indicate that this productivity gap contributes to a difference in wages.

This study analyzed whether the wage gap between exporters and domestic firms may also be attributed to factors other than the productivity gap, while acknowledging the role of differences in productivity. To this end, we first ruled out the influence of other factors that might affect companies' wages, including their characteristics, industry, size, and location, by including those variables in regression analyses (along with productivity).

We analyzed unbalanced panel data from Korean manufacturing companies for the 10-year period 2007-2016. First, we compared the wages of exporters and domestic firms. Before 2010, the real average wages offered

---

[4] In some cases, the wages of exporting companies may be lower because government policies such as free export zones give preferential treatment to exporting companies (in terms of the observation of working conditions).

by exporting companies were higher than those of domestic market-oriented companies. We also compared labor productivity and found that, for exporting firms, it has been declining since before 2011, while for their domestic market-oriented counterparts it has risen. In terms of firm size, the wages of large corporations were 24-34% higher than those of SMEs, and in terms of location, the wages of companies in the Seoul metropolitan area were lower than those of companies in non-metropolitan areas.

Multiple panel regression analysis showed that the wage premium of exporting companies existed even when major variables, such as productivity, industry, company size, and location, were controlled for. However, no wage premium emerged for firms that had particularly large export proportions. In addition, a cross-sectional analysis was conducted to determine how the annual wage premium of export companies changed from 2007 to 2016. Export companies showed a significantly higher wage premium from 2007 to 2010. From 2011 to 2013, positive coefficients were obtained, but wage did not differ between exporters and domestic firms. Finally, from 2014 to 2016, the wages of exporting companies were lower, albeit not significantly.

Although the changes identified in this study are compelling findings, they are difficult to explain. This study has proposed external and internal factors that may account for the changes. Based on these findings, it appears that Korean manufacturing exporters can no longer pay higher wages simply by virtue of their status as export companies. However, the wage gap appears to have been caused by productivity differences. Overall, this is consistent with the results of previous studies and suggests that the Korean economy may achieve wage growth via productivity improvement rather than government support aimed at increasing exports.

Appendix

Table 17A-1. Ratio of the Number of Large firms and SMES

	SMEs	Large firms
2007	77.93	22.07
2008	78.38	21.62
2009	78.19	21.81
2010	78.71	21.29
2011	79.95	20.05
2012	82.10	17.90
2013	85.11	14.89
2014	83.69	16.31
2015	83.55	16.45
2016	82.52	17.48

Appendix 17A-2. Ratio of Large firms to SMEs by areas

	Seoul Metropolitan		Non-Seoul Area	
	Large firms	SMEs	Large firms	SMEs
2007	0.17	0.83	0.26	0.74
2008	0.16	0.84	0.26	0.74
2009	0.16	0.84	0.26	0.74
2010	0.15	0.85	0.26	0.74
2011	0.14	0.86	0.25	0.75
2012	0.12	0.88	0.22	0.78
2013	0.11	0.89	0.18	0.82
2014	0.11	0.89	0.20	0.80
2015	0.11	0.89	0.21	0.79
2016	0.12	0.88	0.21	0.79

CHAPTER 18

RELATIONSHIPS BETWEEN POLARIZATION AND OPENNESS IN KOREAN ECONOMY

1. Introduction

It seems undeniable that the rapid growth of the Korean economy during the past 50 years was only possible because of the expansion of international trade, and exports were particularly important in this expansion. According to growth accounting, the economic growth is due to two factors: input growth and productivity growth. Trade with other countries was critical for both, and the Korean economy owes its success to international trade. But international trade has other economic side effects that are not as desirable. First, consider the income distribution problem. In particular, polarization in various areas can emerge in the context of international trade expansion. International trade gives rise to significant gains in the exporting industry, which can result in benefits for holders of capital resources, exporting companies and workers associated with these fields. The Heckscher Ohlin theory of international trade can give us some important ideas about who benefits and who loses in this situation. If the wealthy classes enjoy gains from international trade, undesirable income distribution effects will result. Second, the positive effects from exports have, of late, been decreasing in the Korean economy. It is unknown at present whether there is significant spillover from exports to other areas; for example, in 1990, exports of 1 billion KRW lead to the employment of 58.6 workers in 1990, but this had dropped to 12.6 workers by 2005, and further to 7.7 workers by 2012 (Institute for International Trade, 2014).

This study investigates the relationship between international trade and polarization. We will look at the relationship between international trade and industry using industry data from whole industries and individual firms. In particular, we calculate GINI-similar coefficients and other measures to obtain the polarization indices, and we perform regression analysis on the time series and panel data of these indices. This study finds that there is a positive relationship between export and polarization.

There are several ways to define polarization; we consider it to be the gap in peoples' incomes, the gap between exporting industries and other industries, and the gap among firms in a particular industry. These gaps can be widened by international trade. First, the Heckscher-Ohlin theory of international trade states that, in the long run, free trade benefits the factors of production that are abundant and hurts factors of production that are scarce. Second, a gap between exporting industries and importing industries may exist in the short run. Third, within an industry, exporting companies will become larger while the other companies will become smaller. Fourth, if the exporting companies are large firms, the gap between large firms and small and medium sized firms will be larger. As a result, international trade will result in the polarization of the economy.

Even in many advanced countries, it has been reported that increased trade has negative income distribution effects. This study uses trade data at the industry and firm levels, and investigates the effects of international trade on the polarization of the economy. This research is expected to determine whether the expansion of international trade in Korea widened the gap in the economy, and to identify the factors affecting polarization.

2. Literature

When we consider the relationship between economic growth and income inequality in developing countries, the effects of economy globalization should be investigated. Many empirical studies including Feenstra and Hanson (1997) have addressed this topic. Most of them have pointed to the increases in income differences caused by economic globalization (Sato and Fukushige, 2007). An important study comes from Feenstra and Hanson (1997); they investigated the effects of Foreign Direct Investment (FDI) on the skilled labor share of wages in Mexico from 1975-1988. FDI was found to increase the demand for, and the wages of, skilled labor, and this effect was particularly large in FDI concentrated regions. Another example relates to U.S industry. Borjas and Ramsey (1995) argued that employment changes in trade concentrated industries can explain the inequality in the U.S. Hanson and Harrison (1999) analyzed the relationship between trade reform and rising wage inequality, focusing on the 1985 Mexican trade reform. Wage inequality in Mexico rose after the reform, which is puzzling in a Heckscher-Ohlin context if we assume that Mexico has a comparative advantage in producing low skill-intensive goods.

More recently, Lim and McNelis (2014) examined the relationship between the Gini coefficient, trade-openness, aid, and FDI flows. Panel data estimates are provided for the overall data set (42 low to middle income countries). It finds empirically that trade openness is more able to change income inequality than either FDI or foreign aid, but that its effectiveness depends on the stage of development. The countries with high labor intensity in production and greater openness generate lower inequality in response to favorable shocks to export demand and trade.

Many papers have attempted to address this question by using data for the Korean economy, but the results are not consistent. For example, even within a single paper we find mixed results. Mah (2002, 2003) studied the impact of changes in trade values and FDI inflows on the Gini coefficients for Korea. Mah (2002) found that Gini coefficients tend to increase with trade liberalization measures and FDI inflows, and concluded that the progress of globalization caused income inequality to deteriorate in Korea, which supports the Feenstra-Hanson (1997) hypothesis. On the other hand, Mah's regression results indicated that neither changes in the openness ratios, regardless of the measures, nor those in the FDI inflows were significant in influencing the Gini coefficients. Sato and Fukushige (2009) analyzed the determinants of the Gini coefficient for income and expenditure for the Korean economy. Their results suggest that the effect of economic globalization has two routes, and two different speeds, in affecting income inequality. Recently, Kang (2014) examined the relationship between globalization and income distribution in Korea.[1] The study investigates the effects of trade openness, inward and outward FDI flows, and per capita GDP on income distribution from 1992 to 2011. It found that, as trade openness and per capita GDP increased, income inequality was reduced. Meanwhile, income equality deteriorates as inward and outward FDI flows increase. The negative effect of inward FDI flows on income inequality is greater than that of outward FDI flows.

---

[1] Of course, there are a lot of studies on the relationship between openness and income distribution written in the Korean language, which we do not mention here to save space.

This study differs from those mentioned above in the sense that we do not focus on the relationship between international trade and income inequality, but on the relationship between polarization and international trade. Here, we use concentration as a proxy for polarization; namely, the concentration of industries and the concentration of firms. Thus, we will use concentration indices like HH (Hirschman-Herfindahl) and Gini coefficients. The Gini coefficients used in this study are not used to indicate income distribution. We report how much concentration occurs among industries and firms, and we explore the effects of international trade on this concentration or polarization. This research, therefore, uses production data instead of wage data or per capita income data, making it relatively unique.

3. Changes in Industry Structure

The industry structure of the Korean economy has changed from primary industries such as agriculture and fisheries, to secondary industries such as automobiles and semi-conductors over the past few decades. By using OECD STAN data (rev.3) we obtained the following results.[2]

3.1 Changes in Industry Structure

These numbers are shown in Table 18-1. In Korea, primary industry (agriculture and fishery) has been reduced to less than 3%, from 30% during the last four decades, while secondary industry (mining and manufacturing) grew from 20% to 30%. The service sector is almost 70%, and has increased from 50% in 1970.

---

[2] Industry classification in STAN data is given in the appendix. (We did not recalculate the original data using a deflator because we are only interested in changes in industry structure.

Table 18-1. Industry Shares

	1970	1975	1980	1985	1990	1995	2000	2005	2009
Agriculture and fishery*	0.291	0.269	0.160	0.133	0.087	0.062	0.046	0.033	0.026
Mining and Manufacturing**	0.215	0.248	0.280	0.311	0.298	0.297	0.315	0.304	0.301
Service***	0.494	0.483	0.560	0.557	0.615	0.642	0.639	0.663	0.673

Note: * ISIC (International Standard Industry Classification) C01-C05. ** ISIC C10-C37. *** ISIC C40-C99

3.2 Industry Structure Change in Manufacturing

Even within manufacturing, the Korean economy has experienced dynamic changes in industry structure (Table 18-2). From the table, we see a reduction in food products, beverages and tobacco, textiles, textile products, leather and footwear, wood and products of wood, and cork, while basic metals and fabricated metal products, machinery and equipment, and transport equipment have been steadily increasing.

3.3 Industry Change in Terms of Technology Level

It is generally acknowledged that the Korean economy has moved toward capital and technology intensive industries. In particular, we can observe that, as the Korean Economy has grown, it has moved toward high tech industries, from low tech industries. According to the classification by OECD, we can confirm the trend change. Table 18-3 shows those findings.

In the table, HI, MH, ML, LO stand for high, mid high, mid low, and low, respectively. The Korean economy has been rapidly transformed from low and mid-low technology industries, to mid-high and high technology industries.[3]

---

[3] The specific industries for each technology are in the appendix (OECD, 2011).

Table 18-2. Changes in Industry Structure inside Manufacturing

	1970	1975	1980	1985	1990	1995	2000	2005	2009
Food products, beverages and tobacco	0.196	0.131	0.108	0.091	0.073	0.064	0.062	0.052	0.051
Textiles, textile products, leather and footwear	0.280	0.264	0.233	0.186	0.133	0.087	0.082	0.051	0.041
Wood and products of wood and cork	0.030	0.020	0.008	0.008	0.008	0.008	0.006	0.005	0.004
Pulp, paper, paper products, printing and publishing	0.059	0.054	0.038	0.052	0.053	0.062	0.048	0.041	0.041
Chemical, rubber, plastics and fuel products	0.142	0.170	0.199	0.167	0.144	0.162	0.151	0.170	0.155
Other non-metallic mineral products	0.063	0.063	0.065	0.063	0.066	0.051	0.041	0.035	0.038
Basic metals and fabricated metal products	0.027	0.051	0.102	0.129	0.138	0.138	0.126	0.165	0.142
Machinery and equipment	0.081	0.132	0.166	0.179	0.235	0.275	0.337	0.330	0.338
Transport equipment	0.085	0.085	0.052	0.092	0.117	0.127	0.123	0.135	0.175
Manufacturing n.e.c. and recycling	0.037	0.031	0.029	0.033	0.032	0.025	0.023	0.016	0.014

* Manufacturing is from ISIC C15-37.

Table 18-3. Changes toward high Technology Industries

	1985	1990	1995	2000	2005	2009
HI	0.120	0.157	0.191	0.234	0.227	-
MH	0.208	0.268	0.284	0.273	0.287	-
ML	0.302	0.275	0.279	0.271	0.321	0.295
LO	0.370	0.301	0.247	0.222	0.165	0.142
H&MH	**0.328**	**0.424**	**0.475**	**0.507**	**0.514**	**0.562**

* H, M, LO stand for High, Middle, Low technology, respectively. In the case of 2009, OECD did not provide for the HI and MH separately.

Figure 18-1. Ratio of trade to GDP

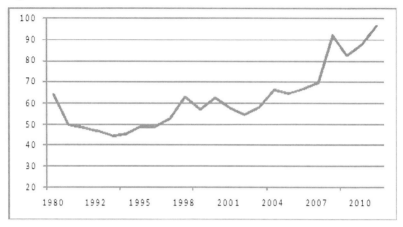

Source: KOSIS and Bank of Korea

3.4 The Ratio of International Trade to GDP

As is well known, the Korean economy depends heavily on international trade. The degree of dependence of the Korean economy on foreign trade has been increasing since the opening of the economy in the 1970s and, during this time, the growth strategy of the Korean economy was export-oriented. The ratio of international trade to GDP, which is sometimes referred to as openness, has recently been around 100%. Figure 18-1 shows the trend of this ratio.

This ratio rose rapidly in the 1970s (not shown in the figure) (Jang, 1999). After a period of slow change and decrease in the 1980s, the ratio began increasing again, and has continued ever since. Of interest is the fact that the trend of these ratios looks similar to the degree of concentration in the manufacturing industry. We anticipate finding similar patterns as we continue our research and calculations.

4. Polarization of Production and International Trade

International trade in the Korean economy has been increasing rapidly since the 1970s and the total amount of international trade has recently exceeded one trillion dollars. On the one hand, it would not be an exaggeration to say that international trade has made the economy grow and that the Korean people enjoy today's income level. On the other hand, it would be fair to say that international trade may have caused some amount of polarization within the economy.

During the decades of economic development, Korea experienced drastic changes in industry structure. The percentage share of manufacturing increased significantly. In addition, there were big changes, even within the manufacturing industry. All these changes seem to be related to international trade. Naturally, exporting industries have grown and importing industries have shrunk. These changes might result in the polarization of industries. In this section, we report on the degree of polarization by using manufacturing industry data.

4.1 Measures

We are going to use the degree of concentration as the proxy for the polarization index. In particular, we borrow some measures from other areas of economics, such as CR3 (concentration ratio 3), CR5, H-H (Hirschman-Herfindahl) index, and GINI (Gini's coefficients). For example, if we consider the polarization in an industry with n firms, CR3 and CR5 are the share of the top three or five firms, and H-H is the sum of squares of each of the firms in the industry; $HH=\sum s_i^2$, where s_i indicates the share of i-th firm. Gini was originally proposed to be a measure of income inequality, and is the most commonly used measure of inequality. A Gini coefficient of zero expresses perfect equality, that is, all values are the same. For the calculation, the following formula is used (Jasso, 1979):

$$G = \frac{1}{2\mu n^2} \sum_{i=1}^{n} \sum_{j=1}^{n} |y_i - y_j|$$

Where $y_{i(j)}$ indicates the sales of a firm i(j) and μ is the average of the sales, and n is the number of firms. Usually, GINI is calculated based on i-th percentile of the population, but in this study the number of firms does not equal one hundred; therefore, we use a GINI-similar (GINI-s) instead of GINI itself.[4] Therefore, the absolute size of GINI-s could be quite different from the usual GINI, and we should note that only the trend or the 'change' itself is meaningful. If we want to obtain the degree of concentration toward a few industries in the whole economy, *i(j)* can indicate an industry. By the same token, the degree of concentration of an industry can indicate how the industry is concentrated toward some firms if we use *i(j)* for the firms in the industry.

4.2 Industry Production

First, we report CR3, CR5, H-H, GINI-s for 26 manufacturing industries in the Korean economy in Figure 18-2.

All the indices have very similar shapes; four indices had a decreasing trend in the early 1990s and then increasing trends after the mid-90s. It seems that the manufacturing sector was dispersed in the 1990s, but began to focus on some specific sectors in the 2000s, meaning that polarization mainly occurred in the mid and late 2000s. It is a relief to see that this increasing tendency has not continued in more recent years.

---

[4] In this study we use DASP (Distributive Analysis Stata Package), which is an external software of STATA.

Figure 18-2. Trend of polarization of 26 industries

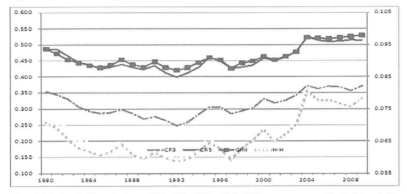

Note: Right hand side axis shows HH while CR3, CR5, GINI-s are expressed by left hand side axis.

4.3 International Trade

The structure of international trade has changed greatly in Korea, and the change occurred along with the polarization of the economy; most exports and imports centered on a few items. We report the calculated results from the concentration indices in order to see the polarization trends. In the year 2009, the five largest exporting industries were ship building, semi-conductors, mobile phones, display panels, and motor vehicles, and these five items account for 43.5% of total exports. This shows that Korea's export economy is concentrated on only a few industries. By the seventies, light industries such as textiles and shoes were major exporting items, but high-tech and capital intensive items have been the main exports since the 1980s.

In the 2000s, another important phenomenon was that exports changed from being mostly final goods, to being mostly intermediate goods. The share of parts, components, and half-finished goods being exported has been growing a lot recently due to the increase in the production of final goods overseas. Nowadays, intermediate goods are produced in foreign countries with final goods as manufacturing factories moved abroad. Due to this trend, the export market of Korean products is transferring from advanced countries to developing countries where manufacturing factories are located. As this has been happening, Korean exports have been concentrating on a few items like shipbuilding, IT (semi-conductor, flat display panel, mobile phones), and cars. In particular, exports of display panels have risen sharply since the mid-2000s when the export of the LCD panel for TVs began.

For an understanding of the background to this we report the degree of concentration of export items by using UN Comtrade data. From SITC three digit data with 'rev.2', we used 255 sub industries and calculated the concentrations. About 230 out of 255 industries have reported exports. The GINI-s in Figure 18-3 show that the concentration of the Korean export economy has been increasing since the mid-1990s.

In Figure 18-3, two lines are shown. If the GINI-s is a large number, it means that the exports and imports are centered on only a few items.[5] Basically, it seems that Korean economy exports are more concentrated than Korean economy imports, but both lines have been increasing in recent years.

---

[5] But we have to note that the absolute size of GINI-s cannot be compared with the usual GINI in the income distribution. Here, GINI-s looks very large (0.7~0.8) comparing the usual GINI (in general 0.3~0.5). This large number may have been obtained given that we are managing 255 sub-industries rather than just one hundred classes, as in usual GINI. Therefore, note that 'change' or trend of GINI-s rather than absolute size itself can be meaningful.

Figure 18-3. Concentration of trade in the Korean economy: data from 255 sub industries

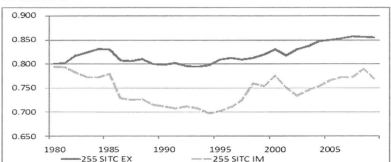

Interestingly, we find a similar U-shape for both industrial products and international trade. It seems that the production concentration is positively correlated with international trade concentration. In addition, these U-shapes look to be related to the degree of dependence on foreign trade, shown in Figure 18-2.

4.4 Trade Partners

What about Korea's trading partners? Was the concentration tendency related to exporting or importing countries? We report two indices that indicate the degree of concentration of trading partners. All the data are from Comtrade Data of UN.

One distinct characteristic is that Korea's exports and imports have been concentrating on a few countries, and five countries account for more than 50%. In past years, Korea has exported the most to the US and then to Japan. In the 2000s, however, Korea exported the most goods to China, with the US and Japan ranking second and third, respectively. As for importing

Figure 18-4. CR5, CR10, and H-H's of trade partners

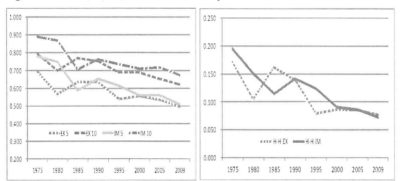

partners, in the 2000s Korea imported the largest amount from Japan, with the US in second place, but now China is the number one source of imports into Korea.

Figure 18-4 shows CR5 (concentration ratio 5) and CR10, which indicate the share of the top five or ten trading partners. Even though those numbers are still relatively large, we see a decreasing tendency in concentration, which means that Korea's efforts to diversify trading partners have been successful. Such a tendency can also be found from the HH index in the figure.

5. A Regression of Trade and Production: Firm Level Data

In this section, we analyze the polarization of production and international trade by using firm level manufacturing data from 1985-2013. We use the KISvalue data provided by Korea Investors Service Inc. The KISvalue database contains data from almost 20,000 firms, of which 10,756 firms operate in 23 manufacturing industries. We selected 2,018 firms from this

Figure 18-5. Increasing trend of GINI-s by using firm level data

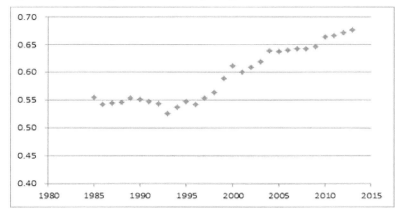

number that were consecutively included in the dataset for 29 years. We summed the firm level data to get production and trade data at the industry level. Thus, the data are different from the results above, which were obtained from industry level, UN Comtrade and STAN data.

Two types of GINI-s were calculated from the data. One is GINI-s for a particular industry in a specific year using data from an individual firm. From this we obtained 23*29 panel data (Appendix Table 18-2). The other is 29 time series GINI-s using the industry data, which was calculated from firm level data. This GINI-s might show the degree of concentration among the industries for a particular year. Figure 18-5 shows the second GINI-s (The numbers are shown in the last column of Appendix Table 18-2). These figures, calculated from the firm level data, seem to be similar to Figures 18-2 and 18-3, which were calculated using industry level data. Since the data source is not the same as before, these figures do not necessarily have to be exactly the same as the previous ones, but the basic trends look similar in recent years: concentration and polarization are increasing in Korean manufacturing.

Table 18-4. Exports and Polarization in Time Series Data

	Coef.	Std. Err.	t-value	Robust Std. Err.	t-value
Export Ratio	0.162	0.093	1.80	0.060	2.72
constant	0.563	0.019	29.13	0.015	37.11
$R^2 = 0.1070$	$n = 29$				

Now we report the results from regression analyses to see the relationship between the GINI-s and the trade dependence ratio.

First, Table 18-4 indicates the results for the time series data of the manufacturing industry as a whole. The number of data, 29, indicates 29 years. We used a robust standard errors estimation by using the sandwich estimator of variance. The dependent variable is GINI-s, and the independent variable is the ratio of exports to total production in each year. We summed up the total amount of exports and production of the firms in the data set. The regression results show that the export ratio is significant at the 10% significance level when we use the usual standard errors, and significant at 1% when we use the robust errors. In all, it seems reasonable to conclude that the export ratio has a positive relationship with GINI-s.

Second, we report the regression result by using the panel data: GINI-s in each industry for every year. Several panel data regression models are used: fixed effect model, random effect model, two-way effects model, and two-way GLS model. The two-way GLS model was used in order to consider the heterogeneity of the error terms in the panel data. Here, we also find a positive relationship between the export ratio and polarization. When the export ratio is large in an industry, the GINI-s also tends to be large.

Table 18-5. Exports and Polarization in Panel Data[6]

	Fixed Effect	Random Effect	Two-Way Effect	Two-Way GLS
export rate	0.023 (1.57)	0.025* (1.68)	0.048*** (3.25)	0.029*** (2.98)
constant	0.627*** (239.84)	0.626*** (21.9)	0.567*** (66.3)	0.598*** (100.3)
R^2	0.2075	0.2075	0.2075	
n	667	667	667	667

* $p<.1$; ** $p<.05$; *** $p<.01$, the numbers in parenthesis are t-values.

6. Conclusion

International trade usually changes the production patterns of an economy; the share of exporting industries tends to increase while the share of importing industries tends to decrease. Thus, it is natural for an economy to experience concentration in export-centric industries. This concentration might also occur within individual industries; the exporting firms tend to grow, and the share of other firms tends to decrease. All these changes can result in polarization of the economy. This study investigates if a polarization trend exists in the Korean economy by using industry level and firm level data.

In addition, we explore the relationship between polarization and international trade. Since much criticism has been focused on the idea that international trade has resulted in polarization and income inequality in the Korean economy, this study tries to determine the effects of international trade on polarization. We borrowed an index that is similar to the GINI coefficient and other indices to measure the degree of polarization, and

---

[6] We implemented Hausman test to check whether to use fixed effect model or random effect model. But we report all the results for both model in order for reader to identify those.

performed regression analysis with this index, and the export ratio. Time series and panel data were used. We find that there is a positive relationship between export ratio and polarization, which indicates that international trade or openness may lead to polarization in the Korean economy.

Appendix

Table 18A-1. Industry Classification in Korea

KSIC2	Manufacturing	OECD classification by tech level
C10	Manufacture of Food Products	L
C11	Manufacture of Beverages	L
C12	Manufacture of Tobacco Products	L
C13	Manufacture of Textiles, Except Apparel	L
C14	Manufacture of wearing apparel, Clothing Accessories and Fur Articles	L
C15	Tanning and Dressing of Leather, Manufacture of Luggage and Footwear	L
C16	Manufacture of Wood Products of Wood and Cork; Except Furniture	L
C17	Manufacture of Pulp, Paper and Paper Products	L
C18	Printing and Reproduction of Recorded Media	L
C19	Manufacture of Coke, hard-coal and lignite fuel briquettes and Refined Petroleum Products	ML
C20	Manufacture of chemicals and chemical products except pharmaceuticals, medicinal chemicals	MH
C21	Manufacture of Pharmaceuticals, Medicinal Chemicals and Botanical Products	H
C22	Manufacture of Rubber and Plastic Products	ML
C23	Manufacture of Other Non-metallic Mineral Products	ML
C24	Manufacture of Basic Metal Products	ML
C25	Manufacture of Fabricated Metal Products, Except Machinery and Furniture	ML
C26	Manufacture of Electronic Components, Computer, Radio, Television and Communication Equipment & Apparatuses	H
C27	Manufacture of Medical, Precision and Optical Instruments, Watches and Clocks	H
C28	Manufacture of electrical equipment	MH
C29	Manufacture of Other Machinery and Equipment	MH
C30	Manufacture of Motor Vehicles, Trailers and Semitrailers	MH
C31	Manufacture of Other Transport Equipment	MH
C32	Manufacture of Furniture	L
C33	Other manufacturing	L

Table 18A-2. GINI-s by Industries and by Years

KSIC	C10	C11	C13	C14	C15	C16	C17	C18	C19	C20	C21	C22
1985	0.55	0.52	0.64	0.47	0.26	0.12	0.53	0.30	0.80	0.68	0.58	0.47
1986	0.56	0.54	0.65	0.50	0.37	0.33	0.53	0.32	0.82	0.68	0.59	0.55
1987	0.59	0.59	0.67	0.51	0.35	0.40	0.55	0.31	0.82	0.69	0.60	0.50
1988	0.59	0.57	0.68	0.49	0.41	0.49	0.57	0.23	0.81	0.71	0.58	0.53
1989	0.60	0.59	0.67	0.50	0.45	0.48	0.58	0.24	0.79	0.71	0.56	0.52
1990	0.62	0.61	0.65	0.52	0.45	0.39	0.58	0.28	0.80	0.71	0.59	0.51
1991	0.64	0.62	0.65	0.54	0.46	0.53	0.59	0.30	0.81	0.71	0.58	0.53
1992	0.64	0.63	0.65	0.54	0.47	0.52	0.61	0.35	0.81	0.71	0.57	0.54
1993	0.64	0.63	0.63	0.54	0.50	0.44	0.61	0.30	0.80	0.68	0.56	0.54
1994	0.64	0.66	0.64	0.59	0.49	0.49	0.63	0.31	0.81	0.71	0.56	0.52
1995	0.65	0.67	0.63	0.60	0.51	0.46	0.65	0.31	0.81	0.73	0.55	0.51
1996	0.64	0.64	0.62	0.60	0.52	0.47	0.66	0.32	0.80	0.73	0.54	0.51
1997	0.64	0.64	0.60	0.62	0.49	0.50	0.66	0.34	0.83	0.73	0.55	0.53
1998	0.66	0.61	0.60	0.55	0.46	0.52	0.65	0.36	0.83	0.74	0.56	0.56
1999	0.66	0.61	0.59	0.52	0.50	0.53	0.62	0.36	0.82	0.75	0.54	0.54
2000	0.66	0.67	0.57	0.52	0.48	0.51	0.64	0.34	0.81	0.76	0.54	0.54
2001	0.65	0.67	0.57	0.52	0.49	0.52	0.64	0.35	0.81	0.76	0.54	0.53
2002	0.66	0.67	0.55	0.52	0.47	0.52	0.65	0.34	0.82	0.75	0.54	0.52
2003	0.67	0.68	0.57	0.51	0.49	0.51	0.64	0.32	0.83	0.75	0.54	0.49
2004	0.66	0.63	0.56	0.51	0.49	0.53	0.64	0.32	0.83	0.77	0.55	0.50
2005	0.66	0.65	0.58	0.51	0.48	0.52	0.64	0.29	0.83	0.77	0.55	0.54
2006	0.67	0.64	0.58	0.53	0.47	0.50	0.63	0.32	0.83	0.77	0.55	0.55
2007	0.67	0.63	0.59	0.53	0.47	0.47	0.63	0.34	0.83	0.78	0.56	0.55
2008	0.65	0.62	0.59	0.55	0.47	0.51	0.64	0.35	0.83	0.79	0.56	0.56
2009	0.65	0.63	0.60	0.55	0.47	0.51	0.65	0.39	0.83	0.79	0.56	0.58
2010	0.65	0.64	0.63	0.55	0.50	0.50	0.63	0.38	0.83	0.80	0.55	0.57
2011	0.65	0.68	0.60	0.55	0.52	0.51	0.62	0.41	0.83	0.80	0.55	0.58
2012	0.65	0.72	0.61	0.56	0.53	0.53	0.63	0.43	0.83	0.80	0.53	0.59
2013	0.65	0.72	0.61	0.57	0.56	0.48	0.63	0.41	0.83	0.80	0.54	0.59

KSIC	C23	C24	C25	C26	C27	C28	C29	C30	C31	C32	C33	Total
1985	0.70	0.80	0.51	0.81	0.50	0.64	0.70	0.83	0.73	0.54	0.55	0.55
1986	0.70	0.79	0.50	0.80	0.52	0.67	0.71	0.86	0.74	0.49	0.55	0.54
1987	0.71	0.80	0.47	0.79	0.51	0.67	0.71	0.85	0.73	0.50	0.55	0.55
1988	0.70	0.81	0.46	0.80	0.51	0.68	0.69	0.86	0.73	0.59	0.61	0.55
1989	0.70	0.82	0.46	0.83	0.54	0.68	0.67	0.85	0.76	0.51	0.61	0.55
1990	0.70	0.81	0.46	0.83	0.54	0.69	0.69	0.85	0.79	0.47	0.66	0.55
1991	0.72	0.82	0.49	0.84	0.55	0.69	0.71	0.85	0.80	0.44	0.65	0.55
1992	0.72	0.82	0.48	0.85	0.53	0.71	0.75	0.85	0.83	0.48	0.64	0.54
1993	0.71	0.83	0.48	0.86	0.49	0.71	0.76	0.85	0.83	0.47	0.62	0.53
1994	0.71	0.82	0.49	0.88	0.51	0.71	0.75	0.86	0.85	0.48	0.61	0.54
1995	0.72	0.80	0.47	0.89	0.51	0.73	0.74	0.85	0.86	0.44	0.63	0.55
1996	0.72	0.80	0.44	0.88	0.53	0.74	0.74	0.85	0.85	0.42	0.59	0.54
1997	0.72	0.80	0.43	0.87	0.55	0.75	0.75	0.84	0.86	0.44	0.56	0.55
1998	0.72	0.82	0.47	0.87	0.55	0.77	0.78	0.84	0.87	0.44	0.52	0.56
1999	0.72	0.80	0.44	0.88	0.56	0.75	0.75	0.84	0.86	0.41	0.49	0.59
2000	0.74	0.80	0.44	0.89	0.56	0.73	0.74	0.85	0.85	0.44	0.49	0.61
2001	0.74	0.80	0.44	0.88	0.54	0.72	0.74	0.87	0.86	0.45	0.43	0.60
2002	0.71	0.80	0.44	0.89	0.51	0.72	0.74	0.87	0.86	0.45	0.45	0.61
2003	0.70	0.81	0.45	0.89	0.51	0.74	0.72	0.86	0.86	0.45	0.39	0.62
2004	0.71	0.81	0.46	0.90	0.51	0.76	0.71	0.86	0.85	0.46	0.37	0.64
2005	0.70	0.82	0.47	0.90	0.51	0.76	0.72	0.85	0.85	0.47	0.36	0.64
2006	0.71	0.81	0.47	0.90	0.53	0.75	0.73	0.85	0.85	0.49	0.39	0.64
2007	0.72	0.81	0.50	0.91	0.55	0.72	0.73	0.85	0.86	0.49	0.39	0.64
2008	0.73	0.82	0.53	0.92	0.52	0.73	0.73	0.85	0.85	0.47	0.42	0.64
2009	0.73	0.81	0.51	0.92	0.51	0.71	0.76	0.86	0.85	0.46	0.42	0.65
2010	0.73	0.82	0.49	0.93	0.48	0.71	0.74	0.85	0.85	0.50	0.40	0.66
2011	0.75	0.83	0.52	0.93	0.49	0.72	0.73	0.85	0.85	0.53	0.41	0.67
2012	0.74	0.82	0.52	0.94	0.51	0.71	0.75	0.85	0.87	0.56	0.42	0.67
2013	0.73	0.81	0.52	0.94	0.50	0.69	0.75	0.85	0.87	0.57	0.46	0.68

Table 18A-3. Share of Top five or ten Trade Partners

	1975	1980	1985	1990	1995	2000	2005	2009
EX 5	0.695	0.566	0.636	0.633	0.538	0.554	0.535	0.497
EX 10	0.794	0.697	0.771	0.753	0.689	0.689	0.650	0.622
IM 5	0.781	0.749	0.587	0.650	0.614	0.558	0.559	0.509
IM 10	0.889	0.869	0.704	0.763	0.732	0.709	0.715	0.673

* EX indicates that Korea exports to these countries and IM means Korea's import from these countries.

Table 18A-4. Hirschman Herfindahl Index for Trading Partners

	1975	1980	1985	1990	1995	2000	2005	2009
EX	0.171	0.105	0.161	0.139	0.079	0.086	0.085	0.077
IM	0.196	0.151	0.115	0.142	0.124	0.092	0.086	0.073

CHAPTER 19

AN OPTIMAL TARIFF FOR ENVIRONMENTAL PROTECTION IN A DEVELOPING ECONOMY

1. Introduction

The discussion of environmental problems in economic literature dates back as far as the Symposium on Natural Resources in the Review of Economic Studies' 1967 issue. This issue largely addressed planning problems related to the use of natural resources. Unlike other traditional inputs like labor and human capital, natural resources such as coal and minerals are not reproducible once they are put into production processes. Instead, they create pollution and are considered a cause of global climate change. Since the British industrial revolution, the global temperature has risen 2°C above the pre-industrial level, which has drawn worldwide attention among economists and politicians. The Paris Accord of 2015 came to an agreement among 175 signatory nations to reduce the temperature no higher than the 2°C increase which had already occurred.

Not only are there pollutants causing health problems from the use of natural resources, but the productivity capacity of nature, which provides the energy for production, is also affected. An ecological perspective of production processes suggests that the use of natural resources is governed by the physical law of energy provision in production. Ecologists consider "the source of energy" as the ultimate provider of services for human needs, with resulting waste products, or "sinks." Under this circular flow of the "source" and "sink," human needs are met. This flow is comparable to the standard circular flow found in economics textbooks, which involves the "service markets" and "goods markets.

Georgescu-Roegen's (1971) book, *The Entropy Law and the Economic Process*, drew economists' attention to the importance of the "entropy law" of physics in explaining the process of economic development. According to this law, economic development involves the transformation of a system from a state of low entropy to a state of high entropy. For example, the use of coal for locomotives and heating can be interpreted as a transformation from a state of low entropy to one of high entropy. In this physical transformation process, energy is harnessed to meet human needs.

One of the distinguishing features of the production process under the "entropy law" is its "irreversibility," which may vary depending on the type of natural resources used. For instance, when coal is burned for energy, it leaves behind ashes and cannot return to its original form. It may take a long time for new coal deposits to form. On the other hand, the use of land for agriculture, livestock husbandry, and construction does not seem to face the same irreversibility issue as coal. However, the productive capacity of the land can become eroded through use, as evidenced by crop rotations in agriculture, and it can also become polluted by manure and other agricultural chemicals. The same applies to sea resources. In other words, the resilience of nature may be affected by climate change, which may be caused by air pollution resulting from industrialization.

From an economist's viewpoint, the physical interpretations of the production process involve external problems both on the production side and the consumer side. Since Hagen's argument in 1958 for protection in the case of externalities in production, it has been widely accepted in trade literature that government intervention is a suboptimal policy. These externality problems justify the introduction of government taxes or subsidies as a second-best optimum policy. In the context of a global economy, this externality problem raises the question of whether free trade is still the first-best optimum policy for economists.

We assume that physical capital goods tend to rely on 'high-entropy' natural resources in a fixed bundle, while "low-entropy" resources are more commonly utilized in conjunction with human capital. We refer to a developing economy whose comparative advantage lies in the production of physical capital goods using "high-entropy" natural resources as a "brown economy." An advanced economy whose comparative advantage lies in the production of human capital-intensive goods using "low-entropy" resources is referred to as a "green economy." There is also a third type of economy, endowed with both labor and natural resources, which we call a "resource economy". The "resource economy" possesses natural resources at various levels of entropy and trades with both the "brown" and "green" economies.

Under this framework of global trade, the "brown economy" specializes in producing "brown goods" due to its comparative advantage in physical capital goods. On the other hand, the "green economy" specializes in producing "green goods" due to its comparative advantage in human-capital intensive goods. In free trade, the "brown economy" exports its "brown goods" to both the "green economy" and the "resource economy," while importing "green goods" from the "green economy" and natural resources associated with the production of "brown goods" from the "resource economy." Similarly, the "green economy" exports its "green goods" to both the "resource economy" and the "brown economy" and imports natural resources associated with their production in return.

We are interested in examining the impact of free trade on global environmental issues from the perspective of developing economies' environmental protection. Free trade can lead to a scale effect and a composition effect, which can increase the use of "high-entropy" resources by "brown economies" and generate pollution, causing damage to the environment. These two adverse effects can be mitigated by the Kuznets environmental curve, which suggests that environmental degradation initially increases with economic growth, but eventually decreases as income levels rise and environmentally friendly techniques are adopted. Therefore, as demand for "green goods" increases along with income, environmentally-friendly techniques may emerge in "brown economies." The overall effect of free trade on the environment depends on the balance between these three effects.

Copeland and Taylor (1994) examine the environmental impact of trade between the Global North and South. They find that free trade has a negative "composition effect" on developing economies in the South, while the North benefits environmentally by allocating resources towards cleaner goods. Overall, the negative impact on the South outweighs the positive effects on the North, making free trade a suboptimal policy for addressing global environmental problems. However, Copeland and Taylor's (2001) study on sulfur dioxide shows that for this particular pollutant, the "technique effect" outweighs both the scale and composition effects of free trade. This suggests that free trade can still be the best policy even when environmental problems are at play.

We introduce a social planner for the "brown economy" who considers the environmental damage caused by capital accumulation. This planner intervenes in free trade by setting an optimal tariff rate for imports of green goods. The planner's optimal level of the capital stock for the brown economy is compared to the steady state level under free trade. If the steady state level of the capital stock in the brown economy does not exceed the level chosen by the social planner, then the first-best optimality of free trade remains intact.

Section 2 outlines the model used in this study. Section 3 examines the international trade equilibrium of the model. Section 4 focuses on the social planner's optimal capital accumulation problem under free trade, and proposes an optimal tariff for developing economies. Finally, section 5 provides a conclusion.

2. A Model

The final goods are indexed based on their order of environmental friendliness with respect to their production techniques. The production process involves two inputs: physical capital and human capital. It is assumed that an intensive use of physical capital relative to human capital is less environmentally friendly, as it pollutes the air and deteriorates the environment. Each production technique is distinguished by its level of pollution emissions. A cleaner technique emits fewer pollutants as inputs and is more human-capital intensive.

A continuum of goods is indexed by technology $z \in (0,1)$, which requires physical capital along with natural resources such as land in a fixed proportion and human capital in a Cobb-Douglas form. Equation (19-1) expresses the production function for the generation τ of a good z.

$$Y_\tau(z) = K_\tau(z)^{\alpha(z)}(uL_\tau(z))^{1-\alpha(z)}$$

$$= K_\tau(z)^{\alpha(z)}(uh_\tau N(z))^{1-\alpha(z)}. \tag{19-1}$$

Green goods

Employment of the capital by the amount of $K_\tau(z)$ and that of labor by the amount of $uL_\tau(z)$ produces a good indexed by z for the amount of $Y_\tau(z)$. As is usual, the parameter $\alpha(z)$ is the distributive share for the owner of the physical capital good, while the parameter $(1 - \alpha(z))$ is that for human capital. The per capita output of a good z for a generation τ denoted by $\tilde{y}_\tau(z)$ in efficiency unit of labor is written as:

$$\tilde{y}_\tau(z) = f(\tilde{k}_\tau(z)) = \tilde{k}_\tau(z)^{\alpha(z)},$$

where the amount of capital and labor employed for the production of a good z, by a generation τ, is $K_\tau(z)$ and $L_\tau(z)$, respectively, while $\tilde{k}_\tau(z)$ is the per capita capital stock in efficiency unit of labor:

$$\tilde{k}_\tau(z) \equiv K_\tau(z)/uL_\tau(z) ; \tilde{y}_\tau(z) \equiv Y_\tau(z)/uL_\tau(z).$$

We introduce Assumption 1 concerning a continuum of techniques associated with the production of final goods indexed by z.

Assumption 1: $\alpha'(z) > 0$.

Assumption 1 suggests that the higher the index, the less environmentally friendly the technique. This implies that the importance of the physical good in production increases while that of human capital decreases with an increase in z.

Competition in the factor market ensures the factor share expression of Equation (19-2) for a given wage rate of an effective unit of labor denoted by $w_{\tau e}$ and the rental rate r_{τ} of the physical capital good:

$$\frac{w_e}{r_\tau} = \left(\frac{1-\alpha(z)}{\alpha(z)}\right)\frac{K_\tau}{(u_\tau hN)}. \qquad (19\text{-}2)$$

This factor share equilibrium indicates that the greater the amount of physical capital relative to human capital, the less environmentally friendly the production technique is used for a given wage-rental ratio of $w/r(w_e/r)$. An alternative interpretation of Equation (19-2) is that more time is spent on education in an economy with a greater amount of human capital stock, h.

We can summarize the discussion of this section as follows: For a given wage-rental ratio and technology, the higher the time spent on education $(1 - u)$ of a given unit of time of a generation τ, the higher the amount of human capital stock h.

Entropy

In Equation (19-1), $K_\tau(z)$ represents a composite of physical capital and natural resources such as land or minerals used for the production of a good by a generation τ. The productivity capacity of natural resources erodes with the use of physical capital for production by a fraction of $0 < c < 1$. The productivity capacity of natural resources is denoted by $\bar{R}$. A natural scientist suggests that there is a resilient force in nature to recover the damages done to it. A parameter of $0 < \xi < 1$ captures the resilience of nature. To sustain a long-run growth rate, we assume that $0 < c < \xi < 1$. This is a viability condition for natural resources.

The following expression for $s(\tilde{k}_\tau)$ is based on the ratio of the amount of degradation of nature associated with the use of per capita physical capital goods in efficiency units of labor to its resilience capacity:

$$0 < s(\tilde{k}_\tau) \equiv \frac{c\tilde{k}_\tau}{\xi\bar{R}} < 1 \,; 0 < c < \xi, \forall \tau.$$

Presumably, since the productive capacity $\tilde{k}_\tau$ is smaller than $\bar{R}$, $s(\tilde{k}_\tau)$ is smaller than one as indicated by the above inequality.

The damages done to nature by a generation τ, denoted by d_τ, is represented by the following expression:

$$d_\tau \equiv -\lambda s(\tilde{k}_\tau) \log s\,(\tilde{k}_\tau). \tag{19-3}$$

This is Georgescu-Roegen's formula, which is used to explain economic development in the context of entropy in physics. In his book *The Entropy Law and the Economic Process* (1971), Georgescu-Roegen argues that economic development is associated with an increase in entropy, which leads to environmental distortions such as deforestation, depletion of the ozone layer, depletion of mineral resources, air pollution, and climate change. Equation (19-3) captures these damages as d_τ. The social planner values these damages using the coefficient λ, which is measured in units of consumer goods. We assume that this value is given to the social planner and remains constant.[1]

Figure 19-1 displays how damages change with the increase of physical capital. The horizontal axis represents the ratio of the share of natural

---

[1] The social planner's valuation of the future value of natural assets depends on their time preference rate for the future, as well as on nature's resilience rate ξ.

Figure 19-1. Change of damages with the increase of physical capital

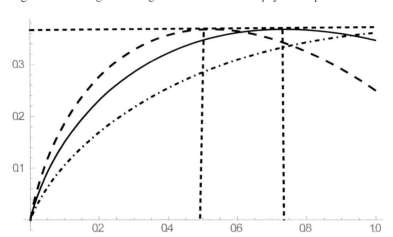

resources in fixed capital formation to the resilience rate of nature for its preservation, which is denoted by $s(\tilde{k}_\tau)$. The vertical axis measures the damages in units of consumer goods. It shows that the damages increase along the curve $0d$ as physical capital accumulates, reaching a maximum at the ratio of e^{-1}, and then decrease.

In the following, we will restrict the ratio of physical capital to nature with respect to environmental damages between 0 and e^{-1}, ensuring that d_τ is an increasing function of $\tilde{k}_\tau$. This restriction guarantees sustainable economic growth by fulfilling the condition of the viability of natural resources. On the steady-state physical capital stock $\tilde{k}^*$, the damages d^* occur, as shown in Figure 19-1. The damages decrease to the level of d^{**} as the accumulation of physical capital decreases to $\tilde{k}^{**}$, as indicated by the arrows in the figure. The increase in the resilience parameter ξ of nature in the entropy lowers the damages incurred by capital accumulation. Note that the damage curve $0d(\xi)$ in Figure 19-1 shifts downwards to $0d(\xi')$ by the rise of the resilience rate to ξ' from ξ. In section 4, we will discuss the role of the optimum tariff of the South in reducing environmental damages by lowering the physical capital to the lower level of $\tilde{k}^{**}$ from the initial level of $\tilde{k}^{*}$.

An indirect utility function

We adopt the DFS assumption of a constant share of spending on a good z, where $0 < b(z) < 1$ (Dornbusch et al., 1977). This assumption will enable us to present a trade balance of the continuum of goods in terms of the per capita income of the trading economies, as we will see later on. The representative consumer's indirect utility function can be expressed as follows:

$$v(c) = \int_0^1 b(z)\, ln[c(z)dz],$$

where $c(z)$ denotes per capita consumption, which is expressed in terms of per capita income and the price of good z, $p(z)$: $c(z) \equiv b(z)I/Lp(z)$, where (I/L) is the per capita income of an economy. Therefore, the per capita consumption of an economy in generation τ (denoted by $c_\tau(\bar{z})$) is a weighted average of the goods consumed, with the weight being the share of the good consumed in relation to its price by an individual. This is expressed as a density of the consumption of goods with $0 < z < 1$ by the following formula:

$$c_\tau(\bar{z}) = \int_0^1 \frac{b(z)}{p(z)} \frac{I_\tau}{N} dz,$$

where (I_τ/N) is an income of a representative individual in a generation τ.

Savings of a family unit

When a representative individual in a family unit leaves bequests for future generations at the beginning of a period, they are maximizing the stream of consumption for those succeeding generations. This can be expressed through the following formula:

$$\int_0^\infty \frac{c(\bar{z})_\tau^{1-\sigma}-1}{1-\sigma} e^{-\rho\tau} d\tau, \tag{19-4}$$

where the discount factor, denoted as $0 < \rho < 1$, represents the altruism of the current generation towards future generations. We assume that the level of altruism of a newly born individual remains the same over an infinite time horizon. Additionally, each family unit is assumed to be risk-averse with a risk aversion factor of $1 < \sigma$, which is assumed to be identical across future generations.

The savings generated by a generation τ are in the form of physical capital, which is denoted by $\dot{k}_\tau$. As a result, the constraints faced by a representative individual of that generation can be expressed as follows:

$$\dot{k}_\tau = f(\tilde{k}_\tau) - c_\tau(\bar{z}) - (\delta + 1 - u)\tilde{k}_\tau, \tag{19-5}$$

where $c_\tau(\bar{z})$ represents the amount of per capita consumption by a generation τ, measured in efficiency units of labor, and δ is the rate of depreciation on the physical capital.

The problem of maximizing bequests, as described above, is equivalent in form to the classical intertemporal optimization problem in an infinite horizon. Equation (19-3) indicates that there exists a steady-state per capita physical capital stock, denoted as $\tilde{k}^s$. The optimal solution to equation (19-

4) also reveals the presence of a shadow value of the capital stock, denoted as q^s, which is associated with $\tilde{k}^s$. However, it's worth noting that this per capita physical stock is lower when the human capital stock of the economy is lower.

The balanced growth rate of an economy tends to be higher when a greater fraction of an individual's time is dedicated to education. However, it's important to note that this optimal accumulation problem for an individual doesn't take into account the externalities associated with the use of physical capital. Specifically, an individual doesn't consider the damages done to the environment, as expressed in equation (19-5), when making decisions about capital accumulation. This problem is better addressed by a social planner, who can determine the optimal tariff rate for the South.

3. A Trade Equilibrium

The world economy comprises two distinct economies: a developing economy (the South) and an advanced economy (the North). These two economies differ in their relative endowments of human capital. The advanced economy is relatively more endowed with human capital compared to the developing economy. According to the Heckscher-Ohlin-Samuelson model, the developing economy is expected to specialize in the production of physical capital-intensive goods and import the human capital-intensive goods.

The unit cost function of a good z for a given generation τ in perfect competition is expressed as:[2]

---

[2] This expression is due to equation (4) of the 'CT model'. Hereafter, we will delete the notation τ unless it is necessary to use it.

$$c(w, r; h, z) = \kappa(z) r^{\alpha(z)} \left(\frac{w}{h}\right)^{1-\alpha(z)};$$

$$\kappa(z) \equiv \alpha(z)^{-\alpha(z)} (1 - \alpha(z))^{-(1-\alpha(z))}. \qquad (19\text{-}6)$$

The direction of trade is determined by the following inequality:

$$\frac{w}{w^*} \geq \frac{h}{h^*} \left(\frac{r^{*s}}{r^s}\right)^{\frac{\alpha(z)}{1-\alpha(z)}} \equiv 1/A(z; h/h^*, r^{*s}/r^s). \qquad (19\text{-}7)$$

As long as a good z satisfies the above inequality (19-7), the North has a comparative advantage in the good and exports it to the South. If a good z has the reversed inequality of (19-7), the South has a comparative advantage in it. The right-hand side of the inequality (19-7), denoted by $1/A(z)$, indicates the relative productivity of the South to that of the North with respect to a good z for a given steady-state rate of return on physical capital of the two, denoted by r^{*s} and r^s respectively. Note that the schedule $A(z)$, which represents the relative productivity of the North to that of the South, is a monotonically decreasing function of an index z. This represents a chain of comparative advantage in the goods indexed by z.

Balance of trade

A trade equilibrium is reached when the inequality of equation (19-7) becomes an equality. Let the trade equilibrium hold at the good indexed by $\bar{z}$. Then, $\varphi(\bar{z}) = \int_0^{\bar{z}} b(z) dz$ is the share of world spending on Northern goods, and the balance of trade is satisfied by the following expression:

$$I = \varphi(\bar{z})(I + I^*),$$

Figure 19-2. A trade equilibrium

where I and I^* denote the incomes of the South and the North, respectively. They are the sum of the returns on capital and the effective wage rates on raw labor:

$$I = w_e N + rK;$$
$$I^* = w_e^* N^* + r^* K^*.$$

The trade equilibrium condition of equation (19-7) implies that the wage rate of the South relative to that of the North is a monotonically increasing function of z. Intuitively, as the world's demand for physical capital-intensive goods – in which the South has a comparative advantage – increases, the income of the South rises relative to that of the North. The schedule $B(z)$ in Figure 19-2 shows the trade balance schedule between the North and the South as an upward-sloping schedule with respect to the horizontal good index z.

Figure 19-3. A free trade and technology

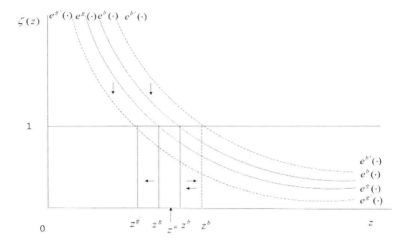

Both the relative productivity schedule and the trade balance equilibrium schedule, represented by $A(z)$ and $B(z)$ in Figure 19-2, determine the comparative advantage of the two economies at the level of the green good, $\hat{z}$.

We can summarize the direction of trade as follows: The North has a comparative advantage in the range of goods indexed by $z \in 0, \hat{z})$, while the South has a comparative advantage for the higher range of goods indexed by $z \in \hat{z}, 1$. Therefore, the North exports the greener goods to the South and imports the less green goods from the South.

Environmental indifference curve

This concept relates to the relative resistance of nature against damages caused by an industry i, to its technology level. The environmental indifference curve shows that damages done at a relatively high rate can be offset by a cleaner technology, resulting in an unchanged environmental level across industries and the economy. The vertical axis of Figure 19-3 represents the ratio of damages caused by industrialization to nature's resilience rate ζ, while the horizontal axis shows the technology level of $\alpha(z)$.

The environmental indifference curve is downward-sloping. Before trade, a green economy's environmental curve is denoted by the solid curve $e^g(\cdot)$, while a brown economy is represented by the solid curve $e^b(\cdot)$. Due to a higher per capita income and demand for green environments, the green economy's environmental curve lies below the brown economy's curve. An industry attains the maximum entropy associated with its production at a ratio of 1 on the relative resistance rate of nature. Green technology refers to a product that is relatively more human capital-intensive at this ratio of one. We are interested in examining how free trade affects the level of technology's greenness.

Environmental distortions in free trade

An allocation of the world's endowment of physical capital to human capital in free trade enlarges the scale of physical capital operation in the South. The North specializes in green goods due to a relatively higher endowment of human capital. Using the entropy defined in equation (19-3), the environmental distortions on a global level, denoted by d^w, can be expressed as the weighted average of the entropy of the South and of the North on the per capita physical capital stock of the world, where the weight is the share of the world population between the two. Equation (19-8) represents the world environmental distortions in per capita before trade. This is the sum of the entropy of the two trading economies in isolation. The share of the South in the world population is denoted by n, and that of the North is denoted by n^*:

$$d^w = nd(\tilde{k}) + n^* d(\tilde{k}^*). \tag{19-8}$$

By engaging in free trade, the South expands its production of the less green goods in which it has a comparative advantage, while a greater amount of labor is allocated to the production of greener goods in the North. Due to this scale effect of free trade, the share of the world population engaged in the less green goods in the South increases, while the share in the North decreases. Equation (19-9) represents the world environmental distortions after trade, denoted by d^{wo}.

$$d^{wo} = n^o d(\tilde{k}) + n^{*o} d(\tilde{k}^*), \tag{19-9}$$

where n^o represents the share of the world's population in the South who are affected by $d(\tilde{k})$ distortions after trade, while n^{*o} represents the share in the North affected by $d(\tilde{k}^*)$ distortions. It is worth noting that the environmental distortions caused by the South $(d(\tilde{k}))$ are greater than those caused by the North $(d(\tilde{k}^*))$ due to the entropy restriction within the range of $0 < s(\tilde{k}) < e^{-1}$. With free trade, $n^o > n$ and $n^{*o} < n^*$, which leads to an increase in environmental distortions after trade, as indicated by the inequality of "d33".

In summary, the discussion on the effect of free trade on environmental distortions at the global level suggests that the world's environments deteriorate with free trade for $0 < s(\tilde{k}) < e^{-1}$. The larger the discrepancy in environmental distortions between the South and the North in terms of entropy, the greater the environmental distortions caused by Southern capital accumulation. In the definition of $d(\cdot)$, we note that this difference is amplified by the difference in human capital endowment between the two regions. On the other hand, the difference in the level of human capital between the North and the South affects time allocation between work and education, according to the factor market equilibrium condition of equation (19-2). This explains why the discrepancy in growth rate differences becomes greater as the human capital endowment of the two regions increases. This result is consistent with that of a CT model, in which the growth rate difference between the North and the South amplifies environmental distortions caused by free trade.

An imposition of tariff

Introducing a tariff on free trade disrupts equation (19-2) by generating differential effects on the factor prices of the country imposing the tariff. For example, the imposition of a tariff by the South favors the wage rate of human capital while negatively impacting the rentals on physical capital goods. This leads to individuals in the South devoting more time to education. Human capital formation affects the steady-state ratio of physical capital per unit of labor in efficiency units. To discuss the capital accumulation effects of the South's tariff, we introduce Assumption 2, which assumes that the cutting-edge green good "z" is smaller than 1/2.

Assumption 2: $0 < \hat{z} < 1/2$.

As the rate of tariff increases, the prices of green goods with an order between 0 and 1/2 rise. Assumption 2 ensures that the share of human capital is greater than that of physical capital. Due to the Jone's magnification effect, the wage rate for human capital increases at a greater rate than the rental rate for physical capital, which is caused by an increase in the price of the relevant good. The relative increase in the wage rate compared to the rental rate implies that individuals with human capital allocate more of their time towards education, in accordance with the factor market equilibrium condition of equation (19-2).

The relative productivity schedule of the North and South, as shown in equation (19-7), indicates that the $1/A(z)$ schedule shifts leftwards to the $1/A^o(z)$ schedule, as illustrated in Figure 19-2. This is due to the increase in human capital in the South and the fall in rental rates resulting from the imposition of tariffs on green goods with an index of 0<z<1/2. Trade equilibrium is reached at the cutting edge $\hat{z}^o$, as shown in Figure 19-2. The composition of goods leans towards green technology at the global level due to the South's imposition of tariffs. The techniques employed by the North after trade become greener than those before trade, and likewise, the techniques of the South also become greener.

In conclusion, the South's imposition of tariffs on green goods contributes to solving environmental problems by making techniques more environmentally friendly at the global level. Additionally, the increase in the growth rate of the South due to the imposition of tariffs narrows the growth gap between the North and South.

Figure 19-4 displays a phase diagram for capital accumulation and its shadow price, showing the per capita physical capital, $\tilde{k}^s$, moving towards a new steady state, $\tilde{k}^{ss}$, which will be reached by the imposition of a tariff.

4. A Policy Proposal to Solve Environmental Problems

There are various instruments available to address environmental problems. The first one is to provide subsidies to producers of goods with a lower environmental impact, as measured by the green goods index. This approach

Figure 19-4. Phase diagram for the capital accumulation and its shadow price

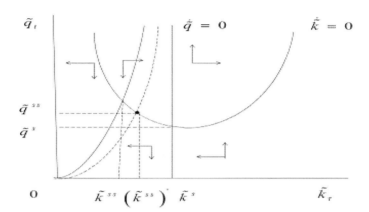

aims to promote the adoption of greener technologies in the economy. An indirect means of achieving this goal is to increase the price of goods with a lower index rating. In the case of a developing economy in the South, imposing a tariff on imported green goods is an alternative measure for raising their prices. As a social planner concerned with environmental protection, we need to consider the tariff rate of the South.

A social planner's optimum tariff

A social planner is concerned about the negative utility of polluted air and environmental damage caused by consumption in generation τ. We denote this adverse consumption as d_τ, which is subtracted from the total amount of consumption c_τ. As a result, the social planner's net consumption, denoted by $\tilde{c}_\tau$, is equal to $(c_\tau - d_\tau)$.

The primary objective of a social planner's optimum tariff problem is to determine the optimal rate of capital accumulation to solve the infinite planning horizon model presented in equation (19-10).

$$\int_0^\infty \left(v(c_\tau) - d_\tau(\tilde{k}_\tau)\right)e^{-\rho\tau}d\tau$$

$$s.\,t.$$

$$\dot{\tilde{k}}_\tau = f(\tilde{k}_\tau) - c_\tau(\bar{z}) - (\delta + 1 - u)\tilde{k}_\tau,$$

$$d(\tilde{k}_\tau) = -\lambda s(\tilde{k}_\tau)\log s(\tilde{k}_\tau). \quad (19\text{-}10)$$

This planning problem is similar to an individual's optimum problem presented in equation (19-4), except that the objective function includes the term $d(\tilde{k}_\tau)$ to represent environmental damage. The optimal steady state of $\tilde{k}^{ss}$ would be lower than the solution $\tilde{k}^s$ of the individual's optimal problem in equation (19-4). The optimum tariff rate is the rate at which physical capital accumulation is reduced to the optimal level of an individual's physical capital accumulation in the steady state. It is important to note that the higher the value of λ, which represents the social planner's evaluation of environmental damages, the higher the optimum tariff rate. Furthermore, Figure 19-3 shows that the higher the nature's resilience rate ξ, the higher the optimum rate of capital accumulation, as indicated by $\left(\tilde{k}^{ss}\right)'$ on the horizontal axis. The corresponding optimum tariff rate for this steady-state level of physical capital stock is lower.

5. Conclusion

This study examines environmental problems in a developing economy (in the South) that engages in trade with an advanced economy (in the North). The North is relatively more endowed with human capital, while the South is relatively more endowed with physical capital. Physical capital-intensive goods are considered to be damaging to the environment, while human capital-intensive goods are considered to be environmentally friendly.

Imposing a tariff by the South on green goods imported from the North not only reduces environmental damages on a global level but also contributes to making the techniques of the goods more environmentally friendly. This study also shows that reducing environmental problems through tariffs can decrease the growth gap between the North and the South. This finding is consistent with a 'CT trade model' in which a divergence of growth rates between the two regions contributes to environmental problems at a global level.

The optimum rate of tariff associated with the capital accumulation of the South also depends on the planner's valuation of natural assets and the abatement costs of pollution. This trade-off between abatement costs and sustainability is related to the urgency of investing in pollution abatement and preserving natural resources from the damages caused by present consumption. This issue has been subject to controversy, with Nordhaus (2007) and Weitzman (2007) criticizing Stern's skeptical view on the urgency of future natural disasters (Stern, 2007). In this study, the optimum rate of tariff is related to the resilience of nature. A higher resilience of nature leads to a lower optimum rate of tariff.

CHAPTER 20

EFFECTS OF ENVIRONMENTAL REGULATIONS ON KOREAN EXPORTS

1. Introduction

Since the Industrial Revolution, resource depletion, environmental damage (e.g., to the ozone layer), and the extinction of many species have occurred in association with industrialization and urbanization. It is now widely believed that a global body that can protect the environment while also guiding economic development is required. At present, there are approximately 200 multilateral environmental agreements, some of which use strong measures such as trade regulations to promote environmental protection. Although few trade measures were initially implemented for environmental reasons, the number of such measures is gradually increasing; this is highly likely to result in conflict with the GATT/WTO, which favor free trade.

Most studies on international trade and the environment have focused on whether strengthening environmental standards reduces the competitiveness of companies (i.e., in terms of productivity or production costs), or on whether trade liberalization negatively affects the environment. This study is concerned with how environmental regulations affect trade patterns. In particular, we assess how strengthened environmental regulations in other countries affect Korean exports, which is an important issue given Korea's high dependence on trade.

Strengthening environmental regulations often increases production costs, which weakens the competitiveness of companies, decreases exports, and increases imports. When environmental regulations are strengthened in developed countries, polluting industries may be relocated to developing countries through foreign direct investment (FDI), and developed countries lose their comparative advantage. Therefore, environmental regulations have been labeled "another non-tariff barrier". However, studies analyzing empirical data from developed countries often fail to find clear evidence to support this view. Although the results differ by country, industry, and period, in many cases evidence that strengthened environmental regulations negatively affect trade patterns is lacking. Nevertheless, more recent studies have indicated that such effects may arise in the specific context of polluting industries.

In Korea, it is widely believed that strengthening environmental standards reduces the international competitiveness of companies. However, the relationship between environmental standards and economic activities, such as international trade, is still not fully understood. In light of the so-called Green Round, it is necessary to obtain more empirical data on this topic.

In this study, we performed regression analyses to determine how Korean exports are affected by the environmental regulations of other countries. We reviewed various studies that focused on developed countries and empirically analyzed the relationship between environmental regulations imposed in importing countries and Korean exports. A gravity model was used as a basis for our cross-sectional analysis. We analyzed Korean export data for 2001 produced by the OECD in 2003. The level of environmental regulations in 82 importing countries was assessed based on data from the World Bank and criteria provided by the World Economic Forum (Davos

Forum; http://www.weforum.com).

In section II of this chapter, theories of international trade and environmental regulations and related existing research results are briefly summarized, and in section III, an empirical analysis model is derived and variables and data are explained. In section IV, regression analysis was conducted using data extracted from the OECD database. Finally, implications were derived from the results of the empirical analysis.

2. Literature Review of Environmental Regulations and Trade

Research on the relationship between environmental regulations and trade has been conducted in two directions. The first is the question of how trade liberalization affects environmental pollution in each country or in the world. As trade liberalization progresses, competition in the global market intensifies from the perspective of companies in each country. In this competitive environment, they may ignore environmental pollution problems, leading to environmental degradation in each country. [1] Numerous empirical studies have been performed on this topic, as summarized by Jayadevappa (2000). Case studies have tended to focus on developing countries such as China (Chai, 2002) and Indonesia (Strutti & Anderson, 2000).

In contrast, this study focuses on analyzing how environmental regulations affect international trade. Many perceptions in this field suggest that as environmental regulations are strengthened, the production cost of

---

[1] Such competition among companies is known as the "race to the bottom". In the face of global competition, companies compete to reduce production costs and thus cannot afford to address environmental issues.

enterprises will rise, which may result in relocation abroad through FDI, a decrease in exports, or an increase in imports. In the case of the United States, the estimated cost increase was $184 billion in 2000 (Cole and Elliott, 2003). Therefore, in developed countries with strong environmental regulations, competitiveness in the environmental pollution industry weakens, and comparative advantage disappears. Ultimately, the environmental pollution industry is transferred to developing countries or replaced by imports.

It should be noted that many empirical studies have failed to demonstrate that environmental regulations have a decisive effect on trade patterns, possibly because such regulations were historically minor. Moreover, the impact of environmental factors on FDI seems to be smaller than that of wages, among other factors. A brief summary of recent studies on environmental regulations and trade patterns is provided below.

Most previous studies used the Heckscher-Ohlin-Vanek (HOV) model and factor endowment theory to analyze the impact of environmental regulations on trade patterns. Janicke et al. (1997) showed that the strengthening of environmental regulations in a given country is not a critical determinant of the net exports of its polluting industries; this finding was supported by Xu and Song (2000). An extensive OECD report (1997) concluded that relocating to developing countries to avoid environmental regulations does not provide advantages for industrial enterprises, which was subsequently corroborated by Ferrantino and Linkins (1999).

Using a gravity model similar to that employed in this study, van Beers and van Den Bergh (1997) analyzed data from 21 OECD countries for the period 1975–1992, and showed that the strengthening of environmental regulations reduced both exports and imports. However, Harris et al. (2000) noted errors in the ordinary least squares analysis of van Beers and van Den Bergh (1997), and modified the gravity model to demonstrate that environmental regulations had no effect on exports or imports. Grether and De Melo (2003) found no significant relationship between environmental regulations and trade flows in an analysis of polluting and resource-dependent industries. According to the Heckscher-Ohlin (HO) model, the effect of environmental regulations on trade is small relative to other production factors such as capital and labor. Moreover, if polluting industries are also capital-intensive, it is difficult to relocate production facilities.

Ederington and Minier (2001) conducted a regression analysis to determine whether the strengthening of US environmental regulations led to a competitive disadvantage. Production factors (human resources and capital) and costs associated with pollution reduction were included in their model, which demonstrated that stronger environmental regulations increased imports.

Cole and Elliott (2003) conducted a cross-sectional analysis of data from 1995 pertaining to polluting industries in 60 countries, and found that the effect of environmental regulations on net exports was not significant. They attributed this result to the lack of consideration of inter-industry trade by the HOV model; the impact of environmental regulations on trade was greater in a subsequent analysis considering both inter- and intra-industry trade.

Mulatu et al. (2004) conducted a regression analysis including capital, skilled labor, unskilled labor, research and development, and pollution abatement costs as independent variables. For the US and Germany, environmental regulations led to a comparative disadvantage for polluting industries, whereas in the case of the Netherlands this was only seen for wood and steel industries.

Results have differed among studies using the HO model because quantifying environmental regulations is difficult. Moreover, analysis targets and methods vary widely and, in some cases, exports from developing countries to developed countries were not considered.

Most polluting industries are large-scale, capital-intensive, resource-dependent industries, for which the cost of pollution reduction measures is lower than the cost of securing resources (Jug & Mirza, 2004). In Korea, studies have focused mainly on countermeasures to offset environmental regulations in developed countries; few studies have analyzed the relationship between environmental regulations and trade patterns. However, some Korean studies have assessed the effects of environmental regulations on the overall economy, typically using computable general equilibrium models.

Kang et al. (1997) analyzed data for the period 1980–1994 and showed that the comparative advantage (RCA) index for environmentally sensitive products decreased as the environmental regulations of economically advanced countries became stricter. The RCA changes were attributed to changes in Korea's trade structure and environmental standards. Subsequently, Kang et al. (2000) analyzed dynamic spillover effects of trade liberalization, whereas other studies on the relationship between trade patterns and environmental legislation performed static analyses.

While most previous studies analyzed the effects of strengthened environmental regulations in a given country on exports, this study uses a gravity model to analyze how changes in environmental regulations in other countries have affected Korean exports.

3. Model and Data

3.1 Gravity Model

When changes in environmental regulations necessitate pollution-reducing measures, companies may experience reduced productivity and infrastructure replacement costs. However, in countries where environmental regulations are not enacted due to lack of capital or technology, or to indifference toward environmental pollution, production costs do not increase because no measures to mitigate pollution are required. The production costs associated with the implementation of environmental regulations can also differ among countries according to environmental conditions, socioeconomic factors, overall policy goals, and the ways in which environmental regulations are enforced. This complicates cross-country comparison of production costs associated with environmental regulations.

We modified the equation of Greenaway and Milner (2002) to yield the following basic gravity model, which includes economic openness, distance, and economic scale variables:

$$\ln\bigl(Ex_{ij}\bigr) = \beta_0 + \beta_1 \ln\bigl(D_{ij}\bigr) + \beta_2 \ln\bigl(POP_j\bigr) + \beta_3 \ln\bigl(GNI_j\bigr)$$

$$+ \beta_4 \, ln(OPEN_j) + \varepsilon_{ij} \qquad (20\text{-}1)$$

where Ex_{ij} is the export amount of country i to country j, D_{ij} is the distance between country i and country j, POP_j is the population of country j, GNI_j is the national income per capita of country j, and $OPEN_j$ is the degree of economic openness of country j.

In the above formula, POP_j and GNI_j together provide an estimate of the size of the economy of a given country. According to gravity model, Korean exports will show a positive relationship with the size of the economy of the importing country, whereas exports will decrease as the distance from a trading partner country increases, such that β_1 for D_{ij} is expected to have a negative value. The economic openness of a given country can be calculated based on its trade dependence index as follows: *Openness = (Exports + Imports)/Gross domestic product.* For countries with high economic openness, the amount of exports is high such that β_4 is expected to have a positive value.

3.2 Environmental Regulation

The strengthening of environmental regulations in other countries can be expected to increase Korean exports. Economically advanced countries tend to have stricter environmental regulations. According to a World Bank report of United Nations countries, the level of environmental regulations is highly positively correlated with the level of economic development (Dasgupta et al., 1995). When highly developed countries strengthen their environmental regulations, the competitiveness of their own products decreases such that countries exporting to those countries have a competitive advantage.

Developing countries tend to tolerate environmental pollution to a certain extent, to achieve economic growth; environmental regulations are strengthened as income levels rise. Because it is important to classify and analyze countries according to their degree of economic development, DEV_j, which is a dummy variable representing the stage of economic development, was included in our model. The World Bank classifies countries into high-, upper-middle-, lower-middle-, and low-income groups. We analyzed the influence of environmental regulations in countries belonging to these groups using the following equation:

$$\ln(Ex_{ij}) = \beta_0 + \beta_1 \ln(D_{ij}) + \beta_2 \ln(POP_j) + \beta_3 \ln(GNI_j) + \beta_4 \ln(OPEN_j)$$

$$+ \beta_5 \, ln(ENVREG_j) + \beta_6 \, ln(ENVREG_j) * DEV_j + \varepsilon_{ij} \qquad (20\text{-}2)$$

where $ENVREG_j$ represents the level of environmental regulations in country j.

3.3 Data Source and Description

Trade-related data were extracted from a CD-ROM produced by the OECD International Trade Data in 2003. The data can be filtered by country, region, industry (according to the Standard International Trade Classification [SITC]), and year. By analyzing export data for polluting industries, we were able to determine the impact of environmental regulations in individual countries on the trade patterns of Korea. Distances between countries can be calculated using the population, urban distribution, and land area data provided by CEPII (http://www.cepii.fr/ anglaisgraph/bdd/distances.htm) as inputs to gravity models. Population serves as a proxy for economic scale and can be analyzed in terms of growth rate, structure, density, and concentration. Countries with large populations also have large markets and trade volumes. In this study, we analyzed gross national income (GNI), which represents the disposable income per capita of the importing country. The GNI data were extracted from the website of the World Bank (http://www.worldbank.org).

3.4 Indicators of the Level of Environmental Regulations

Elucidating the relationship between the level of environmental regulations of a given country and exports is difficult. Exports are a function of both the size of the economy of the importing country and the level of environmental regulations. Moreover, unlike various related variables, the level of environmental regulations cannot be measured directly. Therefore, the major difficulty for trade analysis models is quantification of environmental regulations. Various proxies for the level of environmental regulations have been used, including CO_2 emissions, energy consumption, and the costs associated with pollution prevention measures (i.e., pollution abatement costs and expenditure).

The Environmental Sustainability Index (ESI) of the World Economic Forum (Davos Forum) was analyzed in this study. One of the main variables used to calculate the ESI is the ENVELOP environmental governance index, which provides a measure of the level of environmental regulations in a given country. Korea's ENVELOP index ranking is 47th out of 142 countries. Major advanced countries, including the US and several European countries, occupy the top ranks. The UK is the top-ranked country, followed by Switzerland. In this study, ENVELOP was used as the main measure of the level of environmental regulations. First, we analyzed correlations of the ENVELOP index with proxy variables for environmental regulations used in previous studies, such as pollutant (per capita CO_2) emissions and energy consumption (kg of oil equivalent per capita). The correlation coefficients of the ENVELOP index with pollutant emissions and energy consumption were 0.441 and 0.612, respectively, and the correlation coefficient between energy consumption and CO_2 emissions was 0.910. These results indicate that ENVELOP can serve as a proxy for the level of environmental regulations.

3.5 Classification of Industries

This study distinguished between polluting and non-polluting industries. In a US study, Grossman and Krueger (1993) classified polluting industries based on the ratio between pollution abatement costs and added value, whereas Low and Yeats (1992) classified industries for which pollution abatement costs corresponded to ≥ 1% of sales as polluting industries. According to this latter classification, steel, metal manufacturing, cement, and agricultural chemical industries are all polluting industries. Finally, Tobey (1990) considered industries for which pollution abatement costs exceed 1.85% of the total cost of production as polluting industries.

The effects of environmental regulations are greater for industries that experience significant cost increases due to environmental regulations (Ederington et al., 2003). Previous studies focusing on developed countries analyzed the effects of environmental regulations on the entire industrial sector, polluting industries, and non-polluting industries (Cole and Elliott, 2003). In this study, we employ the classification system of Low and Yeats (1992), which is based on the SITC and is the most widely used classification system in the literature.

Table 20-1 summarizes OECD data on the proportions of Korea's total exports and imports accounted for by 19 polluting industries. Korea's polluting industries accounted for 14.0% of the total exports and 14.7% of the total imports in 2021. The table shows that the proportions of exports and imports increased and decreased, respectively, over the period 1994–2001.

In total, we analyzed the data of 82 countries for which the total value of exports from Korea exceeded $30 million. Countries lacking data on

Table 20-1. Proportions of Korea's Total Exports and Imports accounted for by Polluting Industries

Year	1994	1995	1996	1997	1998	1999	2000	2001
Export	12.0%	11.8%	12.2%	13.4%	14.6%	13.4%	14.0%	14.0%
Import	16.7%	17.2%	16.5%	14.8%	14.6%	14.6%	14.4%	14.7%

Data source: OECD International Trade by Commodity Statistics CD Rom (2003)

environmental regulations or other important variables were not considered. Data pertaining to the level of environmental regulations of the analyzed countries are shown in Appendix Table 20-1.

4. Empirical Analysis Results

4.1 Correlations among Explanatory Variables

Before performing regression analysis to analyze the relationship between environmental regulations and exports, correlations among explanatory variables were analyzed to check for multicollinearity. If multicollinearity is present, it is difficult to isolate the effect on the dependent variable of each independent variable. Larger correlation coefficients indicate greater multicollinearity. The correlation coefficient between environmental regulations and per capita income was relatively large ($r = 0.762$), which may be due to the strong environmental regulations in high-income countries. If both income and environmental regulation variables are included in analysis models, it may be difficult to separate the effects of per capita income and the level of environmental regulations on trade. Therefore, we also conducted an analysis excluding GNI per capita.

4.2 Relationship between Level of Environmental Regulations and Total Exports

A regression analysis of total exports was performed to evaluate the relationship between the level of environmental regulations in foreign countries and Korean exports. The regression model also included the population, openness, and income level of importing countries, which were significantly positively associated with total exports. In contrast, distance showed a significant negative association with total exports (Table 20-2). Overall, the results indicate that gravity models are suitable for analyzing Korean trade data.

After adding environmental regulation variables to the basic model, the β value of the ENVELOP index became non-significant. However, after excluding GNI per capita, the β value (1.554) was significant. Overall, the results show that Korea tends to export more to countries with high-level environmental regulations.

In the analysis of OECD countries only, the impact of environmental regulations on exports was smaller than in the analysis including all countries, although stronger regulations still had a positive effect on Korean exports. For the model including the stage of economic development dummy variable, a significant relationship between GNI and the level of environmental regulations was seen. However, after omitting that dummy variable, the relationship between GNI and the level of environmental regulations became non-significant for low-income countries (β= -0.715, t = -1.130).

Table 20-2. Regression Results of Environmental Regulations of Foreign Countries and Total Exports of Korea

	Expected sign	Base model	Add environment variable	Excluding income variable	Add environment variable without GNI	OECD countries	Stage of economic development
Distance	-	-0.478 (-2.272)	-0.482 (-2.274)	-0.610 (-2.305)	-0.580 (-2.466)	-0.602 (-2.505)	-0.603 (-2.709)
Population	+	0.762 (7.635)	0.760 (7.538)	0.593 (4.849)	0.657 (6.002)	0.591 (5.323)	0.716 (6.933)
Openness	+	0.554 (2.382)	0.552 (2.361)	0.361 (1.239)	0.451 (1.736)	0.361 (1.361)	0.429 (1.791)
GNI per capita	+	0.489 (6.898)	0.465 (4.461)				
ENVELOP	+		0.138 (0.317)		1.554 (4.675)	1.083 (4.206)	-0.715 (-1.130)
ENVELOP × DEV(HI)							0.846 (3.988)
ENVELOP × DEV(UM)							0.723 (3.136)
ENVELOP × DEV(LM)							0.364 (1.685)
R^2		0.627	0.792	0.397	0.530	0.510	0.618

* Numbers in parentheses are t values (the same below)

Figure 20-1 shows the relationship between the level of environmental regulations and Korean exports after controlling for variables such as distance, population, and economic openness. To obtain residuals, regression analysis was performed after excluding environmental regulation variables. In a further regression analysis, the environmental regulatory variable *ENVELOP* was included as an explanatory variable and the residuals were dependent variables. Logarithms were used for the environmental regulation variables and exports. Figure 20-1 shows that there was a positive relationship between the level of environmental regulations of importing countries and Korean exports.

Figure 20-1. Relationship between the level of environmental regulations of importing countries and Korean exports

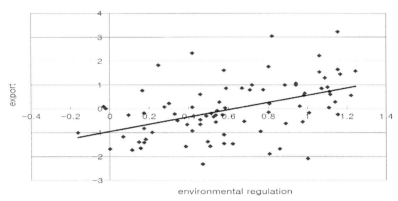

Unlike many previous empirical studies, we demonstrated a significant relationship between environmental regulations and Korean exports. There are several potential explanations for this result. First, Korea's industrial sector is characterized by a high proportion of polluting industries (14%) relative to the worldwide average; moreover, this proportion is increasing every year. Second, the effect of environmental regulations on trade may be greater today than in the past. As exemplified by the concept of the Green Round, legislation to mitigate environmental pollution is being introduced worldwide.

4.3 Polluting Industries

Because the effect of environmental regulations on exports varies among industries, we used the SITC industry classification to distinguish between 17 different types of industries considered to be polluting industries by Low and Yeats (1992).[2]

As shown in Table 20-3, Korean exports were higher to countries with high-level environmental regulations. In particular, environmental regulations in foreign countries on chemical, other organic chemistry, other chemistry, wood manufacturing, paper product, steel, and metal industries were associated with an increase in Korean exports. The effect of environmental regulations on these industries was larger than that on the entire industrial sector ($\beta = 1.554$).

The high level of sensitivity of polluting industries to environmental regulations manifests as decreased competitiveness (i.e., a relative increase in the competitiveness of Korean products). On this basis, if environmental regulations are strengthened in Korea in the future, the competitiveness of Korean industries could also decline. The results of the regression analysis including the stage of economic development variable are shown in Table 20-4. In general, the economic development stage had little effect on exports, although higher economic development stages were associated with larger coefficients for the other chemicals, plywood, paper products, steel, non-ferrous metals, and metal manufacturing industries.

---

[2] According to the classification of Low and Yeats (1992), there are 19 types of polluting industries. However, the pulp and coal industries were excluded from our analysis because of the small numbers of importing countries (6 and 2, respectively).

Table 20-3. Results of Regression Analysis of the Relationships of Various Factors with Korea's Exports

	334 petroleum products	515 chemicals	516 Other Organic Chemistry	523 Other non-organic chemistry	524 radioactive material	562 Fertilizer	598 Other Chemistry
Distance	-2.881 (-3.126)	-0.366 (-0.890)	-1.005 (-2.242)	-1.186 (-2.690)	-2.033 (-2.949)	0.219 (0.209)	-1.094 (-2.756)
Population	0.851 (1.806)	1.269 (6.259)	1.289 (5.907)	0.748 (3.216)	0.405 (1.039)	1.870 (2.949)	1.290 (7.054)
Openness	0.780 (0.695)	0.516 (1.062)	1.195 (2.343)	0.545 (1.018)	0.395 (0.453)	1.629 (1.198)	0.618 (1.351)
ENVELOP	1.836 (1.303)	3.280 (5.088)	4.186 (5.545)	0.922 (1.187)	2.272 (1.624)	1.690 (0.606)	2.350 (4.105)
R^2	0.330	0.544	0.656	0.419	0.339	0.481	0.599
n	52	64	52	50	33	16	77

	634 plywood	635 wood manufacturing	641 Paper board	642 paper products	661 cement, etc.	67 steel	68 non-ferrous metal	69 metal fabrication
Distance	-1.715 (-2.758)	-0.778 (-1.616)	-1.886 (-3.470)	-1.641 (-4.471)	-0.479 (-0.68)	-1.296 (-2.99)	-1.361 (-2.87)	-1.389 (-3.91)
Population	0.600 (1.749)	0.764 (3.265)	0.618 (2.491)	0.607 (3.538)	0.403 (1.057)	0.777 (3.84)	1.104 (5.04)	0.709 (4.29)
Openness	-0.373 (-0.462)	0.876 (1.544)	-0.885 (-1.426)	0.174 (0.418)	0.524 (0.597)	-0.327 (-0.66)	0.391 (0.71)	-0.04 (-0.10)
ENVELOP	-0.907 (-0.828)	3.391 (4.036)	0.219 (0.278)	2.092 (3.98)	-0.354 (-0.29)	2.001 (3.25)	1.371 (1.99)	2.951 (5.869)
R^2	0.401	0.384	0.351	0.497	0.068	0.432	0.474	0.554
n	34	51	76	78	43	81	74	81

Note; the numbers in column headings are SITC codes

Table 20-4. Regression Analysis including the Stage of Economic Development

	334 petroleum products	515 chemicals	516 Other Organic Chemistry	523 Other non-organic chemistry	524 radioactive material	562 Fertilizer	598 Other Chemistry
Distance	-3.024 (-3.104)	-0.453 (-1.117)	-0.985 (-1.993)	-1.149 (-2.517)	-1.463 (-1.969)	-0.143 (-0.119)	-1.136 (-2.912)
Population	0.803 (1.647)	1.297 (6.915)	1.375 (6.037)	0.823 (3.394)	0.680 (1.640)	1.240 (1.370)	1.374 (7.712)
Openness	0.855 (0.741)	0.340 (0.755)	1.231 (2.387)	0.601 (1.139)	0.903 (0.998)	0.472 (0.264)	0.582 (1.341)
ENVELOP	3.522 (1.131)	-0.485 (-0.397)	2.697 (1.543)	-1.645 (-1.013)	-0.056 (-0.018)	-3.773 (-0.393)	-0.821 (-0.743)
ENVELOP × DEV(HI)	-0.581 (-0.535)	1.432 (3.542)	0.413 (0.717)	1.017 (1.949)	0.572 (0.645)	1.447 (0.558)	1.197 (3.229)
ENVELOP × DEV(UM)	-0.017 (-0.010)	1.005 (2.243)	0.607 (0.968)	0.580 (1.048)	-0.474 (-0.501)	3.018 (1.017)	1.023 (2.541)
ENVELOP × DEV(LM)	0.289 (0.274)	0.780 (1.908)	-0.076 (-0.138)	0.821 (1.641)	-0.452 (-0.569)	1.941 (0.861)	0.561 (1.477)
R^2	0.349	0.635	0.676	0.483	0.428	0.556	0.654
n	52	64	52	50	33	16	77

	634 plywood	635 wood manufacturing	641 paperboard	642 paper products	661 cement, etc.	67 steel	68 non-ferrous metal	69 metal fabrication n
Distance	-1.742 (-2.798)	-0.685 (-1.370)	-2.108 (-3.760)	-1.785 (-4.864)	-0.524 (-0.70)	-1.438 (-3.37)	-1.539 (-3.24)	-1.508 (-4.96)
Population	0.756 (2.116)	0.789 (3.322)	0.592 (2.345)	0.638 (3.784)	0.316 (0.762)	0.836 (4.23)	1.193 (5.50)	0.816 (5.794)
Openness	-0.176 (-0.224)	0.798 (1.417)	-0.947 (-1.541)	0.137 (0.342)	0.463 (0.507)	-0.329 (-0.70)	0.356 (0.67)	-0.052 (-0.15)
ENVELOP	-6.409 (-2.506)	1.207 (0.747)	-1.740 (-1.120)	-0.415 (-0.402)	-0.886 (-0.34)	-1.262 (-1.05)	-1.881 (-1.39)	-1.583 (-1.847)
ENVELOP × DEV(HI)	2.049 (2.236)	0.760 (1.578)	0.882 (1.689)	1.001 (2.890)	0.220 (0.262)	1.268 (3.141)	1.269 (2.750)	1.720 (5.975)
ENVELOP × DEV(UM)	1.600 (1.579)	0.221 (0.393)	0.949 (1.664)	1.013 (2.674)	0.407 (0.438)	1.301 (2.96)	1.279 (2.53)	1.641 (5.25)
ENVELOP × DEV(LM)	1.153 (1.208)	0.330 (0.623)	1.115 (2.044)	0.816 (2.312)	0.721 (0.811)	0.900 (2.19)	0.779 (1.60)	0.958 (3.27)
R^2	0.508	0.438	0.391	0.554	0.090	0.504	0.530	0.704
n	34	51	76	78	43	81	74	81

Table 20-5. Environmental Pollution Industry and Other Industries

	Environmental pollution industry		Other industry	
	(1)	(2)	(3)	(4)
Distance	-1.355 (-4.553)	-1.432 (-5.006)	-0.544 (-2.363)	-0.552 (-2.584)
Population	0.778 (5.605)	0.845 (6.366)	0.622 (5.793)	0.683 (6.889)
Openness	0.094 (0.279)	0.086 (0.275)	0.436 (1.669)	0.426 (1.810)
ENVELOP	1.997 (4.731)	-0.653 (-0.809)	1.656 (5.071)	-0.711 (-1.178)
ENVELOP × DEV(HI)		0.993 (3.660)		0.895 (4.414)
ENVELOP × DEV(UM)		0.987 (3.352)		0.724 (3.289)
ENVELOP × DEV(LM)		0.529 (1.916)		0.392 (1.902)
R^2	0.607	0.672	0.530	0.634

4.4 Comparison between Polluting and other Non-Polluting Industries

Table 20-5 shows the results of regression analysis of polluting and non-polluting industries. Although both types of industry were significantly affected by environmental regulations, the effects were greater on polluting industries. Moreover, industries in high-income countries were more affected by environmental regulations than those in low-income countries.

5. Summary and Conclusion

In this study, we empirically analyzed the relationship between the level of environmental regulations in foreign countries and Korean exports using a gravity model. We found that stronger environmental regulations in foreign countries reduced the competitiveness of their products, which was associated with an increase in exports of Korean products. For the chemicals, other organic chemistry, other chemistry, wood manufacturing, paper products, steel, and metal manufacturing industries, the effects of environmental regulations were greater than those on the entire industry. Furthermore, environmental regulations had greater effects on high-income countries and polluting industries.

Appendix

Table 20A-1. Covered Countries and their Environmental Regulation Levels

Country	Regulation level	Country	Regulation level
1. Angola	1.18	42. Kuwait	1.35
2. Argentina	2.24	43. Lebanon	1.41
3. Australia	2.23	44. Liberia	1.28
4. Austria	3.17	45. Libya	0.97
5. Belgium	2.67	46. Sri Lanka	1.97
6. Bangladesh	1.24	47. Morocco	1.86
7. Brazil	2.17	48. Mexico	1.80
8. Canada	2.97	49. Mongolia	1.66
9. Switzerland	3.39	50. Malaysia	1.95
10. Chile	3.01	51. Nigeria	0.85
11. China	1.52	52. Nicaragua	1.52
12. Colombia	1.71	53. Netherlands	3.17
13. Costa Rica	2.74	54. Norway	2.68
14. Czech Republic	2.36	55. New Zealand	3.05
15. Germany	3.21	56. Oman	1.72
16. Denmark	3.03	57. Pakistan	1.78
17. Dominican Republic	1.58	58. Panama	2.27
18. Algeria	1.07	59. Peru	1.69
19. Ecuador	1.10	60. Philippines	1.32
20. Egypt	1.71	61. Poland	2.43
21. Spain	2.42	62. Portugal	2.23
22. Finland	2.92	63. Paraguay	1.20
23. France	3.04	64. Romania	1.16
24. United Kingdom	3.47	65. Russian Fed.	1.58
25. Ghana	1.19	66. Saudi Arabia	2.05
26. Greece	1.78	67. Sudan	1.12
27. Guatemala	2.03	68. Singapore	2.89
28. Hong Kong China	1.52	69. El Salvador	1.48
29. Honduras	1.63	70. Slovenia	2.14
30. Hungary	2.65	71. Sweden	3.13
31. Indonesia	1.74	72. Syrian Arab Rep.	1.19
32. India	1.78	73. Togo	1.64
33. Ireland	2.56	74. Thailand	1.79
34. Iran	0.98	75. Tunisia	1.47
35. Israel	2.72	76. Turkey	1.77
36. Italy	2.56	77. Ukraine	1.00
37. Jordan	1.67	78. Uruguay	2.61
38. Japan	2.89	79. United States	3.17
39. Kazakhstan	1.17	80. Uzbekistan	1.19
40. Kenya	1.60	81. Venezuela	1.58
41. Cambodia	2.24	82. Vietnam	1.39

Source: World Economic Forum (2002), ESI

ENDNOTE

This book is a compilation of research works that the authors have written over the years. While some chapters in this book are published for the first time, most chapters are revised versions of previously published papers. The following is a list of papers related to each chapter.

(Chapter)

02: Kim, Shin-Haing. Unpublished paper

03: Kim, Shin-Haing. Unpublished paper

04: Kim, Shin-Haing and Kim, Taegi. Unpublished paper

05: Kim, Shin-Haing. Unpublished paper

06: Kim, Shin-Haing. 2007. "Finance and Growth of the Korean Economy from 1960 to 2004". *Seoul Journal of Economics.* 20(4). 377-418.

07: Wu, Chao, Kim, Taegi, and Oh, Keunyeob. 2019. "Shift from Input-based Growth to Productivity-based Growth in Korean Manufacturing Industry". *Asian Economic Journal.* 33(4). 363-379.

08: Kim, Shin-Haing and Kim, Taegi. 2018. "Tobin's q of a Multi-Product Firm and an Endogenous Growth of a Firm". *Seoul Journal of Economics.* 31(4). 377-399.

09: Kim, Shin-Haing and Kim, Taegi. 2020. "Investment and Adjustment Costs of Korean Firms in View of Tobin's q". *Asia-Pacific Journal of Accounting & Economics*. 27(3). 300-311.

10: Kim, Taegi. 2012. "Dynamic Changes of Export Specialization Industries in Korea". *Korea Trade Review*. 37(2). 49-72. (in Korean)

11: Kim, Taegi. 2018. "Inter-Industry Labor Mobility and Changes of Labor Productivity in Korea". *Journal of Industrial Economics and Business*. 31(1). 113-131. (in Korean)

12: Kim, Taegi. 2010. "Measurement of Export Prices and Product Quality in Korean Exports". *Korean Economic Studies*. 28(2). 123-144. (in Korean)

13: Han, InSoo, Oh, Keunyeob, and Yoo, Jinman. 2012. "Changes in Competitiveness of LCD Industry of East Asia". *International Telecommunications Policy Review*. 19(1). 1-26.

14: Kim, Taegi and Park, Changsuh. 2003. "R&D, Trade, and Productivity Growth in Korean Manufacturing". *Review of World Economics (Weltwirtschaftliches Archiv)*. 139(3). 460-483.

15: Kim, Taegi and Kim, Hong-Kee. 2015. "The Comparative Analysis of Total Factor Productivity between Exporting Firms and Domestic Firms". *Korean Economic Studies*. 33(1). 145-167. (in Korean)

16: Kim, Taegi and Oh, Keunyeob. 2012. "The Effects of Patent System on Innovation and Productivity: Evidence from Korea's Firm Level Data". in *The Economics of Intellectual Property in the Republic of Korea*. (Chapter 4). WIPO.

17: Yang, Ling and Oh, Keunyeob. 2018. "Wage Premium of Exporting Firms in Korean Manufacturing". *Korean Economic Studies*. 36(3). 65-90. (in Korean)

18: Yoo, Jinman, Wu, Chao, and Oh, Keunyeob. 2015. "Relationships between Polarization and Openness in Korean Economy". *Asian Social Science*. 11(24). 79-89.

19: Kim, Shin-Haing, Unpublished paper

20: Oh, Keunyeob and Myung, Chang-Yeon. 2005. "An Empirical Study of the Relation between Environmental Regulation and Export of Korea". *Environmental and Resource Economics*. 14(3). 627-653. (in Korean)

REFERENCES

Abel, Andrew B., and Eberly, Janice C. 2011. "How Q and Cash Flow Affect Investment without Frictions: An Analytic Explanation". *The Review of Economic Studies*. 78(4). 1179-1200.

Aghion, Phillippe, and Howitt, Peter. 1992. "A Model of Growth Through Creative Destruction". *Econometrica*. 60(2). 323-351.

Agustinus, P. 2007. "Foreign Ownership and Firm Financing Constraint in Indonesia". *MPRA Paper* 6500. University Library of Munich, Germany.

Aiginger, Karl. 1997. "The Use of Unit Values to Discriminate between Price and Quality Competition". *Cambridge Journal of Economics*. 21. 571-592.

Alonso-Borrego, C., and Bentolila, S. 1994. "Investment and Q in Spanish Manufacturing Firms". Oxford Bulletin of Economics and Statistics. 56 (1). 49-65.

Alvarez, R., and Lopez, R. A. 2005. "Exporting and Performance: Evidence from Chilean Plants". Canadian Journal of Economics, 38(4). 1384-1400.

Amado, João, and Cabral, Sónia. 2008. "The Portuguese Export Performance in Perspective: A Constant Market Share Analysis". Economic Bulletin. Autumn. 201-221.

Amendola, Mario, and Gaffard, Jean-Luc. 2009. "From Traverse to Out-of-Equilibrium". in *Capital, Time and Transitional Dynamics*. edited by H. Hagemann and R. Scazzieri. London: Routledge. 250-261.

Amendola, Mario, and Gaffard, Jean-Luc. 2014. "Time to Build and Out-of-Equilibrium growth process". *Structural Change and Economic Dynamics*. 29(C). 29. 19-27.

Amendola, Mario, and Gaffard, Jean-Luc. 1998. *Out of Equilibrium*. New York: Oxford University Press.

Amendola, Mario, Gaffard, Jean-Luc, and Patriacrcal, Fabrizio. 2017. "Inequality and Growth: The Perverse Relation between the Productivity and the non-Productive Assets of the Economy". *Journal of Evolutionary Economics*. 27. 531-554.

Amsden, Alice H. 1989. *Asia's Next Giant: South Korea and Late Industrialization*. New York and Oxford: Oxford University Press.

Arellano, M., and Bond, S. 1991. "Some Tests of Specification for Panel Data: Monte Carlo Evidence and an Application to Employment Equations". *The Review of Economic Studies*. 58(2). 277-297.

Arip, M. A., Yee, Lau Sim, and Satoru, Madono. 2010, "Commodity-Industry Classification Proxy: A Correspondence Table between SITC Revision 2 and ISIC Revision 3". MPRA Paper. 27626, University Library of Munich, Germany.

Arnold, J M., and Hussinger, K. 2005. "Export Behavior and Firm Productivity in German Manufacturing: A Firm-level Analysis". *Review of World Economics*. 141(2). 219-243.

Arrow, K.J. 1962. "The Economic Implications of Learning by Doing". *Review of Economic Studies*. 29. 155-173.

Arrow, K.J., and Levhari, David. 1969. "Uniqueness of the Internal Rate of Return with Variable Life of Investment". *Economic Journal*. 79. 560-566.

Arturupane, C., Djankov, S., and Hoekman, B. 1999. "Horizontal and Vertical Intra-Industry Trade between Eastern Europe and the European Union". *Weltwirtschaftliches Archiv*. 135(1). 62-81.

Ash, R. 1965. *Information Theory*. New York, London, and Sydney: John Wiley & Sons.

Attanasio, O., Goldberg, P., and Pavenik, N. 2003. "Trade Reforms and Wage Inequality in Columbia". *Journal of Development Economics*. 74. 331~366.

Aw, B. Y., and Hwang, A. 1995. "Productivity and Export Marker: A Firm Level Analysis". *Journal of Development Economics*. 47(2). 209-231.

Aw, B. Y., Chung, S., and Roberts, M. J. 1998. "Productivity and the Decision to Export: Micro Evidence from Taiwan and South Korea". *NBER Working Paper*. 6558.

Aw, B. Y., Chen, X., and Roberts, M. J. 2000. "Productivity and Turnover in the Export Market: Micro Evidence from Taiwan and South Korea". *The World Bank Economic Review*. 14. 65-90.

Aw, Bee Yan, and Roberts, Mark J. 1986. "Measuring Quality Change in Quota-Constrained Import Markets". *Journal of International Economics*. 21(1). 45-60.

Bai, Jushan, and Perron, Pierre. 1998. "Estimating and Testing Linear Models with Multiple Structural Changes". *Econometrica*. 66(1), 47-78.

Balassa, B. 1965. "Trade Liberalisation and Revealed Comparative Advantage". *The Manchester School*. 33. 99-123.

Balassa, B. 1979. "The Changing Pattern of Comparative Advantage in Manufactured Goods". *The Review of Economics and Statistics*. 61(2). 259-266.

Bank of Korea. Database. Yearly. (in Korean).

Bank of Korea. 2004. *Financial Markets in Korea*. (in Korean).

Bank of Korea. *Input-Output Tables: 1970-95 CD-ROM*. (in Korean)

Barro, R.J. 1991. "Economic Growth in a Cross Section of Countries". *Quarterly Journal of Economics.* 106. 407-444.

Baumol, William J. 1967. "The Macroeconomics of Unbalanced Growth: The Anatomy of Urban Crisis". *American Economic Review.* 57(3). 415-426.

Becker, G.S., Murphy, K.M., and Tamura, R. 1990. "Human Capital, Fertility, and Economic Growth". *Journal of Political Economy.* 98. 512-537.

Becker, Gary S. 1962. "Investment in Human Capital: A Theoretical Analysis". *Journal of Political Economy.* 70(5). 9-49.

Ben-David, Dan. 1996. "Trade and Convergence among Countries". *Journal of International Economics.* 40. 279-298.

Benedictis, Luca De and Tamberi, Massimo. 2004. "Overall Specialization Empirics: Techniques and Applications". *Open Economies Review.* 15(4). 323-346.

Bernard, A. B. and Jensen, J. B. 2004. "Why Some Firms Export". *The Review of Economics and Statistics.* 86(2). 561-569.

Bernard, A. B., Jensen, J. B., and Lawrence, R. Z. 1995. "Exporters, Jobs, and Wages in US Manufacturing: 1976-1987". *Brookings Papers on Economic Activity. Microeconomics.* 1995. 67-119.

Bernard, A. B. and Jensen, J. B. 1997. "Exporters, Skill Upgrading, and the Wage Gap". *Journal of International Economics.* 42(1). 3-31.

Bernard, A. B. and Wagner, J. 1997. "Exports and Success in German Manufacturing". *Review of World Economics.* 133(1). 134-157.

Bernard, A. B. and Jensen, J. B. 1999a. "Exceptional Exporter Performance: Cause, Effect or Both?". *Journal of International Economics.* 47(1). 1-25.

Bernard, A. B. and Jensen, J. B. 1999b. "Exporting and Productivity". *NBER Working Paper.* 7135.

Bernholz, P., Malte, F., and Winfried, R. 1978. "A Neo-Austrian Two-Period Multisector Model of Capital". *Journal of Economic Theory.* 17. 38-50.

Beyer, H., Rojas, P., and Vergara, R. 1999. "Trade Liberalization and Wage Inequality". *Journal of Development Economics.* 59(1). 103–123.

Bliss, C. J. 1975. *Capital Theory and the Distribution of Income.* Amsterdam: North-Holland.

Blundell, R., Bond, S., Devereux, M., and Schiantarelli, F. 1992. "Investment and Tobin's Q: Some Evidence from Panel Data". *Journal of Econometrics.* 51 (1-2). 233-257.

Boorstein, Randi and Feenstra, Robert C. 1987. "Quality Upgrading and its Welfare Cost in U.S. Steel Imports, 1969-74". *NBER Working Paper.*

2452.

Borjas, G. and Ramey, V. 1995. "Foreign Competition, Market Power, and Wage Inequality". *Quarterly Journal of Economics*. 110(4). 1075~1110.

Bottazzi, L. and Peri, G. 2001. "Innovation and Spillovers in Regions: Evidence from European Patent Data". University of Bocconi. working paper.

Braconier, H., Ekholm, K., and Knarvik, K. H. M. 2001. "In Search of FDI-Transmitted R&D Spillovers: A Study Based on Swedish Data". *Weltwirtschaftliches Archiv*. 137(4). 644-665.

Brander, James A. and Spencer, Barbara J. 1983. "International R&D Rivalry and Industrial Strategy". *Review of Economic Studies*. 50. 707-722.

Breau, S. and Rigby, D. L. 2006. "Is There Really an Export Wage Premium? A Case Study of Los Angeles Using Matched Employee-employer Data". *International Regional Science Review*. 29(3). 297-310.

Breusch, T. S. and Pagan, A. R. 1979. "A Simple Test for Heteroscedasticity and Random Coefficient Variation". *Econometrica*. 47(5). 1287-1294.

Brown, Gilbert T. 1973. *Korean Pricing Policies and Economic Development in the 1960s*. Baltimore and London: The Johns Hopkins University Press.

Burmeister, Edwin. 2009. "A Retrospective View of Hicks's Capital and Time: A Neo-Austrian Theory". In *Capital, Time and Transitional Dynamics*. edited by Harald Hagemann and Roberto Scazzieri. London: Routledge. 250-261.

Byun, Jae Jin and Lee, Sang-Hyop. 2005. "Horizontal and Vertical Intra-Industry Trade: New Evidence from Korea, 1991-1999". *Global Economy Journal*. 5(1). 1-31.

Cantwell, J. 1989. *Technological Innovation and Multinational Corporations*. Oxford. Blackwell.

Caves, D. W., Christensen, L. R., and Diewert, W. E. 1982. "Multilateral Comparisons of Output, Input, and Productivity Using Superlative Index Numbers". *Economic Journal*. 92(365). 73-86.

Caves, D. W., Christensen, L.R., and Diewert, W. E. 1982. "The Economic Theory of Index Numbers and the Measurement of Input, Output, and Productivity". *Econometrica*. 50(6). 1393-1414.

Chai, Joseph. 2002. "Trade and Environment: Evidence from China's Manufacturing Sector". *Sustainable Development*. 10. 25-35.

Chandler, A.D. 1992. "What Is a Firm? A Historical Perspective". *European Economic Review*. 36. 483-492.

Chandler, Alfred D. 1990. *"Scale and Scope"*. Cambridge, Mass.: Harvard University Press.

Chang, S. C. 2005. "The TFT-LCD Industry in Taiwan: Competitive Advantages and Future Developments". *Technology in Society. 27*. 199-215.

Chang. Sea-Jin. 2003. *Financial Crisis and Transformation of Korean Business.* Cambridge: Cambridge University Press.

Chen, R., Sadok, E.G., Guedhami, O., and Wang, He, 2017. "Do State and Foreign Ownership Affect Investment Efficiency? Evidence from Privatizations". *Journal of Corporate Finance.* 42(C), 408-421.

Chen, X. and Fougere, M. 2009. "Inter-provincial and Inter-industry Labor Mobility in Canada, 1994-2005". EcoMod2009 21500033.

Chenery, H. 1983. "Interactions between Theory and Observations in Development". *World Development.* 11. 853-861.

Chin, Judith C. and Grossman, Gene M. 1988. "Intellectual Property Rights and North-South Trade". *NBER Working Paper.* 2769.

Cho, Y. J. 1989. "Finance and Development: The Korean Approach". Oxford *Review of Economic Policy.* 5(2). 88-102.

Choi, Han-Joo, and Lee, Ki-Hoon. 2010. "Sources of Industrial Growth in the Korea Analyzed by IO-SDA". *Journal of Industrial Economics and Business.* 23(2). 727-747. (in Korean)

Choi, Nakgyoon and Lee, Hongshik. 2010. "Analysis of Comparative Advantage Patterns and its Policy Implications". Research Report. 10-01, KIEP. (in Korean)

Chun, Hyunbae, Cho, Janghee, and Jung, Hur. 2013. "Productivity Difference and Globalization Strategies of Firms". Economics Studies. 61(1). 5-30. (in Korean)

Clark, J. B. 1923. *The Distribution of Wealth: A Theory of Wages, Interest and Profits.* New York: Macmillan.

Clerides, S. K., Lach, S., and Tybout, J. R. 1998. "Is Learning by Exporting Important? Micro-dynamic Evidence from Colombia, Mexico, and Morocco". *The Quarterly Journal of Economics.* 113(3). 903-947.

Coe, D.T. and Helpman, E. 1995. "International R&D Spillovers". *European Economic Review.* 39. 859-887.

Coe, D.T., Helpman, E., and Hoffmaister, A. W. 1997. "North-South R&D Spillovers". *The Economic Journal.* 107. 134-149.

Coelli, T. 1996. "A Guide to DEAP Version 2.1: A Data Envelopment Analysis (Computer) Program". *CEPA Working Paper.* 96/08. University of New England. Australia.

Cohen, W., Goto, A., Nagata, A., Nelson, R., and Walsh, J. 2001. "R&D Spillovers, Patents, and the Incentives to Innovate in Japan and the United States". Druid Conferences. working paper.

Cole, M. A. and Elliott, R. J. R. Do Environmental Regulations Influence Trade Patterns? Testing Old and New Trade Theories". The World Economy. 26(8). 1163-1186.

Cole, David C. and Park, Yung Chul. 1983. *Financial Development in Korea 1945-1978.* Cambridge, Massachusetts: Harvard University Press.

Cooper, R.W. and. Haltiwanger, J.C. 2006. "On the Nature of Capital Adjustment Costs". *Review of Economic Studies.* 73(3). 611–33.

Copeland, B. R. and Taylor, M. S. 1994. "North-South Trade and the Environment". *Quarterly Journal of Economics.* 109(3). 755-787.

Copeland, B. R. and Taylor, M. S. 2001. "Is Free Trade Good for the Environment". *American Economic Review.* 91(4). 877-908.

Dalum, Bent, Laursen, Keld and Villumsen, Gert. 1998. "Structural Change in OECD Export Specialisation Patterns: De-specialisation and 'Stickiness'". *International Review of Applied Economics.* 12(3). 423-443.

Dasgupta, S., Mody, A., Roy, S., and Wheeler, D. 1995. "Environmental Regulation and Development". *World Bank Policy Research. Working Paper* 1448.

De Locker, J. 2007. "Do Exports Generate Higher Productivity? Evidence from Slovenia". *Journal of International Economics.* 73. 69-98.

De Long, J. B., and Summers, L. H. 1991. "Equipment Investment and Economic Growth". *Quarterly Journal of Economics.* 106(2). 445-502.

Deardorff, A. 1974. "Factor Proportions and Comparative Advantage in the Long Run: Comment". *Journal of Political Economy.* 82(4). 829-833.

Deardorff, A. V. 1992. "Welfare effects of global patent protection". *Economica.* 59. 35-51.

Deaton, Angus. 1979. "The Distance Function in Consumer Behavior with Applications to Index Numbers and Optimal Taxation". *Review of Economic Studies.* 46 (3). 391-405.

Diamond, P. 1965. "National Debt in a Neoclassical Growth Model". *American Economic Review.* 55. 1126-50.

Diwan, Ishac and Rodrik, Dane. 1991. "Patents, appropriate technology, and north-south trade". *Journal of International Economics.* 30. 27-47.

Dixit, A. and Stiglitz, J. 1977. "Monopolistic Competition and Optimum Product Variety". *American Economic Review.* 67. 297-308.

Dollar, D. 1992. "Outward-oriented Developing Economies Really Do Grow More Rapidly: Evidence from 95 LDC, 1976-1985". *Economic Development and Cultural Change.* 40. 523-544.

Domar, Evsey D. 1946. "Capital Expansion, Rate of Growth and Employment". *Econometrica.* 14. 137-147.

Donaldson, H. B. and Mehra, R. 1984. "Comparative Dynamics of an Equilibrium International Asset Pricing Model". *Review of Economic. Studies.* 51. 491-508.

Dornbusch, R., Fischer, S., and Samuelson, P. A. 1977. "Comparative Advantage, Trade and Payments in a Ricardian Model with a Continuum of Goods". *American Economic Review.* 67(5). 823-839.

Durkin, John T. and Krygier, Markus 1998. "Comparative Advantage and the Pattern of Trade within Industries". *Review of International Economics.* 6(2). 292-306.

Durkin, John T. 2000. "Differences in GDP per Capita and the Share of Intra-industry Trade: The role of Vertically Differentiated Trade". *Review of International Economics.* 8(4). 760-774.

Eaton, J. and Kortum, S. 2001. "Trade in capital goods". *European Economic Review.* 45. 1195-1235.

Ederington, J., Levinson A., and Minier, J. 2003. "Footloose and Pollution-free" *National Bureau of Economic Research Working Paper.* 9718.

Ederington, J. and Minier, J. 2001. "Is Environmental Policy a Secondary Trade Barrier? An Empirical Analysis". *Canadian Journal of Economics.* 36(1). 137-154.

Edwards, S. 1998. "Openness, Productivity and Growth: What Do We Really Know?". *Economic Journal.* 108. 383-398.

Eichengreen, B. and Hausmann, R. 1999. "Exchange Rates and Financial Fragility". *NBER Working Paper.* 7418.

Engelbrecht, H.J. 1997. "International R&D Spillovers, Human Capital and Productivity in OECD Countries: An Empirical Investigation". *European Economic Review.* 41. 1479-1488.

European Central Bank. 2005. "Competitiveness and the Export Performance of the Euro Area". Occasional Paper Series. 30.

Faber, Malte and Proops, J.L.R. 1991. "The Innovation of Techniques and the Time-Horizon: a neo-Austrian Approach". *Structural Change and Economic Dynamics.* 2. 143-159.

Faber, Malte and Winkler, Ralph 2006. "Heterogeneity and Time from Austrian Capital Theory to Ecological Economics". *American Journal of Economics and Sociology.* 65. 803-825.

Faber, Malte. 1975. "Superiority and Hicks' new concept of technical change". *Kyklos.* 28. 474-496.

Faber, Malte. 1979. *Introduction to Modern Austrian Capital Theory.* Berlin, Heidelberg, New York: Springer-Verlag.

Faini, Riccardo and Heimler, Alberto. 1991. "The Quality of Production of

Textiles and Clothing and the Completion of the Internal Market". *CEPR Discussion Papers.* 508.

Falvey, R.E. and Kierzkowski, H. 1987. "Product Quality, Intra-Industry Trade, and (Im)perfect Competition". in *Protection and Competition in International Trade.* Edited by H. Kierzkowski. Oxford: Basil Blackwell.

Färe, R. and Grosskopf, S. 1996. *Intertemporal Production Frontiers: With Dynamic DEA.* Boston: Kluwer Academic Publishers.

Färe, R., Grosskopf, S., Norris, M., and Zang, Z. 1994. "Productivity Growth, Technical Progress, and Efficiency Change in Industrialized Countries". *American Economic Review.* 84. 66-83.

Färe, R., Grosskopf, S., and Norris, M. 1997. "Productivity Growth, Technical Progress, and Efficiency Change in Industrialized Countries: Reply". *American Economic Review.* 87. 1040-1044.

Fazzari, Steven M., Glenn Hubbard, R., and Petersen, Bruce C. 1988. "Financing Constraints and Corporate Investment." *Brookings Papers on Economic Activity.* 1. 141-195.

Feenstra, R. C. 2000. *World Trade Flow, 1980-1997.* Center for International Data, Institute of Governmental Affairs, University of California, Davis, U.S.A.

Feenstra, R. C., and Hanson, G. 1997. "Foreign Direct Investment and Relative Wage: Evidence from Mexico's Maquiladoras". *Journal of International Economics.* 42. 371-393.

Feenstra, R. C., Madani, D., Tzu-Han, Y., and Chi-Yuan, L. 1999. "Testing Endogenous Growth in South Korea and Taiwan". *Journal of Development Economics.* 60. 317-341.

Feenstra, R. C., Lipsey, R. E., and Bowen, H. P. 1997. "World Trade Flows, 1970-1992, with Production and Tariff Data". *NBER Working Paper.* 5910.

Feenstra, R.C. 1996. "Trade and Uneven Growth". *Journal of Development Economics.* 49. 229-256.

Feenstra, Robert C. 1988. "Quality Change Under Trade Restraints in Japanese Autos. *Quarterly Journal of Economics.* 103. 131-146.

Fernandes, A. M. and Isgut, A. 2015. "Learning-by-Exporting Effects: Are They for Real". *Emerging Markets Finance and Trade.* 51(1). 65-89.

Ferrantino, M. J. and Linkins, L. A. 1999. "The Effect of Global Trade Liberalization on Toxic Emissions in Industry". *Weltwirtschaftliches Archiv.* 135(1). 128–5.

Findlay, R. 1978. "An Austrian Model of International Trade and Interest Rate Equalization". *Journal of Political Economy.* 86. 989-1007.

Findlay, R. 1996. "Modeling Global Interdependence: Centers, Peripheries, and Frontiers". *American Economic Review Papers and Pro ceedings.* 86. 47-51.

Findlay, R. and Kierzkowski, H. 1983. "International Trade and Human Capital: A Simple General Equilibrium Model". *Journal of Political Economy.* 91. 957-978.

Findlay, R. and Jones, R.W. 2001. "Input Trade and the Location of Production". *American Economic Review Papers and Pro ceedings.* 91(2). 29-33.

Findlay, R. 1970. "Factor Proportions and Comparative Advantage in the Long Run". *Journal of Political Economy.* 78(1). 27-34.

Findlay. R. 1984. "Growth and Development in Trade Models". In *Handbook of International Economics.* Edited by Ronald W. Jones and Peter B. Kenen. Volume 1. Chapter 4. Amsterdam: North-Holland. 185-236.

Flam, H. and Helpman, E. 1987. "Vertical Product Differentiation and North-South Trade". *American Economic Review.* 76. 810-22.

Fontagne, L. and Freudenberg, M. 1997. "Intra-Industry Trade: Methodological Issues Reconsidered". *CEPII, document de travail N.97-01.* 31.

Fontoura, M.P. and Serôdio, P. 2017. "The Export Performance of the 2004 EU Enlargement Economies since the 1990s: a Constant Market Share Analysis". *International Advances in Economic Research.* 23. 161–174.

Fu, D. and Wu, Y. 2013. "Export Wage Premium in China's Manufacturing Sector: A Firm Level Analysis". *China Economic Review.* 26. 182-196.

Winter, G. 1987. "Appropriating the returns from industrial research and development". *Brookings Papers on Economic Activity.* 783-831.

Galian, S. and Sanguinetti, P. 2003. "The Impact of Trade Liberalization on Wage Inequality: Evidence from Argentina". *Journal of Development Economics.* 72(2), 497~513.

Garrison, R.W. 2000. *"Capital and Time in Ecological Economics: Neo-Austrian Modelling".* *Quarterly Journal of Austrian Economics.* 3(3). 85-88.

Gatto, M. D., Mauro, F., Gruber, J. W., and Mandel, B. R. 2011. "The Revealed Competitiveness of U.S. Exports". *International Finance Discussion Papers.* 1026. Board of Governors of the Federal Reserve System (U.S.).

Georgescu-Roegen. 1971. *Entropy Law and Economic Development.* Cambridge: Harvard University Press.

Ginarte, Juan C. and Park, Walter G. 1997. "Determinants of patent rights: A cross-national study". *Research Policy.* 26(3). 283-301.

Gini, C. 1936. "On the Measure of Concentration with Special Reference to Income and Statistics". Colorado College Publication. General Series. 208, 73–79.

Glynn, J., Perera, N., and Verma, R. 2007. "Unit Root Tests and Structural Breaks: a Survey with Applications". *Journal of Quantitative Methods for Economics and Business Administration*. 3(1). 63-79.

Goldsmith, Raymond W. 1969. *Financial Structure*. New Haven. CT: Yale University Press,

Gould, D.M. and Gruben, W.C. 1996. "The Role of Intellectual Property Rights in Economic Growth". *Journal of Development Economics*. 48 (2). 323–350.

Greenaway, D. and Yu, Z. 2004. "Firm-level Interactions Between Exporting and Productivity: Industry-specific Evidence". *Review of World Economics*. 140(3). 376-392.

Greenaway, D., Hine, R., and Milner, C. 1994. "Country Specific Factors and the Pattern of Horizontal and Vertical Intra-Industry Trade in the U.K.". *Welwirtschaftliches Archiv*. 130. 77-99.

Greenaway, D. and Milner, C. 1986. *The Economics of Intra-Industry Trade,* Basil Blackwell, Cambridge, MA.

Greenway, D. and Milner, C. 2002. "Regionalism and Gravity". *Scottish Journal of Political Economy*. 49(5). 574-585.

Greenwood, J., Hercowitz, Z. and Krusell, P. 1997. "Long-run Implications of Investment-specific Technological Change". *American Economic Review*. 87(3). 342-362.

Gregory, A.W. and Hansen, B.E. 1996. "Residual-Based Tests for Cointegration in Models with Regime Shifts". *Journal of Econometrics*. 70. 99-126.

Grether, J. and Melo, J. 2003. "Globalization and Dirty Industries: Do Pollution Havens Matter?" *National Bureau of Economic Research Working Paper*. 9776

Griliches, Z. 1990. "Patent Statistics as Economic Indicators: A Survey". *Journal of Economic Literature*. 18. 1661-1707.

Griliches, Z. 1995. "R&D and Productivity: Econometric Results and Measurement Issues". In *Handbook of the Economics of Innovation and Technological Change*. Edited by P. Stoneman. Oxford: Basil Blackwell. 52-89.

Griliches, Z., and Lichtenberg, F. 1984. "Interindustry Technology Flows and Productivity Growth: A Reexamination". *Review of Economics and Statistics*. 66. 324-329.

Griliches, Z., and Mairesse, J. 1984. "Productivity and R&D at the Firm Level". In *R&D, patents and productivity.* edited by Zvi Griliches. Chicago: Univ. of Chicago Press. 339-374.

Grossman, G. M., and Helpman, E. 1990. "Comparative Advantage and Long-run Growth". *American Economic Review.* 80. 796-815.

Grossman, G. M., and Helpman, E. 1991. "Trade, Knowledge Spillovers, and Growth". *European economic review. 35*(2-3). 517-526.

Grossman, G. M., and Helpman, E. 1991. *Innovation and Growth in the Global Economy.* Cambridge, MA: MIT Press.

Grossman, G. M., and Helpman, E. 1991a. "Endogenous Product Cycles". *The Economic Journal.* 101. 1214-1229.

Grossman, G. M., and Helpman, E. 1991b. "Quality Ladders in the Theory of Growth". *Review of Economic Studies.* 58. 43-61.

Grossman, G. M., and Krueger, A. B. 1991. "Environmental Impacts of a North American Free Trade Agreement". *NBER Working Papers* 3914.

Grossman, G. M., and Krueger, A. B. 1995. "Economic Growth and the Environment". *Quarterly Journal of Economics.* 110(2). 353-377.

Grubel, H. G., and Lloyd, P. J. 1975. *Intra Industry Trade.* London: MacMillan Press.

Gurley, J. G., and Shaw, E. S. 1955. "Financial Aspects of Economic Development". *American Economic Review.* 45(4). 515-38.

Gurley, J. G., and Shaw, E. S. 1967. "Financial Structure and Economic Development". *Economic Development and Cultural Change.* 15(3). 257-68.

Gurley, J. G., Patrick, H. T., and Shaw, E. S. 1965. "The Financial Structure of Korea". United States Operations Mission to Korea.

Hagemann, Harald and Kurz, Heinz D. 1976. "The Return to the Same Truncation Period and Reswitching of Techniques in Neo-Austrian and More General Models". *Kyklos.* 29. 678-708.

Hagen, Everett E. 1958. "An Economic Justification of Protectionism". *Quarterly Journal of Economics.* 72(4). 496-514.

Hakura, D., and Jaumotte, F. 1999. "The Role of Inter- and Intra- industry Trade in Technology Diffusion". *IMF Working Paper.* 99/58.

Hall, B. H. 1990. "The manufacturing Sector Master File: 1959-1987". *NBER Working Paper.* 3366.

Hallak, Juan C. and Schott, Peter K. 2008. "Estimating Cross-Country Differences in Product Quality". *NBER Working Paper.* 13807.

Hallak, Juan C. 2006. "Product Quality and the Direction of Trade". *Journal of International Economics.* 68(1). 238-265.

Han, I. S 2007. "Development Strategies of LCD Industry in Taiwan. International Conference on Development and Globalization of

Innovation Cluster in Pan-Yellow Sea Rim". Management and Economics Research Institute (MERI). Chungnam National University (in Korean).

Han, I. S 2008. "Success Factors of Korean LCD Industry". *Discussion Paper*. Management and Economics Research Institute (MERI). Chungnam National University (in Korean).

Hanson, G. and Harrison, A. 1999. "Trade and Wage Inequality in Mexico". *Industrial and Labor Relations Review*. 52. 271-288.

Harberger, Arnold C. 1998. "A Vision of the Growth Process". *American Economic Review*. 88: 1-32.

Harrigan, J. 1997. "Technology, Factor Supplies, and International Specialization: Estimating the Neoclassical Model". *American Economic Review*. 87(4). 475-494.

Harris, M., Konya, L., and Matyas, L. 2000. "Modelling the Impact of Environmental Regulations on Bilateral Trade Flows: OECD 1990-1996". *Melbourne Institute Working Paper*. 11/00.

Harris, R. 2002. "Foreign Ownership and Productivity in the United Kingdom-Some Issues When Using the ARD Establishment Level Data". *Scottish Journal of Political Economy*. 49. 318-335.

Harrison, A, and Scorse, J. 2006. "Improving the Conditions of Workers? Minimum Wage Legislation and Anti-sweatshop Activism". *California Management Review*. Conference: Conference on Social Metrics. Volume: 48.

Harrison, A. 1991. "Openness and Growth: a Time-series, Cross-country Analysis for Developing Countries". Policy Research Working Paper. WPS 809. Washington: World Bank.

Harrison, A., and Hanson, G. 1999. "Who gains from trade reform? Some remaining puzzles". *Journal of Development Economics*. 59. 125–154.

Hart, P.E. and Prais, S.J. 1956. "The Analysis of Business Concentration: A Statistical Approach". *Journal of the Royal Statistical Society*. 119(2), 150-191.

Hayashi, Fumio 1982. "Tobin's Marginal q and Average q: A Neoclassical Interpretation". *Econometrica*. 50(1). 213-224.

Hayashi, Fumio and Inoue, Tohru 1991. "The Relation Between Firm Growth and Q with Multiple Capital Goods: Theory and Evidence from Panel Data on Japanese Firms". *Econometrica*. 59 (3). 731-753.

Hayek, F.A. 1941. *The Pure Theory of Capital*. London: Routledge & Kegan Paul.

Helliwell, J.F. 1992. "International Growth Linkages: Evidence from Asia and the OECD". *NBER Working Paper*. 4245.

Helliwell, J.F. and Chung, A. 1992. "Aggregate Productivity and Growth in an International Comparative Setting". in *International Productivity and Competitiveness*. Edited by B.G. Hickman. New York: Oxford University Press.

Helpman, E. and Krugman, Paul R. 1985. *Market Structure and Foreign Trade: Increasing Returns, Imperfect Competition and the International Economy*. Cambridge, MA: MIT Press.

Helpman, Elhanan, 1993, "Innovation, Imitation, and Intellectual Property Rights". *Econometrica*. 61. 1247-1280.

Helpman, Elhanan. 1981. "International Trade in the Presence of Product Differentiation, Economies of Scale and Monopolistic Competition". *Journal of International Economics*. 11. 305-340.

Hicks, John R. 1969. *A Theory of Economic History*. Oxford: Clarendon Press.

Hicks, John R. 1973. *Capital and Time*. Oxford: Clarendon Press.

Hicks, John R. 1977. *Economic Perspectives-Further Essays on Money and Growth*. Oxford: Clarendon Press.

Hong, Ki-Suk, 2006. "The Microdata Analysis on Recent Corporate Investment in Korea". *Economic Analysis*. 12(1). 1–52. (in Korean).

Hong, Wontack and Park, Yung Chul. 1986. "The Financing of Export-Oriented Growth in Korea". In *Pacific Growth and Financial Interdependence*. edited by A. Tan and B. Kapur: Allen and Unwin.

Hong, Wontack. 1976. *Factor Supply and Factor Intensity of Trade in Korea*. Seoul: KDI Press.

Hong, Wontack. 1989. "Factor Intensities of Korea's Domestic Demand, Production and Trade: 1960-85". *International Economic Journal*. 3. 97-113.

Hong, Wontack. 2002. *Catch-up and Crisis in Korea*. Northampton, MA: Edward Elgar Publishing Limited.

Hoshi, T. and Kashyap, A. K., 1990. "Evidence on q and Investment for Japanese Firms". *Journal of The Japanese and International Economics*. 4. 371-400.

Hoshi, Takeo, Kashyap, Anil, and Scharfstein, David. 1991. "Corporate Structure, Liquidity, and Investment: Evidence from Japanese Industrial Groups". *Quarterly Journal of Economics*. 106(1). 33-60.

Hu, A. G. Z., and Jaffe, A. B. 2001. "Patent Citations and International Knowledge Flow: The Cases of Korea and Taiwan". *NBER Working Paper. 8528*.

Hulten, Charles. 1992. "Growth Accounting when Technical Change is Embodied in Capital". *American Economic Review*. 82(4). 964-980.

Hummels, David and Klenow, Peter. 2005. "The Variety and Quality of a

Nation's Exports". *American Economic Review.* 95. 704-723.

Hung, J., Salomon, M., and Sowerby, S. 2004. "International trade and US productivity". *Research in International Business and Finance.* 18(1), 1–25.

Hurley, Dene T. 2003. "Horizontal and Vertical Intra-industry Trade: The case of ASEAN Trade in Manufactures". *International Economic Journal.* 17(4). 1-14.

Hwang, Soo-Kyeong 2008. "Structural Analysis of Employment and Labor Productivity in the Service Industry". Labor Policy Studies (Korea Labor Institute). 8(1). 27-62. (in Korean)

Hyundai Research Institute. 2010. "The Efficiency of Economic System is the Resource of Potential Growth". *VIP Report.* 10(36). (in Korean).

Jaffe, Adam. 1986. "Technological Opportunity and Spillovers of R&D: Evidence from Firms' Patents, Profits, and Market Value". *American Economic Review.* 76. 984-1001.

Jang K. 1998. "The Effects of Openness on the Economic Growth and Inflation". *Economic Analysis*, Bank of Korea. 4(1). (in Korean)

Janicke, M., Binder, M., and Monch, H. "'Dirty Industries': Patterns of Change in Industrial Countries". *Environmental and Resource Economics.* 9, 467–1, 1997

Jasso, G. 1979. "On Gini's Mean Difference and Gini's Index of Concentration". *American Sociological Review.* 44(5). 867–870.

Jayadevappa, R. and Chhatre, S. 2000. "International Trade and Environmental Quality: a Survey". *Ecological Economics.* 32. 175-194.

Johansen, S. 1988. "Statistical Analysis of Cointegration Vectors". *Journal of Economic Dynamics and Control.* 12(2). 231-254.

Jones, R.W. 2000. *Globalization and the Theory of Input Trade.* Cambridge, MA: MIT Press.

Joo, D. Y. 2008. "Display Industry Outlook and Coping Strategies". *KIET Industrial Economic Review.*

Jovanovic, B. 1995. "Learning and Growth," NBER Working Papers 5383.

Jug, J. and Mirza, D. 2004. "Environmental Regulations and Trade in Europe: The Role of Differentiation". *European Trade Study Group 2004 conference paper.*

Jung, S.C., Yoon, M.S. and Jang, J.K. 2004. *Correlations between Patents, Technology Innovation, and Economic Development.* Policy Study 2004-15. Science & Technology Policy Insititute (STEPI)

Jwa, Seung-Hee. 2018. "Understanding Koea's Saemaul Undong Theory, Evidence, and Implication". *Seoul Journal of Economics.* 31(2). 195-236.

Kandogan, Y. 2003. "Intra-industry Trade of Transition Countries: Trends and Determinants". *Emerging Markets Review.* 4(3). 272-286.

Kang, M. 2014. "The Study on the Effect of Trade Openness and FDI on Income Distribution". *International Commerce and Information Review.* 16(4). 151~167.

Kang, Man-ok, and Cha, Gun Ho. 1997. "Effects of Environmental Regulation on the competitiveness". Samsung Economic Research Institute. (in Korean)

Kang, Moon-soo. 1990. *Money Markets and Monetary Policy in Korea.* Seoul: Korea Development Institute.

Kang, Sang In, Kim, Tae wan, Han, W.J., Kang, Kwang kyu, and Choi, Daeseung. 2000. "A Study of Endogenous Sustainable Growth Model Considering Environmental Aspect". Korea Environment Institute. (in Korean)

KDI. 2003. "Comprehensive Study on Korea's Industrial Competitiveness". Research Report 2003-07. 197~217. (in Korean)

Keller, W. 2001. "International Technology Diffusion". *NBER Working Paper.* 8573.

Keller, W. 2002. "Trade and the Transmission of Technology". *Journal of Economic Growth.* 7. 5-24.

Keller, W. 2000. "Do Trade Pattern and Technology Flows Affect Productivity Growth?" The *World Bank Economic Review.* 14 (1): 17-47.

Kim, E. 2000. "Trade Liberalization and Productivity Growth in Korean Manufacturing Industries: Price Protection, Market Power, and Scale Efficiency". *Journal of Development Economics.* 62. 55-83.

Kim, Eun Mee. 1997. *Big Business, Strong State: Collusion and Conflict in South* Korean *Development. 1960-1990.* Albany: State University of New York Press.

Kim, Geuk-Soo. 2004. "A Study on Korea's Intra-Industry Trade and Determinants: Analysis of International Division of Labor Patterns with Major East Asian Countries". Korea International Trade Association. Trade Research Institute. (in Korean)

Kim, Hyunho. 2007. "Analysis on R&D Activity and Productivity by Firm's Exporting Status". Policy Research. STEPI. 1-78. (in Korean)

Kim, J. I., and Lau, L. 1994. "The Sources of Economic Growth of the East Asian Newly Industrializing Countries". *Journal of the Japanese and International Economics.* 8 (3). 235-71.

Kim, Jiyun, Lee, Keun, and Choo, Kineung. 2008. "Estimation of the Market Value of Korean Firms (Tobin Q) between 1980 and 2005: Comparison of Various Estimation Methods and their Usefulness

Experiment". *Seminar Paper of Korea Securities Association.* (in Korean).

Kim, Jong-Il and Lau, L.J. 1994. "The Sources of Economic Growth of the East Asian Newly Industrializing Countries". *Journal of Japanese and International Economies.* 8. 235-271.

Kim, Kyung Soo, Kim, Woo-Taek, Park, Sang-Soo, and Jang, Dae-Hong. 1996. "Estimation of Tobin Q for Korean Listed Companies". *Analysis of Korean Economy.* 2. 147-175. (in Korean).

Kim, Shin-Haing 2007. "Finance and Growth of the Korean Economy from 1960 to 2004". *Seoul Journal of Economics.* 20(4). 377-418.

Kim, Shin-Haing and Yang, Donghyu. 2014. "Post-Malthusian Population Model of the British Industrial Revolution in a Lewis's Unlimited Supply of Labor Model". *Seoul Journal of Economics.* 27(4): 421-443.

Kim, Shin-Haing and Kim, Taegi. 2020. "Investment and Adjustment Costs of Korean Firms in view of Tobin's q". *Asia-Pacific Journal of Accounting & Economics.* 27(3). 300-311.

Kim, Shin-Haing and Kim, Taegi. 2018. "Tobin's q of a Multi-Product Firm and an Endogenous Growth of a Firm". *Seoul Journal of Economics.* 31(4). 377-399.

Kim, Shin-Haing. 1994. "Capital Gains in a Neo-Austrian Framework". *Structural Change and Economic Dynamics.* 2. 361-82.

Kim, Shin-Haing. 2009. "Hicks's Traverse in a Small Open Economy". In *Capital, Time and Transitional Dynamics.* edited by Harald Hagemann and Roberto Scazzieri, London: Routledge. 250-261.

Kim, Shin-Haing. 2016. "Austrian Model of Trade and Growth of a Developing Economy". *Seoul Journal of Economics.* 2. 235-268.

Kim, Shin-Haing. 2019. "Weitzman's Recombinant Growth Model Once Again". (monograph)

Kim, Shin-Haing. 2019. "Wicksell's Natural Rate of Interest and Hayek's Trade Cycle in Austrian approach" (manuscript)

Kim, Taegi 2007. "Correlation between Production Structures and Trade Patterns". *International Economic Studies.* 13(1). 107-126. (in Korean)

Kim, Taegi. 2009. "An Analysis of Trade Openness using Industry-Level Gravity Model". *International Economic Studies.* 15(1). 131-153. (in Korean)

Kim, Taegi and Park, Changsuh. 2003. "R&D. Trade and Productivity Growth in Korean Manufacturing". *The Review of World Economy.* 139(3). 460-483.

Kim, Taegi and Kim, Hongkee. 2015. "The Comparative Analysis of Total Factor Productivity between Exporting Firms and Domestic Firms". *Journal of Korean Economics Studies.* 33(1). 145-167. (in Korean)

Kim, Taegi and Zhan, Jun-Heng. 2006. "Industrial Structure, Regional Trade Bias, and China's FTA with Korea and Japan". *Seoul Journal of Economics.* 19(4). 381-404.

Kim, Taegi and Kim, Kap Yong. 1997. "Productivity Growth in Korean Exporting and Importing Industries". *International Economic Studies.* 3(1). 57-80. (in Korean)

Kim, Taegi and Chang, Sun-Mee. 2002. "The Effects of Trade on Korean Economic Growth". *Economics Studies.* 50(1). 173-207. (in Korean)

Kim, Taegi. 2009. "A Comparison of Product Quality in Korea's Intra-Industry Trade with China and Japan". *East Asian Studies.* 2(2).71-94. (in Korean)

Kim, Taegi, Maskus, K., and Oh, Keun-Yeob. 2014. "Effects of Knowledge Spillovers on Knowledge Production and Productivity Growth in Korean Manufacturing Firms". *Asian Economic Journal.* 28(1). 63–79.

Kim, Taegi, Maskus, K., and Oh, Keun-Yeob. 2009. "Effects of Patents on Productivity Growth in Koran Manufacturing". *Pacific Economic Review.* 14(2). 137–154.

Kim, Taigi. 2016. "The Causes and Consequences of Labor Productivity Changes: International Comparison for Korea". *Industrial Relations Research.* 26(2). 59~83. (in Korean)

Kim, Taegi and Ju, Kyungwon. 2007. "Korea's Horizontal and Vertical Intra-Industry Trade and FDI in Trade with East Asian Countries". *East Asian Economic Review.* 11(1). 27-58. (in Korean)

Kim, Woo-Yung, Park, Soonchan, and Lee, Chang-Soo. 2005. "The Effects of Trade Liberalization on Employment and Wage Inequality in the Korean Manufacturing Sector". KIEP.

KIS VALUE. Database, http://www.kisvalue.com/web/index.jsp

Kongsamut, Piyabha, Rebelo, Sergio, and Xie, Danyang. 2001. "Beyond Balanced Growth". *Review of Economic Studies.* 68(4). 869-882.

Koo, Jaewoon and Maeng, Kyunghee. 2006. "Foreign Ownership and Investment: Evidence from Korea". *Applied Economics.* 38(20). 2405-2414.

Krueger, A. O. and Tuncer, B. 1982. "Growth of Factor Productivity in Turkish Manufacturing". *Journal of Development Economics.* 11. 307-326.

Krugman, P. 1979a. "A model of Innovation, Technology Transfer, and The World Distribution of Income". *Journal of Political Economy.* 87. 253-266.

Krugman, P. 1979b. "Increasing Return, Monopolistic Competition, and International Trade". *Journal of International Economics.* 9. 469-79.

Krugman, P. 1981. "Intra-industry Specialization and Gains from Trade". *Journal of Political Economy*. 89. 959-973.

Krugman, P. 1994. "The Myth of Asia's Miracle". *Foreign Affairs*. 73. 62-78.

Kurz, Heinz D. 2000. "Wicksell and the Problem of the 'Missing' Equation". *History of Political Economy*. 32(4). 765-788.

Kwon, H. U. 2004. "International R&D Spillovers between Korean and Japanese Manufacturing Industries". Institute of Economic Research. Hitotsubashi University, Discussion paper No. 36.

Lach, S. 1995. "Patents and Productivity Growth at the Industry Level: A First Look". *Economics Letters*. 49. 101-108.

Laitner, John 2000. "Structural Change and Economic Growth". *Review of Economic Studies*. 67(3). 545-561.

Lancaster, Kelvin. 1966. "A New Approach to a Consumer Theory". *Journal of Political Economy*. 74. 132-57.

Lancaster, Kelvin. 1979. *Variety, Equity, and Efficiency*. New York: Columbia University Press.

Lancaster, Kelvin. 1980. "Intra-Industry Trade Under Perfect Monopolistic Competition". *Journal of International Economics*. 10. 151-175.

Lau, M. and Wan, H.Y. Jr. 1991. "The Theory of Growth and Technology Transfer: Experience from the East Asian Economies". *Seoul Journal of Economics*. 4. 109-122.

Lawrence, Robert Z. and Weinstein, David E. 2001. "Trade and Growth: Import Led or Export Led? Evidence from Japan and Korea". in *Rethinking the East Asia Miracle* edited by Joseph E. Stiglitz and Shahid Yessuf, New York, N.Y.: Oxford University Press.

Lee, Byeong-hee, Kim, Joo-seop Park, Seong-jae, and Ryu, Jang-soo. 2004. "Qualifications and Labor Market Research". Research Report 2004-06, Korea Labor Institute. (in Korean)

Lee, Dongyeol. 2013. "Determinants of Labor Productivity in Manufacturing and Service Industries in Korea". Bank of Korea WP 2013-22 2013-22. (in Korean)

Lee, Eun-seok, Park, Chang-hyun, Park, Se-joon, and Kim, Joo-young. 2013. "Analysis of Labor Mobility between Industries and its Implications". Monthly Bulletin. 16-34, Bank of Korea. (in Korean)

Lee, Jong-Wha. 1996. "Government Interventions and Productivity Growth in Korean Manufacturing Industries". *Journal of Economic Growth*. 1. 391-414.

Lee, Jaedeuk and Park, Jaejin. 2009. "Empirical Analysis on Dynamics of Comparative Advantage of Korea, Japan and China Using Kernel Density Curves and Markov Transition Matrices". *International*

Economic Studies. 15(1). 55-87. (in Korean)

Lee, Jong-Wha. 1995. "Capital Goods Imports and Long-Run Growth". *Journal of Development Economics*. 48. 91-110.

Lee, Junyeop. 2004. "A Study on the International Division of Labor in North Asia Based on the Intra-Industry Trade among Korea, China and Japan". *Korean Economic Studies*. 10. 209-225. (in Korean)

Lee, Keun. 2019. *The Art of Economic Catch-up: Barriers, Detours and Leapfrogging in Innovation Systems*. Cambridge: Cambridge University Press.

Lee, M. H. 2010. *Research Report: Display*, Dong Bu Securities Research Center. (in Korean)

Lee, Si-Wook and Choi, Yong-Seok. 2009. "The Effects of Plants` Export Activity on Total Factor Productivity in Korea". Korean Economic Analysis. Korea Institute of Finance. 15(1). 77-125. (in Korean)

Lichtenberg, F. R., and van Pottelsberghe de la Potterie, B. 1998. "International R&D Spillovers: A Comment". *European Economic Review*. 42. 1483-1491.

Lim, G. C., and McNelis, Paul D. 2014. "Income Inequality, Trade and Financial Openness". RES_SPR Conference on Macroeconomic Challenges Facing Low-Income Countries. IMF.

Linder, S.B. 1961. *An Essay on Trade and Transformation*. Stockholm: Almqvist and Wiksells.

Liu, J. T., Tsou, M. W., and Hammitt, J. K. 1999. "Export Activity and Productivity: Evidence from the Taiwan Electronics Industry". *Review of World Economics*. 135(4): 675-691.

Low, P. and Yeats, A. "Do 'Dirty' Industries Migrate?". *World Bank Discussion Paper*. 159. 1992.

Lucas, R.E.Jr. 1988. "On the Mechanics of Economic Development". *Journal of Monetary Economics*. 22. 3-42.

Lucas, R.E.Jr. 1993. "Making a Miracle". *Econometrica*. 61(2). 251-72.

Lucas, R.E.Jr. 2009. "Trade and Diffusion of the Industrial Revolution". *American Economic Journal: Macroeconomics*. 1(1). 1-25.

Lucas, Robert E. Jr., 1967. "Adjustment Costs and the Theory of Supply". *Journal of Political Economy*. 75 (4). 321-334.

Luthria, M. and Maskus, K. E. 2004. "Protecting Industrial Inventions, Authors' Rights, and Traditional Knowledge: Relevance, Lessons, and Unresolved Issues". in *East Asia Integrates: A Trade Policy Agenda for Shared Growth*. Edited by Kathie Krumm and Homi Kharas, Washington DC: The World Bank. 95-114.

Mah, J. S. 2002. "The Impact of Globalization on Income Distribution: The Korean Experience". *Applied Economic Letters*. 9(15). 1007-1009.

Mah, J. S. 2003. "A Note on Globalization and Income Distribution: The Case of Korea: 1975-1995". *Journal of Asian Economics.* 14(1). 157-164.

Malinvaud, Edmond. 1986. "Les causes de la montée du chômage en France". *Revue française d'économie.* 1-1. 50-83

Mao, Rui and Yao, Yang 2012. "Structural Change In A Small Open Economy: An Application To South Korea". *Pacific Economic Review.* 17(1). 29-56.

Maskus, K. E. 2000. *Intellectual Property Rights in the Global Economy.* Washington DC: Institute for International Economics.

Maskus, K. E. and McDaniel, C. 1999. "Impacts of Japanese Patent System on Productivity Growth". *Japan and the World Economy.* 11. 557-574.

Maskus, K. 1983. "Evidence on Shifts in the Determinants of the Structure of U.S. Manufacturing Foreign Trade, 1958-76". *Review of Economics and Statistics.* 65. 415-422.

Mathews, J. A. 2005. "Strategy and the Crystal Cycle". *California Management Review. 47(2).* 6-32.

Matsuyama, Kiminori. 2009. "Structural Change in an Interdependent World: A Global View of Manufacturing Decline". *Journal of the European Economic Association.* 7 (2-3). 478-486.

McDonald, I. M, Solow, R. M. 1981. "Wage Bargaining and Employment". *The American Economic Review.* 71(5). 896-908.

McKinnon, Ronald I. 1973. *Money and Capital in Economic Development.* Washington, D.C.: Toe Brookings Institution.

McKinnon, Ronald I. 2002. "After the Crisis, the East Asian Dollars Standard Resurrected: An Interpretation of High-frequency Exchange Rate Pegging". In *Rethinking the East Asia Miracle. Edited by* Joseph E. Stiglitz and Shahid Yusuf. Washington: The World Bank. 197-246,

McMillan, Margaret and Rodrik, Dani. 2011. "Globalization, structural change and productivity growth". in *Making Globalization Socially Sustainable.* Edited by Marc Bacchetta, and Marion Jansen. WTO.

Melitz, M. J. 2003. "The Impact of Trade on Intra-industry Reallocations and Aggregate Industry Productivity". *Econometrica.* 71(6). 1695-1725.

Meller, P. 1995. "Chilean Export Growth, 1970–90: an Assessment". in *Manufacturing for Export in the Developing World: Problems and Possibilities.* Edited by Gerry Helleiner. 21-53.

Milanovic, B. and Squire, L. 2005. "Does Tariff Liberalization Increase Wage Inequality? Some Empirical Evidence". NBER Working Paper. 11046.

Mulatu, A., Florax, R., and Withagen, C. 2004. "Environmental Regulation and International Trade" *Tinbergen Institute Discussion Paper.* 2004-

020/3.

Munch, J R, Skaksen, J R. 2008. "Human Capital and Wages in Exporting Firms". *Journal of International Economics.* 75(2): 363-372.

Nadiri, M. I., and Kim, S. 1996. "R&D, Production Structure and Productivity Growth: A Comparison of the US, Japanese, and Korean Manufacturing Sectors". *NBER Working Paper.* 5506.

Nakata, Y. 2007. "Japan's Competitiveness in TFT-LCD Industry: Analysis on the Decline and a Proposal for Core National Management". *RIETI Discussion Paper.* (in Japanese)

Nam, Chong-Hyun, and Lee, Jae Ho. 2003. "Human Capital Accumulation and Changes in Comprative Advantage: The Case of Korea". *International Economic Studies.* 9(1). 69~93. (in Korean)

Nam, D.J., Cho, l..H., Yang, T. H. 2010. *2010 The Second Half Display Industry Outlook.* SK Securities Co. (in Korean)

Nam, S. W. 1994. "Korea's Financial Reform since the Early 1980s". In *Financial Reform-Theory and Experience. Edited by* Gerard Caprio, Jr., Izak Atiyas, and James A Hansen. New York: Cambridge University Press. 184-222.

Negishi, T. 1982. "Wicksell's Missing Equation and Böhm-Bawerk's Three Causes of Interest in a Stationary State". *Zeitschrift für Nationalökonomie.* 42. 161-174.

Nelson, Richard and Pack, Howard 1999. "The Asian Miracle and Modern Growth Theory". *Economic Journal.* 109(July). 416-436.

Nelson, Richard R. and Phelps, Edmund S. 1966. "Investment in Humans, Technological Diffusion, and Economic Growth". *American Economic Review.* 56. 69-75.

Ngai, R. L. and Pissarides, C. A. 2007. "Structural Change in a Multisector Model of Growth". *American Economic Review.* 97(1). 429-443.

Nordhaus, William D. 2007. "A Review of the Stern Review on the Economics of Climate Change". *Journal of Economic Literature.* 45. 3: 686-702.

OECD. *ANBERD Research and Development Database.*

OECD. *STAN Database for Industrial Analysis 1970-1997.*

OECD. Economic Outlook available on http://www.oecdsource.org.

OECD. Unit Labor Cost, http://stats.oecd.org/wbos/Index.aspx?DatasetCode=ULC_QUA.

OECD. *Science, Technology and Industry Scoreboard.*

Oh, G., and Rhee, C. 2002. "The Role of Corporate Bond Markets in the Korean Financial Restructuring Process". In Korean *Crisis and Recovery.* Edited by David Cole and Se-Jik Kim. International Monetary Fund and Korea Institute for International Economic Policy. 229-600.

Oh, Keun-Yeob and Joo, Hye-Young. 2000. "Horizontal and Vertical Intra - Industry Trade in Korea : Country - Specific Factors". *International Trade Studies*. 5(1). 3-24. (in Korean)

Oh, Keun-Yeob, Kim, B., and Kim, H. 2006. "An Empirical Study of the Relation between Stock Price and EPS in Panel Data". *Applied Economics*. 38: 2361–2369.

Oh, Keun-Yeob. 1996. "Purchasing Power Parity and Unit Root Tests Using Panel Data". *Journal of international Money and Finance*. 15(3). 405-418.

Oh, Keun Yeob and Joo, Hye Young. 2000. "Horizontal and Vertical Intra - Industry Trade in Korea: Country-Specific Factors". *International Trade Studies*. 5(1). 3~24. (in Korean)

Oh, Young-seok and Hwang, Yun-jin. 2003. "An Analysis of the International Division of Labor Patterns in Korean Industry: An Integrated Analysis of intra-industry trade and inter-industry trade". KIET. *Research Report*. 479. (in Korean)

Ok, Wooseok, Jeong, Se-Eun, and Oh, Yonghyup. 2007. "Trade, International Division of Labor, Skill-Demand Structure and Wage Inequalities: With a Focus on the Korea-China Trade". Korean *Economic* Analysis. 13(3). 73-132. (in Korean).

Pakes, A. and Griliches, Z. 1984. "Patents and R&D at the Firm Level: A First Look". In: *R&D, patents and productivity*. Edited by Zvi Griliches. Chicago: Univ. of Chicago Press. 55-72.

Panzar, John C. and Willig, Robert D. 1981. "Economies of Scope". *American Economic Review*. 71(2). 268-272.

Parante, S. L. and Prescott, E. C. 1994. "Barriers to Technology Adoption and Development". *Journal of Political Economy*. 102. 298- 321.

Park, B. S. 2005. "Rising China and Changes in Model for Regional Development in East Asia". *Issue Paper*. Samsung Economic Research Institute. (in Korean)

Park, Jae-Jin 2009. "The Empirical Analysis of Dynamic Comparative Advantage of Korea and China". *Trade Journal* (Korea Trade Research Association). 34(1). 405-432. (in Korean)

Park, Walter G. and Ginarte, Juan Carlos. 1997. "Intellectual Property Rights and Economic Growth". *Contemporary Economic Policy.* 15(3). 51- 61.

Pasinetti, Luigi L. 1978. "Wicksell Effects and Reswitchings of Technique in Capital Theory". *Scandinavian Journal of Economics.* 181-9.

Perron, P. 1997. "Further Evidence on Breaking Trend Functions in Macroeconomic Variables". *Journal of Econometrics.* 80(2). 355-385.

Phelps, E.S. 1961. "The Golden Rule of Accumulation: A Fable for Growthmen". *American Economic Review.* 51. 638-43.

Piketty, T. 2013. *Capital in the Twenty-first Century*, Cambridge, Massachusetts: The Belknappress of Harvard University Press.

Piketty, T. and Zucman, G. 2014. "Capital is Back: Wealth-Income Ratios in Rich Countries 1700-2010". *Quarterly Journal of Economics.* 1255-1310.

Proudman, J. and Redding, S. 2000. "Evolving Patterns of International Trade". *Review of International Economics.* 8(3). 373-396.

Pyo, Hak K. 2002. *Accumulation and Distribution of National Wealth in Korea (1953-2000).* Seoul: Institute of Economic Research. Seoul National University.

Quah, Danny T. 1996. "Empirics for Economic Growth and Convergence". *European Economic. Review.* 40. 1353-1375

Quah, Danny T. 1997. "Empirics for Growth and Distribution: Stratification, Polarization, and Convergence Clubs". *Journal of Economic Growth.* 2. 27-59.

Ranis, G. 1977. "Economic Development and Financial Institutions". In *Economic Progress, Private Values, and Public Policy. Edited by* Bela Balassa and Richard Nelson. Amsterdam: North-Holland Publishing Company. 27-55.

Ray, S. C., and Desli, E. 1997. "Productivity Growth, Technical Progress, and Efficiency Change in Industrialized Countries: Comment". *American Economic Review.* 87. 1033-1039.

Redding, Stephen. 2002. "Specialization Dynamics". *Journal of International Economics.* 58(2). 299-334.

Rhee, Y. H., Park, K. J., Rhee, M. H., and Choi, S. S. 2005. *The Centennial History of Stocks and Bonds in Korea.* Seoul, Korea: Korea Stock Depository. (in Korean)

Ricardo, D. 1821. *On the Principles of Political Economy and Taxation.* In *The Works and Correspondence of David Ricardo.* Vol. 1. edited by Sraffa, P. and M.H. Dobb. 1951. Cambridge: Cambridge University Press.

Roberts, M. and Tybout, J. 1997. "The Decision to Export in Colombia: An Empirical Model of Entry with Sunk Costs". *American Economic Review.* 87. 545-564.

Roland-Holst, D. 2003. "Global Supply Networks and Multilateral Trade Linkages: A Structural Analysis of East Asia". *ADB Institute Discussion Paper Series.* 15.

Romer, P. M. 1986. "Increasing Returns and Long-Run Growth". *Journal of Political Economy.* 94. 1002-1037.

Romer, Paul M. 1990. "Endogenous Technological Change". *Journal of Political Economy.* 98. 571-5102.

Rosenberg, N. 1970. "Economic Development and the Transfer of Technology: Some Historical Perspectives". *Technology and Culture.* 11(4). 550-575.

Sachs, J.D., and Warner, A. 1995. "Economic Reform and the Process of Global Integration". *Brookings Papers on Economic Activity.* 26(1). 1-118.

Sato, S., and Fukushige, M. 2009. "Globalization and Economic Inequality in the Short and Long Run: The Case of South Korea 1975-1995". *Journal of Asian Economics.* 20(1). 62-68.

Schank, T, Schnabel, C, and Wagner, J. 2007. "Do Exporters Really Pay Higher Wages? First Evidence from German Linked Employer–employee Data". *Journal of International Economics.* 72(1). 52-74.

Scherer, F. M. 1982. "Inter-Industry Technology Flows and Productivity Growth". *Review of Economics and Statistics.* 64. 627-634.

Segerstrom, Paul S. 1991. "Innovation, Imitation, and Economic Growth". *Journal of Political Economy.* 99. 807-827.

Sharma, K. 2004. "Horizontal and Vertical Intra-industry Trade in Australian Manufacturing: Does Trade Liberalization Have any Impact?". *Applied Economics.* 36. 1723-1730.

Shintaku, J. 2008. "Manufacturing Technology Strategy in Korean LCD Industry". *Akamon Management Review.* 7(1), 55-74. (in Japanese).

Shioji, Etsuro. 2015. "Productivity, Demand and Inter-Sectoral Labor Allocation in Japan". *Japan Labor Review.* 12(2). 65-85.

Singh, L. 2004. "Domestic and International Spillovers in Manufacturing Industries in South Korea". *Economic and Political Weekly.* January 31. 498-505.

Slaughter, M.J. 2001. "Trade Liberalization and Per Capita Income Convergence: A Difference-in-Differences Analysis". *Journal of International Economics.* 55. 203-228.

Solow, R. 1956. "A Contribution to the Theory of Economic Growth". *Quarterly Journal of Economics.* 70. 65–94.

Solow, R.M. 1960. "Investment and Technical Progress". in *Mathematical methods in the social sciences* edited by K.J. Arrow, S. Karlin, and P. Suppes. Stanford, California: Stanford University Press.

Song, Byung-Nak. 1997. *The Rise of the Korean Economy.* Hong Kong: Oxford University Press.

Sposi, Michael J. 2015. "Evolving Comparative Advantage, Sectoral Linkages, and Structural Change". Globalization and Monetary Policy Institute. Working Paper No. 231.

Stephan, Gunter. 1995. *Introduction into Capital Theory: A Neo-Austrian Perspective.* Berlin, Heidelberg: Springer-Verlag.

Stern, Nicholas. 2007. *The Economics of Climate Change.* Cambridge: Cambridge University Press.

Stiglitz, Joseph E. 1993. "The Role of the State in Financial Market". *World Bank Economic Review.* 7(1). 19-52.

Stiglitz, Joseph E. 1996. "Some Lessons from the East Asian Miracle". *The World Bank Research Observer.* 11(2). 151-177.

Stokey, N.L. 1991. "Human Capital, Product Quality, and Growth". *The Quarterly Journal of Economics.* 106(2). 587-616.

Stokey, N.L. 1989. "Learning by Doing and the Introduction of New Goods". *Journal of Political Economy.* 96(4). 701-717.

Strutti, Anna and Anderson, Kym. 2000. "Will Trade Liberalization Harm the Environment? : The Case of Indonesia to 2020". *Environmental and Resource Economics.* 17. 203-232.

Summers, Lawrence H. 1981. "Taxation and Corporate Investment: A q-Theory Approach". *Brookings Papers on Economic Activity.* 1981(1). 67-127.

Summers, R., and Heston, A. 1991. "The Penn World Table (Mark 5): An Expanded Set of International Comparisons 1950-1988". *Quarterly Journal of Economics.* 106. 327-368.

Tehle, Vaclav. 2012. Structural Change in the Course of Economic Development, Charles University in Prague.

Timmer, Marcel P, and Szirmai, Adam. 2000. "Productivity Growth in Asian Manufacturing: The Structural Bonus Hypothesis Examined," *Structural Change and Economic Dynamics.* 11(4). 371-392.

Tobey, J. A. 1990. "The Effects of Domestic Environmental Policies". *Kyklos.* 32(2). 191-209.

Tobin, James. 1969. "A General Equilibrium Approach to Monetary Theory". *Journal of Money, Credit and Banking.* 1(1). 15-29.

Torstensson, Johan. 1994. "Property Rights and Economic Growth: An Empirical Study". *Kyklos.* 47. 231-247.

Tsou, M. W., Liu, J. T., and Huang, C. J. 2006. "Export Activity, Firm Size and Wage Structure: Evidence from Taiwanese Manufacturing Firms". *Asian Economic Journal.* 20(4). 333-354.

Uy, Timothy, Yi, Kei-Mu, and Zhang, Jing. 2013. "Structural Change in an Open Economy". *Journal of Monetary Economics.* 60(6). 667-682.

Uzawa, Hirofumi. 1969. "Time Preference and the Penrose Effect in a Two-Sector Model of Economic Growth". *Journal of Political Economy.* 77(4). 628-652.

Van Beers, Cees, and Jeroen C. J. M. Van Den Bergh, 1997. "An Empirical Multi-Country Analysis of the Impact of Environmental Regulations on Foreign Trade Flows". *Kyklos.* 50(1). 29-46.

Van Biesebroeck, J. 2005. "Exporting Raises Productivity in Sub-Saharan African Manufacturing Firms". *Journal of International Economics.* 67(2). 373-391.

Wakelin, K. 2001. "Productivity Growth and R&D Expenditure in UK Manufacturing Firms". *Research Policy.* 30. 1079-1090.

Wang, J. C., and Tsai, K. H. 2003. "Productivity Growth and R&D Expenditure in Taiwan's Manufacturing Firms" *NBER Working Paper* 9724.

Weitzman, Martin L. 2007. "A Review of the Stern Review on the Economics of Climate Change". *Journal of Economic Literature.* 45(3). 703-724.

Weitzman, Martin. 1998. "Recombinant Growth Model". *Quarterly Journal of Economics.* 113(2). 331-360.

Were, M., and Kayizzi-Mugerwa, S. 2009. "Do Exporting Firms Pay Higher Wages? Evidence from Kenya's Manufacturing Sector". *African Development Review.* 21(3). 435-453.

Widodo, Tri. 2008. Dynamic Changes in Comparative Advantage: Japan "Flying Geese" Model and its Implications for China". *Journal of Chinese Economic and Foreign Trade Studies.* 1(3) .200-213.

Woo-Cumings, M. 2001. "Miracle as Prologue: The State and the Reform of the Corporate Sector in Korea." in *Rethinking the East Asia Miracle. edited by* Joseph E. Stiglitz and Shahid Yusuf. Washington: The World Bank. 343-77.

World Economic Forum. 2002. "2002 Environmental Sustainability Index (ESI)". Yale Center for Environmental Law and Policy.

Wörz, Julia. 2005. "Dynamics of Trade Specialization in Developed and Less Developed Countries". *Emerging Markets Finance and Trade.* 41(3). 92-111.

Xu, X., and Song, L. 2000. "Regional Cooperation and the Environment: Do 'Dirty' Industries Migrate?". *Weltwirtschaftliches Archiv.* 136(1). 137–7.

Xu, X., and Wang, Y. 1999. "Ownership Structure and Corporate Governance in Chinese Stock Companies". *China Economic Review.* 10(1). 75-98.

Yang, Donghyu, and Kim, Shin-Haing. 2013. "An Escape from the "Malthusian Trap": A Case of the Chosun Dynasty of Korea from 1701 to 1891 Viewed in Light of the British Industrial Revolution". *Seoul Journal of Economics.* 26 (2). 173-201.

Young, A. 1991. "Learning by Doing and the Dynamic Effects of International Trade". *Quarterly Journal of Economics.* 106. 587-616.

Young, A. 1995. "Tyranny of Numbers: Confronting the Statistical Realities of the East Asian Growth Experiences". *Quarterly Journal of Economics.* 110(3). 641-680.

Young, A. T., Higgins, M. J., and Levy, D. 2013. "Heterogeneous Convergence". *Economics Letters.* 120(2). 238-241.

Zhou, Q. 2009. "Trade and Mobility: The Political Economy of Interindustry Labor Mobility in Globalization". University of Chicago.

Zivot, E., and Andrews, K. 1992. "Further Evidence on the Great Crash, the Oil Price Shock and the Unit Root Hypothesis". *Journal of Business and Economic Statistics.* 10. 251-70.